A practical guide to

LEGAL WRITING
& LEGAL METHOD

second edition

A *practical guide* to

LEGAL WRITING & LEGAL METHOD

second edition

John C. Dernbach
WIDENER UNIVERSITY SCHOOL OF LAW

Richard V. Singleton II
HEALY AND BAILLIE

Cathleen S. Wharton
UNIVERSITY OF GEORGIA SCHOOL OF LAW

Joan M. Ruhtenberg
INDIANA UNIVERSITY SCHOOL OF LAW AT INDIANAPOLIS

Fred B. Rothman & Co.
Littleton, Colorado 80127
1994

Library of Congress Cataloging-in-Publication Data

A practical guide to legal writing and legal method / John C. Dernbach
. . . [et al.]—2d. ed.
    p.   cm.
  Rev. ed. of: A practical guide to legal writing and legal method
/ John C. Dernbach. 1st ed. 1981.
  Includes bibliographical references and index.
  ISBN 0-8377-0561-4
  1. Legal composition. 2. Law—United States—Language. 3. Law
—United States—Methodology. I. Dernbach, John C., 1953-
KF250.P72 1994
808' .06634—dc20   94-16472
                            CIP

© 1994 John C. Dernbach
& Richard V. Singleton II

Second printing 1996

 Text is printed on 10% post
consumer recycled paper

Printed in the United States of America

To our families & friends—
for their love, support, and patience

Acknowledgments

A GREAT MANY PEOPLE, both students and teachers, encouraged us to publish a second edition. Their support has made the second edition a reality.

Susan Brody helped bring Joan Ruhtenberg and Cathy Wharton into the project. As a result, the second edition combines the practical experience of John Dernbach (government) and Richard Singleton (private practice) with their substantial teaching experience.

At Widener University School of Law, Dennis Corgill, Mary Kate Kearney, Maureen Kordesh, Randy Lee, Robert Mensel, Michael Murtaugh, Robyn Meadows, Kathy Nelson, and Susan Raeker-Jordan provided extensive and constructive comments on many of the new chapters. In the administration, Arthur Frakt's support was invaluable. Beth Schaeffer went above and beyond the call of duty in typing and formatting parts of the manuscript. Paul Litwin provided helpful research assistance. Jill Ramsfield of Georgetown University Law Center provided invaluable comments on many of the new chapters in this second edition.

The administration, faculty, and staff at the University of Georgia School of Law were extremely supportive throughout the writing of this book. Peg McCann, Allison Hale, and Barbie Frake provided comments and suggestions that have made this a better book. Jane Kobres, Valarie Blyden, Gracie Wilson, and many other secretaries at Georgia were unendingly patient in typing and formatting much of the manuscript. Laura Ivey wrote the first draft of the memorandum in Appendix A.

Cynthia Adams, Deborah McGregor, Thomas Newby, and Andrew Solomon—all members of the legal writing faculty at Indiana University School of Law at Indianapolis—shared their collective experience in teaching the first edition as well as a draft of the second edition. They provided thoughtful comments on everything from the overall pedagogy of the book to the factual details in the exercises. The administration, particularly Deans Norman Lefstein and Thomas Allington, provided support and encouragement from the project's inception.

vii

We are deeply grateful to the Honorable David W. Craig, President Judge, Commonwealth Court of Pennsylvania, the Honorable Lynn N. Hughes, District Judge, Southern District of Texas, the Honorable Sylvia Rambo, Chief Judge, Middle District of Pennsylvania, and Bridget Montgomery, law clerk to Judge Rambo, who reviewed and commented on many of the chapters in Part E.

At Fred B. Rothman & Co., Shannon Wingrove proved to be an exceptional editor. Sheila Jarrett managed the production process efficiently and calmly. Paul Rothman was unfailingly helpful and patient.

The late Fred B. Rothman believed in this book from the beginning. His decision to publish the first edition made all the rest possible.

Our greatest debt is to our students, both past and present, at five different schools over fifteen years. We hope they have learned as much from us as we have learned from them.

Summary of Contents

Part C
BASIC CONCEPTS OF LEGAL WRITING

Part D
THE OFFICE MEMORANDUM

Part E
BRIEFS

APPENDIXES

Table of Contents

Part B
BASIC CONCEPTS OF LEGAL METHOD

Part D
THE OFFICE MEMORANDUM

APPENDIXES

Introduction

A GOOD LAWYER is much more than a professional. A good lawyer is a craftsman, applying his or her talents with imagination, diligence, and skill. Although the practice of law requires a combination of negotiation, counseling, research, and advocacy skills, there is one skill upon which all others depend. The good lawyer, the craftsman, must be able to write effectively.

Effective legal writing combines two elements—legal method and writing. Legal method is a process of applying legal rules to specific factual situations and drawing justifiable and well-organized conclusions. Law school, it is often said, is designed to teach you to "think like a lawyer." The myriad of legal rules presented in torts, civil procedure, property, and other courses are important, but law school courses should also instill the logic or method of law. A good lawyer knows how to resolve a particular problem, even though he or she may not yet know the relevant legal rules.

A thorough understanding of the legal problem-solving process is of little value, however, unless the analysis can be communicated on paper. Good legal writing is in many ways the same as good writing in general. Legal writing is clear, precise, and complete, yet fully understandable to a lay person. Although it may seem surprising, good legal writing is not a legalistic style of Latin phrases and archaic words.

Effective legal writing is hard work. Nothing is included without good reason, and nothing of significance is omitted. Each word, each sentence, is chosen or structured with care. If the document reads smoothly and intelligently, it is not usually because it was easy to write. The reverse is more often true; the document that was easy to write is often muddled. The beauty of good craftsmanship is that the final product masks the painstaking and difficult process by which it was created. The good writer—the craftsman—makes it *look* easy.

The good writer also understands his or her audience. Not surprisingly, the audience is mostly lawyers. It includes friendly or supportive lawyers, lawyers for the opposing side, lawyers who are judges, and lawyers who are clerks. They have different experiences and legal skills, but you should assume that they understand legal method and legal writing and that they bring certain expectations to what they read. They don't necessarily know the law relevant to a particular problem, so they expect that a memorandum or brief will explain it. They have a good nose for the strengths and weaknesses of legal conclusions, so they expect conclusions to be explained and counterarguments answered. They are sensitive to the real-world consequences of decisions based on legal documents, so they take these documents seriously. And they are busy, often extremely busy and working under a deadline, so they expect memos and briefs to be as direct, easy to read, and understandable as the material will allow.

This book is designed as a legal writing text, primarily for first-year law students. Its value as a learning tool is based on two classroom-tested premises. First, the fundamental principles of legal writing and legal method can be reduced to a series of fairly simple guidelines. Second, these guidelines can best be learned by practice, particularly by working through highly focused exercises. More than a decade of experience with the first edition of this book has confirmed these premises.

This book provides practical guidance in the basic skills of legal writing and legal method.[1] Each chapter covers a specific topic such as organization, precedent, or advocacy. Most chapters set out a short series of principles or guidelines. These guidelines are explained, justified, and then illustrated with hypothetical legal problems. The book shows good and bad ways of applying these guidelines to the problems and explains why one way is better than the others. Exercises of varying complexity, which afford an opportunity to learn and apply the rules, are provided at the end of each chapter (except Chapters 15 and 19). The illustrations and exercises are based on altered or abridged versions of real cases and statutes, citations to which are set out in the Bibliography.

The book is divided into five parts. The first three parts focus on analytical and writing lessons that are common to most legal documents. These three parts introduce the law (Part A) and explain basic concepts of legal method (Part B) and legal writing (Part C). Although the examples used in these parts tend to be based on legal memoranda, the guidelines in these parts also apply to briefs and other legal documents. The last two parts of the book show how these guidelines apply to

---

[1] Legal research, basic grammar, and citation form are not discussed. These subjects are covered in detail elsewhere, and there is little value in summarizing them here.

the writing of memoranda (Part D) and briefs (Part E) and give additional guidelines for writing these documents.

Although the book offers a step-by-step approach to legal writing and legal method, you need to be aware that legal writing is a recursive process. You may outline a memorandum or brief, begin writing, and then find you need to change your outline. You may find, as you edit your explanation of how a particular statute is applicable to your case, that the statute is not applicable. The steps in this book do not, in other words, move inevitably from "earlier" to "later" because you will often find yourself going back to "earlier" steps.

The book integrates and synthesizes many of the fundamental lessons of other law courses. It explicitly states the basic principles of legal method and provides a way of learning this method by the thinking and writing necessary to analyze specific legal problems.

The materials in this book are intended to be straightforward, manageable, and easy to understand. After the guidelines are understood in this context, they can be applied to legal writing assignments and to more complex situations. With time and analysis, the finer points of legal writing and legal method can be mastered. Ultimately, this book provides tools that will be helpful wherever you go in the practice of law.

Part A

INTRODUCTION TO LAW

1

Rules and Policies

DEFINING LAW IS a difficult philosophical problem, but law can generally be understood as the rules and underlying policies for guiding or regulating behavior in society. Rules describe what behavior is permissible or impermissible, what procedures must be followed to achieve certain ends, and what happens to those who do not follow them. Legal rules are intended to provide a means of resolving disputes peaceably, predictably, and more or less efficiently. They define relationships among individuals and groups and help people arrange or conduct their business with greater security.

Legal rules come about when the legislature enacts a statute, when a court resolves a dispute, when Congress ratifies a treaty with another nation, or when a government agency promulgates administrative regulations. Legal rules differ from other rules because their creation and enforcement require the participation of government. The police, courts, and other governmental bodies are responsible for ensuring compliance with these rules.

Rules vary considerably in their clarity and precision. Some rules are created one case at a time, particularly in the common law. They may apply to more situations than the case at hand, but they may not. Some rules are phrased in broad or general language. Many federal constitutional rules, for example, prohibit persons from being denied "freedom of speech" or "equal protection of the laws." Much tort law turns on what is "reasonable" in particular cases. Rules like this offer attorneys and judges considerable freedom for interpretation. Other rules are much more specific. Statutes tend to be more detailed than constitutions, and administrative regulations tend to be even more detailed. An administrative regulation, for example, may require a person who uses explosives to be certified by the state after paying a $200 fee and passing a competency test. Such regulations offer less room for interpretation. Common law rules, such as those involving property conveyancing, can also be quite specific.

This range reflects, at each extreme, contrasting approaches to the creation and application of law. In some situations, law is made on a case-by-case basis. This typically occurs in the common law, when a court fashions or applies a rule to the case before it. Other laws confront problems in groups. Statutes and administrative rules are often written in this manner. This approach is more bold, relies on the premise that problems can be understood in categorical terms, and makes law about particular situations in advance. Each approach works to solve certain problems, but neither approach works for all problems.

Policies are the specific underlying values or purposes for legal rules. Policies reflect varying and sometimes inconsistent views about what is socially good. Much property law survives from feudal times for no reason other than the convenience of adhering to custom. A good deal of more recent lawmaking, on the other hand, is directed toward the achievement of specific political goals. Policies also vary greatly in abstractness, even for the same rules. A building code provision requiring a certain kind of fire extinguisher for apartment buildings will probably be premised on technical judgments concerning the safety or efficiency of certain products or materials. These technical judgments, in turn, will be premised on certain moral or value judgments about the degree of protection that ought to be afforded tenants of apartment buildings. Sometimes policies are articulated clearly, but frequently they are stated unclearly or not at all. Often, a single rule is buttressed by several policy considerations.

Because legal rules are based on social judgments, they tend to act as a shorthand way of deciding what is just in a specific factual situation. Instead of simply asking what is right, for example, a court will first apply the relevant legal rule. The Twenty-sixth Amendment to the United States Constitution states that a United States citizen who is 18 years of age or older cannot be denied the right to vote simply because of the person's age. The answer to the question "Can Isaac vote in the national presidential election?" depends on whether Isaac is a United States citizen and is 18 years of age or older. There are good reasons for restricting the national voting privilege to United States citizens. But we all know of 10 and 12 year olds who could vote more intelligently than some adults. Could we fairly select and include these children while excluding certain adults? Probably not. The age of 18 is simply an appropriate place to draw a line. Line drawing is one of the most important policy questions in creating and applying legal rules.

Because legal rules are created to achieve socially desirable goals, they are not etched in stone for eternity, nor do they necessarily reflect the "natural" order of things. Change in underlying values or policies will often be followed by change in the legal rules.

The evolution of the law regarding gender-based discrimination is illustrative. The Fourteenth Amendment to the United States Constitution, which went into effect in 1868, provides in part that no state shall "deprive any person of life, liberty, or property, without due process of law." In 1872, the Supreme Court of the United States decided that this provision of the Constitution did not prevent Illinois from refusing to license an otherwise qualified woman to practice law in that state. The legislature had said, in effect, that only men could be lawyers. Justice Bradley, writing for himself and two other justices, commented:

> The paramount destiny and mission of woman are to fulfil the noble and benign offices of wife and mother. This is the law of the Creator. And the rules of civil society must be adapted to the general constitution of things, and cannot be based upon exceptional cases. . . . I am not prepared to say that it is one of her fundamental rights and privileges to be admitted into every office and position, including those which require highly special qualifications and demanding special responsibilities. [1]

Although the Court's sex discrimination decisions leave open some important questions about equality, there can be little question that its outlook has undergone a marked change in the past century. It is difficult to imagine the Court drawing the same conclusion today as it did in 1872, particularly with the increasing number of women enrolled in law schools, practicing law, and judging cases. As Justice Brennan, referring to the *Bradwell* case, wrote in a 1974 opinion:

> There can be no doubt that our Nation has had a long and unfortunate history of sex discrimination. Traditionally, such discrimination was rationalized by an attitude of "romantic Paternalism" which, in practical effect, put women, not on a pedestal, but in a cage.[2]

This change in the Court's attitude, and ultimately in the law, came as a direct result of changing public views about the role of women. This is not to suggest that judicial (or even legislative) decisions are made only after a poll is taken; the point is rather that public attitudes and values influence the environment in which these decisions are made.

The law, in turn, is a source of social norms and expectations. What the law requires, permits, or prohibits often comes to be associated with what is good or right. Just as the Supreme Court's early decisions helped maintain or create patterns of sex discrimination, so its more recent opinions can be credited with helping to lessen it.

The conclusion that rules are created to carry out socially desirable goals has an important corollary; rules should never be applied to a factual situation without consideration of the consequences. This may seem like a paradox. If the rule is

[1] Bradwell v. Illinois, 83 U.S. (16 Wall.) 130, 141–42 (1872).
[2] Frontiero v. Richardson, 411 U.S. 677, 684 (1974) (footnote omitted).

thoughtfully designed to achieve a particular goal, after all, then every application of that rule to a factual situation ought to further that goal; there should be no need to examine its fairness in each case. The practical difficulty with this proposition, however, is the impossibility of knowing in advance the full range of situations to which the rule might ultimately apply. As a result, the rule may not work the desired result in all cases. It is even possible for rules to achieve exactly the opposite of what was intended.

The old legal adage "hard cases make bad law" is rooted partly in the tremendous difficulty that lawyers and judges have when a rule is clearly applicable to a factual situation in which it would work a manifestly unjust result. Sometimes the rule is flexible enough that the problem can be solved by interpretation. Sometimes the rule provides for exceptions. Sometimes it is more important to maintain the integrity of the category than it is to work justice in all cases. And sometimes it is necessary to change the law.

Other hard cases require a judge to reconcile competing policy considerations. At what point, for example, does a criminal defendant's right to a fair trial limit the public's right to full media reporting of that trial? To what extent can a person's right to run her own business as she sees fit be limited by society for the protection of her employees? You will constantly be probing the cases you read for the justness of their rules and policies.

Law practice and legal education tend to focus on hard cases. Easy cases don't necessarily require a lawyer at all. One doesn't need a law degree to know that a person who drives 70 miles per hour in a residential neighborhood is breaking the speeding law. Lawyers are most necessary when hard cases do arise. Their training and experience help them solve problems that others cannot resolve.

Suppose, for example, the rule is that the named beneficiary in a will inherits the property of the deceased. The rule respects the wishes of the deceased and provides a way for the orderly distribution of the dead person's property. But what if the beneficiary murders the person who wrote the will to collect the inheritance? The rule contains no exceptions or room for interpretation. If it is applied as written, the beneficiary will collect the inheritance. Although the basic purposes of the rule would be served, applying the rule seems terribly wrong. A court's best alternative in this situation is to change the rule: A beneficiary may not inherit property from a person he has murdered.[3]

The importance of recognizing that value choices support legal rules, therefore, cannot be overstated. You will need to explain and weigh competing policies in your office memos. As an advocate, moreover, you will be writing briefs to

---

[3] Riggs v. Palmer, 22 N.E. 188 (N.Y. 1889).

explain why certain policies outweigh others, and you will have to appeal to the values of your audience to do so.

Value choices are also important for their moral implications. Obviously, your work as a lawyer will be important to your clients, but on a larger scale, your work will affect the way society operates. Lawyers have obligations to their clients, but they also have obligations to society. That tension is not always easy to resolve. If you successfully help a company develop a shopping mall near a city, for instance, you will have a significant effect on local land use, transportation, and housing patterns. If you successfully represent a landowner's group seeking to block that development, you prevent those effects but cause others. Whichever side you represent, you will be arguing for the social good your clients ostensibly seek. "Justice" and "the social good" have many meanings, and you will develop and refine your own understanding of these concepts as you study law.

The following exercises are intended to show you some of the difficult problems judges and legislators face. As you answer the questions in the exercises, ask yourself where your policy or value judgments come from, whether other judgments might be more appropriate, and what consequences your judgments would have.

Exercise 1-A

1. Assume you are a state legislator voting on the following bills. State whether you would vote for or against these bills and explain your decisions.

    (a) A bill requiring persons who ride motorcycles to wear protective helmets. *for*

    (b) A bill requiring companies that produce food or beverages for public consumption to place warning labels on products known to contain cancer-causing agents. *for*

    (c) A bill requiring couples applying for a marriage license to undergo twelve hours of psychological counseling and testing before the license is granted so they can better determine whether marriage is appropriate for them. *against*

    (d) A bill prohibiting any person from smoking tobacco. *against*

2. Are your decisions consistent with one another? Explain.

3. Do you think it is important that your decisions be consistent? Is it more important that judicial decisions be consistent? Explain.

Exercise 1-B

1. Assume you are a trial judge. Decide each of the following cases according to your idea of a just result, and explain the reasons for your decision. Do not refer to any of the other cases in making your decision, and do not invent additional facts.

(a)   Sally Hyde was arrested and charged with possession of marijuana at the annual "Hash Bash," an unofficial celebration of spring that drew 2,000 people. She objected to her prosecution because most of the other people there also possessed marijuana. There were no other arrests for drug possession, and the police said she was arrested at random "as an example to others." Does Hyde have a valid defense? Explain.

(b)   Hiram Price was arrested and charged with armed robbery shortly after three men stole $20,000 from Crabtree National Bank. Two of the men escaped. Price objected to his prosecution on the ground that he should not be tried unless the other two were tried with him. Does Price have a valid defense? Explain.

(c)   Jennifer Flick was arrested for driving sixty-four miles per hour in a fifty-five mile-per-hour zone. She objected to her prosecution because she had just been passed by two trucks and a car, all traveling five to ten miles per hour faster than she. Most of the other vehicles were traveling at the speed limit. Does Flick have a valid defense? Explain.

(d)   Denise Gilman was arrested for cohabitation with a male friend. She is an outspoken and militant advocate for better housing, integrated schools, and improved social services in Motor City. The cohabitation law had not been enforced for years. She objected to her arrest on the ground that she was being unfairly singled out. Does Gilman have a valid defense? Explain.

2.   Using your decisions in these four cases and the reasons you gave, frame a rule that will reconcile your conclusions. Remember that your statement of the rule should be clear and precise. Justify your rule.

2

Sources of Law

THE UNITED STATES has many sources of law because of our federal system. The United States Constitution is the nation's charter and the source of authority for federal laws and the federal courts. The Constitution delineates the limits of federal power and reserves considerable authority to the states. Each state has authority over persons and activities within its boundaries. State governments, in turn, delegate some authority to local governments. Each of these governmental units may, within certain constraints, make law.

Understanding how laws arise and how they affect our activities requires an understanding of two key concepts: (1) the relationships among laws within a single jurisdiction and (2) the relationships among federal, state, and local governments in the system. This chapter describes these two concepts and briefly describes source material for researching the law.

The Hierarchy of Laws

Four basic kinds of laws exist: constitutions, statutes or ordinances, administrative regulations, and judge-made law.[1] These sources form a hierarchy with constitutions at the top and judge-made laws at the bottom. Constitutions include the United States Constitution as well as state constitutions. Within a jurisdiction, the constitution is the highest authority; statutes, regulations, and common law must not conflict with the constitution.

Statutes create categorical rules to address particular problems. The Food, Drug, and Cosmetic Act, for example, was adopted by Congress to ensure the safety and healthfulness of the nation's food supply. A statute is controlling as to the subject it encompasses, unless the statute is unconstitutional.

---

[1] This summary is limited to the basic internal laws of the United States. International agreements and laws of other countries are not described here.

The federal government and most states have many agencies with diverse responsibilities (e.g., labor, veterans' affairs, transportation, commerce, environmental protection). Administrative regulations are rules promulgated by such agencies to help implement specific statutes. For example, the "laws" relating to declarations of nutritional information required on the packages of certain foods are largely administrative regulations promulgated by the Food and Drug Administration under the Food, Drug, and Cosmetic Act. Properly adopted administrative regulations have the same legal effect as statutes, so long as they are consistent with the Constitution and relevant statutes.

Judicial decisions often interpret or apply constitutions, statutes, or regulations. At other times, when such law is not applicable, they interpret or apply a body of judge-made law known as the common law. In either situation, law is made whenever a court decides a case. Once a constitutional provision, statute, or regulation has been construed by a court, that construction of the statute becomes law.

The charts below illustrate the order of authority within the federal government and within a state government:

United States
United States Constitution
Food, Drug, and Cosmetic Act, passed by Congress to ensure the safety and healthfulness of the nation's food supply
Administrative regulations promulgated to effectuate the Act, such as rules relating to the declaration of nutritional information required on the packages of certain foods
Judicial decisions construing the Act or the regulations

California
California Constitution
California Environmental Quality Act, passed by the California Legislature to protect and enhance the quality of the environment in the State of California
Administrative regulations promulgated to effectuate the Act, such as the rule that an environmental impact report must be filed before a construction project is approved
Judicial decisions construing the Act or the regulations

The Hierarchy of Jurisdictions

The United States has fifty-three sovereign systems of law—federal law and the laws of each of the states and territories. Although these systems are parallel, they sometimes intersect. Federal law controls when they do. Article VI of the United States Constitution provides that the Constitution and federal laws made pursuant to the Constitution "shall be the supreme law of the land." Therefore, a state may not act, through its legislature or its courts, in a way that is inconsistent with applicable provisions of the United States Constitution or with federal statutes and regulations. For example, the federal Voting Rights Act restricts or bars entirely devices used to discourage voting by racial and ethnic minorities, such as poll taxes, literacy tests, and voting and registration instructions written only in English. A state whose laws conflict with this Act must change its laws to conform to the federal statute.

Subdivisions of the state, including counties, townships, cities, boroughs, villages, or parishes, may also make laws. These laws, usually called ordinances, must comply with the applicable provisions of the state and federal constitutions and state and federal statutes.

The Hierarchy and Jurisdiction of Courts

The federal court system and most state court systems consist of three tiers: the trial courts, the middle-level court of appeals, and the court of last resort. Within each system, the jurisdiction of the courts, that is, the authority of courts to hear a case, is limited by geography and subject matter. In the federal system, the trial courts are known as district courts because the jurisdiction of each is limited to cases brought within its geographic district. A district might be an entire state (such as Maine) or a portion of a state (such as Texas, which currently has four federal judicial districts). The jurisdiction of the middle tier, the federal appeals courts, is also limited by geographic boundaries. The fifty states and the territories are currently divided into eleven judicial circuits, with the District of Columbia Circuit forming the twelfth and the Federal Circuit forming the thirteenth. Each federal court of appeals has jurisdiction to hear appeals from districts within its circuit, and may affirm or reverse district court decisions. The final level of appeal is to the United States Supreme Court, which may affirm or reverse federal court of appeals decisions as well as certain decisions by a state's highest court.

The chart below illustrates the hierarchy of courts within three jurisdictions:

Jurisdiction	Federal	Florida	Indiana
Highest court	United States Supreme Court	Florida Supreme Court	Indiana Supreme Court
Middle-level appeals court	United States Court of Appeals for the First Circuit	Court of Appeals of Florida, Fifth District	Indiana Court of Appeals, Second District
Trial court	United States District Court for the District of Massachusetts	Circuit Court for Seminole County	Marion County Superior Court

The power of a court to hear certain types of cases is known as subject-matter jurisdiction. The subject-matter jurisdiction of the federal courts is limited by the United States Constitution and Congress. Federal courts have no authority to hear cases which fall outside those limitations. As a general matter, the federal courts have subject-matter jurisdiction over (1) civil actions that arise under the Constitution, laws, or treaties of the United States (federal-question jurisdiction); (2) cases involving admiralty or maritime law; (3) civil cases in which the amount in controversy exceeds $50,000 if the plaintiff and defendant are citizens of different states (diversity jurisdiction); and (4) cases involving federal crimes. Congress has also created specialized civil courts, such as federal bankruptcy courts, whose jurisdiction is limited to a particular area of the law.

The jurisdiction of state courts is similarly defined by the state's constitution and legislature. A trial court's jurisdiction is limited by geography (usually all or part of a county or municipality) and by subject matter and amount in controversy. The court system in a municipality or county may include criminal courts and civil courts of limited or general jurisdiction. The latter are often called circuit courts, superior courts, district courts, or county courts.

A state court may hear questions of federal law as well as state law. For example, a defendant who has been charged with violating a local ordinance and who believes the ordinance violates the right to assemble guaranteed by the United States Constitution may raise the constitutional claim in state court. Federal courts may also hear questions of state law, but they must apply the law of the state under whose laws the claim arose. If the law of the state is unclear, the federal court must either make an educated guess about what the highest court of that state would do if confronted with the question before it or, if state law permits, certify the question to the state's highest court.

Within each jurisdiction, the decision of the highest court is binding on the lower courts. A decision of the United States Supreme Court on a federal question would be binding on all courts that entertain the identical federal question. As explained more fully in Chapter 4 (Precedent and Stare Decisis), when the question is one of state law, state courts are bound by their court of last resort, but they are free to accept or reject decisions by courts of other states and decisions by federal courts interpreting their state law. Judicial decisions outside the jurisdiction may be persuasive but are never binding.

Source Material for Researching the Law

The sources of law described above—constitutions, legislation, regulations, judicial decisions—are referred to as primary authority. They are "law," and the outcome of legal disputes turns on their applicability and interpretation.

Other resources, in which people write about the law or collect and offer general theories about selected rules of law, are known as secondary authority. Included in this category are treatises, restatements of the law, articles in law reviews and other legal periodicals, annotations, and legal encyclopedias. These resources may describe the law in a general way or suggest what the law should be, but they are not sources of law. Although secondary authority may assist in persuading a court that a given result is correct or better, it cannot mandate that result. Nevertheless, some secondary authority has greatly influenced the courts, and many courts have adopted various statements in secondary authority as the law of the jurisdiction. Once a court has adopted a rule proposed or stated in secondary authority, that rule becomes primary authority.

The following is a brief overview of the main sources in which primary and secondary authority are located.

Primary Authority

Federal statutes are published chronologically as they are enacted, first in pamphlet form called "slip laws" and then in a series of books called *United States Statutes at Large*. They are also published by subject matter in the *United States Code* (U.S.C.), the official version, in *United States Code Annotated* (U.S.C.A.), published by West Publishing Company, and in *United States Code Service* (U.S.C.S.), published by Lawyers Cooperative Publishing Company. The publication of state statutes follows a similar pattern. Recent enactments are first published in pamphlet form and then in books organized by subject matter. U.S.C.A., U.S.C.S., and all state codes are annotated, which means that the compilations include the history of successive amendments to a code section, references to analogous statutes, references to secondary authority and finding aids, and brief annotations or descriptions of cases construing a particular section.

Constitutions are published in the same manner as statutes. The United States Constitution is published in U.S.C., U.S.C.A., and in U.S.C.S., for example. State constitutions are also usually published with state statutes.

Administrative regulations are printed in the *Federal Register*, which is published five days per week by the United States Government Printing Office. The *Federal Register* also contains proposed regulations and various notices. Regulations are then published by subject matter in the *Code of Federal Regulations* (C.F.R.), the official source for United States government regulations. In many states, administrative regulations are published in a state version of the *Federal Register* (e.g., *Pennsylvania Bulletin)* and then codified by subject matter (e.g., *Pennsylvania Code*).

Judicial opinions are published in hardbound volumes, roughly in chronological order, with pamphlet supplements that contain opinions too recent to be published in hardbound. Decisions by the United States Supreme Court are published in *United States Reports* (U.S.), the official version, the *Supreme Court Reporter* (S. Ct.), published by West Publishing Company, and *United States Supreme Court Reports, Lawyers' Edition* (L. Ed.), published by Lawyers Cooperative Publishing Company. West publishes decisions by the federal appeals courts in *Federal Reporter* (F.), *Federal Reporter, Second Series* (F.2d), *Federal Reporter, Third Series* (F.3d), and by the federal district courts in *Federal Supplement* (F. Supp.). Not all federal district court and court of appeals decisions are published.

Most states publish their own court decisions. West also publishes state court decisions by region. It has divided the country into seven regions:

Atlantic (A. and A.2d): Connecticut, Delaware, Maine, Maryland, New Hampshire, New Jersey, Pennsylvania, Rhode Island, Vermont, the District of Columbia.

Northeastern (N.E. and N.E.2d): Illinois, Indiana, Massachusetts, New York, Ohio.

Northwestern (N.W. and N.W.2d): Iowa, Michigan, Minnesota, Nebraska, North Dakota, South Dakota, Wisconsin.

Pacific (P. and P.2d): Alaska, Arizona, California, Colorado, Hawaii, Idaho, Kansas, Montana, Nevada, New Mexico, Oklahoma, Oregon, Utah, Washington, Wyoming.

Southeastern (S.E. and S.E.2d): Georgia, North Carolina, South Carolina, Virginia, and West Virginia.

Southwestern (S.W. and S.W.2d): Arkansas, Kentucky, Missouri, Tennessee, Texas.

Southern (So. and So. 2d): Alabama, Florida, Louisiana, Mississippi.

Because of the efficiency of the West national reporter system, some states have discontinued the publication of official versions of their decisions. Their published decisions are available only in West's regional reporters.

Secondary Authority

This category includes encyclopedias, annotations, scholarly publications, and restatements.

Encyclopedias. Two encyclopedias found in virtually every law library attempt to cover the entire scope of Anglo-American jurisprudence—*American Jurisprudence, Second Series* (Am. Jur. 2d), published by Lawyers Cooperative, and *Corpus Juris Secundum* (C.J.S.), published by West. Some encyclopedias are devoted to the law of a particular state. If a state encyclopedia is published by one of the two national publishers, West or Lawyers Cooperative, topics are arranged to conform to the national encyclopedia. Like other encyclopedias, the topics in legal encyclopedias are arranged alphabetically with cross-references in the index.

Annotations. American Law Reports (A.L.R.) publishes selected cases along with annotations that survey the law within a discrete area suggested by a particular case. The cases are selected for their interest to the practicing lawyer. A selected case might represent, for example, a new development in the law or one approach to an issue on which the jurisdictions have split. An annotation on the issue you are researching will give you not only an overview of the law nationwide but also citations to the most useful cases in each jurisdiction.

Scholarly Publications. Scholars and practitioners publish books within their particular area of expertise called treatises (multivolume sets) or hornbooks (single volumes). In addition, legal periodicals throughout the country, most of them run by law students, publish numerous scholarly articles each year on current topics of interest to the legal community. These publications cover subjects in more depth than legal encyclopedias or A.L.R. annotations, and the research is usually comprehensive. They frequently propose solutions to particular legal problems.

Restatements of the Law. About the turn of the century, a group of lawyers formed the American Law Institute. In 1932, the Institute initiated a series of publications consisting of black-letter rules that generally reflect the majority view on a given common law issue. So far, the American Law Institute has issued restatements of the law on the following subjects: Agency, Conflict of Laws, Contracts, Foreign Relations Law of the United States, Judgments, Property—Landlord and Tenant, Property—Donative Transfers, Torts, and Trusts. Each rule is followed by a Comment that further explains the rule or the reasons for its adoption and Illustrations that demonstrate how the rule applies in specific situations. In format, a Restatement resembles a code. It is divided into sections, with each section stating a separate rule.

Here is an example from the Restatement (Second) of Agency:

§ 14. Manifestations of consent.

An agency relationship exists only if there has been a manifestation by the principal to the agent that the agent may act on his account, and consent by the agent to act.

This code-like structure has led many law students to believe that a restatement is more authoritative than it actually is. Restatements are only secondary authority. They are written by authors who describe what the law is in some jurisdictions or what it ought to be, but who have no authority to make laws. Courts and legislatures, however, sometimes adopt a particular restatement provision. When that occurs, the restatement provision is the law of that jurisdiction.

This description of the origin of laws, the hierarchy of authority in our federal system, and the published sources of laws and commentary about the laws should enable you to put the resources you will find in a law library in the proper perspective. The following exercises will test your understanding of the information in this chapter.

Exercise 2-A

You represent Charles Hollister, who has been accused of raping his companion while the two were on a date. Hollister admits that he had sexual intercourse with the victim but claims that she consented. The prosecution has sought to introduce into evidence testimony which will show that Hollister has been publicly accused of rape several times in the past and prosecuted for rape once. Hollister would like you to offer a motion to exclude this evidence if you can find sufficient legal authority to support the motion. You have found the following:

1.   A section of the code of your state which says that evidence of prior wrongs is usually inadmissible but may be admissible to show the accused person's criminal intent.

2.   A law review article on the difficulty of proving criminal intent in date rape cases.

3.   A decision by a middle level court in another state in which the court held that if the accused rapist admits the act, his intent is irrelevant, the only issue being the consent of the victim.

4.   A decision by a federal court of appeals, applying the law of another state, in which the court held that prior rapes are irrelevant to both the defendant's intent and the victim's consent, and are therefore inadmissible.

5.   A section of the code of your state that defines rape as compelling another person to engage in a sexual act by force or threat of force.

6.   A decision by the highest court of another state in which the court held that evidence of prior rapes is relevant to show the defendant's awareness that the victim had not consented and therefore his intent to rape.

7.   A decision by the highest court of another state in which the court held that prior acts of rape are not admissible because they are unfairly prejudicial and have no bearing on the defendant's intent at the time of the rape for which he is on trial.

8.   A dissent by a judge in the case described in 7. The judge believed that the prior acts were similar enough to show the defendant's characteristic behavior and thus to rebut the defense that the victim consented.

Divide these sources into three categories: (A) primary authority that is binding, (B) primary authority that is persuasive, and (C) secondary authority. List the sources in category (B) in order of precedential value, from most persuasive to least persuasive. You may conclude that the precedential value is equal.

Exercise 2-B

Your client is Sandra Eckert, who operates a refinery. Several of Eckert's neighbors have brought suit against her in state court, alleging that her negligent operation of the refinery resulted in the seepage of pollutants into the aquifer, contaminating their soil and well water. The plaintiffs claim damages for various health problems and for the diminution of the value of their property. Eckert has an insurance policy which provides that it does not cover damages arising out of the release of pollutants unless the release was "sudden and accidental." The insurer has denied coverage on the ground that the release was gradual rather than sudden. In researching the issue of insurance coverage, you have found the following:

1.   A law review article discussing the treatment of the "sudden and accidental" clause by various courts.

2.   An A.L.R. annotation on an insurer's liability for damages resulting from pollution.

3.   An opinion by the highest court of another state defining "sudden and accidental" in a case with similar facts.

4.   An opinion by a federal district court defining "sudden and accidental" in a case with similar facts and applying the law of another state when that state's courts had not decided this specific issue.

5.   An opinion by a federal district court defining "sudden and accidental" and applying the law of your state. The case involves pollution, but the facts are not otherwise similar.

6.   An article in a national legal periodical on allocating the costs of pollution damage.

7.   An opinion by the highest court of your state involving an automobile liability policy in which the court set out certain principles regarding the construction of insurance policies.

8.   An opinion by a federal court of appeals defining "sudden and accidental" in a case with similar facts, construing the law of another state and relying on decisions by intermediate level courts in that state.

9.   An opinion by the same court described in 8 deciding the same issue but reaching the opposite conclusion based on decisions by an intermediate level court in still another state.

Divide these sources into three categories: (A) primary authority that is binding, (B) primary authority that is persuasive, and (C) secondary authority. List the sources in category (B) in order of precedential value, from most persuasive to least persuasive. You may conclude that the precedential value is equal.

3

Case Analysis and Case Briefs

COURTS IN OUR SOCIETY decide what the law means and how it should be applied to specific situations. As noted in Chapter 2 (Sources of Law), courts sometimes interpret rules that are codified in statutes, regulations, or constitutions. At other times they make their own rules as they decide cases, forming the common law.

Judicial decisions are the result of a great deal of time and hard work on the part of lawyers, judges, and all other participants in the litigation process. Disputes are first heard in trial courts. Whether one party is suing another for breach of contract, or whether the state is prosecuting someone for manslaughter, the trial court hears the case first. The trial court has two responsibilities. First, it decides what actually occurred in the case. For example, where was the defendant on the night of June 25? Sometimes the parties agree on the facts, but often they do not. Different witnesses may have different stories. The court will hear the testimony of these witnesses and it will examine other evidence to determine which version of the facts is correct. Sometimes a jury determines the facts; sometimes that job belongs to the judge. Second, the trial court is required to determine what legal rules should be used to decide a particular case. Counsel for the opposing parties will argue their positions, but the judge makes the final decision. In light of both the law and the facts, the court then decides which party prevails.

The losing party may challenge the decision in a higher or appellate court if that party believes the trial judge made a mistake that affected the outcome in stating or applying the relevant legal rules. Appellate courts must usually accept the factual record from the trial court; the only remaining issues are legal ones. The appellate court will examine the legal rule or rules at issue, sometimes upholding

18

the trial court decision and sometimes reversing it. Unlike trial courts, whose responsibilities are limited largely to ascertaining what actually happened and doing justice in individual cases, appellate courts must think about a range of situations far beyond the facts of the case and about the broader policy implications of what the trial court has done. Because appellate courts review decisions by many trial courts under them, they also help ensure that the rules are understood and applied uniformly.

Courts record their decisions in opinions, which describe what the dispute was about and why the court decided the case as it did. These opinions deserve careful study. Because courts rely on earlier cases in resolving disputes, cases have enormous value in predicting what a court might do in a specific situation and in persuading a court to reach a particular conclusion. Your ability to understand what these cases mean is thus a necessary skill in analyzing or writing about any legal problem.

More fundamentally, cases demonstrate the basic methods of legal reasoning that you will use in studying and practicing law. Courts must decide whether particular laws do or do not apply to factual situations, and must explain their reasoning. Similarly, the study and practice of law will require you to decide whether certain laws apply to certain facts. You, too, must explain your reasoning. You can learn a great deal about legal reasoning by studying the ways that courts analyze problems. At the same time, you should realize that judicial decisions (including the cases described in this book) contain both good and bad examples of legal reasoning. Over time, you will learn to recognize the difference.

A case brief is a written summary of your analysis of a case, which should help you prepare for class or write an assignment. (Case briefs are not to be confused with trial and appellate court briefs discussed in Part E of this book, which are written to persuade a court to adopt your client's position.) Many formats exist for case briefing, but they all include the elements described in this chapter.

Although judicial opinions can contain many things, five components are critical. These are a description of the facts, a statement of the legal issue or issues presented for decision, the relevant rule or rules of law, the holding (the rule of law applied to the particular facts of the case), and the policies and reasons that support the holding.

Consider, for example, the following judicial opinion:

State v. Jones (1971)

(1) Jones appeals his conviction for possession of marijuana. (2) When the police stopped and searched Jones's van, they found an ounce of marijuana in a backpack in the far rear of the vehicle. (3) Although Jones admitted he knew the marijuana was there, he defended against the charge by claiming that the backpack and drugs

belonged to a hitchhiker who had been riding with him and who had accidentally left them in the van. (4) In this state, it is presumed that drugs are in the possession of the person who controls them. (5) The issue in this case is whether the marijuana was within Jones's control even though it was in a backpack in the rear of his van. (6) That the backpack and drugs may have been owned by someone else is irrelevant. (7) Public policy dictates that possession should not be synonymous with ownership because the difficulty of proving ownership would permit too many drug offenders to evade prosecution. (8) It is sensible to assume that anything inside a vehicle is within the control of the driver. (9) We hold that Jones possessed marijuana because the backpack was within Jones's van and thus under his control. Affirmed.

All of the essential elements of a case are in the above example. Sentences (1), (2), and (3) tell you the facts of the case. Sentence (1) sets out the procedural facts; sentences (2) and (3) give the legally relevant facts. Sentence (5) is the issue presented for decision by the appellate court. Sentence (4) gives the rule of law applicable to this factual situation. Sentence (9) is the court's holding. Sentences (6), (7), and (8) are reasons and policies that support the holding. Although few cases lend themselves to such ready analysis, each case should contain these elements.

You should, however, be aware of three major difficulties. The first is learning how to think in reverse. The opinion is the end product of a lawsuit. You have to start with this end product and work backward to unravel what the dispute was about, what happened in the trial court, and what happened on appeal. This process is akin to discovering the secret of a competitor's product through reverse engineering. The second difficulty is understanding the interplay among the basic components of a judicial opinion. All the components of a case—facts, issues, rules, holdings, reasons, and policies—are related. One element cannot be understood without understanding the others. Case analysis is thus largely a recursive process. You will constantly revise your understanding of the elements as you begin to fit them together. The third difficulty is that not all of the elements may be expressed. Because all five elements should be present in any opinion, you must read between the lines to pinpoint an element as precisely as you can when you do not see it identified.

The remainder of this chapter is designed to give you a method for analyzing cases. Each component of a case will be discussed separately with an emphasis on identifying and understanding that component. Because of the web-like nature of a judicial opinion, no method will result in instant identification or understanding of the components. As you gain experience at briefing cases, you will develop a format that suits your particular abilities and needs. The following method should prove helpful as a starting point and framework for your analysis.

1. Read the opinion carefully.

Several readings are usually required before you can completely understand a case. During your initial reading you will gain a general understanding of who the parties were, how the dispute originated, and what effect the court's decision had on the parties. You will also form tentative theories concerning the basic components of the opinion, which you will test and clarify during later readings. After you have acquired a basic understanding of the facts of the case and the "real world" implications of the court's decision, you can figure out what the court decided.

2. Identify the holding.

The holding is the actual decision in the case. It is the answer to the legal question presented to the court. Identifying the holding requires you to study the opinion and determine what the court *actually decided* in the case. Holdings can be either express or implied. Express holdings are easy to identify because they are announced as such. In an express holding, for example, a court might state:

> We hold that driving a car at eighty miles per hour is prima facie reckless driving.

Although identifying express holdings appears easy from this example, there is a hidden danger. Courts sometimes inadvertently state they are ruling one way when, in fact, they are deciding the case a different way, or they identify as a holding something that is really reasoning or policy. To avoid being misled, concentrate on what the court actually did in the case, rather than on what it said.

Implied holdings are usually harder to identify than express holdings because you can rely only on the court's actions. The court gives its ultimate decision and the reasons supporting it, but does not tell you what rule it has formulated or followed. In an implied holding, for example, a court might state:

> The trial court found the defendant guilty of reckless driving without any testimony that the defendant was, in fact, operating his car in a reckless manner. Anyone who drives at eighty miles per hour is forced to dodge and weave through traffic at a high rate of speed. This conduct is inherently reckless and endangers the well-being of others. Affirmed.

The court's holding is the same as in the first example, but here the judge did not expressly state it. Both holdings, however, are equally important.

Do not confuse implied holdings with the reasons for the decision. Sometimes these two elements are hard to distinguish. Remember that the holding is the actual decision and that the reasons or policies are the justifications given for the decision. The two concepts can be distinguished by a simple but useful idea: Each issue has only one holding, but each holding may be supported by several reasons.

■ Study the following judicial opinion and the three proposed holdings for the case:

State v. Klein (1969)

Casey Klein appeals his conviction for burglary. Klein was apprehended reaching into a house with ten-foot-long tree snips he had modified into a long pair of tweezers. He admitted to the police that he intended to steal a mink coat lying on a chair near an open window.

Appellant Klein denies that he could properly have been convicted of burglary. The maximum offense, he argues, is attempted larceny, because that crime requires only an attempt to steal the property of another. The prosecutor, however, correctly sought and won a conviction for burglary.

Generally, burglary occurs only if the defendant is physically present in the house; he must actually penetrate the enclosure of the dwelling. Although the defendant in this case never entered the house, he did extend his tree snips through the window. There is no meaningful difference between the snips and his arm because the penetration by the snips was merely an extension of Klein's person. Crime has run rampant in recent decades and this type of activity must be discouraged. Burglary carries a greater penalty than attempted larceny and this penalty will more effectively deter such crimes. We therefore hold that the need to deter such activities renders the defendant's actions burglary.

ANSWER A: A defendant may properly be convicted of burglary during a high crime period when his conviction will deter similar actions, even if he was not physically present in the building.

ANSWER B: For the purposes of burglary, tree snips are the same as a human arm.

ANSWER C: The protrusion of tree snips held by defendant into a dwelling satisfies the penetration element of burglary even if the defendant's body does not enter the dwelling.

The actual holding of the case is contained in Answer C. It shows how the relevant legal rule was found applicable to the facts of this case. Answer C does not justify the holding; it is simply a statement of what the court decided. This is the rule that subsequent courts will apply or distinguish.

Answer A is what the court said it was holding, but not what it actually held. Deterring crime is a reason the court gave for deciding the case the way it did, but reasons and holdings are different things. The holding, again, is what the court actually decided in the case. Answer A reflects the court's confusing way of stating a policy justification for the decision, but it is not the court's holding.

Answer B sounds more like a holding and less like a reason than Answer A. It does not, however, offer a very useful holding. A tree snips may be the same as a human arm, but that statement fails to explain what legal rule is involved. In addition, the court *reasoned* that there was no meaningful difference between a tree snips and a human arm for purposes of satisfying the penetration requirement. Thus, Answer B is also more like a reason.

3. Identify the issue.

Cases usually develop because the parties disagree over the application of one or more rules of law to a particular set of facts. The issue is the legal question that must be resolved before a case can be decided. Notice the interplay between holdings and issues: Holdings are the legal answers to the issues.

The issue in a case, like the holding, can be express or implied. Many times the court will tell you the issue. For example: "The question presented in this case is whether a snowmobile is a motor vehicle within the meaning of the Michigan Motor Vehicle Code." This is an express issue. Sometimes a court will tell you the issue is one thing when a close reading of the case will demonstrate that it is something else. Sometimes the court will not tell you the issue. When this happens, you must read the case carefully and identify the issue based on the holding and the reasons that support the holding. The holding helps identify the issue because the holding is the answer to the issue. Once you have identified the holding in a case, you should have little trouble spotting the issue.

Study the following opinion and three suggested issues:

Johnson v. Silk (1969)

Alice Silk and Fran Johnson, university students who had recently met, decided to use Silk's small sports car to drive to their hometown for the weekend. Silk told Johnson she would pay all their traveling expenses to repay Johnson for tutoring Silk before the midterm examination in Silk's Chinese philosophy class. Shortly after they started out, Silk lost control of her car and it struck a construction barrel on the side of the road. Johnson suffered severe injuries and brought suit against Silk to recover damages. The trial court granted Silk's motion to dismiss, and Johnson appealed.

The state Automobile Guest Statute bars guest passengers from suing drivers for injuries they sustain in automobile accidents. The statute applies only if the passenger did not confer a substantial benefit on the driver that motivated the driver to provide the ride.

The trial court found that Johnson was barred from recovery because she "paid nothing for the ride." The issue in this case is whether Johnson assumed the risk of her own injury by riding on a busy highway in a small sports car. Johnson tutored Silk, and she did so before the ride with every expectation of repayment. It is not necessary that the substantial benefit motivating the ride be cash. Silk owed a favor to Johnson that she felt obligated to repay, and under general principles of fairness actually was bound to repay. The Guest Statute therefore is inapplicable. Reversed.

ANSWER A: Whether a passenger injured in an accident while riding in a small sports car on a busy highway is barred by assumption of risk from suing the driver of that car for damages.

ANSWER B: Whether a court can disregard the Automobile Guest Statute to reach a just and fair result.

ANSWER C: Whether a passenger's tutoring of a driver before a midterm examination constitutes a substantial benefit that bars application of the Automobile Guest Statute.

The correct statement of the issue is Answer C. The court had to decide whether the Automobile Guest Statute applied to this situation. Application of the statute turned on whether the passenger conferred a substantial benefit on the driver. This is the real issue. The court determined that Johnson's tutoring of Silk constituted a substantial benefit because Silk had an obligation to repay Johnson by providing the ride. The court, therefore, held the statute inapplicable, and this holding provides further evidence of the issue.

Answer A is what the court said the issue was, but it is not what the court decided. Because the issue and the holding are so closely related, you must look elsewhere for the issue. Assumption of risk, as you may know, is a defense to negligence. Most of this opinion, however, deals with the Automobile Guest Statute, and this is a good clue that the issue concerns the statute and not assumption of risk. Although few courts will err as obviously as this one did, you must remember that word and deed are not necessarily the same thing in judicial opinion writing.

Answer B may be your first reaction to what happened in this case, but issues must be defined in a legal context, not a political one. Fairness is mentioned in the opinion, but it was a reason for the decision, even though the court mistakenly said it was the holding. This mistake points to an important lesson. Although holdings and issues are closely related, you must be very sure you have identified the correct holding before you use it to infer the issue. Answer B does not define the legal issue.

4. Identify the rule.

Once you have determined the issue and holding, you should identify the rule. The rule is the general legal principle relevant to the particular factual situation presented. The rule can be a synthesis of prior holdings in cases with similar facts. It can also be a statutory provision.

Identifying the rule involved in a particular case is relatively easy. The court will usually state what rule it is applying or why it is refusing to apply a certain rule. When the court does not state the rule, and you are unfamiliar with the area of law, you will have to infer the rule from the issues, holdings, and facts of the case.

Rules, issues, and holdings are closely related. The issue is generally how the relevant rule will be applied to the case. The holding is the resolution of the issue—the determination of how the rule should be applied to the case. Stated another way, the holding is the rule modified by the facts of a particular case.

The following examples are illustrative:

Whitman v. Whitman (1971)

James Whitman's will left all of his property to his brother, George. James's wife challenged the validity of the will after James died, claiming that it did not express James's clear intent. She sought to present evidence, including her own testimony, that James actually wanted to give a substantial portion of his estate to her. The trial court excluded the evidence, and we affirm. The rule in this state is that an unambiguous will is conclusive as to the testator's intent unless it would contravene law or public policy. All other evidence must be excluded. Because James's wife sought to present precisely such evidence, and the will was not ambiguous, the trial court properly ruled the evidence inadmissible. We find no legal or public policy reason to depart from the intent expressed in the will.

Identifying the rule in this case is simple because the court explained that "the rule in this state" is that an unambiguous will is conclusive as to the testator's intent. But consider this opinion:

Central Credit Co. v. Smith (1963)

Olan Company began to operate as a business before it was properly incorporated. Prior to proper incorporation, the company made sales and incurred debts. Olan's creditors are seeking to hold Smith and Jones, the incorporators and sole shareholders, personally liable for these debts. A corporation does not legally exist until it has been properly incorporated. Once a business is properly incorporated, a creditor must look to the corporate entity to satisfy its claim. The trial court properly found Smith and Jones personally liable for the debts. Affirmed.

Because the precise rule used by the court is not stated here, you must identify it by inference. The legal rules stated by the court and its holding in this case help the inquiry. A corporation's legal existence begins with proper incorporation, the court said. After that time, the corporation's shareholders are not personally liable for its debts. The court also held these shareholders personally liable for debts they incurred before incorporation. The court thus applied a corollary of the rules stated: A shareholder of a corporation can be held personally liable for debts incurred when the company is not properly incorporated.

5. Identify the facts.

Once you understand the rule, holding, and issue, you will be able to identify the relevant facts of the case. After the initial reading of the case, you have a general knowledge of the facts. Now you are ready to reread them and determine which facts were important to the decision.

Judicial opinions usually contain a lengthy description of the facts because the court wants the reader to understand the situation completely. You should identify two kinds of facts—legally relevant facts and procedurally significant facts.

Legally relevant facts are those the court considered important in deciding the case. Sometimes these facts are events that did occur, and sometimes they are events that did not occur. These facts are outcome-determinative; they affected the court's decision. Because facts are inextricably tied to legal issues and rules, it is impossible to know which facts are relevant without first knowing what the court decided. Sometimes a court will state precisely those facts it thought significant in deciding the case. At other times you will have to guess those facts from the court's holding and reasons. There is no rule that indicates which facts are outcome determinative, and no single fact is necessarily legally significant.

Procedurally significant facts describe at what stage in the case an error may have occurred in the lower court. These facts are routinely stated in appellate opinions. Procedural facts are important because the procedural posture of the case affects what legally relevant facts are available to the appellate court. When the parties agree on the facts, the trial court simply determines and applies the relevant law. If the parties disagree on the facts, a trial is held in which each side presents witnesses and other evidence to support its story. Appellate courts are then confronted with more numerous and less consistent facts than if a case is resolved before trial. The procedural posture of the case also affects what the appellate court can do if it disagrees with the trial court. If the factual record is complete, the appellate court's decision should end the controversy; if the record is not complete, the appellate court will remand the case for more fact finding.

☐ Consider the following opinion and factual statements:

Lost River Ditch Co. v. Brody (1923)

The defendant owns a small riparian tract on Apple Blossom Creek. In the fall of 1922 he began diverting 45,000 gallons of water a day from a pumphouse on that tract to a nonriparian parcel one-half mile from the stream. The defendant claimed he needed the water because he had just doubled the size of his herd. The plaintiff, who owned another riparian tract downstream on the creek, sued the defendant for damages, claiming that any diversion of water from the watershed was impermissible. Although the plaintiff was unable to prove any actual damages, the jury awarded him one dollar in nominal damages. We reverse. Diversion of water from the creek to a nonriparian tract without some evidence of damage does not provide a basis for recovery of nominal or any other damages.

ANSWER A: The defendant, who owned a small riparian tract on Apple Blossom Creek, diverted 45,000 gallons of water per day in the fall of 1922 to supply water for his recently doubled cattle herd. The plaintiff, a downstream riparian owner on the same creek, sued the defendant for damages, claiming that any diversion of water from the riparian tract was prohibited. A jury awarded the plaintiff one dollar in nominal damages even though he was unable to prove actual damages.

ANSWER B: The defendant, who owned a riparian tract on a creek, diverted water from the creek to a nonriparian tract. The plaintiff, a downstream riparian owner on the same creek, sued the defendant for diverting the water. The plaintiff could not show actual damages, but a jury awarded him nominal damages.

Answer B is better because it contains only those facts the court used to decide the case and those facts needed to explain what happened in the trial court. Answer B contains nothing else; it is simple and succinct. Answer A is a slightly rewritten version of the facts stated in the case. It includes interesting details, but the name of the creek, the quantity of water diverted, the actual amount of the nominal damages, and other details have nothing to do with the legal rule or the significant facts of this case. Answer A also omits an important fact by ignoring the type of tract to which the water was diverted. Because the rule is applicable only to water diverted to a nonriparian tract, Answer A should have stated that the water was diverted from the creek to a nonriparian tract.

6. Identify the reasons and policies.

Reasons are the steps in the logical process a court uses in arriving at its holding. Reasons can be simple explanations of how a legal rule or policy is applicable or inapplicable to the case, or they can be more involved explanations of why the analysis from one area of the law is applicable to an entirely different area of the law. When studying cases, you should determine the exact reasoning process the court employed to arrive at its holding on an issue. Only through understanding the reasons behind a court's decision can you understand what the decision actually means or how broadly or narrowly the case might be interpreted.

Chapter 1 (Rules and Policies) defines policies as the underlying purposes of legal rules. They are similar to but broader than reasons. Whether a court is modifying the law in bold strokes to reach certain goals or whether it is carefully limiting the scope of earlier decisions, it will usually advance some policy justification for its decision. Even when a court admits it reached a harsh or unfair result for the parties, it will still try to show how the decision is in the best interest of the public. In other cases, when the law dictates an outcome the court dislikes, the court may complain about the law and even suggest the desirability of legislative change, but it will still explain the policies underlying the law and the outcome. Policies are important because they define the future direction of the law.

The easiest way to identify policies is to first identify the holding. Once you have determined what the court decided, look for the social justifications for the court's decision. An illustration used earlier in this chapter involved a defendant who attempted to take a fur coat through a window using tree snips. The court in that case held that use of tree snips satisfied the penetration element of burglary even though no part of the defendant's body entered the building. The court stated a broad policy in support of its conclusion by emphasizing the high crime rate and the deterrent value of the more severe penalty for burglary.

Some opinions contain no policy justification at all. In the water diversion illustration given earlier in this chapter, for example, the court stated a rule and reversed the trial court without explaining the basis for the rule or its holding. A court is less likely to provide an explanation in cases such as this, when the rule and its application are fairly well settled. Look to earlier decisions, if necessary, to determine the policies underlying the rule.

The close relationship between reasons and policies sometimes makes it difficult to tell the two apart, but the following test is useful: Reasons indicate how the court arrived at its holding; policies tell you why this holding is socially desirable. An opinion can make sense without any policy justifications, but it cannot make sense without reasons explaining how the court arrived at its conclusion.

Sometimes, you will find that the court's explanation is incomplete or ambiguous. When that occurs, say so. If only one interpretation is logical, explain it. If several interpretations are possible, you may want to explain them.

In the burglary case, for example, the court stated that tree snips were an extension of Klein's arm. The court's reasoning is not explained, beyond the statement that there is "no meaningful difference" between the snips and Klein's arm. You might reconstruct the court's reasoning as follows:

> The requirement that the burglar must penetrate the enclosure would mean nothing if a burglar could circumvent the requirement by devices that extend the reach of the burglar's arm. Therefore, we will enlarge this requirement by redefining penetration to include a mechanical extension of a burglar's person.

This reconstruction explains how the court arrived at its holding. The announced policy to deter crime, in addition, helps to justify the court's extension of one of the burglary requirements.

7. Check for congruency.

Once you have some idea of the important facts, the issue, the rule of law, the holding, and the reasons and policies, check these elements against one another to make sure they are congruent. There is an interplay among them that should be obvious by now. The court's holding will be a combination of the relevant rule of law and the significant facts. The issue is the holding stated in the form of a question: How does this rule of law apply to the particular facts of this case? The answer to the issue will be the holding. Policies and reasons form a basis for the holding. Such interaction makes the case an interlocking whole and underscores why you cannot understand any one element without reference to the others. Always pause when you have gone this far to make sure the elements are congruent.

You might test for congruency by using the following model:

Facts	What happened?
Rule	The law
Issue	Does the law apply to these facts?
Holding	The law does or does not apply to these facts
Reasons & Policies	Why the law does or does not apply to these facts

If you are using the same law and the same facts in each element, and they accurately reflect the court's decision, you have a good case brief. When the court's holding changes the law, however, you will find that the law described in the holding differs from the law described in the rule. Your case brief should reflect that change.

8. In multiple-issue cases, analyze each issue separately.

A case can contain more than one issue because there may have been several disagreements about the law that the appellate court was asked to resolve. Although an appellate court will frequently dispose of an entire case after resolving only one of these disagreements, many times an opinion will contain a discussion of several issues with a corresponding holding for each issue. When a case contains several issues, analyze each issue separately. For each issue you must identify the rule, relevant facts, holding, and reasons and policies supporting the court's decision. Although the issues may be closely related, your analysis of each should be distinct. Once you have identified each issue presented in an opinion, follow the steps outlined in this chapter for dissecting each one.

Each of the elements discussed above may be written out in a case brief. As already stated, a case brief is a short summary of a case that may be useful to you in preparing for class or when researching a problem. It gives you a ready reference so you do not have to reread a case to remember what it was about.

Below is an opinion and a sample case brief:

Roberts v. Zoning Commission (1988)

Appellant Edwin Roberts owns a parcel of land. He applied to the city Zoning Commission to rezone the parcel from R-3 (single-family residential) to O-I (office-institutional). The Commission denied his application, finding that all surrounding parcels are zoned for and contain single-family homes. Roberts produced evidence that the parcel was appraised at between $50,000 and $90,000 under the current zoning, but would be worth $200,000 to $250,000 if rezoned.

Following the denial of his rezoning request, Roberts filed this action alleging that the Zoning Commission had taken his property without compensation, in violation of the state and federal constitutions. To demonstrate a taking, the challenger to a zoning classification has the burden of presenting clear and convincing evidence that he has suffered a significant detriment.

The trial court properly dismissed the landowner's complaint because Roberts failed to meet his burden. Merely showing a disparity in the market value of property as currently zoned versus its value if rezoned is not, by itself, sufficient to establish a significant detriment. Offers for real estate depend on the method of marketing and the asking price. Because the landowner did not attempt to market the property at an asking price consistent with its value under current zoning, no significant detriment has been shown. We must bear in mind that zoning ordinances exist to ensure the greater good of the community even though specific zoning may not always be in the best interest of an individual. Affirmed.

Here is a sample brief of this case. The five parts of the case brief are set out in a different order here than the order described earlier in this chapter. Looking for the holding first, and then the issue, rule, facts, and reasons and policies, is a good way to study a case. But you may want your written case brief to have the five parts in the order shown in the example below. Case briefs are for your use. You should feel free to adopt a format that works best for you.

Roberts v. Zoning Commission (1988)

Facts: A landowner applied for a rezoning of his property. His request was denied even though his property would have been worth substantially more under the new zoning. He did not try to market the parcel under the existing zoning classification. The landowner then sued, alleging an unconstitutional taking. The trial court's dismissal of this complaint was affirmed.

Rule: The government may not take property without compensation. To show a taking from a rezoning denial, a landowner must demonstrate by clear and convincing evidence that he has suffered a significant detriment.

Issue: Has the landowner suffered a significant detriment?

Holding: No. A landowner cannot show a significant detriment unless he attempts to market the property at an asking price consistent with its value under current zoning.

Reasons and policies: A significant detriment does not occur when the landowner is deprived of a potential increase in property value. A difference in market value depends on such variables as how the land is marketed. Zoning may not always serve the best interest of the individual, but it serves the greater good of the community.

The following exercises are designed to introduce you to case analysis. Each opinion contains all of the components discussed in this chapter. Using the format provided above for case analysis, write a brief for each one. The goal is to identify the various components as precisely as possible.

Exercise 3-A

Toad v. Ulrich (1972)

The appellee, Michael Toad, operates a roadside stand where he sells hand-carved, three-legged wooden stools to tourists. Toad's business started slowly, but it has increased substantially in recent years. Toad now derives a modest income from his enterprise. From the start, he has advertised and referred to his stools as "Toad Stools." After Toad operated his stand for one year, the appellant, Bruce Ulrich, began operating a similar stand and selling similar stools, which Ulrich also called "Toad Stools." When Ulrich first opened his stand, Toad asked him not to use the name "Toad Stools," but Ulrich did so for two years. Toad made no further effort to prevent the use of the name until he started this suit.

Toad filed suit alleging that the appellant had infringed on his trademark. Toad requested $5,000 in damages for lost sales and an injunction barring Ulrich from using the name "Toad Stool." The trial court awarded Toad $4,500 in damages and granted his request for an injunction. Appellant Ulrich now contends that the trial court erred in finding a trademark infringement because Toad did not actively defend his use of the name.

Common law trademark principles can protect the name of a business or product, but that protection is not absolute. A person must actively defend that trademark against known infringements. If he or she does not actively defend the name, a competitor is free to use that name after two years. "Actively defend" means making diligent efforts, including lawsuits if necessary, and Toad has not made diligent efforts according to the traditional rule.

We must, however, distinguish between large businesses that have the capacity and the resources to litigate such claims, and small businesses that do not have these resources and should not be held to the same standards. The smaller the business, the easier it should be to satisfy the active defense requirement. When Toad approached Ulrich and asked him not to use the name, he satisfied that requirement. Therefore, Toad is entitled to common law trademark protection. Affirmed.

Exercise 3-B
Bronson v. Road Runner Shoe Co. (1976)

The appellee, Road Runner Shoe Co., is a Maryland corporation that manufactures and sells running shoes. Twenty of the company's 100 employees work at its Maryland headquarters, while the remainder work at offices throughout the United States. The company, which sells to major retailers, has a fleet of trucks for delivering its shoes. The company employed George Granger as a general helper and driver for one of its delivery trucks.

Johnny Bronson filed suit against the company for injuries he sustained when one of the company's trucks, driven by Granger, jumped the median strip and struck him while he was jogging. It is undisputed that Bronson was using extreme care while jogging and was wearing a bright red jogging outfit. Bronson claimed he would never be able to jog again and that he has had emotional problems since the accident. Granger, who had not received permission to use the truck, had visited his girlfriend during his lunch hour. The company gives Granger one hour to eat lunch, and he was speeding back to work when the incident occurred. Granger was nineteen years old at the time and a " hard worker who comes from a reputable family." Granger was earning money so he could go to college and major in business administration. Granger was arrested once when he was sixteen for drag racing on a public highway, but his case was dismissed. Granger had worked for the company two years when the incident occurred.

The trial court granted the company's motion for summary judgment. On appeal, Bronson argues that the company should be liable on the theory of *respondeat superior*. We agree.

The general rule is that an employer is liable for the acts of employees when they are acting within the scope of their authority. In this case, Granger did not have permission to use the truck during lunch and did not usually drive it then. However, Granger normally had exclusive possession of the keys during working hours, and the company had never objected to Granger's private use of the truck. Employers should be held liable for the torts of their employees. It is too easy for an employer to shrug off legal responsibility by saying the employee was not authorized to commit the act. Very few employers expressly authorize employees to commit tortious acts. Employers, by their position of authority, have control over employees. Employees who do not behave responsibly should be discharged. Reversed.

Exercise 3-C

State v. Phillips (1975)

The appellant set fire to an unoccupied building. The building had been deserted for many years and had been condemned as a "firetrap." The appellant poured several gallons of gasoline throughout the first floor of the building and then ignited it. The building burned to the ground in thirty minutes. The trial court found her guilty of arson, a felony in this state. The appellant does not contest that conviction here.

On the way to put out the fire, a fireman was killed when he fell off the back of the fire truck and was run over by a car that was speeding and following the truck too closely. There was no way the driver of the car could have avoided the fireman. The driver of the car was charged and convicted of speeding and careless driving.

The appellant was also found guilty of murder under the felony-murder rule. She appealed this conviction. The felony-murder rule provides that if someone is killed during the commission of a felony, the defendant is guilty of murdering that person. The purpose of the rule is to deter people from committing felonies, particularly those which are inherently dangerous to human life. In this case, there is no doubt the fireman was killed during the commission of a felony.

Fires and arson are inherently dangerous to people in buildings, bystanders, the surrounding neighborhood, and firemen summoned to combat the blaze. The appellant should have known that a fire truck would be summoned to put out the fire, but could not foresee someone would be following the truck too closely. Public policy dictates that there must be a limit to liability. The felony-murder rule borders on strict liability in criminal law. Any expansion should be carefully scrutinized. As with any principle of strict liability, there must be a causal connection. Reversed.

4

Precedent and Stare Decisis

JUDGES HAVE MUCH FREEDOM to modify legal rules and principles in accordance with social norms and their views of justice and common sense. The concepts of precedent and *stare decisis* serve as important checks on this judicial freedom and ensure that the law develops in an orderly fashion.

One of the fundamental notions of our legal system is that courts look to previous decisions on similar questions for guidance in deciding present cases. Previous decisions on similar questions are known as precedent, and their usefulness is premised on the idea that an issue, once properly decided, should not be decided again. Reliance on precedent ensures that similar cases are decided according to the same basic principles and helps courts to process cases more efficiently. Durable rules also reinforce the social norms they define, encourage confidence in the legal system, and assist people in planning their activities.

The values that surround the notion of precedent are reinforced by the principle of *stare decisis*. Whereas precedent merely requires that courts look to previous decisions for guidance, *stare decisis* requires that a court follow its own decisions and the decisions of higher courts within the same jurisdiction. A state trial court, for example, must follow the decisions of appellate courts in that state; an intermediate appellate court must follow its own decisions and the decisions of the state's highest appellate court. Federal courts of appeal generally must follow their own prior decisions and those of the United States Supreme Court, but they are not bound by decisions of federal district courts or other federal courts of appeal.

Precedent, then, can be of two types—binding or persuasive. When the doctrine of *stare decisis* applies, precedent is binding and a court must reconcile the result in a given case with past decisions. Only after explaining why previous cases are inapplicable may a court fashion new rules or modify existing ones; a court may never ignore or contradict binding precedent. When the doctrine of *stare decisis* does not apply, as with decisions from other jurisdictions or lower courts in the same jurisdiction, courts are free to follow, or refuse to follow, previous decisions. Although not binding, such decisions may be persuasive. The reasoning of other courts often illuminates the issues and suggests solutions to a problem.

The concept of binding precedent may seem absolute. But in practice, *stare decisis* is a flexible concept. Because a judicial opinion may be interpreted in different ways, judges have significant latitude even when dealing with binding precedent. Differing interpretations result from internal tension between the facts and holding of a case and its underlying reasons or policies. Viewed most narrowly, a case stands for a particular result regarding that set of facts. Courts often do confine cases to narrow factual categories, but such interpretations give the case relatively little importance. Viewed more broadly, a case stands for the articulated reasons or policies. Because the court was concerned primarily with the facts of the case before it, you travel on increasingly risky ground the further you venture from those facts. The best guides in venturing from those facts are the reasons and policies given in the opinion.

The various ways in which a case can be interpreted highlight the fundamental role that *stare decisis* plays in the process of legal analysis. In his well-known book, *The Bramble Bush*, Professor Karl Llewellyn defined this range of interpretation in terms of "strict" and "loose" views of precedent. The "strict" view, applied to "unwelcome" precedent, limits the reach of prior cases to show that they are not applicable to the case at hand. It requires careful distinguishing of the facts and policies. The "loose" view, applied to "welcome" precedent, maximizes the reach of these cases to show how they are applicable. As Llewellyn pointed out, both approaches are "respectable, traditionally sound, [and] dogmatically correct."[1]

The varying levels of case interpretation permit flexibility within the confines of *stare decisis*. This flexibility is necessary to the legal system because it allows the law to adapt to evolving conditions and to accommodate new factual situations.

Although there is much flexibility, the stabilizing effect of *stare decisis* should not be underestimated. When the rules are well defined and the factual situations are clearly similar or plainly different, *stare decisis* mechanically dictates the result. Even when the rule is ambiguous or the factual situation complex, *stare decisis* at least defines the starting point for analysis. This tension between restraint and

---

[1] KARL LLEWELLYN, THE BRAMBLE BUSH 66–69 (1930).

freedom, between stability and change, embodies the essence of our common law system.

Determining the precedential value of rules or ideas in a court's opinion requires a close reading of the case. Statements made by a court that do not bear on the issues before it are known as *dicta* (from the Latin phrase *obiter dictum*, literally, "said in passing"). *Dicta* have little precedential value because a court is supposed to decide only the issues before it and *dicta,* by definition, are not part of the reasoning process that led to the decision. Courts sometimes rely on *dicta* nonetheless because *dicta* reflect other judges' concerns and often indicate how a court would rule in the future, given a particular set of facts.

Courts may also rely on the ideas and reasoning of concurring and dissenting judges. Appellate courts consist of a panel of judges who may not agree on how a dispute should be resolved or why a particular decision should be reached. If the court is divided, one of the judges in the majority will write the opinion of the court. Judges who disagree with the decision reached by the majority and refuse to join the court's opinion are said to dissent. Judges who agree with the decision but either disagree with the majority's reasons or would have reached the same decision on other grounds are said to concur. These judges frequently write separate opinions.

Unlike *dicta,* which may indicate how a court would rule in the future, a concurring or dissenting opinion indicates only that a judge disagreed strongly enough to write a separate opinion. Nevertheless, these opinions can be a valuable resource. Often, a dissenting or concurring opinion sharpens the focus of the debate. It may offer a different interpretation of precedent, emphasize social policies disregarded by the majority, or frame the legal question in a different way. A court that is considering a change in the law of its jurisdiction or facing an issue of first impression will read concurring and dissenting opinions on the issue in question with great interest. And dissenting opinions in an earlier case are sometimes adopted by a majority of the court in later cases.

The following two cases illustrate how precedent and *stare decisis* function. They concern the question whether a landlord should be held liable for negligently exposing tenants to foreseeable criminal activities. After deciding the first case, *Brainerd v. Harvey,* in 1972, the same state appellate court was presented with an opportunity four years later, in *Douglas v. Archer Professional Building, Inc.* to expand the scope of the rule to cover a different factual situation.

Brainerd v. Harvey (1972)

The plaintiff is an elderly man who lived in a small building in a high crime area. The building had poor lighting on its front porch and a continuously unlocked outer door. As the plaintiff was about to enter the building one night, the outer door was jerked open by an unknown youth who had been hiding inside. The youth struck and robbed the plaintiff. The plaintiff brought suit against the landlord, but the trial judge granted the defendant's motion for a directed verdict of no cause of action.

We reverse. We have from time to time held that persons are liable for negligently exposing others to foreseeable criminal activities, and this is such a case. The inadequate lighting and locks were physical defects in a common area of the building under the landlord's control; this would be a far different case if the building had not contained such defects. The landlord's negligence in failing to repair them made it more likely than not that the plaintiff would be victimized by a criminal attack.

The trial court also erred in refusing to grant the plaintiff a jury trial. The plaintiff demanded a jury trial. He did not waive that right by waiting until the pretrial conference to make his demand. Remanded for a jury trial.

Douglas v. Archer Professional Building, Inc. (1976)

In 1968, a mental health clinic leased and began occupying an office on the fifth floor of the Archer Professional Building. About two years later, an outpatient at the center stabbed Carol Douglas, a physician with an office in the building, while both of them were riding in the building's elevator. Dr. Douglas brought suit against the owner of the building. At trial, the director of the clinic testified that the stabbing was the first such incident in his ten years of experience with such programs. There was also testimony that before the incident other tenants in the building had voiced concern over use of the elevators and stairwells by the clinic's patients. Dr. Douglas won a jury verdict for $115,000 in damages. We affirm.

We stated in *Brainerd v. Harvey* that landlords are liable for damages caused when they negligently expose others to foreseeable criminal attacks in common areas of buildings they lease. In both this case and *Brainerd*, the attack occurred in an area of the building under the landlord's control and used by all tenants. Just as the landlord in *Brainerd* knew or should have known about the absence of adequate lighting and locks in the apartment building, the defendant here knew or should have known about the potentially dangerous condition in the professional building. When the landlord is informed by his tenants that such a condition exists, he has a duty to investigate and take any possible preventive measures. The jury could properly find that the landlord's failure to do so was negligence.

Fisher, J., dissenting. The court here imposes unwarranted and unreasonable burdens on landlords by vastly extending their potential liability. In *Brainerd v. Harvey*, we expressly limited the landlord's liability to his failure to detect and repair dangerous physical conditions in common areas of leased buildings. Unlike the front door, this professional building had no physical defect that enabled the assault to occur. In *Brainerd*, we also limited liability to foreseeable criminal attacks, rather than those based merely on the subjective fears of some tenants in the building. The majority opinion suggests a medieval fear of persons who receive mental health care and will impede the state's goal of returning mental patients to the community.

Although the majority and dissenting opinions reach opposite conclusions in the *Douglas* case, they both rely on *Brainerd* for the basic principles of decision. Both opinions acknowledge that landlords are liable when they negligently expose their tenants to foreseeable criminal attacks in common areas of buildings they lease. The principle of *stare decisis* requires that the court start from that position, rather than craft new and different rules.

The division of the court in *Douglas* illustrates the flexibility of *stare decisis*. The majority interpreted *Brainerd* broadly as "welcome" precedent. When the landlord is informed by his tenants of their subjective fears of a potentially dangerous condition in a common area of the building, the majority ruled, he has a duty to investigate the situation and take precautionary measures. The court departed from *Brainerd* by refusing to limit the landlord's liability to situations in which there was tangible evidence suggesting the possibility of a criminal attack. The court responded to the different factual situation presented in *Douglas* by pushing the law in a different direction, even as it reasoned that it was merely following the *Brainerd* decision.

The dissenting opinion interpreted *Brainerd* more narrowly as "unwelcome" precedent. *Brainerd*, it concluded, conditions the landlord's liability on the presence of physical defects in the building and objective evidence suggesting the possibility of a criminal attack, neither of which were present in *Douglas*. To support its narrow reading of *Brainerd*, the dissent also raised an objection about the effect of the court's decision on landlords in general and outpatient mental clinics in particular. The dissenting opinion is buttressed by *dicta* from *Brainerd* that states the case would be different if the building did not have physical defects. The statement is *dicta* because it was not necessary to the resolution of the *Brainerd* case and was thus disregarded by the majority in *Douglas*.

These two cases illustrate the tension between change and stability that is central to the study and practice of law. Certain factors militate in favor of stability. The *Brainerd* decision altered business expectations and forced landlords to modify their practices to avoid liability. In addition, because the corporate owner was found liable in the second case, it paid damages pursuant to a rule that was not articulated until the owner was found to have breached it. After *Douglas*, landlords for other office buildings no doubt made significant changes in their leasing procedures and plans. Uncertainties would be magnified by any perception that the law was subject to further modification.

Other factors counseled for change. The injury to Carol Douglas underscored the majority's view that landlords should keep their common areas free of foreseeable criminal activity. Even if the risk seemed most apparent after the harm occurred, the court concluded that a subjectively perceived risk of great bodily harm should be sufficient to warrant extra protective measures by the landlord. In addition, even though the defendant is liable under a new formulation of the rule, such liability is the only realistic incentive for encouraging a plaintiff to seek relief in court. *Douglas* was based on an evolving view of the landlord-tenant relationship. Although the arguments vary somewhat from case to case, the tension between change and stability remains.

Two additional considerations are necessary for a full understanding of the mechanics and policies of precedent and *stare decisis*. First, appellate courts are supposed to decide only as many issues as are necessary for the disposition of a case. As Chapter 3 (Case Analysis and Case Briefs) points out, sometimes this requires courts to decide multiple issues. Each holding on an issue—regardless of the number of holdings—is precedent for later decisions. The court's holding in *Brainerd* concerning the plaintiff's demand for a jury trial, as well as its holding on the negligence issue, are both precedent and will have to be considered by future courts rendering decisions on the same issues.

Second, because appellate courts tend to make and apply law while trial courts simply apply law, appellate courts have greater freedom in treating precedent than trial courts. Appellate courts sometimes find it impossible to use previous cases and still reconcile their decisions with their own values or social norms. When this happens, a court may simply overrule the previous cases and chart a new course rather than show how these cases may be distinguished. Courts usually justify overruling previous decisions by pointing to the outdated principles or poor reasoning that supported them. These decisions are often spectacular, as when the United States Supreme Court, in the 1954 case of *Brown v. Board of Education*,[2] held that a state could not constitutionally require racial segregation in public schools, overruling its 1896 *Plessy v. Ferguson*[3] decision permitting "separate but equal" accommodations. Cases may also be more subtly overruled; a series of decisions, for example, may chip away at the scope of an earlier rule or undercut its policy basis.

[2] 347 U.S. 483 (1954).
[3] 163 U.S. 537 (1896).

The exercises that follow are intended to show the stability and flexibility inherent in the concepts of precedent and *stare decisis.*

Exercise 4-A

Assume you are a trial judge in a civil action in which Elizabeth Fowler, the defendant, claims the court has no jurisdiction because service was obtained "by trickery and fraud." Fowler, a resident of another state, knew she was the possible subject of two civil actions in your state, one for a $5,000 damage deposit she had not returned to a merchant, and the other for a $200,000 insurance swindle. She wanted to resolve the first potential suit but not the second. To do this, she arranged a vacation in your state so she could pay off the merchant, who said he wanted "to avoid litigation over the deposit." She met the merchant at the airport and paid his deposit. The merchant, who secretly worked for the allegedly defrauded insurance company, then served her with papers for the insurance scheme. The following case is the only relevant precedent in your state:

Eckersly v. Ramon (1951)

The appellant, Sean Eckersly, a resident of this state, sought to bring an action against Hal Ramon, a nonresident, for breach of contract. To secure service of process on Ramon, Eckersly requested several of Ramon's acquaintances to persuade Ramon that his mother, who also lives in this state, was terminally ill. Ramon agreed to come to this state to visit her. In reality, Ramon's mother was hiking in the Rocky Mountains. Ramon was met at the airport by Eckersly's agent, who served Ramon with papers in the contract action.

The trial court rejected Ramon's claim that it lacked jurisdiction because service was fraudulently obtained. We disagree. When plaintiffs resort to such shocking fraud to obtain service of process, the integrity of the entire judicial system is undermined. The trial court had no power to render judgment in this case. Reversed.

1. Decide whether your court has jurisdiction, using the *Eckersly* case as precedent. Justify your decision.

2. Is your answer to 1 consistent with your sense of a just result? Explain.

3. Could you have used *Eckersly* to support a decision contrary to the one you reached in response to 1? Explain.

Exercise 4-B

Assume that you are a state appellate court judge. Elliot Buckler was charged with reckless endangerment under the Motor Vehicle Code after the car he was driving left the road early one morning and struck a tree, killing a passenger. The trial judge instructed the jury that it could return a guilty verdict only if it was convinced beyond a reasonable doubt that the evidence showed Buckler had operated his motor vehicle in reckless disregard of the lives or safety of others. The judge then read a separate provision of the Motor Vehicle Code, which prohibits driving while under the influence of alcohol. Although Buckler was not charged for violating this provision, there was evidence that he had been drinking heavily. The judge told the jury it could use Buckler's violation of this provision to determine his guilt for reckless endangerment. Buckler was convicted. On appeal, he seeks a new trial by challenging the trial judge's instruction that guilt for driving while under the influence of alcohol could be used to establish guilt for reckless endangerment.

There are two relevant cases in the state:

State v. Waterford (1909)

This action began on a criminal complaint charging defendant with reckless endangerment. The complaint charged that defendant recklessly ran his motor vehicle against the decedent and the horse that the decedent was riding, killing both. The defendant filed a demurrer, claiming that the complaint did not indicate the offense with sufficient clarity to notify the defendant specifically for what crime he was to be tried. The trial court overruled the demurrer, and the defendant was convicted. We affirm.

Operators of motor vehicles have a duty to obey the laws regarding the use of motor vehicles. Disregard of or inattention to this duty, as defined in any of the motor vehicle laws, constitutes recklessness. The complaint therefore properly used the words "reckless endangerment" to describe the manner in which the defendant acted, particularly considering his manifest drunkenness. This was not an innocent accident.

State v. Seperic (1958)

A criminal complaint charged the defendant with reckless endangerment in violation of the Motor Vehicle Code. He was convicted after a jury trial. The defendant argues on appeal that the statute violates the state constitution because it does not state with sufficient clarity what it prohibits. We disagree.

Motor vehicles play such an important role in our lives that reckless driving has come to have a commonly understood meaning—driving with wanton disregard for the lives or safety of other persons. The acts prohibited are sufficiently definite to persons of ordinary intelligence. The standard requires not only reckless operation but also operation that endangers the lives or safety of others. Nothing else is needed to establish reckless endangerment. Affirmed.

1.   The court in *Seperic* did not mention the *Waterford* decision. Does the holding in the later case nonetheless affect the validity of the earlier case? Explain.

2.   How would you decide Buckler's case? Why? How would you use these cases to explain your decision?

3.   Could you use *Waterford* to support a decision contrary to the one you reached in response to 2? Could you use *Seperic* to support a decision contrary to the one you reached in response to 2? Explain.

Exercise 4-C

Assume you are a trial judge. In the case before you, Marie Elson, an elderly blind woman, defaulted on the land contract for her home. The real estate company wants to repossess the house and keep $15,000 in payments she has made thus far on the $21,000 contract. Elson does not contest her default, and she is willing to let the real estate company repossess the house. She does, however, insist on the return of the $15,000.

The following case is the only relevant precedent in your state:

Aaron v. Erickson (1947)

Susan Aaron defaulted on a $30,000 land contract after making $12,000 in payments. The trial court denied Aaron's request for return of the $12,000. We affirm. There is a fundamental difference in our law between land contracts and mortgages. A land contract is an installment plan under which the purchaser does not get title to the property until the last payment. Those who buy property on a mortgage have it financed through a third party and receive title immediately. It may be a hard result, but those who buy property on a land contract take the risk of losing everything for failure to make payments. If this were a mortgage, we would reach a different result.

The following case is from the highest court of another state:

Deal v. Novack (1990)

In 1976, Samuel Deal entered into a land contract with Larry Novack for $60,000. Deal defaulted in 1986 after making $24,000 in payments. The court of appeals affirmed the trial court's holding that Novack was entitled to repossess the property and retain Deal's payments. We reverse. Had Deal entered into a typical mortgage arrangement, he would have title to the property and the mortgagee who provided the purchase price would have a lien on the property to secure the loan. Upon his default and the mortgagee's foreclosure, he would lose the property but his $24,000 would be returned. To hold that a land contract is conceptually different from a mortgage is to elevate form over substance. In both cases, the seller gives up possession of the property in exchange for the purchase price. In the case of a land contract, the seller retains legal title to the property as security for the price. In the case of a mortgage, the mortgagee retains a lien on the property as security. It is inequitable to hold that the defaulting buyer under the first arrangement must forfeit 40% of the purchase price while the defaulting buyer under the second arrangement forfeits nothing.

      Pearle, J., concurring. A buyer who enters into a land contract must make a clear showing of inequity in order to avoid forfeiture of his payments. Otherwise, the court's opinion can be read as a wholesale repudiation of the land contract as an accepted instrument of commerce.

1.   Is Elson entitled to have the money refunded? Justify your decision.

2.   Is your answer to 1 consistent with your sense of a just result? Explain.

3.   Could you have used the cases to support a decision contrary to the one you reached in response to 1? Explain.

Exercise 4-D

Assume you are a judge confronted with the following cases:

1.   Ernie Tubbs and Ray Hoffman negotiated every word of the contract by which Tubbs sold his elaborate stereo system to Hoffman for $2,700. The contract provided that Tubbs would deliver the stereo to Hoffman's house, and that Hoffman would be obligated to accept the stereo and pay the full price even if it was damaged in transit. The stereo was damaged when Tubbs' truck was involved in an accident. Hoffman accepted the stereo, but he insisted on a deduction from the full price. Can Tubbs collect the $2,700 from Hoffman?
        Decide this case according to your idea of a just result, and state a rule that explains your decision.

2.   Beth Goldberg insured her house on Louisiana's Gulf Coast for $90,000. The contract was identical in form to all other home insurance policies sold by the company. Goldberg's home was severely damaged by flooding from a hurricane, and she made a claim on her policy. The company denied the claim, stating that a line in the middle of the seven-page contract specifically excluded hurricane flooding from coverage. Beth Goldberg had never read the contract. Can she recover for damage to her home?
        (a)   Decide this case for Goldberg in a manner that is not inconsistent with your answer to 1. State a rule that explains your decision in both cases, and describe the basis for your rule.
        (b)   Decide this case for the insurance company in a manner that is not inconsistent with your answer to 1. State a rule that explains your decision in both cases, and describe the basis for your rule.
        (c)   Are you more comfortable deciding the case for Goldberg or for the insurance company? Explain.

3.   Waldo Graff bought a refrigerator from his neighborhood appliance dealer for $400. Because he could not pay the full purchase price, he agreed in a contract to the dealer's financing scheme, which required a $30 payment each month for five years. Graff has a third-grade education and is not good with figures, so he did not know (nor was he told) that the refrigerator would actually cost him $1,800. After he had paid the dealer $500, a friend explained the contract to him. He made no further payments. Can the dealer collect the remaining $1,300?
        (a)   Decide this case for the dealer in a manner that is not inconsistent with your decision in 2(a). State a rule that explains your decision and describe the basis for it.

(b)   Decide this case for the dealer in a manner that is not inconsistent with your decision in 2(b). State a rule that explains your decision and describe the basis for it.

(c)   Decide this case for Graff in a manner that is not inconsistent with your decision in 2(a). State a rule that explains your decision and describe the basis for it.

(d)   Decide this case for Graff in a manner that is not inconsistent with your decision in 2(b). State a rule that explains your decision and describe the basis for it.

(e)   Which of the above decisions do you prefer? Why?

Part B

BASIC CONCEPTS OF
LEGAL METHOD

5

Identifying and Selecting Issues for Analysis

THE FIRST STEP in solving a legal problem is to select the questions that require analysis from the broad range of questions suggested by the facts of the case. Some questions that occur to you initially will not require analysis because you will discover that they are not relevant, that is, they are not essential or even helpful in answering the inquiry. Other questions might prove to be relevant, but they are excluded from detailed analysis because they have clear answers. Questions that must be resolved before a legal problem can be solved are known as issues, and they occur whenever there can be some reasonable disagreement about whether, or how, a legal rule should apply to a set of facts.

Selecting issues is a tentative and ongoing process, requiring you to change or sharpen the focus of your inquiry as you think about the problem and the legal authority that will govern the outcome. The process involves four distinct steps, which are best illustrated in the context of a specific problem.

☐ Fred Brookson, a lifelong resident of Klamath Falls, Oregon, contacted your firm to see whether he can file suit against Wendell Carter for injuries sustained as a result of an incident that occurred in southern Oregon. About three months ago, Brookson and his wife, Ellen, from whom he is now separated, participated in a demonstration concerning recent acts of violence against doctors practicing in a local abortion clinic. The demonstration occurred on a wharf extending into the Coos River. A group of people, including Wendell Carter, gathered around the demonstrators and began to heckle them. The two groups exchanged remarks and eventually the hecklers threw rocks and bottles at the demonstrators. When Carter threw a rock that struck and injured Ellen, Fred became angry and approached Carter. Carter said he regretted injuring Ellen because he had been aiming at Fred. The two men exchanged heated remarks. Then, without any provocation, Carter pulled out a knife, screamed, and lunged at Brookson, intending to stab him. As Brookson jumped back to avoid being injured, he almost bumped into an unidentified demonstrator. The demonstrator, who apparently thought he was being attacked, struck Brookson several times and seriously injured him. Both Brooksons required hospital treatment. Fred Brookson's medical expenses exceeded $55,000; his estranged wife's expenses were approximately $2,000. Both have lost weight, exhibit chronic anxiety, and have periods of severe insomnia.

Your supervising attorney wants you to write a memo assessing Fred Brookson's chances of success in an action against Carter for the damages Carter inflicted on him. Carter grew up in California but has spent the last three years attending college and living with his brother in Oregon. Your supervising attorney believes it best to bring this action in federal district court because of the unpopular nature of the incident which gave rise to the injuries. Can a federal district court exercise jurisdiction in this case? What claims can Fred Brookson raise?

Your preliminary research has turned up two statutory provisions and three cases. The statutory provisions are federal; they are taken from the United States Code. The first case was decided by the United States court of appeals for your circuit. The other two cases were decided by the highest court of your state.

§ 1332. Diversity of Citizenship; Amount in Controversy; Costs

(a)   The district courts shall have original jurisdiction of all civil actions where the matter in controversy exceeds the sum or value of $50,000, exclusive of interest and costs, and is between—

(1)   citizens of different States;

(2)   citizens of a State and citizens or subjects of a foreign state;

(3)   citizens of different States and in which citizens or subjects of a foreign state are additional parties; and

(4)   a foreign state . . . as plaintiff and citizens of a State or of different States.

For the purposes of this section . . . an alien admitted to the United States for permanent residence shall be deemed a citizen of the State in which such alien is domiciled.

§ 1333. Admiralty, Maritime and Prize Cases

The district courts shall have original jurisdiction, exclusive of the courts of the States, of:

(1)   Any civil case of admiralty or maritime jurisdiction, saving to suitors in all cases all other remedies to which they are otherwise entitled.

(2)   Any prize brought into the United States and all proceedings for the condemnation of property taken as prize.

Krebs v. Beechwood Aircraft Co. (1986)

Appellant Krebs filed suit in federal district court after the small plane in which he was flying crashed into the ocean off the Washington coast because of a defective engine mount. Krebs claimed admiralty jurisdiction under section 1333 of the United States Code. The district court dismissed for want of jurisdiction and we affirm.

Federal courts are courts of limited jurisdiction. Absent an express grant of jurisdiction by Congress or the Constitution, the federal courts have no power to hear a case. Section 1333 vests the federal courts with jurisdiction over cases that are maritime in nature. Maritime jurisdiction under section 1333(1) is appropriate when a potential hazard to maritime commerce arises out of an activity that bears a substantial relationship to traditional maritime activity. Claims dealing with navigation, shipping, and commerce by sea are typical subjects for maritime jurisdiction. Airplane crashes are not so linked. Although such crashes may present a potential hazard to maritime commerce, aircraft operations do not bear a substantial relationship to traditional maritime activity. Nor is this a case under Section 1333(2) involving a prize, such as a ship seized in wartime or a newly discovered undersea treasure.

Jansen v. McLeavy (1987)

Mabel Jansen brought suit against the defendant for negligence and intentional infliction of emotional distress after the defendant's car ran a stop sign and killed her young son. She witnessed the accident from her front yard. The jury awarded her $175,000 for the defendant's negligence in causing the death of her son and $250,000 for intentional infliction of emotional distress. The defendant appeals only the latter award, and we reverse.

For intentional infliction of mental distress, proof of four elements is required to establish the cause of action: (1) the conduct of the defendant must be intentional toward the plaintiff; (2) the conduct must be extreme and outrageous; (3) there must be a causal connection between the defendant's conduct and the plaintiff's mental distress; and (4) the plaintiff's mental distress must be extreme and severe. On this appeal, the defendant vigorously argues that the first element has not been met. The tort of intentional infliction of emotional distress requires some evidence that the defendant intended to inflict the emotional distress on the plaintiff. Although Jansen's mental distress was great, the driver did not intend to cause that distress. While some jurisdictions have allowed recovery in similar circumstances on a theory that the defendant's conduct made it probable that mental suffering would result, we will continue to require intentional infliction in this state.

Powers v. Locke (1989)

While plaintiff Anthony Powers and defendant James Locke were waiting in line to board a school bus, Locke shoved Powers in an effort to take his place in line.

Powers fell through a glass door and suffered multiple injuries. Powers sued Locke for battery. The trial court entered a directed verdict in favor of Powers.

A defendant commits battery when he acts intending to cause a harmful or offensive contact with the plaintiff or a third person, and thereby causes a harmful or offensive contact with the plaintiff. Because battery is intended to protect a person's body from intentional and unwanted contact, its protection extends to anything so closely connected with the person's body as to be regarded a part of it, but it does not extend to contact that is legally consented to or otherwise privileged. One who commits battery is liable for no more than nominal damages unless the person contacted proves actual harm.

Locke's argument that the evidence does not support a finding that he intended to cause injury to Powers is without merit. The tort of battery requires only that the defendant intend the contact that caused the harm, not the harm itself. Here, the evidence is uncontroverted that Locke intended to shove Powers. Locke also argues that Powers consented to the battery by agreeing to engage in a "shoving match" with Locke. Because the evidence presented at trial is conflicting on this issue, a directed verdict was improper. Reversed and remanded.

---

1. Focus only on questions within the scope of the problem.

Legal memos and briefs should discuss only those questions necessary to resolve the question presented; they should not be cluttered with unfocused dissertations or answers to questions, no matter how interesting, that were not asked. This is not to say that these questions are unimportant; they are simply outside the scope of the problem.

Two considerations are especially important in determining what legal questions are within the scope of a particular problem. First, if you have been given express instructions about the precise legal questions you should address, then you should, of course, disregard all other questions. If you have not been given express instructions, the scope of your discussion will usually be dictated by the relationship of your client to the other parties, by the relief sought, or by the procedural posture of the case. You should, for example, discuss only questions that concern your client's rights against the named adversary and not consider questions that pertain to additional parties. Second, the questions that should be discussed will vary with the procedural context of the case. Exclude questions that are not important at a given point in the procedural development of a case. For example, potential defenses to a suit would be proper questions in the context of a motion for summary judgment but improper questions in the context of a motion to dismiss. If you are uncertain about the scope of a problem, you should seek clarification from the person who assigned it.

In the Brookson case, look for legal questions dealing with the encounter between Fred Brookson and Wendell Carter. The diversity jurisdiction question is clearly within the scope of the memorandum because the instructions specifically direct you to consider this issue. Possible questions concerning a cause of action on behalf of Fred Brookson for battery and intentional infliction of emotional distress are within the scope of the memorandum. Both of these issues are dictated by the procedural context of the anticipated case, which requires you to assess the chances of success if Fred Brookson files suit. The law and facts suggest a possible cause of action by Fred Brookson against the unidentified demonstrator. The questions raised by this potential suit, however, are outside the scope of the memo because you are asked only to examine causes of action against Carter. Likewise, Ellen Brookson's possible cause of action against Carter is outside the scope of the memo. Because Fred Brookson is the party for whom the lawsuit is contemplated, your only concern is with possible avenues of relief for him.

2. Identify all relevant questions.

The next step is to identify potentially applicable legal rules. These rules, in rough form, are the counterparts of the possible issues in a case. A legal question arises from the possible application of a legal rule to a set of facts. To identify the issues in a case, you have to ask whether these rules apply or, if there is no question that they apply, what effect they will have on the outcome.

Many rules may seem to apply at first, but only a few are likely to prove useful in analyzing a particular problem. A rule applies to a situation when it so closely corresponds to the situation that it affects the rights and responsibilities of the persons involved. A statutory rule applies when it covers the facts of the case. A common law rule applies when the decided cases are more analogous to the client's case than they are different. Some rules will clearly apply; others will be plainly irrelevant and can be eliminated immediately. Keep under consideration rules that do not fit easily into either category. It is better to weed out a rule later as irrelevant than to discard a potentially applicable rule prematurely.

To identify potentially applicable rules, you must first decide what large body of law applies to your problem and do preliminary reading in that area. After you have identified a body of law, such as torts, determine what kind of tort or torts might have been committed and what defenses might be available. Reading background material such as treatises, digests, annotations, and legal encyclopedias will focus your attention on the broad spectrum of rules encompassed by a particular body of law.

Once you have gained a general understanding of the large body of relevant law, you should tighten the focus of your inquiry by examining and comparing primary sources of rules, such as cases, statutes, constitutions, and administrative regulations. You must examine all reasonable sources of legal rules and determine which of these rules, if any, match your factual situation closely enough to have a plausible effect on the outcome. At the simplest level, rules will be applied to the specific situations for which they were created. At a more abstract level, rules may be applied to different situations if it is sensible to do so.

Relevant questions are of two kinds. The first involves legal rules that plainly affect the outcome because there can be little dispute that they apply. The second involves rules that may or may not affect the outcome. Given the value and limits of a lawyer's time, a lawyer cannot explore every question in this second category and must use judgment to determine which are plausible enough to consider. There is a certain threshold of plausibility concerning the possible application of rules to the facts of your problem. Questions that do not reach this threshold are not relevant and should be discarded.

The threshold is not always easy to determine, and there can be reasonable disagreement about whether a problem involves a particular question. For example, suppose that an ordinance imposes on a city a duty to keep sidewalks in good repair, and case law has established that this duty gives rise to a cause of action against the city by pedestrians injured while traveling over sidewalks in disrepair. The rule, that the city is liable to pedestrians injured because of the city's failure to keep sidewalks in good repair, would clearly apply to a pedestrian who tripped over a broken sidewalk slab. At first glance, the rule does not seem to apply to persons injured while riding a bicycle or roller skating over a broken sidewalk because none of these people are pedestrians. Further research might reveal, however, that cyclists and skaters could be in the same category as pedestrians because they customarily travel on sidewalks.

In the Brookson case, you need to answer two questions: (1) what claims can reasonably be brought against Carter, and (2) how can this case be brought in federal court? Thus, the bodies of applicable law are civil procedure and torts.

As you read in Chapter 3 (Case Analysis and Case Briefs), each case usually contains a statement of the rule applied by the court. Identify this rule, and read it carefully. Each word in the rule may be legally significant. That is, each word may form the basis for determining whether the rule applies to the facts of your case. As a practical matter, however, most courts cluster the words of the rule into elements. The elements of a legal rule are those things that need to be satisfied or met for the rule to apply to a particular situation.

In identifying relevant questions, review the rules and their elements carefully, and decide whether their application is plausible. A good test for determining a relevant question is whether you can make a plausible argument for each side, even though you may not be persuaded by the argument for one side. As indicated earlier, at this stage in your research and thinking, potentially applicable rules should be included.

The jurisdictional rule regarding diversity of jurisdiction appears to be relevant. Section 1332(a) gives the federal district courts original jurisdiction to hear certain cases. Just like common law rules, statutory rules may be divided into elements. Section 1332(a) applies to (1) civil actions (2) where the amount in controversy exceeds $50,000, exclusive of interest and costs, and (3) the parties fall into one of four categories. These categories are (a) citizens of different states, (b) citizens of a state and citizens or subjects of a foreign state, (c) citizens of different states and in which citizens or subjects of a foreign state are additional parties, and (d) a foreign state as plaintiff and citizens of a state or of different states.

Each of these elements is plausibly met in this case. An action by a private citizen to recover damages is a civil action, which satisfies the first element. The term "civil action" distinguishes this potential lawsuit from a criminal case. Fred Brookson's medical expenses exceed $55,000, which satisfies the element requiring that the amount in controversy exceed $50,000. The third element can be satisfied if the parties fall into one of the four categories. It is plausible that Brookson and Carter are citizens of different states and thus fall into the first of these categories. Brookson is an Oregon citizen. Although Carter has attended college and lived three years in Oregon, he grew up in California. This point will require additional legal research and analysis, because Carter's residency in Oregon as a college student for the past three years may make him an Oregon citizen. An elements chart forces you to review the other three categories. Because those elements involve foreign states or citizens of foreign states, however, you would consider them no further after your review.

An elements chart, such as the one on the following page, shows whether the individual elements of a rule are, may be, or are not applicable to the facts of your case:

Diversity Jurisdiction ELEMENTS CHART		
Element	**Facts of Our Case**	**Element Met?**
Civil action	Action by private citizen to recover damages	Yes
Amount in controversy exceeds $50,000	Medical costs exceed $55,000	Yes
Parties fall into one of the following categories: a. citizens of different states	Parties are Oregon resident and person who grew up in California but lived in Oregon for the past three years as a college student	Maybe
b. citizens of a state and citizens or subjects of a foreign state	Same	No
c. citizens of different states and in which citizens or subjects of a foreign state are additional parties	Same	No
d. a foreign state as plaintiff and citizens of a state or different states	Same	No

You may have identified the jurisdictional rule regarding admiralty jurisdiction because the incident took place on a wharf over a river. Your research already shows section 1333 to be inapplicable. The *Krebs* case identifies two elements required for jurisdiction under section 1333(1): (1) a potential hazard to maritime commerce (2) arising out of an activity that bears a substantial relationship to traditional maritime activity. It is plausible that the demonstration on the wharf created a potential hazard to maritime commerce. But it is not plausible to state that an abortion demonstration bears a substantial relationship to traditional maritime activity. Nor is it plausible to state, under section 1333(2), that the case involves a prize. Section 1333 is so plainly irrelevant that it should not be mentioned in the memorandum.

In situations like this, when it is fairly easy to discern that a rule is inapplicable, an elements chart may be unnecessary. An elements chart on this question, however, might look like this:

Admiralty Jurisdiction ELEMENTS CHART		
Element	**Facts of Our Case**	**Element Met?**
1333(1) Potential hazard to maritime commerce	Demonstration on wharf over river	Maybe
Arising out of an activity that bears a substantial relationship to traditional maritime activity	Demonstration involved abortion	No
1333(2) Proceeding for condemnation of property taken as a prize	Civil claims arising from a demonstration	No

The cases indicate that several tort rules potentially apply. The court in *Jansen v. McLeavy* explicitly identifies the specific elements necessary for intentional infliction of emotional distress. According to the court, all four elements need to be met. Otherwise, intentional infliction of emotional distress has not occurred. You should go through the elements one by one, and look for corresponding facts in Fred Brookson's case, to see whether this rule might apply.

A review of each element shows that Fred Brookson may have a cause of action for intentional infliction of emotional distress. The first element requires that the defendant's conduct be intentional in regard to the plaintiff. At first it may appear that this element has been met because Carter lunged at Brookson with a knife. But the language of the rule is unclear about what must be intended. Although Carter intended to stab Brookson, it is not clear whether Carter intended to cause Brookson emotional distress. At this point, you cannot say for certain whether the element is met. The *Jansen* case does not address this issue, and you will need to find cases that do.

The second element is plainly met. Under that element, the defendant's conduct must be extreme and outrageous. By lunging at Brookson with a knife, Carter engaged in extreme and outrageous conduct.

The third element requires a causal connection between the defendant's conduct and the plaintiff's mental distress. This element may or may not be met. Brookson was beaten up by another man when he moved to avoid Carter's knife. To meet this element, however, you will need to show a causal connection between Carter's action and Brookson's emotional distress. This connection plausibly exists. But the odd chain of events, and the possibility that Brookson's emotional distress could have other causes, means it may not exist. Legal research is needed involving cases that have specifically addressed this element. Factual research on the causes of his distress may also help.

The final element requires the plaintiff's mental distress to be extreme and severe. Brookson's chronic anxiety and severe insomnia meet that element.

Because two of the elements are easily met, and two might plausibly be met, Carter may be liable for intentional infliction of emotional distress. While additional research will be necessary, intentional infliction of emotional distress appears to be a relevant question. You might use a chart like the following to depict the results of this analysis:

Intentional Infliction of Emotional Distress ELEMENTS CHART		
Element	**Facts of Our Case**	**Element Met?**
The defendant's conduct must be intentional toward the plaintiff	When Carter lunged at Brookson with a knife, he must have intended physical harm to Brookson	Maybe
Conduct must be extreme and outrageous	Carter tried to stab Brookson	Yes
Must be a causal connection between the defendant's conduct and the plaintiff's mental distress	Brookson beaten up by another when he avoided Carter's knife	Maybe
The plaintiff's mental distress must be extreme and severe	Brookson has chronic anxiety and severe insomnia	Yes

Carter may also have committed battery. The *Powers* case defines battery:

> A defendant commits battery when he acts intending to cause a harmful or offensive contact with the plaintiff or a third person, and thereby causes a harmful or offensive contact with the plaintiff.

This rule requires an analysis different from the rule in *Jansen* because the court has not divided it into elements. As already stated, each word in this rule may be important. To use each word as an element, however, would be cumbersome and confusing to both you and the reader. You should therefore try to identify elements by clustering the words into specific concepts or ideas. When the court does not expressly describe individual elements, you can identify them in two ways. You should first look at how the court has clustered words or phrases in its decision. If the court hasn't done that, or hasn't done it clearly, cluster the words or phrases yourself. Sometimes you may need to do both.

The *Powers* case gives some clues for identifying the elements of battery. The court states that battery occurs if, among other things, the plaintiff intended a harmful or offensive contact. This suggests that intent to cause harmful or offensive contact could be considered one element. It is possible to break this element into smaller pieces (intent, contact, harmful or offensive), but there is no apparent reason for doing so now. An element, again, is a conceptual unit of a rule. The use of elements forces a closer and more rigorous examination of the rule's specific requirements. An element in one situation may be two or more elements in another situation, and only part of an element in still another situation.

If intent to cause harmful or offensive contact is one element, then an act by the defendant is another. The *Powers v. Locke* court states that harmful or offensive contact with the plaintiff is an element, and that a causal connection between the defendant's act and the plaintiff's harmful or offensive contact is also an element. Divided into these elements, the rule is as follows:

> A defendant commits battery when he (1) acts (2) intending to cause a harmful or offensive contact with the plaintiff or a third person, and (3) thereby causes (4) a harmful or offensive contact with the plaintiff.

All four of these elements must be satisfied for a battery to occur. The absence of just one element means that Brookson has no cause of action for battery. Note that several elements include the word "or." When "or" is used in an element, the element may be met in more than one way; it is not necessary for both requirements to be met. The intended contact, for example, must be harmful or offensive, but it need not be both. The intended contact must be with the plaintiff or a third person, but not necessarily both.

Thus divided, the problem readily lends itself to analysis. The first element—an act—is satisfied because Carter lunged at Brookson with a knife. Trying to stab Brookson also satisfies the element requiring intent to cause harmful or offensive contact with the plaintiff or a third party. The fourth element is met by the unidentified demonstrator's beating of Brookson as Brookson tried to avoid Carter's knife. That surely qualifies as a harmful or offensive contact with the plaintiff. It is plausible that the third element, a causal relationship between Carter's act and Brookson's injuries, is also met. As Brookson was avoiding Carter's knife, Brookson almost bumped into another demonstrator. That demonstrator then struck and seriously injured Brookson. Further research will identify cases that specifically address this issue, and you may or may not ultimately conclude that this element is met. But it is plainly worth pursuing.

You may have noticed that the causation element for battery seems similar to the causation element for intentional infliction of emotional distress. When you see these similarities, be careful not to conclude automatically that the elements are the same. For intentional infliction of emotional distress, for example, you are looking to see whether a causal relationship exists between Brookson's emotional distress and Carter's act. It will be easier to show that Brookson's physical injuries arose from the beating than it will be to show that his emotional injuries arose from the beating. His severe insomnia and chronic anxiety may be caused, at least in part, by separation from his wife or his public participation in a politically charged demonstration.

The following chart depicts the analysis for battery:

<table>
<tr><td colspan="3" align="center">**Battery**
ELEMENTS CHART</td></tr>
<tr><td>**Element**</td><td>**Facts of Our Case**</td><td>**Element Met?**</td></tr>
<tr><td>Acts</td><td>Carter lunged at Brookson with a knife</td><td>Yes</td></tr>
<tr><td>intending to cause a harmful or offensive contact with the plaintiff or a third person</td><td>Carter wanted to stab Brookson</td><td>Yes</td></tr>
<tr><td>thereby causing</td><td>Brookson almost bumped into an unidentified demonstrator to avoid Carter, and demonstrator then beat Brookson</td><td>Maybe</td></tr>
<tr><td>harmful or offensive contact with the plaintiff</td><td>Brookson was severely beaten by an unidentified demonstrator</td><td>Yes</td></tr>
</table>

3. Exclude "givens" from detailed discussion.

A "given" is a legal question with a clear answer.[1] Some questions, even though relevant and within the scope of the problem, are so easily resolved that they are not genuine issues. Because legal documents must be concise, you should discuss a question at no greater length than it deserves. A memorandum or brief should usually mention "givens" as necessary to proceed in a logical fashion or to fully

---

[1] Use of the term "given" as a noun is not recommended in a memorandum or brief. It is used in this book as a shorthand way of describing a legal question for which there is obviously only one answer.

describe the context, but "givens" should not be discussed in detail. Tell the reader in two or three sentences what the rule and relevant facts are and what the result will be. If you are unsure about whether a question is a "given," however, discuss it in as much detail as necessary.

The answers in the charts distinguish between "givens" and issues. The third column contains answers to the question whether a particular element has been met in the Brookson case. If the answer is "yes," the applicability of the element is "given." If the answer is "maybe," the applicability of the element is plausible enough to be an issue. (If the answer is "no," as already suggested, the element or rule is clearly inapplicable.)

The diversity jurisdiction rule contains two "givens." It is given that the lawsuit would be a civil action because it would be an action by a private citizen to recover damages. The amount in controversy exceeds $50,000 because Fred Brookson's medical expenses alone are more than $55,000. Your discussion of diversity jurisdiction would briefly explain the applicability of these two elements. Because there is some question whether the parties are from different states, you should spend your time on that issue. Fred Brookson is an Oregon citizen and it is not clear whether Carter is a citizen of Oregon or California. This uncertainty makes diversity jurisdiction an issue.

The tort involving intentional infliction of emotional distress involves two "givens." Because Carter lunged at Brookson with a knife, it is given that his conduct was extreme and outrageous. Because Brookson has chronic anxiety and severe insomnia, it is given that his mental distress is extreme and severe. When you write your analysis, you should briefly explain why these elements have been satisfied, but you need not discuss them in detail. The harder questions are whether Carter intended to cause Brookson's emotional distress, and whether Carter caused that distress. On these two questions, there may be some dispute about the outcome. The analysis of these two questions should be the core of this part of the memo.

Three of the four elements of battery are also given. Carter certainly acted when he lunged at Brookson with his knife, and his intent to cause harmful contact is obvious from his attempt to stab Brookson. Brookson's severe beating by an unidentified demonstrator satisfies the element requiring harmful or offensive contact. (The exception noted in the rule, that it is not battery if the contact is consented to or otherwise privileged, need not be discussed at all because no facts indicate that this exception applies.) There is likely to be no dispute regarding the applicability of these three elements. As a result, your explanation of these elements need not be detailed. The more difficult question is whether Carter's actions caused the injuries Brookson suffered after he almost bumped into the unidentified demonstrator. More research and analysis are required before this question can be resolved.

4. Separate issues and sub-issues.

Some issues can only be resolved by first resolving smaller included issues known as sub-issues. Sub-issues typically occur when a legal rule includes several elements and the application of at least two of these elements may be disputed. The applicability of the rules is thus the issue, and the applicability of each element that may be disputed is a sub-issue.

There is no particular magic that separates issues from sub-issues; what is an issue in one case might be a sub-issue in another. The status of a question as an issue or sub-issue depends on the extent to which you have eliminated some questions because they are irrelevant, outside the scope of the problem, or "givens." The division of questions into issues and sub-issues is simply a useful tool for understanding and stating the relationship among the legal questions in your memorandum or brief.

While sub-issues serve a useful organizational purpose, they should not be fabricated for the sake of convenience. Never divide a question into two parts if the question raises only one issue. Sub-issues must be issues in their own right and they must always be analytically independent of one other.

Keep in mind that issues and sub-issues arise by possible application of the elements of specific legal rules to a factual situation. Issues, therefore, should not be stated in overly general terms, such as whether your client should win the case or whether the court is likely to grant a motion for summary judgment. State issues specifically, focusing on the application of the precise legal rule to the case at hand.

In Fred Brookson's case, intentional infliction of emotional distress depends on whether Carter intended Brookson's emotional distress, and whether he caused it. Thus, intentional infliction of emotional distress is an issue, and there are two sub-issues. Each is independent of the other, and both must be resolved in favor of Fred Brookson for there to be an intentional infliction of emotional distress.

The battery claim, however, involves only one issue. Whether Carter caused Fred Brookson's injuries requires further analysis. Similarly, diversity jurisdiction depends solely on whether there is sufficient diversity of citizenship.

This careful screening of the questions that merit analysis in the Fred Brookson case leaves three tentative issues, one of which has two sub-issues. They should be outlined as follows:

Outline of Legal Questions

1. Whether there is diversity of citizenship between the parties for purposes of federal diversity jurisdiction.
2. Whether Carter is liable to Fred Brookson for intentional infliction of emotional distress.
   a. Whether Carter intended to cause Brookson's emotional distress.
   b. Whether Carter caused Brookson's emotional distress.
3. Whether Carter caused Brookson's battery.

This problem has been cut to its bare legal bones. These issues all merit detailed analysis, and those questions that do not merit detailed analysis have been excluded. Don't forget that "givens" must be included in a discussion even though they do not merit detailed analysis. Keep in mind, too, that your list of issues will be somewhat tentative until you have finished your research. You may find cases in your jurisdiction that clearly resolve something you had thought to be an issue. You may also come across other cases that open up questions you had thought closed, or raise entirely new questions. Sometimes you will find cases that add to your list of elements or modify it. Much will depend on the quality of your research. For example, you may have guessed that Brookson has a potential cause of action against Carter for assault—a possibility you would investigate if you were researching this problem.

Although the four steps discussed above are distinct, they need not be taken in any particular order and some can be combined. The process that you follow will depend upon your knowledge of the relevant law and the nature of the problem. Use these steps as a checklist whenever you are asked to write a document assessing or arguing a client's case.

The following exercises are designed to let you work through the four steps of issue identification.

Exercise 5-A

Recently, Neil McKay telephoned Hugh Green and, as a joke, offered to sell his $50,000 yacht for $5,000 cash. McKay has a reputation as a practical joker. Although Green knew the true value of the boat, he did not know McKay's reputation. Green said to McKay, "You can't be serious," and then told McKay he needed time to think it over and raise the money.

Three days later, Green telephoned McKay to accept the offer but McKay was golfing. Green told McKay's secretary to tell McKay that he had called concerning the boat. The secretary called the golf course and left a message for McKay: "Green called—something about the yacht." By that time McKay was in the clubhouse and was intoxicated. The bartender took the secretary's message to McKay, who then telephoned Green.

Immediately after he started talking with Green, McKay passed out in the phone booth. While McKay was unconscious, Green told him, "I accept the offer," and added, "But I'd like to see your golf clubs thrown into the deal, too." McKay does not remember the telephone conversation and now refuses to sell the yacht to Green. Is there an enforceable contract?

You have found two cases from your state and some secondary authority.

Derek v. Beir (1985)

The appellant, Morse Beir, was a known eccentric with a reputation for playing practical jokes on his neighbors. One day he approached his neighbor, Bob Derek, whom he disliked. Beir stated, "For five bucks I will build a ten-foot-high wall at my own expense between our lots just so I will never have to look at your ridiculous face again." Derek, who was well aware of Beir's reputation, immediately agreed and paid Beir five dollars. Beir failed to build the wall, and the appellee filed this suit for breach of contract. The trial court awarded Derek $3,000 in damages, which represented the cost of building the wall. Beir appealed.

Although the trial court made several errors in this case, we do not have to discuss most of them here because we find the contract unenforceable. The general rule is that a contract is not enforceable unless there is an effective offer. For an offer to be effective, the offeror must intend to make a binding contract. In this state, the test for intent by the offeror is whether a reasonable person in the offeree's shoes would believe that the offeror intended to make a binding contract. We conclude that Derek knew or should have known that Beir was not serious and did not intend to make a contract. Because there was no offer, we do not have to reach the question whether the consideration was so grossly disproportionate that it would shock the conscience of the court to enforce the contract. Reversed.

Caldwell, J., dissenting. It is axiomatic that the appellate court will not set aside a jury finding unless it is clearly contrary to the preponderance of the evidence. The jury in the court below heard testimony from both Derek and Beir as to Beir's true intent and Derek's conception of it. After a correct instruction from the judge on the rule of law in this state, which rule the majority has stated correctly and succinctly, the jury decided that the parties intended to make a contract. It is not up to this court to decide whether the contract was nonsensical or absurd or ill-advised. The court below, after consideration of conflicting evidence, found that the parties intended to enter into a contract. Because that finding was not clearly against the weight of the evidence, I would affirm on the issue of intent to make a valid offer.

Although the majority did not reach the issue of adequacy of consideration, having disposed of the case on other grounds, I would remind the court that any consideration, no matter how small, is generally sufficient to support a contract freely entered into by the parties. Lewis J. Holloway, *A Treatise on Contract Law* 10 (2d ed. 1982).

Anselm v. Kinnet Textiles, Inc. **(1986)**

The appellant, Charles Anselm, offered to sell 200 bales of cotton to the appellee, Kinnet Textiles, Inc. One hundred bales were to be delivered on March 1, and the remaining 100 were to be delivered on April 1. Kinnet sent a messenger to Anselm's office with a written note that stated, "We agree to your offer in all respects if we can instead take delivery on March 5 and April 5." Because Anselm was out of the office, his secretary accepted the note from the messenger and placed it on Anselm's cluttered desk. Anselm did not see it for several weeks and, in the meantime, committed the cotton to another buyer. Kinnet filed suit for breach of contract. The trial court found that the contract was valid and awarded damages to Kinnet. We disagree.

A contract is not formed unless there is a valid acceptance. Because we have not adopted the Uniform Commercial Code in this state, the case is governed by common law. The appellant claims there was not a valid acceptance for two reasons. First, the appellant claims there was no acceptance because he did not see or read the note. We find the delivery and placement of the acceptance on the appellant's desk to be a sufficient communication of the acceptance. Once the offeree has delivered a written acceptance, it would be unreasonable to require the offeree to ensure that the acceptance is read. We do, however, agree with Anselm that the contract is invalid because the acceptance differs from the offer. The rule in this state is that the acceptance must mirror the offer in every respect. If it varies from the offer, it is considered a counteroffer and not an acceptance. Because the dates for delivery in the acceptance here varied from those in the offer, we find there was no acceptance and thus no enforceable contract. Reversed.

Morris, J., concurring. I agree with the majority that there was no acceptance of the offer in this case. However, I disagree that this result must be reached by the application of the mirror-image rule. The creative and regenerative power of the law has been strong enough to break chains imposed by outmoded former decisions. What the courts have power to create, they also have power to modify, reject, and recreate in response to the needs of a dynamic society. The exercise of this power is an imperative function of the courts and is the strength of the common law. It cannot be surrendered to legislative inaction.

Most states have discarded the archaic mirror-image rule and have replaced it with section 2-207 of the Uniform Commercial Code, which treats additional terms in a contract as proposals for additions to the contract unless the acceptance is expressly made conditional on assent to the additional terms. U.C.C. § 2-207. In this case, the acceptance was conditional on Anselm's agreeing to the changed dates. Hence, it was not an acceptance at all but was, instead, a counteroffer. Thus, there was no contract.

Excerpt from Lewis J. Holloway, *A Treatise on Contract Law* 10
(2d ed. 1982)

Generally, an enforceable contract must contain three elements: (1) an offer, (2) an acceptance, and (3) consideration by both parties. Consideration means that each party must incur a legal detriment, i.e., give something of value or a promise to do something one is not already obligated to do. Any consideration is sufficient, no matter how small.

Excerpt from Edna C. Simpson, *Contracts* 30–31
(2d ed. 1985)

A counteroffer is a rejection because it manifests an unwillingness to assent to the offer as made, unless the offeree in making the counteroffer states he still has the original offer under consideration. An acceptance of an offer on condition that the offeror do something more than he has promised in his offer is not an acceptance at all; it is a counteroffer and operates to terminate the original offer. Acceptance conditioned on the seller's delivering additional goods not specified in his offer is a counteroffer and a rejection.

1. List the rule(s), and the elements of the rule(s), in this problem.

2. Are there any questions you would exclude from analysis because they are "givens"? If so, which ones?

3. Identify the issues and sub-issues (if any) in this problem.

Exercise 5-B

Cynthia Mickel, a reporter for the *Star City Banner-Patriot,* was recently assigned to write an investigative series on an organization called Citizens for Law and Order (CLO). She learned from her investigation that CLO is a paramilitary organization whose primary purpose is to arm citizens on behalf of "the Aryan or white elements in our society." The organization is so secretive that its members refused to discuss it with her or even to acknowledge that they were members. Several former members stated that CLO believes that "the whole country is crawling with black, red, and yellow people," that "everybody in power has sold out," and that only CLO "could buck the tide." The organization sponsors target-shooting events for its members, publishes a newsletter discussing different kinds of rifles and handguns, and routinely sends anonymous letters to the *Banner-Patriot.*

Mickel recently learned that the Star City Police Department has been investigating CLO for two years. Although the Department has never arrested any CLO members for illegal activities related to their membership, Mickel has reason to believe the police files are extensive, and that they contain information primarily concerning the structure, activities, and membership of the CLO. She has learned, for example, that the mayor's wife is an officer of the CLO and that the files describe her involvement in detail.

Pursuant to the state Freedom of Information Act, Mickel filed a request with the Police Department seeking all files concerning its CLO investigation. Three days later the Department denied her request, stating in part that "these records are confidential." Two days later, the mayor phoned her, stating that he would sue the newspaper "for every penny it has" if it published a story about CLO. Mickel's editors are reluctant to run the story without corroborating information from the police files. The paper has asked you to determine whether it can obtain the information through a lawsuit against the Police Department.

The state Freedom of Information Act, as amended in 1978, provides:

Sec. 2. As used in this Act:

(a) "Person" means an individual, corporation, partnership, firm, organization, or association.

(b) "Governmental body" means—

    (i) A state officer, employee, agency, department, division, bureau, board, commission, council, authority, or other body in the executive branch of the state government, but does not include the governor or lieutenant governor, the executive office of the governor or lieutenant governor, or employees thereof.

    (ii) An agency, board, commission, or council in the legislative branch of state government.

    (iii) A county, city, township, village, intercounty, intercity, or regional governing body, council, school district, special district, municipal corporation, or a board, department, commission, council, or agency thereof.

(c) "Public record" means a writing prepared, owned, used, in the possession of, or retained by a governmental body.

Sec. 3.

(a) A person desiring to inspect or receive a copy of a public record may make an oral or written request for a public record to the governmental body.

(b) The governmental body shall grant or deny a request in not more than five business days after the day the request is received.

Sec. 4. If a governmental body denies a request, the requesting person may commence an action in circuit court to compel disclosure of the public records. An action under this section may not be commenced unless the requesting person has allowed the governmental body five business days to respond to the request.

Sec. 5. A governmental body may exempt from disclosure as a public record under this Act:

(a)   Records of law enforcement agencies that deal with the detection and investigation of crime and the internal records and notations of such law enforcement agencies which are maintained for its internal use in matters related to law enforcement.

(b)   Information or records subject to the attorney-client privilege.

(c)   Records of any campaign committee, including any committee that receives monies from a state campaign fund.

(d)   Information of a personal nature where the public disclosure of the information would constitute a clearly unwarranted invasion of an individual's privacy [added in 1978].

The highest appellate court in your state has decided the following case:

Holcombe v. Badger Newspapers, Inc. (1976)

The plaintiff, a rape victim, brought an action for damages for invasion of privacy against the defendant newspaper for publishing a factual article about the crime, including her name and address. The trial court dismissed her complaint and we affirm.

The state Freedom of Information Act provides that every citizen has a right to the disclosure of any public record. Although the Act exempts certain public records from disclosure, none of these exceptions pertains to this factual situation. There can be no liability for invasion of privacy at common law when the defendant further discloses information about the plaintiff that is already public. We are sympathetic to the plaintiff's problem, but our duty ends when we have construed the statute. The legislature may amend the Act, but we cannot.

The federal district court in your state has decided the following case:

Wheeler Publishing Co. v. City of Bad Axe (1985)

The Bad Axe Police Department maintains two kinds of records relevant to this case. One is called an "Offense Report," and it includes information concerning the offense committed, the surrounding circumstances, the witnesses, and the investigating officers. The other is called a "Supplementary Offense Report," and it includes information such as the names of potential informants, officers' speculations about a suspect's guilt, and the results of various laboratory tests. The plaintiff, the owner of the *Bad Axe Daily Telegram,* sought to inspect both kinds of reports for its daily newspaper coverage of crime in the Bad Axe area. The Department refused, claiming that the information fit the "police records" exception in section 5(a) of the state's Freedom of Information Act. The plaintiff is challenging that interpretation.

We hold that section 5(a) does not allow the Police Department to withhold the Offense Report. Although the information contained in the Offense Report deals with the detection and investigation of crime, it is not the kind of information that should be solely for the Police Department's "internal use" under section 5(a). The press and the public have a right to information concerning crime and law enforcement activity in the community. In determining the reach of that right in specific situations, however, it is necessary to weigh and balance competing interests. With respect to the Offense Report, the public's right to know about specific crimes is paramount. Access to the Supplementary Offense Report, on the other hand, is protected by section 5(a). To open this material to the press and the public might reveal the names of informants and otherwise jeopardize law enforcement activities. The Department must release Offense Reports but is entitled to retain Supplementary Offense Reports.

1. List the rule(s), and the elements of the rule(s), in this problem.

2. Is it relevant to this problem that the mayor's wife may be able to sue the *Banner-Patriot* for invasion of privacy? Explain.

3. Is it relevant that the Police Department responded to Mickel's request in three days? Explain.

4. What "givens" can be eliminated from detailed consideration?

5. Separate the remaining legal questions into issues and sub-issues.

6

Common Law Analysis

THE PECULIAR WAY lawyers think has been ridiculed for centuries, and often for good cause. Montaigne wrote of several men who had been executed for a crime, even though the actual culprits were discovered after their trial, because the authorities did not want the public to think the judicial process was imperfect. Charles Dickens devoted a lengthy novel, *Bleak House,* to what he described as the "foggiest and muddiest" place in London, the High Court of Chancery.

Although some legal reasoning seems unreasonable, much analysis reflects honest intellectual differences about what the law means or what direction it should take. Perceived unreasonableness also reflects limitations in the analytical process. There are few judicial opinions whose logic is airtight, whose assumptions cannot be questioned, or whose analysis addresses all of the ramifications of the decision. Dissenting opinions often bring these shortcomings (actual and perceived) into sharp relief. Justice Brennan's dissenting opinion in a 1975 United States Supreme Court decision, for example, was strongly critical of the "glaring defect[s]" and "outmoded notions" of the majority opinion.[1]

All these criticisms notwithstanding, there is a method to legal analysis, and it is a sensible one. Previous chapters examined some of the basic principles of legal analysis. This chapter will describe and illustrate the method of common law analysis.[2] The common law is the body of rules and principles found exclusively in

---

[1] Warth v. Seldin, 422 U.S. 490, 520, 521 (1975) (Brennan, J., dissenting).

[2] Statutory analysis is described in Chapter 7. Constitutional analysis, a hybrid of common law and statutory analysis, is not specifically addressed in this book. Constitutions, particularly the United States Constitution, are similar to, but usually more general than, statutes. Judicial decisions interpreting and applying constitutional provisions are thus highly significant because they create a body of "common law" on the meaning of these provisions. But constitutional provisions, like statutes, must also be understood in light of their language and the intent of their drafters.

judicial decisions. It is not created by legislatures, and it is not found in constitutions; the common law is judge-made law. The development of the common law began many centuries ago in England, when early courts were first called on to resolve disputes. These disputes were resolved according to particular principles derived from earlier decisions. Common law analysis has remained virtually unchanged since that time—judges look to earlier cases for guidance in resolving disputes.

The common law develops cautiously because the principles of precedent and *stare decisis* render it comfortable with the familiar, less comfortable with the unknown. As new cases are decided, legal rules evolve and become more complex. Although many areas of the common law have been translated by legal scholars into restatements, the facts and policies of the cases on which these rules are based are still of great importance.

The primary methods of common law analysis are analogy and distinction. Every case involving the possible application of a common law rule involves two basic questions: (1) How are the decided cases similar to my client's case? (2) How are the decided cases different from my client's case? The more analogous these cases are, the more precedent and *stare decisis* dictate the application of their conclusions to the present case. The more distinguishable they are, the more inapplicable they should be. Common law analysis must be undertaken on several related levels. You must first look at the facts of the decided cases and compare them with the facts of your case. You must then examine the reasons and policies stated in the decided cases to see whether these reasons and policies apply to your case. Much of this examination will concentrate on why your significant facts are actually significant. You may find that a policy stated in the decided cases is inapplicable because the facts of your case are significantly different, or you may find that a decided case is applicable to your case for reasons the court did not state. You should always be alert to similarities and differences in both the factual situations and underlying policies.

Analogy and distinction are not simply matters of spotting obvious similarities and differences. A good lawyer will spot threads running through entire lines of cases that the courts themselves may not have made explicit, and use these threads to weave sophisticated arguments for or against the application of these cases.

A sound understanding of both sides of a controversy is the primary goal of common law analysis, or any other legal analysis. Only when you fully understand both sides can you accurately assess the strengths and weaknesses of your client's position. Even when particular cases seem to be favorable to your client, you cannot afford to ignore distinctions between those cases and your client's situation.

You must be prepared to determine whether the similarities are more important than the differences, and why. If you fail to objectively analyze both sides of the problem, you may mislead your client about the strength of her legal position or be unable to properly state and defend that position. Common law analysis must not be a one-sided process.

The basic principles of common law analysis can best be stated and understood in the context of a specific problem.

☐ Your client, Arthur Dooley, a tenant in a large apartment building, had several grievances with the building's manager, Otis Fremont. Dooley designed a one-page flier in which he asserted, "Fremont has a long record of criminal convictions as a landlord." Fremont had received three notices of violation from the local housing commission in the past two years for inadequate lighting and locks. The commission had then threatened to seek a court order requiring correction of the violations, but dropped the matter when Fremont made the necessary repairs. Fremont has no criminal record.

Dooley made 200 copies of the flier at his print shop for distribution to other tenants in the building. On his way back from the print shop, Dooley met Fremont by chance and, after a lengthy conversation, they settled their differences. The fliers were not mentioned. Although Dooley intended to destroy the fliers when he returned to his apartment, he was struck by a teenager riding a skateboard and the fliers were scattered by the wind. Many of the fliers were read by other persons, and Fremont filed suit for libel.

There are three relevant cases. All are from the highest appellate court of the state:

White v. Ball (1966)

Ball appeals from a libel judgment awarded to White and two other employees of the R&T Construction Company. Ball had hired the company to remodel his home. The judgment was based on a letter written by Ball to the company president shortly after the work was completed, in which Ball accused the employees of stealing a valuable watch.

The first issue on appeal is whether the letter was intentionally published. As a general matter, libel consists of the intentional publication of false statements about a person that humiliate the person or subject him to the loss of social prestige. All that is necessary for publication to occur is the delivery of the defamatory matter in written or other permanent form to any person other than the one libeled. It is receipt by a third person that makes the statements so damaging. Because the president of the company, a third person, received and read the letter, the trial court was correct in finding that there was intent to publish.

The second issue is whether the letter was false. On this issue, the trial court erred. A statement is false if the gist, the sting, of the matter is false. Minor inaccuracies in the statement are not sufficient to show that it is false. In this case, the accusation against the employees was, in a technical sense, false. None of the employees took the watch. But the watch was taken by a male friend of one of the employees when he picked her up at the end of the work day. Because of the relationship between the employee and the thief, we believe that the letter was substantially accurate. Reversed.

Simmons v. Deluxe Plaza Hotel (1968)

The manager of defendant hotel wrote Simmons a letter falsely accusing Simmons of staying in the hotel, failing to pay for the room, and taking several articles from the room. The manager was mistaken as to the culprit's identity, so the letter was false. The letter was addressed to Simmons personally and sent by certified mail.

Simmons's wife signed for the letter at his residence and read it. The question on appeal is whether the trial court correctly ruled that the letter was not intentionally published. The evidence shows the manager considered it possible that some third person might receive the letter, though he did not know Simmons was married. This falls far short of a showing that he was reasonably chargeable with appreciation or knowledge of the likelihood that the letter would be opened and read by another. A mere conceivable possibility or chance of such eventuality is not sufficient to demonstrate intent. Affirmed.

Willow v. Orr (1991)

This case arises from a battle between the parties for custody of their four-year-old son, Matthew. Mr. Willow took Matthew from Ms. Orr's home without her consent or knowledge and traveled with him to another state. Ms. Orr looked for them for six weeks and, after she located them, obtained a court order compelling Matthew's return. Mr. Willow then told Ms. Orr, as part of their divorce proceeding, that he might take Matthew again. Thereafter, Ms. Orr wrote a letter to fifteen of her neighbors. The letter said, in part, "Help! Jason Willow kidnapped my child and said he would do it again." Mr. Willow sued Ms. Orr for libel. The trial court granted Ms. Orr's motion for summary judgment.

On appeal, Mr. Willow claims that the letter is false because he did not kidnap the child in the legal sense of that term. Because Mr. Willow's act did not violate any judicial custody order, he did not kidnap Matthew under the state statute. But technical errors in legal terminology and reports of matters involving violations of the law are immaterial if the defamatory charge is true in substance. Because of the nontechnical meaning that "kidnap" has acquired in the child custody context, we hold that Ms. Orr's letter is substantially true. Affirmed.

The problem lends itself to the following preliminary analysis, using the elements chart depicted in Chapter 5 (Identifying and Selecting Issues for Analysis):

Libel ELEMENTS CHART		
Element	**Facts of Our Case**	**Element Met?**
Intent to publish	Dooley wrote and printed 200 fliers, intending to distribute them to Fremont's tenants. They were published accidentally after Dooley no longer intended to publish them.	Maybe
Publication	Fliers were read by third persons.	Yes
of false statements about a person	Fliers said Fremont had a long record of criminal convictions as a landlord. Fremont was cited three times in two years by Housing Commission and corrected violations to avoid court order. Fremont has no criminal record.	Maybe
that humiliate the person —or—	Fliers said Fremont had a long record of criminal violations.	Maybe
subject him to the loss of social prestige	Fliers said Fremont had a long record of criminal violations.	Yes

This analysis suggests that the problem contains two sub-issues—whether Dooley's publication of the fliers was intentional, and whether the fliers were false. It is given that the fliers were published. It is also given that the fourth element is met. Because the accusation of criminal convictions subjected Fremont to the loss of social prestige, it does not matter that there may be some question about whether he was humiliated.

The rest of this chapter provides a method for analyzing one of these sub-issues—whether the "intent to publish" rule should be applied to these facts. (The falsity sub-issue is addressed in Exercise 6-A.) Before analyzing this or any issue, you may find it useful to identify the relevant parts of the cases you will be using. As you read in Chapter 3 (Case Analysis and Case Briefs), briefing cases will often help you understand them. The chart below shows modified briefs of the intent sub-issue from the *White* and *Simmons* cases and includes the relevant facts of our case:

Intent to Publish CASE BRIEFING CHART		
	Our Case	**White**	**Simmons**
Facts	Dooley designed and printed copies of a flier that he intended to distribute to tenants in his apartment building. After he decided not to publish them, they were released by accident.	The defendant wrote a letter to a company president containing allegations about his employees. The company president received and read the letter.	The defendant wrote a letter that was addressed personally to the plaintiff and sent by certified mail. The plaintiff's wife read the the letter. The defendant thought it possible that someone else would read the letter, but did not know the plaintiff was married.
Holding		There was intent to publish.	There was no intent to publish.
Reasons and Policies		Receipt by third person makes statements damaging.	Intent requires reasonable knowledge or appreciation that a letter will likely be read by another. Mere conceivable possibility or chance that a third person would read a letter does not constitute intent.

This case briefing chart helps focus the intent sub-issue. It extracts the facts, holdings, and reasons and policies of the cases concerning this sub-issue. The *Willow* case is not included because it is irrelevant to the sub-issue. It also extracts the relevant facts from Dooley's case. The case briefing chart thus contains the basic information you need to analyze the problem. You may find that using this chart, or a similar chart, will help your analysis. The following outline provides a method for analyzing this or any other common law issue.

1. Determine how the facts of the decided cases support your client's position.

Because each case is decided on the basis of a unique factual setting, it is important to understand that setting as clearly as possible. To understand the setting, first identify similarities and differences between the facts of the decided cases and those of your client's case. In each instance, ask yourself how the facts of a case lend support to your client's position. If a decision is favorable to your client's position, you should show that the decision is factually similar. If the decision is unfavorable, you should try to show that the decision involves different facts.

The holdings in the case briefing chart provide an idea of what cases are likely to be useful to your client. If possible, your client would like to show that he had no intent to publish. *Simmons v. Deluxe Plaza Hotel* is likely to be helpful because the court in that case held that the defendant had no intent to publish. You should look for ways in which the facts of *Simmons* are analogous to the facts of our case.

In *Simmons v. Deluxe Plaza Hotel*, the defendant wrote a letter to the plaintiff containing false accusations against him. The defendant attempted to ensure that the letter would be read only by the plaintiff by addressing it to him personally and sending it by certified mail. Despite these precautions, the plaintiff's wife read the letter. *Simmons* is like the present case because Dooley, like the defendant hotel manager, did not intend to distribute the fliers to third persons after his conversation with Fremont. He intended to destroy the fliers when he returned to his apartment, and it was only by accident that they were released. In any event, he never intended distribution to passersby, just as the defendant in *Simmons* did not intend the plaintiff's wife to read the letter.

The holdings in the case briefing chart also suggest the case your opponent will want to use. Your opponent may try to argue that Dooley intended to distribute the fliers. Because *White v. Ball* held that there was intent, your opponent will try to analogize *White* to our case. You must therefore be prepared to distinguish *White*.

In *White v. Ball*, the defendant wrote a third person, a company president, making false accusations against company employees. The court found intentional publication because the president received and read the letter. *White* is different from Dooley's case in that the release of the fliers was not intended and, unlike the defendant in *White*, Dooley did not address his accusations directly to a third person. This analysis indicates that the interpretation of *White* and *Simmons* most favorable to your client would emphasize the unintentional release of the fliers. Again, you will draw an analogy to *Simmons* and distinguish *White* to support that conclusion.

2. Determine how the facts of the decided cases support your opponent's position.

The omission of certain facts in the previous discussion suggests how your opponent will use the decided cases. Identification of the facts supporting the opposing position requires you to think like your opponent. Actually construct the best opposing arguments. Where you try to show similarities, your opponent will try to show differences. Where you find distinctions, your opponent will find analogies.

Thus, in *White v. Ball*, the defendant prepared a false letter, fully intending to send it to a third person. Similarly, Dooley prepared a false flier with intent to distribute it. In both *White* and the present case, the defamatory material was received and read by third persons. Preparation with intent to publish makes *Simmons v. Deluxe Plaza Hotel* different from these facts. In *Simmons*, the defendant prepared a letter intending that only the plaintiff see it. That an unintended third person read the letter was not enough for publication. In Dooley's case, although passersby rather than tenants read the flier, Dooley intended it for third party distribution when he prepared it. These cases suggest that your opponent's strongest case would be based on Dooley's preparation and printing of the fliers with intent to distribute them. Your opponent would rely on *White* and distinguish *Simmons*.

3. Determine how the reasons and policies of the decided cases support your client's position.

The factual similarities and differences between the decided cases and the present case are significant only to the extent that they are given importance by the reasons and policies of the decided cases. Because the intent issue was of concern in both *White* and *Simmons*, the factual analysis in the present case has focused on the absence or presence of facts that evidence an intent to publish. The analysis has suggested two interpretations, one based on intent at the time of preparation and the other based on intent at the time of distribution. Neither of the decided cases specifically addresses this distinction.

The next level of analysis requires examination of the reasons and policies of the decisions. This examination could show what considerations the courts thought were important to the question of intent. Such considerations assist the analysis of the present case because the courts indicate that some principles are more significant than others, despite different factual settings. The reasons and policies in the case briefing chart provide a basis for this analysis.

The court in *Simmons* refused to find publication simply on the possibility that someone other than the plaintiff would read the letter. The court's conclusion that the defendant "was not reasonably chargeable with appreciation or knowledge of the likelihood that the letter would be opened and read by another" suggests that intent at the time of distribution is required for publication. Dooley originally intended to distribute the fliers after they were printed, but after they were printed he decided not to distribute them at all. At that point, you would reason, the possibility of the accident, just like the possibility of a third person reading the letter in *Simmons*, was speculative. The court in *White v. Ball* focused on receipt of defamatory material by a third person and the subsequent damage caused to the plaintiff's reputation. *White* must be viewed narrowly rather than broadly because, as the court said in *Simmons*, delivery of defamatory material to a third person is not enough. You would conclude that there must be an intent to publish at the time of distribution.

4. Determine how the reasons and policies of the decided cases support your opponent's position.

Your opponent will emphasize reasons that you would subordinate to others and de-emphasize reasons you believe to be significant. Your opponent may also show that your policy arguments are inapplicable because of the different factual situation presented by this case and demonstrate why his policy arguments are relevant and more important. The reasons and policies in the briefing chart provide a starting point.

The court in *White v. Ball*, your opponent would argue, shows primary concern for a person's reputation. This concern is illustrated by the court's observation that receipt by a third person is what makes the defamation damaging. If intent to publish the defamatory material is what made the defendant blameworthy in *White*, then Dooley should also be held blameworthy. By intending to harm Fremont's reputation and by writing and printing a flier to do so, Dooley showed that he was prepared to go to great lengths to injure him. Even assuming his change of mind was genuine, your opponent would reason, Dooley set in motion a series of events that resulted in harm to Fremont.

Simmons is different from Dooley's situation because in *Simmons* there was an unintentional distribution of defamatory material. Dooley, on the other hand, intentionally prepared and printed the flier for distribution. Persons who print 200 copies of a flier, and who hold them so carelessly that an accident sets them loose in the wind, are not unintentionally defaming others. If he had not taken his scheme of damaging Fremont's reputation as far as he did, your opponent would conclude, the fliers would not have been distributed.

You might depict the first four steps in this method by using the chart below:

	Intent to Publish **ANALYSIS CHART**	
	Why Element Is Applicable (Opponent's Case)	**Why Element Is Not Applicable** (Our Client's Case)

Facts	*White* is applicable. The defendant prepared a letter with intent to send it to a third person. Similarly, Dooley prepared the flier with intent to distribute it.
	    Simmons is distinguishable. In that case, the defendant intended only that the plaintiff see the letter when he wrote it. In our case, Dooley intended the fliers to be read by third persons when he prepared them.
		Simmons is analogous. The defendant in that case did not intend the letter to be read by third persons. The letter was addressed to the plaintiff personally and sent by certified mail. Similarly, Dooley did not intend anyone to read the fliers. They were disseminated by accident.
		    White is inapplicable. The defendant wrote a letter to a company president, who then read the letter. In our case, by contrast, Dooley did not intend anyone to read the fliers at the time of their release.

Reasons and Policies	The *White* court stated that receipt by a third person is what makes false statements damaging. Intent to publish fliers makes Dooley blameworthy. Dooley intended to hurt Fremont's reputation, and wrote and printed fliers to do so. Even though he changed his mind, the fliers would not have been released if he hadn't prepared them.
	    Simmons is different because the defendant did not intend publication.
		Intent occurs when there is reasonable appreciation or knowledge that material would be read by third persons. The mere possibility or chance that a third person would read the material does not demonstrate intent. When Dooley decided not to distribute the fliers, the possibility of an accident that would release the fliers was as remote as the possibility that a third person would read the letter in *Simmons*.
		    White is different because the defendant wrote a letter to the company president and had reason to believe that he would read it.

5. Evaluate the strength of your client's case.

The process of constructing and evaluating arguments runs from the technical level of comparing facts to increasingly abstract levels involving basic assumptions and values about the point at which one should be held blameworthy for damage to the reputation of another. Your conclusion should be based on a careful examination and analysis of the facts, policies, and reasons of the decided cases and their application to the present case. You might conclude that there was no publication because the fliers were distributed when Dooley no longer intended to distribute them and because they were distributed accidentally to third persons. This interpretation follows from *White* and *Simmons* and seems to be the most likely outcome here. But you might also conclude that there was publication because the fliers were written and printed for distribution to third persons and because they were distributed to third persons. That conclusion also reasonably follows from *White* and *Simmons*.

Whatever your thoughts are about the strength of your client's case, you must draw a conclusion and you must be prepared to show that your conclusion is more reasonable than any other. Your client wants an answer. Whether you are writing a brief or an office memo, you cannot simply state the competing considerations or describe the relevant cases. You must scrutinize each consideration, weigh it, and then balance it against other considerations. If you cannot come to a satisfactory conclusion, think about it some more. Reaching a well-reasoned conclusion requires careful reading of the cases and thoughtful analysis. There is always a good reason, if not a definitive one, for preferring one side over another. Chapter 8 provides a framework for reaching a conclusion that you should use to check your analysis.

Work through the following exercises using these principles. Although the process may seem mechanical, you will become more comfortable as you gain familiarity with it.

Exercise 6-A

Using the five principles described in this chapter, evaluate the strength of Dooley's position on the falsity of the fliers.

Exercise 6-B

Fourteen-year-old Andrew Quale was struck by a truck while riding his bicycle. Although his injuries seemed slight, his mother, Mary Quale, took him to the hospital. His sole complaint was a headache. After Mary described the accident, Dr. Richard Farmer ordered X-rays. The X-rays did not indicate a skull fracture. Farmer did not examine the back of the boy's head, where there was a red mark, nor did he use the other diagnostic procedures that are standard in such cases. Farmer sent the boy home and asked his mother to observe him. Andrew died early the next morning. The coroner concluded from an autopsy that the boy died from hemorrhaging due to a basal skull fracture.

Mary Quale has asked you to sue Farmer for malpractice. You contacted another doctor as a possible expert witness. He told you that there is no doubt the doctor was negligent. In answer to your question about the likelihood of the boy's survival if there had been proper treatment, he said that the mortality rate for such injuries was about 100% without surgery. Then he added, "There is a reasonable medical possibility —1 chance out of 3, maybe a little higher—that he would have survived with surgery."

Assume that Farmer was negligent. Did Farmer's negligence proximately cause the boy's death? There are two relevant cases in your state:

Moulton v. Ginocchio (1966)

Craig Moulton, who is the administrator of the decedent's estate, brought this action against Samuel Ginocchio, a physician, for negligence in treating the decedent's illness. The trial court dismissed the complaint on the ground that the doctor's negligence did not proximately cause her death. We disagree and reverse. The decedent, a diabetic, went to Ginocchio's hospital with intense abdominal pain, which Ginocchio diagnosed as a stomach "bug." He gave her pain medication and released her. She died several hours later from massive hemorrhaging caused by an intestinal obstruction. Ginocchio claims that there is no basis for concluding with certainty that his negligent diagnosis and treatment caused her death. The law does not require certainty, however; a physician is answerable if he prevents a substantial possibility of survival. Moulton's experts testified categorically and without contradiction that the decedent would have survived had she undergone prompt surgery. Moulton, therefore, satisfied the "substantial possibility" requirement.

Mallard v. Harkin (1969)

Eleanor Mallard brought suit against Joseph Harkin, a physician, for Harkin's allegedly negligent failure to immediately diagnose and perform surgery to arrest a degenerative disease that has now left Mallard paralyzed. The trial court found that Harkin breached his duty of reasonable care but that his actions did not proximately cause Mallard's condition. Only the latter ruling has been appealed. We agree with the trial court and affirm.

We held in *Moulton v. Ginocchio* (1966) that a doctor is liable when his negligence "prevents a substantial possibility of survival" for the decedent. In that case, there was testimony that the decedent would have survived. Traditional standards of proximate cause similarly require evidence that the result was more likely than not caused by the act. Mallard does not meet that standard. Mallard's expert witness testified that prompt surgery would have given Mallard "a possibility" of recovery but that she "probably would not have recovered."

It is an attractive and emotionally appealing idea that a physician should be held liable for the loss of even a remote chance of full recovery from a debilitating disease or injury. But such a rule would result in an unjust situation in which the physician would be held accountable for harm that he did not cause and may not have been able to prevent. We refuse, as a matter of public policy, to hold a physician liable on a mere possibility.

1.   Identify the relevant rule(s), and the elements of the rule(s), in this problem.

2.   Is it significant that both cases are from your state? Explain.

3.   How do the facts of the cases support Quale's case? Farmer's case?

4.   How do the reasons and policies of the cases support Quale's case? Farmer's case?

5.   Evaluate the strength of Quale's position.

Exercise 6-C

Bradley Greenleaf just finished renovating an old house located on a busy street in Porterville. The house, which is now the office for his twelve-person architectural firm, cost $145,000. The renovations, including retrofitting the house with solar panels, cost an additional $195,000. The solar panels provide heating and cooling for the air and water in the building, but they do not provide electricity. His firm, Greenleaf Associates, which specializes in solar design for residences, uses the building as a model for persons who are interested in constructing or retrofitting homes with solar panels. Its extensive "You can do it" promotional campaign relies heavily on the building for that purpose.

Peter Elliot owns the property just west of Greenleaf's office. Recently, Elliot erected two large billboards that shield the sun's rays from the panels by early afternoon and force Greenleaf to rely on conventional energy sources. As a result, Greenleaf is paying substantially more than before in utility bills (about $400 per month, he estimates), and his promotional appeal is less attractive. What good is solar energy, some potential customers ask, if it can be blocked? Greenleaf talked to Elliot about this problem. Elliot apologized for any inconvenience but refused to remove the billboards because he would lose too much money.

Greenleaf has asked you if he has a basis for a lawsuit against Elliot. You have determined that there are no relevant statutes, easements, or zoning provisions. There are, however, three relevant cases from this state.

Shover v. Scott (1889)

Larry Shover brought an action against Wayne Scott, an adjoining landowner, for damage caused by Scott's excavation of adjacent land. The trial court found that the excavation caused Shover's land to cave in, destroyed a barn and some fences, and greatly devalued Shover's property. It ordered judgment for Shover. We affirm.

The maxim that landowners must so enjoy their property as not to injure the property of another has been interpreted in this state to mean that they must enjoy their property without injuring a legal right in the property of another. A landowner has the legal right to lateral support of his lot from the adjoining land. If the support is removed, the owner has a right of action against the person removing the support for the amount of the damages sustained to the land.

Horton v. Eicher (1959)

Stephen Eicher, who owns 200 acres of growing honeydew melons, used a small airplane to dust his melons with calcium arsenate. The compound is toxic to a number of agricultural pests; it is also toxic to bees. John Horton owns sixty-five hives of bees on a parcel of land near Eicher's land. The bees were important to the pollination of Horton's plants and thus contributed to his livelihood. Horton brought this action for nuisance after the spray from Eicher's plane drifted over the hives and killed all of the bees. The trial court awarded $450 in damages, and we affirm. A property owner is entitled to the peaceful enjoyment of his property, free from unreasonable interference by others. This incident unmistakably interfered with Horton's use of his property.

Blum v. Disposal Systems, Inc. (1987)

Disposal Systems, Inc. (DSI) operates a landfill adjacent to Loretta Blum's hog farm. Blum brought a nuisance action against DSI, alleging that noise and vibrations generated by DSI's trash-hauling trucks caused the conception rate of Blum's sows to decrease from 80% to 30%. The trial court found that the alleged facts were true but nevertheless entered judgment for DSI, holding that its use of the land was reasonable and therefore not a nuisance. We reverse.

In private nuisance actions, we must balance the interests of the respective landowners. Whether one's use of property is reasonable is determined by the effect such use has on the neighboring property. Although mere annoyance or inconvenience will not support an action for nuisance, a use of property that essentially confiscates or destroys the neighboring property is unreasonable and constitutes a private nuisance. The landfill operation has had that effect on Blum's hog farm.

The following case is from another state:

Cassells International v. Avery Resorts (1959)

Cassells International, which owns a large resort hotel on an ocean beach, brought suit against Avery Resorts, a neighboring hotel owner, to prevent construction of a ten-story addition to Avery's existing hotel. Cassells claims that the addition will cast a shadow on its beaches and other sunbathing areas and will render these areas unfit for the use and enjoyment of its guests. The trial court refused to enjoin construction of the addition. We agree.

The doctrine of nuisance does not mean that a property owner must never use the property to the injury of another, but rather that the owner may not use the property to injure the legal rights of another. We have found no American case establishing—in the absence of a contractual or statutory obligation—that a property owner has a right to the free flow of light. Affirmed.

1.   Identify the relevant rule(s), and the elements of the rule(s), in this problem.

2.   For each issue, how do the facts of the cases support Greenleaf's case? Elliot's case?

3.   For each issue, how do the reasons and policies of the cases support Greenleaf's case? Elliot's case?

4.   Is it important that the *Cassells* case is from another jurisdiction? Explain.

5.   Evaluate the strength of Greenleaf's position on each issue or sub-issue.

7

Statutory Analysis

STATUTORY ANALYSIS is the process of determining how statutes apply to a given situation and what effect they may have.[1] Statutory analysis differs from common law analysis because it focuses on the meaning of legislative pronouncements rather than judicial ones. Legislatures write rules in broad strokes. Because most statutes are enacted to cover categories of future situations, statutory analysis requires a determination of the effect of these broad rules on particular cases. Statutory analysis therefore focuses on the meaning of the statutory text. The purpose of the analysis is to determine whether the category described by the text does or does not apply to your client's situation.

Common law analysis, by contrast, requires comparing and contrasting factual situations. Common law rules tend to represent a synthesis of the decided cases, and these rules may change as courts decide new cases involving different factual situations. The specific facts of decided cases are thus as important as—if not more important than—the common law rules themselves. In statutory analysis, the text of the statutory rule tends to be more important than the facts of the decided cases. Statutory analysis thus tends to be deductive, while common law analysis tends to be inductive.

Statutory analysis is also different because statutes are less easily modified by courts than are common law principles. The doctrine of separation of powers, under which the legislature writes statutes and courts interpret them, limits courts to ascertaining and carrying out the legislative will. Courts may expand or contract the scope of a statutory rule when the statutory language permits such flexibility, but they may never disregard an applicable statute unless it is unconstitutional. On

---

[1] The basic rules for statutory analysis also apply to the analysis of administrative regulations, local ordinances, and other public laws that contain categorical rules.

the other hand, courts are free to modify or reject common law rules, within the limits of precedent and *stare decisis,* because modifying or rejecting common law rules does not encroach on the prerogatives of another governmental body.

Predicting how a court might apply or fail to apply a statute to your client's case requires an understanding of how courts approach statutory analysis. The courts (and, in some jurisdictions, legislatures) have developed rules or canons of statutory construction. These rules are intended to assist attorneys and courts in interpreting statutes.[2]

Despite these differences, common law and statutory analysis are similar in that both require an examination of potential weaknesses in your position. That is best accomplished, as explained in Chapter 6 (Common Law Analysis), by developing potential opposing positions and evaluating their strength. Every case involving the possible application of a statute or statutory provision involves these questions: (1) How is the statute or statutory provision applicable to my client's case? (2) How is the statute or statutory provision inapplicable to my client's case? The more applicable it is, the more it should dictate the outcome of the case. The more inapplicable it is, the less it should dictate the outcome.

Common law and statutory analysis are also similar when courts have decided relevant cases involving the statute. When that occurs, you must still examine the text of the statute to determine how it applies to your client's situation. But you must also compare and contrast the facts of decided cases with the facts of your case. This kind of statutory analysis is a hybrid of "pure" statutory analysis and common law analysis.

There are two steps in statutory analysis. The first is to determine whether the statute covers the situation at all. Statutes impose restrictions on certain people or activities, provide benefits to certain others, or establish procedures for the orderly accomplishment of certain goals. Your first task is to decide whether the individual, group, or activity in your case is covered by the statute. If the statute is applicable, the second step is to evaluate what effect application of the statute will have on your client's problem. This requires you to determine what conduct is commanded, prohibited, or regulated; whether your client's actions complied with or contravened the statute; and the consequences to your client of noncompliance.

Statutory analysis can best be understood by use of a hypothetical problem.

---

[2] There are numerous canons of construction. A standard work in this area is NORMAN J. SINGER, SUTHERLAND STATUTES AND STATUTORY CONSTRUCTION (5th ed. 1992), which collects all of the rules with citations to representative federal and state cases and reprints selected scholarly articles on the subject.

⬛ Until the recent election, members of the Liberal Party held all seven seats on the Grand View City Council. The Conservatives, who promised in the recent election to significantly reorder the city's budget priorities, now outnumber the Liberals on the Council by four to three. Your client, Joshua Smith, an important member of the Liberal Party, learned that the four Conservative members plan to meet privately within several weeks to write their proposed budget. This budget will then be presented to the full Council. The budget goes into effect once it has been adopted by a majority of the Council. Council meetings require a quorum of five. The Conservatives told Smith that neither he nor any other member of the public would be permitted to attend the meeting. The four members do not constitute any formal Council committee.

Is the Conservatives' position lawful under the state Open Meetings Act? That Act provides:

Sec. 1. Purpose. It is vital in a democratic society that public business be performed in an open and public manner so that the citizens shall be advised of the performance of public officials and of the decisions that are made by such officials in formulating and executing public policy. Toward this end, this chapter is adopted and shall be construed.

Sec. 2. Definitions. As used in this Act:
   (a) "Meeting" means the convening of a public body for the purpose of deliberating toward or rendering a decision on a public policy.
   (b) "Public body" means any state or local legislative body, including a board, commission, committee, subcommittee, authority, or council, that is empowered by law to exercise governmental or proprietary functions.

Sec. 3. All meetings of a public body shall be open to the public and shall be held in a place available to the general public.

The state court of appeals has decided one case concerning this statute:

Times-Journal Co. v. McPhee (1977)

The appellant, Times-Journal Co., brought an action seeking declaratory and injunctive relief against McPhee and the other members of the Bedford Board of Education, claiming that they had violated, and planned to continue violating, the state Open Meetings Act by closing a series of "preliminary" and "informal" meetings to the public. The trial court granted the defendants' motion to dismiss on the ground that no formal actions were taken at these meetings, even though they were attended by the entire board. Therefore, the court reasoned, they were not "meetings" within the meaning of the Act. We reverse.

Section 2(a) defines "meeting" as the convening of a public body "for the purpose of *deliberating toward* or rendering a decision on a public policy" (emphasis supplied). Every step in the decision-making process, including the decision itself, is necessarily part of the deliberation that the legislature intended to affect by enactment of the statute before us. "Preliminary" and "informal" meetings are necessarily part of that deliberative process.

The Open Meetings Act, like many statutes, contains a statement of purposes, definitions, and substantive provisions. To understand a statute, you need to read it carefully. Then reread the substantive provisions. These provisions state what the statute requires, prohibits, or allows. They are, in short, the central parts of the statute. In this case, the substantive provisions are in section 3.

Section 3 would require the caucus of the four Conservative members to be open if it is a "meeting" and if these members constitute a "public body." Words in statutes are ordinarily interpreted according to their customary meaning and usage, as defined in a dictionary. But legislatures often want certain words or phrases in a statute to have a different or more specific meaning. When this occurs, the statute contains its own set of definitions. The terms "meeting" and "public body" are both defined in section 2. The two questions posed by the problem are whether the definitions of these terms have been met.

A "meeting" occurs under section 2(a) if there is (1) a convening (2) of a public body (3) for the purpose of deliberating toward or rendering a decision (4) on a public policy. The first and fourth elements are "givens" because the four Conservative members are meeting to write a budget. The third element is met because of *Times-Journal Co. v. McPhee*. In that case, the court emphasized the deliberative nature of "preliminary" or "informal" meetings to support its conclusion that they were meetings within the meaning of section 2(a). The same type of deliberation would occur at the caucus of the Conservatives. They would be deliberating toward, and possibly deciding, the budget. This construction would most likely be controlling. The second element—whether these four members constitute a "public body"—is a more difficult question. The applicability of this element is also the second question posed by the problem.

The following chart depicts this analysis:

Meeting ELEMENTS CHART		
Element	**Facts of Our Case**	**Element Met?**
Convening	Four Council members meet privately	Yes
of a public body	Four-member Conservative majority of City Council; five required for quorum	Maybe
for the purpose of: deliberating toward —or—	Will write proposed budget, which will then be presented to full Council	Yes
rendering a decision	Will write proposed budget, which will then be presented to full Council	Maybe
on a public policy	Budget	Yes

A "public body" exists under section 2(b) when there is (1) a state or local legislative body, including a board, commission, committee, subcommittee, authority, or council (2) that is empowered by law to exercise governmental or proprietary functions. The Grand View City Council is a local legislative body under the first element, but it is not clear whether a majority of the Council would be held to constitute the Council. It is also unclear whether the second element is met because these four members constitute a majority but not a quorum of the Council.

This analysis may be shown as follows:

Public Body ELEMENTS CHART		
Element	**Facts of Our Case**	**Element Met?**
State or local legislative body, including a board, commission, committee, authority, or council	Four-member Conservative majority of City Council	Maybe
Empowered by law to exercise governmental or proprietary functions	Five members of seven-member Council required for quorum	Maybe

Before analyzing a statutory issue that involves cases, you may find it helpful to develop a case briefing chart like the one shown in Chapter 6 (Common Law Analysis). In this problem, however, a case briefing chart is not likely to be helpful because there is only one relevant case, and it is based primarily on the deliberation issue.

As the chart indicates, the problem has two sub-issues—whether the four members are a "local legislative body" and whether they are empowered to exercise "governmental or proprietary functions." The following principles provide a method for resolving these sub-issues, using the governmental functions sub-issue as an example. (The local legislative body sub-issue is addressed in Exercise 7-A.)

1. Determine how the language of the statute, and the facts of any cases interpreting the statute, support your client's position.

The "plain meaning" rule is a keystone of statutory construction. Courts presume that words and phrases in a statute have a meaning common to drafter and reader alike and that reasonable persons would not disagree over what the meaning is. Courts therefore will not stretch the meaning of a term or phrase beyond its ordinary understanding. Courts also assume that statutory drafters have followed commonly accepted rules of grammar and punctuation.

As already stated, a court will also consider previous cases construing the same or a similar statute. The court will follow the principles of precedent and *stare decisis* whenever previous decisions do not clearly conflict with the plain meaning and clear intent of the statute in question.

According to section 2(b), any entity that has the legal authority to exercise governmental or proprietary functions, including those listed, is a "public body." Although the term is defined in the statute, its applicability to the facts of your client's case is uncertain. Governmental functions would be your focus, however, because proprietary functions are based on ownership. You would argue that the four Conservative members are a public body because they control the Council, an entity that exercises governmental functions. This control exists because they have enough votes to compel adoption of any budget they draft. In that significant sense, their formulation of a budget at a secret meeting would be tantamount to the exercise of a governmental function. They do not need a quorum at this caucus because they can achieve the needed quorum when the full Council meets to consider the budget they have proposed. The *de facto* budget will then become the legal budget. For these reasons, the Conservatives can exercise governmental functions under section 2(b).

2. Determine how the language of the statute, and the facts of any cases interpreting the statute, support your opponent's position.

The same statutory language provides support for the opposite conclusion. Where you try to show how the language of a statute applies to your client's situation, your opponent will try to show that the language of the statute does not. Where you try to analogize cases interpreting the language to support your conclusion, he will show that these cases are inapplicable or that they support his position.

Your opponent will argue that "governmental functions" should not be enlarged by judicial interpretation to include a private meeting of Council members belonging to the same party. They cannot exercise any governmental functions at the secret meeting because the Conservative caucus is short of the needed quorum (even if all the other procedural requirements for calling a City Council meeting could be sidestepped). The full Council must still adopt the budget for it to have the force of law, and that Council meeting will be open to the public.

3. Determine how the policies of the statute, and the policies of any cases interpreting the statute, support your client's position.

Another significant statutory construction rule is that the statute should be interpreted to carry out the legislature's intent. The initial presumption is that the legislature intended to say what it actually said. When the intent is clear from the statutory language and application of the statute unambiguously advances that intent, the court's function is straightforward. When the provision itself is unclear or could be applied in a way that is not in accord with the intent of the statute, the court is likely to engage in statutory interpretation. The overriding concern will then be to ascertain and give effect to the legislature's intent.

The task of ascertaining legislative intent is relatively easy if the purpose of the legislation is explained in a preamble or introductory section of the statute. If it is not, the court will look at the entire statute and try to discern a legislative purpose from its provisions. The legislative history of a statute (published records of hearings, debates, committee reports, proposed bills, and other materials that shed light on what the legislators did and why) can also be a valuable guide to the statute's purpose and the meaning of specific provisions. Courts interpreting federal statutes may consult legislative history because it is printed and accessible. Generally there is little, if any, legislative history for most state statutes because state legislative proceedings are rarely reduced to writing. Occasionally, the drafters will write a commentary explaining the intent of the legislation and giving some guidance on how the provisions are meant to be applied.

Be aware that some courts, particularly federal courts, believe that it is inappropriate to use committee reports, hearing records, legislative debates, and similar materials to interpret statutes. They view the law as being the text of the statute, which the legislature adopted. In their view, statements or materials written by individual legislators, committees, or their staffs should not be used to interpret or modify the statute itself.

Although there is no legislative history for the Open Meetings Act, section 1 of the Act states the legislature's intent. It declares in broad terms the importance of conducting "public business" in an "open and public manner" so that citizens can know what decisions are made and the reasons for these decisions. Section 1 also requires interpretation of the Act to effectuate this goal. The *McPhee* court carried out the purpose of the Act by concluding that each step in the decision-making process ought to be made public.

These policies are particularly applicable here because the most important steps in the decision-making process will occur at the caucus. The Conservative members will resolve many, if not all, of their differences at the caucus and thus foreclose full debate before the full Council. Because the Conservatives will in all likelihood be locked into their positions after the caucus, the debate at the Council meeting will be more form than substance. As a result, an important piece of "public business," the budget, will not be resolved in the "open and public manner" contemplated by the legislature. Section 1 implies that the legislature believed open meetings to be of greater importance than the privacy of political parties, and that decision should be respected.

4. Determine how the policies of the statute, and the policies of any cases interpreting the statute, support your opponent's position.

Your opponent will argue for the merits of other policies in the statute, some expressly stated, some merely implicit in the legislative scheme. He will attempt to show that your policy arguments do not apply to the facts of this case or that they are simply not as important as others that support his client's position.

The statutory emphasis on "public body," "public business," and governmental functions indicates that the legislature did not intend the Open Meetings Act to reach what is essentially private behavior. The planned caucus is only for members of a private political party. *McPhee* supports this conclusion because the court in that case dealt with meetings of the full Board of Education, not with some faction of the Board. To require that private groups open their meetings to the public because of their conceivable impact on public business would stretch the Act far beyond its intended meaning. In any event, the Conservatives and Liberals will almost certainly debate each other at the Council meeting. The Conservative budget proposal and the Council's final budget will tell people what choices were made.

There is no guarantee that debate will be stifled or foreclosed at the City Council meeting. The caucus will merely provide the Conservative members, all of whom are newly elected, with a chance to discuss the budget and arrive at a consensus. No facts support the conclusion that the four members will vote as a bloc on every single budget issue debated before the City Council. They may disagree on some issues initially, or they may change their minds as they listen to the debate or receive new information. Arguments to the contrary are simply speculative.

The following chart shows the first four steps of this analysis:

Governmental Functions ANALYSIS CHART		
	Why Element Is Applicable (Our Client's Case)	**Why Element Is Not Applicable** (Opponent's Case)
Facts	City Council has seven members. Four Conservatives want to meet secretly to adopt a proposed budget. At the Council meeting, they will be able to adopt the budget they wrote secretly.	Five members are required for a quorum. The budget cannot be adopted at the meeting. The meeting is for members of the same political party to develop a budget proposal.
Policies	"Public business" should be conducted in an open and public manner so that citizens know what decisions are made and the reasons for those decisions. The Conservatives will likely resolve many or all differences in the secret meeting. The Council debate will not include much real debate. The public will not know the choices that were made or the reasons for those choices.	The statute was not intended to reach private behavior. The Conservatives may not resolve their differences at the private meeting. At the Council meeting, the Conservatives may not vote together on all issues; they may change their minds. The Liberals and the Conservatives will almost certainly debate each other. The proposed budget by Conservatives and the Council's final budget will inform the public of the choices that were made.

5. Evaluate the strength of your client's position.

Although the issue can be characterized as a technical one involving the definition of several words, it actually raises important and competing policy considerations that need to be reconciled. Ultimately, your client probably has a stronger legal position because the caucus, a majority of the Council, is likely to greatly influence, if not dictate, the budget adopted by the City Council. You should check this result using the factors in Chapter 8 (Reaching a Conclusion). Although there is room for a contrary point of view, the more important point is that you must draw a conclusion and be able to demonstrate that your conclusion is more reasonable than any other. As noted earlier, your client wants an answer. It is not enough to merely list competing considerations; you must scrutinize and evaluate their merits.

This illustration focuses on analysis of the first kind of statutory issue—whether the statute applies to the case. There may be an additional question—what effect application of the statute will have on your client. If Smith is able to obtain relief beforehand, the Conservatives likely will be required to hold an open meeting. If the Conservatives have already met, however, the question is more complicated. What remedy is appropriate? A court will look at the statute to see what guidance, if any, it includes.

The statutory construction rules used in this chapter—"plain meaning" and legislative intent—are relatively straightforward. You should be aware that other statutory construction rules are more subtle. The purpose of these other rules is also to ascertain legislative purpose from the language of the statute. They work by creating a presumption that a particular question should be resolved in a particular way unless the legislature clearly intended otherwise. A court is likely to presume, for example, that the legislature did not intend an unjust or absurd result, and will construe the statute accordingly. It is likely to presume that the legislature was aware of the common law and prior statutes affecting the categories that are the subject of the statute, and will harmonize the statute with prior law if it can.

A rule known by its Latin title, *ejusdem generis* (of the same kind or class), for example, is also widely employed. This rule says that if a general term precedes or follows a list of specific terms, the general term is presumably limited to items of the same kind as those specified in the list.

Suppose your client's car and trailer containing personal items were stolen from a motel parking lot and never recovered. He consults you four months after the theft, wanting to know whether he can recover from the motel owner. In your state, there is a ninety-day statute of limitations for "the recovery or conversion of personal property, wearing apparel, trunks, valises, or baggage left at a hotel or other public lodging." This example presents a classic instance in which a court might apply the *ejusdem generis* rule. The court could reason that the enumerated items—wearing apparel, baggage, and so forth—are the kinds of personal property one might take into a hotel room. A car and trailer do not fit within the enumerated list (are not of the same kind or class) and so are not included within the general term "personal property." That means your client could recover for the loss of his car and trailer because the ninety-day statute of limitations does not apply. He could not, however, recover for the loss of his personal items. The court would reach this conclusion only after deciding that the legislature did not intend the contrary.

You should consult the law in your jurisdiction to see which rules of construction have been adopted. Because it is difficult to argue against a presumption, you should try to fit your case within one or more of the presumptions that have been recognized.

Work through the following exercises with the help of these principles. Try to understand the similarities and differences between common law analysis and statutory analysis, and remember that the process will get easier as you become familiar with it.

Exercise 7-A

Using the guidelines described in this chapter, evaluate the strength of Smith's position on whether the four Conservative members of the City Council constitute a "state or local legislative body."

Exercise 7-B

What arguments would you make for the motel owner in the example involving the theft of a car and trailer from a motel parking lot?

Exercise 7-C

Marianne Preston was a temporary employee of Jade Enterprises, Inc. for six months. As soon as her term of employment ended, she filed a complaint with the state Fair Employment Commission accusing her former employer of sexual harassment. The Commission ordered a hearing before an administrative law judge, who found that Jade had engaged in sexual harassment. The judge ordered Jade to pay Preston compensatory damages of $15,000 for humiliation and emotional pain and distress.

The Fair Employment Act provides in part:

Sec. 1. The purpose of this Act is to eliminate employment discrimination based on race, sex, national or ethnic origin, or handicap by providing effective remedies to the victims of such discrimination.

Sec. 6. Upon a finding that an employer has engaged in employment discrimination, including sexual harassment, the Commission shall order the employer to take such action as will effectuate the purpose of the Act, including, but not limited to, hiring, reinstating, or upgrading employees; awarding back pay; and restoring membership in pension and other employee benefit plans.

Jade plans to appeal the administrative law judge's decision on the ground that the Commission is not authorized under the Act to require an employer to pay compensatory damages.

1. Can reasonable minds disagree over the meaning of the phrase "such action as will effectuate the purpose of the Act, including, but not limited to"? Explain how broadly or narrowly the phrase can be construed.

2. Does the *ejusdem generis* rule of construction apply here? What arguments would you would make for the Commission? What arguments would you make for Jade Enterprises? Do any other rules of construction apply?

3. How do the stated and implicit purposes of the Act support the Commission's position?

4.   How do the stated and implicit purposes of the Act support Jade's position?

5.   How should a court decide Jade's appeal? Explain.

Exercise 7-D

The Metropolitan Social Welfare League is an organization composed of social workers and welfare recipients that advocates welfare reform. For two years the League has urged the City of Lake Rapids to set aside an eighteen-square-block area on the city's east side for low income housing. That area is now vacant. The League has negotiated with city, state, and federal officials on this matter because the mayor said the proposal was "worth looking into" at a news conference ten months ago.

The Swift Land Development Corporation applied eight months ago for a zoning amendment to permit the construction of an auto salvage yard on one block of that eighteen-block area. Several other companies are also interested in zoning amendments. The area is now zoned for multiple-family housing. Six months ago, the city denied Swift's proposal. Swift immediately filed suit to force approval of the amendment. Last week, the city attorney stated that he thought the city might be wrong in this case. The mayor has stated several times that "City Hall represents the people, not narrow special interest groups."

Can the League now intervene as a defendant under State Court Rule 779.1(3)? State Court Rule 779.1(3), which is codified in the state statutes, provides:

> Anyone shall be permitted to intervene in an action:
>
> . . . .
>
> (3)   Upon timely application when the representation of the applicant's interest is or may be inadequate and the applicant may be bound by a judgment in the action.

The Drafting Committee for the rules made this comment in drafting Rule 779.1(3):

> There may be persons having interests so vital that they ought to have been made parties in the first place. They must be allowed to intervene. Therefore, the court is given no discretion in this regard.

There is one relevant case in this state:

Halsey v. Village of Elk Mound (1986)

The appellee petitioned the Elk Mound Planning Commission to rezone two adjacent parcels within the village from single-family residential to multiple-family residential. The Commission denied his request, and the Town Council agreed. The appellee brought suit against the village to prevent it from interfering with his proposed use for the parcels. The appellants, persons with homes within 300 feet of the parcels, sought to intervene. The trial court determined that the appellants could not intervene because they had not met the requirements of Court Rule 779.1(3). We reverse.

The intervention rule requires (1) timely action by the applicant, (2) possible or actual inadequacy of representation by existing parties, and (3) the possibility that the applicant may be bound by a judgment in the action. There was no unreasonable delay here, since the appellants filed their motion to intervene only three weeks after suit was brought. The appellants were not too late to protect their interests. In addition, the rule requires only that existing representation *may* be inadequate. The burden of satisfying this requirement must be minimal. The appellants meet this requirement because the village does not purport to represent the interests of their neighborhood. Finally, we read the term "bound" to mean that, as a practical matter, the appellants' ability to protect their interest may be substantially affected. Since the appellants have met all three requirements, they are entitled to intervene.

1. Identify the relevant rule(s), and the elements of the rule(s), in this problem.

2. Explain the importance, if any, of the Drafting Committee comment. Explain the importance, if any, of the *Halsey* case.

3. How does the language of the rule support the League's position? How do the facts of the *Halsey* case support that position?

4. Assume that the city will oppose a motion to intervene. How does the language of the rule support the city's position? How do the facts of the *Halsey* case support that position?

5. How do the policies in the Drafting Committee comment and the *Halsey* case support the League's position?

6. How do the policies in the Drafting Committee comment and the *Halsey* case support the city's position?

7. Should the League attempt to intervene under Rule 779.1(3)? Explain.

Exercise 7-E

Francine Odegaard was recently elected governor. She received 50.2% of the vote, and her opponent received 49.8%. A state legislative committee set up to monitor the effects of the Election Campaign Finance Act investigated the funding sources of the two candidates and learned that Odegaard's campaign committee received $41,995 from her grandfather after the election. This amount was precisely the debt with which her campaign committee ended the general election. Odegaard's natural parents died when she was very young. She was raised by her grandfather, Rolf Odegaard, although he never formally adopted her. Her grandfather made no other contributions to her campaign. The committee has drafted a report recommending that he be prosecuted for violating section 31 of the Act. The committee has hired you to review its recommendation.

The Election Campaign Finance Act provides in part:

Sec. 2. This Act is intended to regulate political activity, to regulate campaign financing, and to restrict campaign contributions and expenditures without jeopardizing the ability of candidates for state public office to conduct effective campaigns.

Sec. 31. (a) Except as provided in subsection (b), a person other than a campaign committee member shall not make contributions on behalf of the winner of a primary election for the office of governor in excess of $600 for any purpose after the date of such primary election.

(b) A contribution from a member of a candidate's immediate family to the campaign committee for that candidate is exempt from the limitation of subsection (a).

(c) As used in subsection (b), "immediate family" means a spouse, parent, brother, sister, son, or daughter.

Sec. 44. A person who violates the provisions of this Act is guilty of a misdemeanor and shall be fined not more than $1,000.

The highest appellate court in the state has decided the following cases:

Alberts v. Election Commission (1977)

Section 31(a) of the Election Campaign Finance Act prohibits any person from making contributions "on behalf of the winner of a primary election for the office of governor in excess of $600 for any purpose after the date of such primary election." The appellant challenges the validity of a trial court determination that he violated section 31(a) by contributing $1,500 to the unsuccessful candidate for governor in the 1976 general election. He argues that he made the contribution to help retire the candidate's debt from the primary. We affirm.

Section 31(a) of the Election Campaign Finance Act was designed to reduce, if not eliminate, the improper influence a contributor gains from a large contribution near the end of the campaign. More generally, the Act was designed to help improve the integrity, and the appearance of integrity, of the election process. These policy considerations make it particularly important that the phrase "for any purpose" be read for its full meaning. We hold that the phrase includes payments for the purpose of reducing primary debts. Affirmed.

Toland v. Election Commission (1976)

Clyde Swanson lost the general election for governor after winning his party's primary election. His son Raymond handled the finances for Clyde's general election campaign. As treasurer, Raymond received funds from various sources, deposited them in his personal checking account, and then wrote checks from that account to pay for campaign expenses. Clyde's largest contribution, a $15,000 check from Alphonse Toland, was processed in this manner. Toland was convicted of a misdemeanor for violating section 31 of the Election Campaign Finance Act. We affirm that conviction.

Section 31 limits contributions to candidates for governor in a general election to $600 per person, unless the contributor is a member of the candidate's "immediate family." The immediate family exception is premised on a legislative desire to protect freedom of expression by candidates; donating money is a recognized way of expressing a preference. In addition, the Act's purpose of reducing the corrupting influence of outside financial sources has much less force when the contributor is from the candidate's immediate family. Although Swanson's son is a member of his "immediate family" under section 31(b), the son was a conduit, rather than a source, of the funds. The important purposes of the Act should not be undermined by such transparent schemes.

1.   Identify the relevant rule(s), and the elements of the rule(s), in this problem.

2.   For each issue, how does the language of the Act support the committee's position? How do the facts of the cases support that position?

3.   For each issue, how does the language of the Act support Rolf Odegaard's position? How do the facts of the cases support that position?

4.   For each issue, how do the policies of the Act support the committee's position? How do the policies of the cases support that position?

5.   For each issue, how do the policies of the Act support Rolf Odegaard's position? How do the policies of the cases support that position?

6.   Do you think Rolf Odegaard violated the Act? Explain.

8

Reaching a Conclusion

THE FINAL STEP in common law and statutory analysis, as we saw in Chapters 6 and 7, is evaluating the strength of your client's position. A lawyer helps clients to make decisions—often painful and difficult decisions. Clients need advice that is reliable, accurate, and complete. They need to be fully informed of their choices and the relative strengths and weaknesses of each choice. And they don't want to worry about whether the lawyer is right. No lawyer, in turn, wants a client to regret taking her advice.

Evaluating the strength of your client's position requires judgment about the merits of competing considerations. There is no complete guidebook for exercising good judgment, and there is no substitute for experience with difficult problems. Three basic principles nonetheless provide valuable guidance in evaluating the strength of competing legal positions. In general, the strongest legal positions are those that involve little or no extension of existing law, result in a decision that furthers the policies or purposes of the law, and reach a fair or just outcome for the parties. If all of these factors are in your client's favor, your client will almost certainly prevail. If all of these factors are in your opponent's favor, your client will almost certainly lose.

If some factors support your client and some factors support your opponent, drawing a conclusion becomes more difficult. Differences between the outcomes suggested by individual factors reduce the level of certainty that a lawyer can express about a particular position, and must be reflected in a memorandum. To the extent that such differences exist, moreover, they will raise more questions about a particular position. You should therefore devote sufficient time to legal research and analysis, and this should be reflected in your writing.

Each of the three factors must be considered separately in reaching a conclusion about the strength of your client's position. One way to test each factor is to construct an argument for your client's position and your opponent's position, and then see which is stronger according to that factor. The factors are applied and analyzed in the context of the following problem. The answers used to illustrate these factors are set out in shorthand form rather than in the way that you would draft your conclusion.

1. A position is stronger to the extent that it involves little or no extension of existing law.

Judges must determine how the relevant statutes, regulations, cases, and other law apply to the facts of the case. A legal position based on existing law is more likely to win than one involving substantial extension or revision of existing law.

This principle operates on a sliding scale. If no extension at all is required to support a legal position, it is very strong. In cases involving the common law, for example, the strongest position will be one based on existing decisions where your client's situation is plainly analogous or plainly distinguishable. In cases involving statutes, the language of the statute will either include the factual situation or exclude it. In logical terms, the law will describe a category that includes or does not include the factual situation.

A legal position generally is weaker to the extent that it requires a court to extend or revise existing case law, or to interpret a statute in a way that seems to depart from its plain meaning. The other factors described in this chapter may overcome this weakness, however. The most important judicial decisions, in fact, break new legal ground precisely because other factors outweigh a court's deference to existing law.

▮ Your client, Rochelle Timmers, a retired school teacher in her 80s with a perfect driving record, has been injured in a car accident. She was driving to the hospital to visit her husband, who had recently undergone heart surgery. While rounding a corner in the city of Goshen, she unexpectedly encountered a traffic jam caused by the city's traditional St. Patrick's Day parade on a main traffic artery. Timmers was not aware that the traditional parade always traveled down that street. There were no signs, traffic control devices, or police officers to direct traffic or warn motorists. Timmers would like to recover for the damages she suffered when her car collided with another car that was waiting in traffic. Consider whether the city may be liable, because the City Council granted the parade permit and knew from previous years that the parade frequently caused a traffic jam. There are two pertinent cases:

Town of Parkview v. Simon (1983)

While riding her motorcycle, the appellee was injured when she struck the side of an automobile that pulled out into her path. The driver of the automobile was unable to see the appellee approaching because of the shrubbery and tall grass growing in the median, which had been designed and maintained by the town of Parkview. The jury found that the median had been negligently designed and maintained and awarded the appellee damages. The appellant appeals the denial of its motion to set aside the verdict.

Traditionally, a private landowner has no duty to maintain his property so that it does not obstruct a motorist's view. However, when a governmental entity creates a condition it knows or should know is dangerous, it must avert the danger or warn the public. Otherwise, it must be held liable for any resulting damages. This rule strikes a balance between the government's broad right to manage public property as it sees fit and its obligations to the safety of motorists. The town of Parkview built and maintained the median and should have known that failing to properly maintain the shrubbery would create a hazard to motorists. Whether the town did so or not was a question for the jury. The trial court did not err in refusing to overturn the verdict. Affirmed.

Brockton v. City of Adrian **(1981)**

The appellant appeals a summary judgment granted in a wrongful death action. The appellant's decedent drowned when the car in which she was riding went straight through a "T" intersection and into a canal that ran parallel to the intersecting road. The canal is owned by the city. The driver, while approaching the intersection, apparently failed to see four signs: (1) a warning of the approaching "T" intersection; (2) a warning of the decreasing speed limit; (3) a warning of the approaching "STOP" sign; and (4) the "STOP" sign itself. The signs were not obstructed or obscured and met the state requirements for traffic signs. The appellant asserts that the appellee was negligent in failing to warn drivers of the danger posed by the canal located across from the intersection.

The duty to warn was clearly met by the signs, which satisfied the state requirements and were properly maintained. To hold otherwise would improperly penalize diligent municipalities for the negligent conduct of motorists. Judgment affirmed.

The cases show that the city's liability turns on two issues: whether the traffic jam was a hazard and whether the council failed to warn approaching motorists of the hazard. Your summary of the competing arguments might look like this:

Issue 1: Was the traffic jam a hazard?

Client: Yes. The hazard is analogous to the blind median in *Town of Parkview* and the canal in *Brockton*.

Opponent: No. A traffic jam is different from the road feature design in *Town of Parkview* and the adjacent physical hazard in *Brockton*; it is not permanent or dangerous.

Issue 2: Did the city fail to warn approaching motorists of the hazard?

Client: Yes. The failure to warn here is analogous to the failure to warn in *Town of Parkview*. *Brockton*, where warning was given, is thus distinguishable.

Opponent: No, because there was no hazard. The case is thus distinguishable from *Town of Parkview* and *Brockton*. Warning signals weren't given here because they weren't necessary.

This analytical summary indicates that resolution of the problem will turn on whether the unexpected traffic jam was a hazard. Because warning signals weren't provided, the city is liable if the traffic jam is a hazard. If the traffic jam is not a hazard, it doesn't matter that signals weren't provided. Your client would like to analogize the decided cases and state that the traffic jam was a hazard. Your opponent would like to distinguish the decided cases because they involved permanent features and state that the traffic jam was not a hazard. As you assemble arguments for each side, check to see whether the arguments made by one side are answered by the other side. If they are not answered, check to see whether they can be answered, that is, whether you can think of an answer you haven't considered. In this situation, there is no answer so far to the assertion that the decided cases involve permanent features. You would likely answer that this distinction is immaterial because the parade was a hazard. Because the hazard issue does not favor either side at this point, the first factor is a toss-up.

2. A position is stronger to the extent that it furthers the policies or purposes of the law.

Cases are decided to further specific purposes, and statutes are adopted for particular reasons. Courts will look to those purposes and reasons to see whether they will be advanced by their decisions. This is not to say that the purpose of a law automatically overrides the text of that law. Rather, a court will test its conclusions about the result indicated by the law to see whether that result is consistent with the purposes of the law. The more clearly a particular position is consistent with the purposes of the law, the stronger it is.

In common law cases, the policies or purposes are stated in previous court decisions. As noted earlier, courts tend to follow previous decisions rather than chart a new or modified course. In some common law cases, however, the result indicated by the law may be inconsistent with the purposes stated by previous courts. There is no widely accepted theory about how to resolve such differences. It is nonetheless true that in such cases courts will be tempted to modify existing case law to further the underlying purposes.

In statutory problems, as noted in Chapter 7, the policies or reasons may be expressly stated by the legislature in the statute, or they may be inferred from the statute's language or structure. For federal legislation, committee reports and related sources are often helpful. As with common law cases, statutory problems sometimes involve situations in which the language of the statute indicates a result that is inconsistent with its underlying policies. Courts tend to respond to such cases in two ways. In some cases, courts find ways of interpreting statutes to further their underlying purposes, on the theory that courts should assist in the implementation of statutes. This approach is more likely when the statutory language is flexible or general enough to accommodate such a reading. A legal position based on a general or flexible statute will be weakened to the extent that it contradicts or does not further the underlying purposes of the statute.

In other cases, courts read statutes as they are written, regardless of whether the outcome is consistent with the underlying purposes. This is true especially when the language unambiguously indicates a particular result. Increasingly, the federal courts—including the Supreme Court—are taking this approach. A legal position based on an unambiguous statute is likely to prevail even if it contradicts or is inconsistent with the statute's purposes. The rationale is that the legislature, rather than the court, is responsible for correcting problems with statutes.

◻ Your summary concerning the purposes of the law might look like this:

Was the traffic jam a hazard?

Client: Yes. The purpose of the law is to protect motorists from traffic hazards created by the city. The type of hazard does not matter. *Town of Parkview* suggests the purpose of the law is broad enough to extend the term "hazard" to include any danger to motorists created by the city's management of public property. Evidence of the hazard includes its unexpected nature and the accident itself.

Opponent: No. The purpose of the law is to protect motorists from hazards that would not reasonably be known or foreseeable without warning signals. A traffic jam is a foreseeable event in any driving situation, regardless of whether there is a parade.

The summary shows that there are policy arguments for each position. Look carefully, however, at the nature of these arguments. Your client's position focuses on the traffic jam as a hazard. In this part of the analysis, your opponent challenges the premise that a traffic jam is a hazard, saying instead that a traffic jam is foreseeable in any driving situation. Your client's position provides no direct answer to that assertion. While general policy arguments supporting your client's position are appropriate, they must be sensitive to the facts of the case; otherwise, they seem abstract, even irrelevant. Is there a good answer to the assertion that traffic jams are foreseeable in any driving situation? You might argue that this traffic jam occurred in an unexpected place, but the gist of your opponent's position is that traffic jams often occur in unexpected places. Unless you come up with a better answer your case is weakened.

3. When the law does not require a particular result, a position is stronger to the extent that it involves a fair or just outcome for the parties.

One of the worst mistakes a lawyer can make is to assume that the logic of the law matters more than how it affects people. To be sure, there are cases in which the law, its purposes, and the logical structure of an argument dictate a result that the judge might not agree with, but that the judge nonetheless upholds. But when the legal strength of competing positions is otherwise relatively equal, the equities matter a great deal. In such cases, the position that leads to the fairest result is likely to prevail.

As will be explained in more detail in Chapter 23 (Briefs to a Trial Court), sensitivity to the equities is more pronounced at the trial court level than it may be at the appellate court level. Virtually all cases begin in front of trial judges, and trial judges are keenly aware of the facts of a particular case. Their job is to apply the law to real situations involving real people who live in their community and who often watch or participate in the proceedings.

Statements about fairness or justice must be based on particular reasons. Some fairness statements are based on policies expressed in the relevant law. Other fairness statements are based on policies expressed in other laws, and some are based on generally accepted social values.

In this case, the facts of the decided cases and their underlying reasons and policies tend to support your opponent's position, but they do not support it conclusively. Your summary on fairness and justice might look like this:

Client: Timmers had a perfect driving record, is in her 80s, and was on her way to visit her hospitalized husband. It is unfair for Timmers to bear responsibility for the city's failure to warn of the hazard, especially when the city council was aware of the traffic jam and could easily have taken measures to warn unsuspecting motorists such as Timmers. The city will take greater care in warning of future hazards if it is required to compensate Timmers.

Opponent: The accident occurred because of Timmers's negligence. City taxpayers should not be penalized for Timmers's failure to exercise ordinary care in the operation of her car.

The fairness arguments on each side appeal to different values and even to different emotions. Your client's position rests to some extent on sympathy for her situation. Inherent in our culture's concept of fairness is a desire to recognize the needs of people who are in special or difficult situations. But you must be careful how you use facts to gain sympathy. You may want to state that an older driver should not be held to the same standard as other drivers, for example. That statement, however, would hurt your client in two ways. It tacitly admits that your client was not driving as carefully as other drivers, and it seems to condone dangerous driving by senior citizens. You would find it very difficult to defend these positions in court. This example illustrates an important point. You should exclude from your analysis contentions that cannot be even minimally defended.

Your opponent's main fairness argument will likely rest on Timmers's actual behavior and her possible negligence. This argument appears relatively strong in this case because it fits neatly with the claim that she should have been prepared for an unexpected traffic jam. This argument also lessens sympathy for her situation. Because a traffic jam is unlikely to be considered a hazard, a court would probably not hold the city liable in any action brought by Timmers.

The analytical framework used in this chapter requires you to make decisions about the relative strengths of competing positions. It requires you to probe for strengths and weaknesses and to evaluate those strengths and weaknesses in light of the relevant law. It also requires you to develop explanations for the position you take and to be able to explain why that position is better than others.

The following exercises are intended to help you use this framework.

Exercise 8-A

Evaluate the strength of McKay's position based on your answers to Exercise 5-A, pp. 61–64, using the principles described in this chapter.

Exercise 8-B

Evaluate the strength of the *Star City Banner-Patriot*'s position based on your answers to Exercise 5-B, pp. 64–67, using the principles described in this chapter.

Part C

BASIC CONCEPTS OF
LEGAL WRITING

9

Organization

GOOD ORGANIZATION is fundamental to effective legal writing. No matter how well you have stated the question and the significant facts, how thoughtfully you have analyzed the problem, or how skillfully you have used language, your work will be wasted unless it is organized intelligently. As a lawyer, you will be lucky if you are simply asked to rewrite poorly organized documents. More likely, you will be ignored or misunderstood.

Poor organization happens more frequently than you might imagine; readers of legal materials often have no idea what the writer is trying to say. Although failure to communicate effectively can result from many causes, most such failures result from the writer's shoddy organization. Even though a perceptive reader may be able to piece together the writer's ideas anyway, extracting these ideas from a disorganized discussion is not the reader's job. A writer is obligated to make his work as accessible as possible.

Just as legal thinking has its own analytical framework, it also has its own organizational requirements. You will find that the material is sufficiently difficult that you cannot simply use a mental checklist of ideas or a few scribbled notes. Good organization begins with advance planning, and some writers find that advance planning requires a detailed outline. Outlining may help you think through a problem and avoid omitting important points. Outlining may also help you spot organizational deficiencies. Many writers find that charts such as those in Chapters 5, 6, and 7 are more helpful than outlines. These charts serve the same purposes as outlines, and many writers find that they are more conducive to legal writing. While developing a chart or an outline may seem to require extra work at first, it is ultimately a timesaving method of organization. Rewriting an outline or chart is easier than rewriting a paper.

Apart from careful planning, there are four basic principles of good organization.

107

1. Discuss each issue separately.

When there are two or more issues that merit analysis, you must examine each separately. Discuss and draw a conclusion about one issue before moving to the next. Distinct separation of issues helps the reader understand the issues and sharpens your understanding as well.

Separating issues is especially difficult in three types of situations. First, several issues may be hard to distinguish from one another because they are similar or similar-sounding. Effective organization requires a clear understanding of the relevant law. Second, the same reasons or policy considerations are sometimes needed for several issues when these issues are closely related. Never ignore points you have already discussed when they are relevant to a subsequent issue. Instead of completely restating a point you have already made, though, you may simply make brief reference to it. Finally, a case may deal with several issues relevant to your problem, requiring you to discuss that case at several points in your paper. Set out the case's holding and underlying facts pertaining to Issue X when you are discussing Issue X, and discuss the holding and underlying facts pertaining to Issue Y when you are discussing Issue Y. Avoid the temptation to set out all the facts and holdings of the case in one place; it will only confuse the reader. This last point is simply a variation of the basic theme—always discuss each issue separately.

□ Patrick Johnson is charged with assault and robbery in connection with the theft of $300 from First National Bank. The prosecutor alleges that Johnson pointed a gun at a teller and told him to hand over what money he had. After Johnson's arrest, police learned that his gun was not loaded. Does this fact provide a defense to the charges? There are two relevant cases:

State v. Cox (1948)

Gilbert Cox was convicted of robbery for taking $15 from a small grocery. He appeals on the ground that his "weapon," a pointed finger pressed against the inside of his coat, was not lethal. We think he misses the real issue, and consequently we affirm. Robbery requires that the taking be accomplished by either violence or the threat of immediate harm to the victim. Because Cox's act reasonably frightened the clerk into giving away the money, he cannot claim it was only a ruse.

State v. Hines (1962)

Carol Hines appeals her conviction for assault. We affirm. Hines was convicted for placing the eraser end of a pencil against the back of a blind man and threatening to shoot him if he did not turn over his money. He fainted and she fled. She claims that the absence of a real gun frees her from guilt for assault. We disagree. A person is guilty of assault if she intentionally puts another in fear that she may cause him serious bodily injury or death. A genuine handgun would not likely have made much difference to the blind man.

Consider these two discussions:

ANSWER A: Johnson cannot use the fact that his gun was unloaded as a defense to either assault or robbery. In *State v. Hines*, the court held that the defendant's failure to use a real gun was not a defense to assault when she caused a blind man such fear for his life that he fainted. The defendant had pressed a pencil against the victim's back as if it were a handgun. The court said that reasonable fear for one's safety makes it irrelevant that there is actually nothing to fear. Similarly, in *State v. Cox*, the court held that a person can be convicted of robbery if the taking occurs because the defendant caused a reasonable fear of immediate harm to the victim. The court reasoned that the defendant's "weapon," a hidden pointed finger, frightened a clerk into turning over the store's money.

Johnson cannot use the fact that his gun was unloaded as a defense to assault because he intentionally put the teller in fear of serious bodily injury or death by pointing his gun at him. Just like the harmless pencil in *Hines*, the unloaded gun was sufficient to cause the victim reasonable fear for his safety. Nor is the unloaded gun a defense to robbery. Because the threat of immediate harm from Johnson's pointed gun prompted the clerk to give him $300, he is like the defendant in *Cox* who frightened the clerk into surrendering the money.

ANSWER B: Johnson cannot use the fact that his gun was unloaded as a defense to either assault or robbery. He committed assault because he intentionally put the teller in fear of serious bodily injury or death. In *State v. Hines*, the court held that the defendant's failure to use a real gun was not a defense to assault when she had caused a blind man such fear for his life that he fainted. The defendant had pressed a pencil against her victim's back as if it were a handgun. The court stated that reasonable fear for one's safety makes it irrelevant that there is actually nothing to fear. This case is analogous to *Hines* because Johnson intentionally put the teller in fear of serious bodily injury or death by pointing the gun at him. The teller, who did not know the gun was unloaded, complied with his demand. Just like the harmless pencil in *Hines*, the unloaded gun was sufficient to cause the victim reasonable fear for his safety.

Similarly, Johnson committed robbery because his use of the gun threatened the teller into giving him money. In *State v. Cox*, the court held that a person can be convicted of robbery if the taking occurs because of a threat of immediate harm to the victim. The court reasoned that the defendant's "weapon," a hidden pointed finger, frightened a clerk into turning over the store's money. Johnson is like the defendant in *Cox*, who threatened immediate harm to the clerk, because Johnson's pointed gun prompted the teller to give him $300. In both cases, moreover, the victim was not aware that the "weapon" was harmless. It is thus irrelevant that the gun was unloaded.

Although the description of the cases and analysis of the facts in Answers A and B are identical, Answer B is preferable because it is easier to understand. Answer B shows a distinct separation of issues. It describes the assault case and its application to Johnson's situation in the first paragraph, and the robbery case and its application to Johnson's situation in the second. The transition from the description of the case law to analysis of the facts for each issue is smooth and easy to follow.

Answer A, on the other hand, is organized like this: assault, robbery, assault, robbery. It explains the law concerning assault, then explains the law concerning robbery. When it relates the facts to the law, Answer A takes the reader back to assault, then back again to robbery. The organizational pattern is disjointed and hard to follow. Answer A imposes an unfair burden on the reader and is ineffective.

2. Discuss each sub-issue separately.

Each issue, as you have discovered, often has several parts or sub-issues. Each sub-issue involves its own rule, and thus its own set of significant facts. You should deal with each sub-issue in sequence, finishing the discussion of one before continuing to the next. Discuss sub-issues as part of the issue they comprise. If Issue A involves two sub-issues and Issue B also involves two sub-issues, discuss each sub-issue under A before going to any part of Issue B. As with issues, clear separation of sub-issues sharpens your presentation and helps the reader understand your position.

☐ Burns Research Corp., a consulting firm, successfully persuaded the Salem Township Board of Trustees to grant a zoning amendment to reclassify a ninety-seven-acre parcel from agricultural (A) to research office (RO). A local landowner's group, Save Our Heritage Association, is contemplating a lawsuit challenging the amendment on a number of grounds, including spot zoning. The parcel previously was used by a home for delinquent children, whose founders believed in the therapeutic value of agricultural work. Burns plans to lease most of the land for pasture. The surrounding area is made up of homes on five-acre lots as well as farms. There are two relevant cases in the state:

Costello v. Plainview Zoning Commission (1965)

The appellants challenge a decision by the Zoning Commission for the City of Plainview changing the classification of a one-half acre lot from RR (single family residential) to C (commercial). The appellants are homeowners and residents of the fourteen-acre RR zone surrounding the lot. The applicant for the zoning change, a trucking company which is an appellee here, sought permission to build a trucking terminal on the lot. The appellants argued unsuccessfully to the trial court that the Commission's decision constituted unlawful spot zoning.

We agree with the appellants and reverse. The essence of zoning is the division of a municipality into districts defining present or potential suitable uses for property. Spot zoning is unlawful where a parcel of land is singled out for special treatment for the benefit of the owner and to the detriment of other landowners and the community. The zoning change at issue here constituted special treatment for the trucking company because it affected only the small parcel owned by the company. Rezoning also was detrimental to the landowners and the community because the terminal would lead to a decline in property values. Under these circumstances, the Commission's action was impermissible spot zoning.

Persich v. Pole (1974)

Michael Pole, the owner of an undeveloped seven-acre tract zoned R2 (multiple family residential), successfully persuaded the Medford Zoning Commission to rezone the property to C (commercial). He plans to build a shopping center on the tract, lease the center to various retail stores, and use the remainder of the tract for a parking lot. Persich, a homeowner on adjoining property, sued to enjoin the amendment as spot zoning. The trial court agreed with the Commission and we affirm.

We ruled in *Costello v. Plainview Zoning Commission* that spot zoning is impermissible "where a parcel of land is singled out for special treatment for the benefit of the owner and to the detriment of other landowners and the community." Pole is not being unfairly benefited here because the rezoning applies to a large block of land, unlike the half-acre rezoning for the trucking company rejected in *Costello*. In addition, because the record shows the absence of any shopping centers in the area, location of the center on this property will benefit the neighborhood and the city.

Consider these discussions:

ANSWER A: The amendment was not improper spot zoning. "Spot zoning is unlawful where a parcel of land is singled out for special treatment for the benefit of the owner and to the detriment of other landowners and the community." *Costello v. Plainview Zoning Commission*. The court in *Costello* concluded there was spot zoning where a one-half acre lot located in a large residential area was rezoned "commercial" to accommodate a trucking terminal. The court said the essence of zoning is division of a municipality into districts, and it apparently believed a one-half-acre lot was unreasonably small for a district. The court also found that the amendment would lead to lowered property values in the neighborhood.

However, in *Persich v. Pole*, the court concluded that a zoning commission's decision to rezone an undeveloped seven-acre lot from a residential classification to a commercial one for a shopping center and parking lot was not spot zoning. The tract owner was not "unfairly benefited," the court reasoned, because the property was much larger than one-half acre. The court also found a benefit to the neighborhood because of the absence of any shopping centers in the area.

In this case, there is no unfair benefit to Burns because of the large size of the tract and because the basic use of the property will remain the same. The ninety-seven-acre property is larger than the seven-acre tract in *Persich* and thus is a reasonable size for a zoning district. In addition, there is no unfair burden to the surrounding landowners. Like the landowners in *Persich*, the surrounding landowners in the Burns case will actually benefit because they can lease land formerly owned by the home for delinquent children. Unlike the situation in *Costello*, no decline in property values is foreseeable because the essential use of the parcel for agricultural purposes will remain the same.

ANSWER B: The amendment was not improper spot zoning. "Spot zoning is unlawful where a parcel of land is singled out for special treatment for the benefit of the owner and to the detriment of other landowners and the community." *Costello v. Plainview Zoning Commission.*

The amendment is not an unfair benefit to Burns because of the large size of the tract. In *Persich v. Pole*, the court held that a seven-acre undeveloped residential tract that was rezoned commercial was large enough to preclude an unfair benefit. Thus, a ninety-seven-acre tract is large enough to be a zoning district. *Costello*, in which the court held that rezoning created an unfair benefit, is distinguishable because it involved only a half-acre lot. The lot was located in a large residential area, and was rezoned to commercial to accommodate a trucking terminal. The court reasoned that the essence of zoning is division of a municipality into districts, and it apparently believed that a half-acre lot was unreasonably small for a district.

In addition, there is no detriment to the surrounding landowners. The court in *Persich* found a proposed shopping center to be beneficial to the neighborhood, rather than detrimental, because no other shopping centers were located there. Like the landowners in *Persich*, the surrounding landowners in the Burns case will benefit because they can lease land formerly owned by the home for delinquent children. This case is also different from *Costello* because the trucking terminal in that case would have led to lowered property values in the neighborhood. No such problems are foreseeable here because the essential use of the parcel for agricultural purposes will remain the same.

Answer B is more understandable because it is better organized. The spot zoning issue depends on two sub-issues: (1) whether there is an unfair benefit to the owner, and (2) whether there is a detriment to other landowners and the community. Answer B sets out both the description and analysis of the law for each sub-issue separately, completing the discussion of one before moving to the next. Because both the description and analysis for each sub-issue are stated in the same place, Answer B is much easier to follow than Answer A.

Answer A describes both cases before analyzing either sub-issue and is organized like this: private benefit, neighborhood detriment, private benefit, neighborhood detriment, private benefit, and neighborhood detriment. Such zigzagging requires unnecessary effort simply to understand the discussion. This criticism should be familiar to you from the previous discussion on separation of issues. By describing all the law applicable to multiple points first, then trying to analyze the points, the writer risks leaving the reader in hopeless confusion. Stated another way, the sub-issues dictate the organization in Answer B, while the cases dictate the organization in Answer A. The issues and sub-issues, not the cases, should dictate your organization.

3. For each issue or sub-issue, describe the applicable law before applying it to the factual situation.

Each issue or sub-issue involves the application of a legal rule to specific facts. The relevant legal rules, therefore, provide a framework for your analysis and should be stated first. If you state the facts concerning an issue or sub-issue first, without describing the applicable law, the facts will mean nothing to your reader.

Stating the applicable law first enables you to be concise. The Statement of Facts at the beginning of an office memo or brief gives the reader a complete picture of the factual situation. Stating the facts in your Statement of Facts, then stating the facts for a particular issue or sub-issue, then stating the law, and then applying the law to the facts is inherently repetitious. When you write the discussion, therefore, avoid simply restating the facts; apply them. Instead of writing again, "Joe drove through a red light," write, "Because Joe drove through a red light, he violated . . . ." The facts, in other words, must be analyzed in the discussion, not simply restated.

☐   Ronald Jenkins owns a riparian lot on Fredda Lake, a shallow, thirty-acre pond with no inlets or outlets. David McNulty, who also owns a riparian lot on the lake, wants to drain one-third of the lake for water for a small brewery he plans to establish. McNulty's plans would reduce the size of the pond to fourteen acres, making it difficult for Jenkins to use it for fishing or boating. Jenkins, who is your client, wants to know if he can prevent McNulty from carrying out his plans. There is one pertinent case:

Posner v. Fox (1967)

> The appellant, Duane Posner, wants to construct an apartment complex on Lake Minnesota, a 400-acre lake drained by a small stream. He has owned riparian land on the lake for several years. His plans require the diversion of 1,200 acre-feet of water annually. The appellee, Sheila Fox, who also owns riparian land on the lake, seeks to block the diversion of the water. The trial court found that the proposed diversion would permanently reduce water levels by about three feet and would interfere with boating, swimming, and fishing on the lake by Fox and other abutting landowners. The court permanently enjoined the diversion. We affirm. Each riparian owner has certain rights to use the lake for domestic or recreational purposes, but each owner must accommodate the others. Posner's plans would unreasonably interfere with the rights of the other owners.

Consider the following:

ANSWER A: McNulty's proposal can be enjoined because it would constitute an unreasonable interference with Jenkins's use of the lake. McNulty's plans would reduce Fredda Lake from thirty acres to fourteen acres in size. This reduction in size would make it difficult for Jenkins to fish or boat on the lake. The court in *Posner v. Fox* held that a similar action could be enjoined as an unreasonable use of water. The defendant in that case sought to divert water from a 400-acre lake for a proposed apartment complex, thus permanently reducing water levels by about three feet. The court held that proposal to be an unreasonable use because it interfered with recreational uses of the water by the other riparian landowners along the lake. In McNulty's case, as in *Posner*, the proposed diversion would significantly interfere with the recreational use of the lake. Reducing the size of the lake by more than one-half seems an even more unreasonable encroachment than the comparatively slight reduction in water levels found in *Posner*. McNulty's proposal can thus be enjoined.

ANSWER B: McNulty's proposal can be enjoined because it would constitute an unreasonable interference with Jenkins's use of the lake. Each riparian owner of land along a lake must not unreasonably interfere with the rights of other riparian owners to use the lake. *Posner v. Fox.* The court in *Posner* held that the defendant could be enjoined from diverting enough water from a 400-acre lake to permanently reduce water levels by about three feet. The court maintained that the reduction would unreasonably interfere with the rights of other owners to use the lake for recreational purposes. That case is applicable here. McNulty's proposal, which would reduce a thirty-acre pond to fourteen acres, would have an even more drastic effect on the lake than the comparatively slight reduction in water levels found in *Posner*. The proposal here, like the proposal in *Posner*, would have a significant adverse impact on fishing and boating by Jenkins and other riparian owners on the lake. McNulty's proposal can thus be enjoined.

Answer B is preferable because it describes the *Posner* case prior to analyzing the facts of the McNulty situation. This method of organization avoids needless repetition, makes the significance of the stated facts immediately apparent, and clarifies the analysis. Unlike Answer B, Answer A reads like this: facts, applicable law, facts. This method of organization is confusing because the reader is incapable of determining the significance of the facts until the legal rules have been stated. This method is also repetitious because the facts are stated twice. Answer B is more readable, easier to understand, and more concise than Answer A because it is better organized.

4. State the reasons supporting your conclusion on an issue or sub-issue before discussing counterarguments.

The result of your thinking on an issue or sub-issue should be a legal conclusion. This conclusion should be expressed in your thesis sentence. After stating your thesis, explain the reasons for it—reasons you may have come to understand only after thoughtful analysis. The counterarguments, which may have persuaded you at the outset, should be stated at the end. It is at this point in the memo, and only at this point, that you should discuss why the counterarguments are not as compelling as the arguments supporting your position and distinguish any important cases you believe do not apply. This method of presentation makes your discussion easier to follow and also ensures that you will draw a conclusion on each issue and sub-issue.

This principle does not permit you to intuit a particular result and then marshal justifications for it. Rather, this principle, like the others, requires you to distinguish your thought process from your writing. As other chapters indicate, to sharpen your understanding of the issues and determine the strength of your case, you should anticipate how your opponent will respond to your conclusions. This process sharpens your understanding of the issues and helps you determine the strength of your case. Your writing will become disjointed, however, if it reads "on one hand . . . but on the other hand . . . nonetheless . . . still on the other hand." Do not require the reader to watch a game of intellectual badminton. Writers who adopt a back-and-forth style tend to avoid drawing any conclusions, leaving the reader with only a set of considerations rather than a prediction of the probable legal outcome. When closely related arguments are discussed, this style also makes it difficult to state a precise legal conclusion or the reasons for it.

■   Your client, the Wilderness Preservation League, opposes a federal agency's proposed construction of a large hydroelectric dam in a deep western canyon. As required by the 1969 National Environmental Policy Act, the agency has prepared an environmental impact statement (EIS). The Act permits groups such as the League to bring an action in federal district court challenging the adequacy of an EIS. The adequacy of the EIS is one of three potential issues in this case. Consider the following discussions of that issue:

ANSWER A: The agency's EIS is inadequate under the National Environmental Policy Act. The Act requires that an EIS discuss as fully as possible the environmental effects of, and alternatives to, a project. The EIS in this case discussed the environmental effects of flooding on the wildlife and plants of the canyon, on the river, and on areas that would be affected by subsequent development. It did not, however, indicate how long it will take the canyon just upstream from the dam to fill with silt, although it did discuss the siltation issue. This inadequacy is not relevant, though, because courts will not scrutinize an EIS that closely. Because the EIS did not discuss alternatives, however, the agency has violated the Act. The agency did discuss the alternative of "no action," but it did not consider power generation from other sources or whether the power was even needed.

ANSWER B: The agency's EIS is inadequate under the National Environmental Policy Act. The Act requires that an EIS discuss as fully as possible the environmental effects of, and alternatives to, a project. Because this statement did not fully discuss alternatives, particularly power generation from other sources or the need for the power, the agency has violated the Act. The Act does not absolve an agency because it discussed merely some alternatives, and it is thus irrelevant that the agency did discuss the alternative of "no action." The discussion of environmental effects of flooding, however, is probably adequate because there was full discussion of the wildlife and plants of the canyon, the river, siltation behind the dam, and the areas that would be affected by subsequent development. Although there was no indication of the time necessary for large-scale siltation to occur, the courts do not subject a statement to this kind of close scrutiny.

Answer B is preferable because it is easier to understand. Answer B begins by discussing the sub-issue concerning alternatives as the basis for its thesis. The reason for the conclusion on that sub-issue is explained (no full consideration of alternatives), and then the counterargument (discussion of "no action") is refuted. Finally, Answer B draws a conclusion as to the environmental effects sub-issue, explains the basis for that judgment, and dismisses the counterargument. The procedure remains the same, even though the client loses one of these sub-issues and wins the other.

Answer A considers the sub-issues separately, but the discussion of each is muddled by its back-and-forth style. On one hand, it says, these effects have been considered. On the other hand, one effect has not been considered. Answer A concludes that the failure to consider that effect is probably not important. This awkward style follows a zigzag line of reasoning instead of a straight line. The same style is used with the sub-issue concerning alternatives.

There is another basic flaw in Answer A. Because the sub-issue concerning alternatives determines the inadequacy of the EIS in this case, that sub-issue should have been discussed before the sub-issue of environmental effects. Always remember that the points supporting your conclusion, not necessarily those supporting your client's case, should be discussed first.

The following exercises should help you learn to apply these principles.

Exercise 9-A

Several months ago, Colonel Augustus P. Ferguson, who won several medals for bravery in World War I, died at age 104 in the crash of a private plane. His only surviving child is Augustus, Jr. In 1928, the Colonel and his wife executed wills leaving all their property to each other, or in the event the spouse had previously died, in equal shares to their surviving children. His wife passed away in 1977. Shortly after her death, the Colonel became involved with Arizona Properties, Inc. a land development company. He was vice-president of the company at his death. Before he died, he revoked his 1928 will and executed a new will giving his entire $1.3 million estate to Arizona Properties.

Augustus Jr. has asked your senior attorney to challenge the validity of the second will in probate court. The law in this state reinstates the previous will if the later will is invalid. Junior stated that the Colonel's new attorney, also general counsel for Arizona Properties, drafted the second will. This attorney and the Colonel were both avid fishermen and went fishing together two or three weekends each month. The attorney resigned as general counsel a year ago. Junior also said that the corporation financed trips for the Colonel, "allegedly for purposes of learning foreign land development strategies," to Hong Kong, Rio de Janeiro, and Cairo. These trips occurred before he revoked the first will. Junior admitted that his father, from whom he was estranged since the death of his mother, "was not at all senile." You are to write an office memo ascertaining the validity of the second will.

There are two relevant cases in this state:

In re Estate of Steffans (1962)

This case involves the validity of the will of Maxine Steffans, a real estate broker, who left her entire $385,000 estate to her paperboy for eight years, Rodney Prentice. This court has recently required those challenging a will for undue influence to show (1) susceptibility to undue influence, (2) opportunity to influence, (3) disposition to influence, and (4) coveted result. The court below concluded that no such influence occurred, and we agree.

Mr. Prentice testified without contradiction, and the trial court found as fact, that Steffans spoke to Prentice only when he came to collect the biweekly payment for the paper, and that she frequently paid him by putting a small envelope under her doormat to avoid this contact. A neighbor also testified that Steffans, who had a reputation as eccentric, told her that she, Steffans, was willing Prentice her entire estate because he brought the paper on time. Under these circumstances, the claim of undue influence is speculative at best, particularly when the neighbor did not pass this information on to Prentice or anyone else.

In re Will of Kendall (1969)

Harriett Kendall's first will, executed when she was fifty-two, left her entire estate to her husband, Ralph. She entered a nursing home in 1965, when she was eighty-one. Shortly thereafter, she called an attorney to ask some questions about her will. Harriet was bedridden at the time, unable to carry on a conversation for more than several minutes, and prone to forgetfulness.

The attorney made his first visit to the nursing home with Harriet's sister, Mabel. Mabel suggested that she think about writing a new will. On their second visit, about one week later, the attorney and Mabel brought a new will for Harriet to sign. Although she was too weak to sit up to sign it, she was able to mark it with an "X" after Mabel propped her up with some pillows. When Harriet died in early 1966, her husband learned that the second will left her estate to Mabel's only son, Edmund. He also learned that the attorney who drafted the second will was not Harriet's personal attorney, but rather was Mabel's attorney. The trial court nonetheless admitted the second will to probate. We reverse.

There are two tests for determining whether there was undue influence in the execution of a will. The first test, described in *In re Estate of Steffans* (1962), need not be considered here because we find the trial court erred under the second test. Undue influence can occur when there is a confidential relationship between the testator and the one alleged to have exercised undue influence, and there are suspicious circumstances surrounding the making of the will. The existence of a confidential relationship depends on the ease with which the confidant controlled or influenced the drafting of the will. Suspicious circumstances exist when there is a sudden and unexplained change in the attitude of the testator, activity by the beneficiary in procuring the drafting and execution of the will, or similar circumstances. In this situation the activity of the attorney and the beneficiary's mother in procuring a will from an elderly woman meets both requirements.

1. Identify the relevant rule(s), and the elements of the rule(s), in this problem.

2. What issue(s) and sub-issue(s) would you discuss in this memorandum?

3. State as precisely as possible all plausible arguments for and against your client's position on each issue and sub-issue.

4. Using your answers to 3, draw a conclusion about a probate judge's likely decision on each issue and sub-issue.

5. Outline your analysis of the problem as if you were preparing to draft the Discussion in a memorandum.

Exercise 9-B

All-Rite Industries, Inc. operates a coal-fired powerhouse to generate steam and electricity at its factory in Junction City. The powerhouse has a capacity of 500,000 pounds of steam per hour and burns coal containing 0.9% to 1.2% sulfur by weight. All-Rite manufactures chemicals, inks, and dyes at this factory for a variety of commercial products. The short smokestack from the powerhouse emits about 500 pounds of sulfur dioxide per hour.

Farmers downwind of the powerhouse have complained about sulfur dioxide emissions for several years. They can show that sulfur dioxide settles on their alfalfa fields under certain atmospheric conditions, whitening the leaves and reducing the value of the crop by at least 5%. The tax assessor has told several of these farmers that the value of their property is $5,000 to $10,000 lower because of the sulfur dioxide emissions. A physician for several of the farmers attributes their above-average number of respiratory ailments to inhalation of sulfur dioxide.

All-Rite has ignored these complaints. A spokesman for the company states that the factory employs 490 persons and provides millions of dollars of income for the community. By contrast, he says, the farmers' claims are insignificant. The *Junction City Ledger-Gazette* refuses to print letters from the farmers complaining about sulfur dioxide emissions and regularly praises the company in editorials for its "good work and solid contributions to our economy." An article published six months ago in the *Ledger-Gazette* pointed out that coal containing a lower percentage of sulfur releases less sulfur dioxide when burned than coal containing higher amounts of sulfur. The *Ledger-Gazette* cited the relatively low sulfur content of the coal burned at the powerhouse, stating, "When you compare that with the high-sulfur coal used in other states, it is clear that top management at All-Rite is dedicated to the environment."

The farmers have retained your firm to determine whether they have any causes of action against the company, and your senior attorney has asked you to draft a memorandum on the matter.

The state Air Quality Act provides in part:

> **Sec. 11.** The Department of the Environment shall promulgate standards for classes of industries sufficient to assure the highest practicable degree of protection for public health and welfare.

> **Sec. 14.** Any person may bring an action in the appropriate trial court to enforce the provisions of this Act and the regulations promulgated pursuant to it.

The regulations in the state Administrative Code promulgated by the Department of the Environment under the Act provide in part:

> Sec. 405.221(a). It is unlawful for a powerhouse that has a capacity of more than 500,000 pounds of steam per hour to burn fuel that exceeds 1.0% sulfur content by weight.

The following are three relevant cases from your state:

Neely v. Hoff Theater Co. (1970)

The appellee, Hoff Theater Co., operates an outdoor motion picture theater on a large lot adjoining the home of the appellant, Ervin Neely. Neely brought suit against the appellee for trespass to land, claiming that light from the theater and the automobiles of its patrons constituted a physical invasion of his land. The trial court granted summary judgment for the appellee, and we affirm. Trespass to land requires a physical invasion—the presence of some tangible object on another's property. The appellant argues that light is a physical invasion because he can see the presence of light on his property. We think this argument goes too far. If the appellant found the light objectionable, he should have brought his action in nuisance, not in trespass.

Peters v. Hancock (1921)

William Peters sued Molly Hancock in nuisance to enjoin Hancock from operating her saloon, located on a parcel of land adjoining Peters's home. Peters alleged in his complaint that patrons of the saloon "severely disturb the plaintiff's sensibilities and sleep by loitering on the street outside the plaintiff's house and by occasionally using loud and abusive language." The trial judge granted judgment for the plaintiff. This court hesitates to reverse the judgment of the learned trial judge, but the allegations in the complaint do not constitute nuisance. Nuisance requires an unreasonable interference by the defendant landowner with the use or enjoyment of the plaintiff's land. The defendant should exercise what control she can over her patrons, but we do not think their occasional loudness or rudeness is "unreasonable" under the circumstances. Reversed.

Jacobs v. Metzger (1934)

This action arose when the defendant's motor vehicle left a one-lane dirt road to avoid colliding with another motor vehicle speeding from the opposite direction. The defendant's car stopped in the plaintiff's front yard. The plaintiff won damages for trespass in the trial court. We reverse. Although there clearly was a physical invasion of the plaintiff's land by the defendant and his automobile, the defendant was privileged by necessity. The defendant should not be penalized for attempting to save his life by avoiding a collision with a speeding car.

1. Identify the relevant rule(s), and the elements of the rule(s), in this problem.
2. What issue(s) and sub-issue(s) would you discuss in this memorandum?
3. State as precisely as possible all plausible arguments for and against your client's position on each issue and sub-issue.
4. Draw a conclusion about a judge's likely decision on each issue and sub-issue.
5. Outline your analysis of the problem as if you were preparing to draft the Discussion in a memorandum.

10

Describing the Law

THE DESCRIPTION OF THE LAW must convey to your reader the essential legal rules or principles your discussion is based on, and it must fit well with the rest of the discussion. A good explanation of the law makes your analysis credible to your reader. It also improves your analysis because it forces you to identify and state the legal basis for your conclusions. This chapter sets out basic principles for describing the law.

1. Be accurate.

An accurate explanation will enable the reader to understand precisely what the law says, and will provide a logical and coherent basis for the analysis that follows. Readers will often want to study the relevant cases, statutes, or constitutional provisions for themselves. Your credibility will depend on whether your explanation accurately reflects the law. Real choices are based on the analysis presented in legal writing. The quality and defensibility of those choices will depend on the accuracy of your explanation.

Accuracy is also important in legal writing because of the precise meaning given to many words and phrases. The difference between similar sounding words and phrases can be substantial. Take, for example, the difference between "homicide" and "murder." Homicide is any unlawful killing of a human being, but murder is reserved for the most serious homicide. Imprecise use of legal terms can convey a meaning totally different from what you intend and can lead to an analysis of the wrong issue or an analysis that is incoherent.

As you write and rewrite a memorandum or brief, ask yourself whether you are explaining the law as accurately and precisely as possible. If you are having difficulty, you may find it necessary to reread the relevant law and think about it further.

◻   Consider the following case and descriptions of the elements of the law for specific performance of a contract:

Lopez v. Singh **(1993)**

Specific performance is, of course, a remedy available for breach of contract. The plaintiff must show that the remedy at law is inadequate. The remedy at law will be considered inadequate if, for example, the contract involves unascertainable damages or unique items. The plaintiff must also show that the contract is just, reasonable, and supported by adequate consideration. Finally, the plaintiff must show that there is a mutuality of remedies and that the terms of the contract are definite enough to enforce what was promised in the contract.

ANSWER A: Specific performance is available when the following criteria exist: unascertainable damages, unique items, an inadequate legal remedy, definite contract terms, and fair consideration when the contract was made.

ANSWER B: Specific performance is available when the remedy at law is inadequate; the contract is just, reasonable, and supported by adequate consideration; there is a mutuality of remedies; and the terms of the contract are definite enough for the court to enforce what the contract promised.

Both answers describe elements of a claim for specific performance. Answer B is better because it states the law more accurately. The legal analysis that flows from Answer B will be more credible and coherent than the analysis that flows from Answer A. Answer B identifies two elements that are entirely or partly missing from Answer A—a mutuality of remedies; and a contract that is just, reasonable, and supported by adequate consideration. Answer A does say there must be fair consideration (which may or may not be different from adequate consideration), but it does not say the contract must be just or reasonable. Answer A also incorrectly suggests that one element in Answer B (inadequate remedy at law) is really three elements (inadequate remedy at law, unascertainable damages, unique items). Whether there is an inadequate legal remedy will depend on whether the damages cannot be ascertained and whether the items in question are unique. It is not appropriate to list all three as elements.

When you are describing statutory law, be sure to quote the language in the statute that is pertinent to the issue you are analyzing. If you paraphrase, you run the risk of changing the meaning or glossing over issues raised by the statutory language. Statutory issues can hinge on the legislature's choice of one word over another, the grammatical structure of a sentence, or even the punctuation of a particular sentence. If the language at issue is part of a longer statute, set the quoted language in context by paraphrasing the rest of the statute, but make sure that your paraphrase is accurate.

◻   Your client, Toy Kingdom Industries, Inc., was recently named as a defendant in a suit alleging multiple violations of the state Water Quality Act. The suit was brought under the "citizen suit" provision of the Act. The plaintiff, a local resident named Felix Thorpe, warned your client's chief executive officer of a possible suit against his "stinking operation" four weeks ago in a telephone conversation. The question is whether that conversation satisfied the notice requirement in the "citizen suit" provision. Consider the following descriptions of the notice requirement:

ANSWER A: Section 17(b) of the state Water Quality Act provides that no action may be commenced under the citizen suit provision prior to sixty days after the plaintiff has given notice of the alleged violations to the person.

ANSWER B: Section 17(b) of the state Water Quality Act provides that "no action may be commenced under this section prior to sixty days after the plaintiff has given notice of the alleged violation to the person."

ANSWER C: Section 17(b) of the state Water Quality Act requires the plaintiff to give the defendant sixty days' advance notice.

Answer B is best because it simply quotes the notice provision. The exact text of the provision is important here because the telephone conversation occurred only four weeks before the suit and because that conversation does not appear to have focused on violations of the Water Quality Act. In short, there may be two ways in which the plaintiff ignored the notice provision.

Answer A uses the statutory language almost verbatim but does not say so, improperly implying that the language is the writer's own. When you quote, use quotation marks.

Answer C attempts to summarize section 17(b). It doesn't summarize it accurately, however, because it fails to state that the plaintiff must give notice *of the alleged violation* sixty days *before filing suit*. Even if the summary were more accurate, an exact quotation would help ensure that the writer is analyzing the precise language and would boost the reader's confidence in the discussion.

2. Describe only the relevant law.

Describe only the law that may affect the outcome of the client's case. If common law is relevant, describe only the rules, facts, holdings, and reasons and policies that are relevant to the issue or sub-issue being analyzed. Do not include extraneous facts or a description of other holdings in multiple-issue cases. If a statute is relevant, describe only that portion of the statute that may apply to your client's situation. By describing only the relevant law, you will keep yourself and the reader focused. Long statutory quotations and unfocused case descriptions interrupt the flow of your discussion and suggest careless thinking on your part. They may also obscure the relevant law. If you omit anything, however, be sure that it is immaterial to the discussion and does not change the meaning of the statutory provision at issue. Omission of text within a quoted sentence is indicated by a series of three points known as an ellipsis. Omission of text at the end of a quoted sentence is indicated by an ellipsis and a period (four points).

☐   Your client, the Huntington Park Authority, recently purchased lakefront property to develop a new park. It then discovered that several rusting drums with hazardous chemical wastes are buried on the property and are leaking into the lake. It wants to know whether it is liable for cleaning up the property under the state Superfund Act. Your memo concludes that the Huntington Park Authority is liable. Consider these descriptions of the law:

ANSWER A: Section 701 of the Superfund Act provides:

> A person shall be responsible for the release or threatened release of a hazardous substance from a site when any of the following apply:
>
> (1)   The person owns or operates the site when a hazardous substance is placed on the site or comes to be located in or on a site.
>
> (2)   The person owns or operates the site when a hazardous substance is located in or on the site, but before it is released.
>
> (3)   The person owns or operates the site during the time of the release or threatened release.

ANSWER B: Section 701 of the Superfund Act provides that "a person shall be responsible for the release or threatened release of a hazardous substance from a site when . . . (3) The person owns or operates the site during the time of the release or threatened release."

Answer B is better because it quotes only the language on which liability is based. The city did not own the property when the drums were buried, so paragraph (1) does not apply. The chemicals are already being released into the environment, so paragraph (2) does not apply. Because the chemicals are now being released, however, paragraph (3) applies. The ellipsis before paragraph (3) indicates the deletion. Answer B focuses attention on the law that decides the issue. Answer A, on the other hand, does not.

3. Describe the law in enough detail to enable your reader to understand the discussion.

You should be able to analyze each issue or sub-issue solely on the basis of your written explanation of the law, without going to the law itself. Likewise, your reader should be able to independently analyze the issue solely from your description of the law. You will need to add to your explanation if, as you write, you find you are drawing on parts of cases, statutes, or constitutional provisions that have not yet been included in the explanation.

The level of detail in your explanation of the law will vary with the complexity of the analysis. Your analysis of "givens" will probably require only the briefest description of the relevant law. The issues central to your memo or brief, however, will likely require a longer explanation.

▢ Section 1332(a) of the Judicial Code permits federal district court jurisdiction of civil actions against parties other than the United States "when the matter in controversy exceeds the sum or value of $50,000, exclusive of interest and costs," and when the parties are citizens of different states. Approximately 300 citizens of New Mexico, each alleging $100 in damages, wish to bring a class action against a citizen of Delaware in federal court. Does the court have jurisdiction? Consider the following explanations of the law concerning the amount in controversy:

ANSWER A: Section 1332(a) of the Judicial Code requires, as a condition of federal jurisdiction in suits against private parties, that the "matter in controversy exceeds the sum or value of $50,000, exclusive of interest and costs."

ANSWER B: Section 1332(a) of the Judicial Code requires, as a condition of federal jurisdiction in civil suits against private parties, that the "matter in controversy exceeds the sum or value of $50,000, exclusive of interest and costs." In *Zahn v. International Paper Co.*, the court held that multiple plaintiffs with distinct claims must each satisfy this jurisdictional requirement, even if the sum of their individual claims exceeds the required amount in controversy. Although *Zahn* was decided when the required amount in controversy under section 1332(a) was $10,000, subsequent cases have held that each plaintiff must satisfy the $50,000 requirement. *E.g., Kennedy v. Commercial Carriers, Inc.; Coleman v. Southern Norfolk.*

ANSWER C: Section 1332(a) of the Judicial Code requires, as a condition of federal jurisdiction in civil suits against private parties, that the "matter in controversy exceeds the sum or value of $50,000, exclusive of interest and costs." In *Zahn v. International Paper Co.*, the court held that multiple plaintiffs with distinct claims must each satisfy this jurisdictional requirement, even if the sum of their individual claims exceeds the required amount in controversy.

Answer B is best because it contains the most complete and understandable discussion of the law. It describes the statutory rule and then explains that this case was not affected by a legislative increase in the required amount in controversy. Answer B gives the reader confidence because it allows evaluation of the law on which the writer's analysis will be based.

Answer C explains the statutory rule and the *Zahn* case but fails to discuss the effect of the subsequent increase in the amount in controversy. Answer C is thus incomplete and raises questions about the writer's thoroughness.

Answer A is the worst of the three answers because it contains only a description of the statutory provision. Although the description is accurate as far as it goes, it fails to include any explanation of the *Zahn* case or the subsequent change in the amount in controversy.

4. Summarize the law whenever appropriate.

In any discussion of a legal issue, you must identify the sources of the legal rules you apply. How much information you must give about the source of a rule varies. If you are setting out a general and undisputed legal principle, such as in an introductory statement to move the reader from the broad area of the law to the narrow issue under consideration, a bare citation to a case or statute is usually sufficient. As you proceed with the discussion, you should summarize the cases used in your analysis. The amount of detail required in a case summary depends on the complexity of the case and how significant it is to your analysis. A case that is complex, either in its facts or in the legal issues presented, will require a more extensive discussion to allow the reader to see its significance than will a less complex case. Similarly, a case that is central to your analysis should be discussed in detail, while one that is used only for a collateral point could be summarized in a sentence or two. When deciding how much is enough, ask yourself how much the reader needs to know to be able to understand the point you are making.

When writing about issues that involve only a handful of relevant cases, you can describe each case in some detail. Many legal problems, however, involve more relevant cases than you can reasonably describe. For these problems, you must summarize the general legal principles and then describe several representative cases to illustrate your point. In selecting representative cases, you may choose to examine in detail the few leading cases in an area, because these cases are followed by many other courts. Another approach is to examine the cases whose factual situations are most analogous or most different. Decisions by higher courts or courts from your jurisdiction are ordinarily preferable to lower court cases or cases from another jurisdiction.

☐   Your client, Susan Wennerberg, was seriously injured while skiing near a small town that has a private hospital. Although she had heard many times that this hospital treated injuries, she was refused emergency treatment. She wants to know whether she can successfully sue the private hospital for the aggravation of her injury that occurred during the drive to the public hospital. Consider the following ways of describing the relevant law:

ANSWER A: Traditionally, a private hospital has had the right to select those persons who could enjoy its benefits. Private hospitals have been able to lawfully reject emergency patients because they had policies of not accepting members of certain health insurance plans, *O'Neill v. Montefiore Hospital*, or persons with contagious diseases, *Birmingham Baptist Hospital v. Crews*. This right was so well-established that the *Crews* court said a private hospital needs no reason at all to refuse service to a particular emergency patient.

The principal exception to this right to refuse treatment now occurs when there is an unmistakable emergency and the patient has relied on the well-established custom of the hospital to render aid in such cases. In the leading case for this exception, *Wilmington General Hospital v. Manlove*, a private hospital refused emergency treatment to the plaintiffs' four-month-old infant, who had a sore throat, diarrhea, and a 102-degree temperature. The nurse explained that the hospital could not give treatment because the baby was under a physician's care. The baby died of pneumonia several hours later. In affirming the trial court's denial of the hospital's motion for summary judgment, the court stressed the importance of the time lost in fruitless attempts to obtain medical aid.

ANSWER B: Traditionally, a private hospital has had the right to select those persons who could enjoy its benefits. In *Birmingham Baptist Hospital v. Crews*, the parents of a two-and-a-half-year-old girl suffering from diphtheria brought her to the defendant hospital, where she was diagnosed and treated with antitoxin. The hospital staff told the parents that the hospital did not accept patients with contagious diseases and refused to allow her to stay. She died within five minutes of returning home. In deciding that the hospital was not liable for the child's death, the court reasoned that a private hospital can lawfully refuse service to emergency patients and that preliminary treatment should not prejudice that right of refusal.

Similarly, in *O'Neill v. Montefiore Hospital*, a private hospital refused admission to a man who complained of heart attack symptoms, because he was a member of a particular health insurance plan. The man subsequently died. Although there was some question whether the hospital undertook to aid the man by certain other actions, the court held that the hospital had no obligation to treat him in the first place.

The principal exception to this right of refusal now occurs when there is an unmistakable emergency and the patient has relied on the well-established custom of the hospital to render aid in such cases. In the leading case for this exception, *Wilmington General Hospital v. Manlove*, a private hospital refused emergency treatment to the plaintiffs' four-month-old infant, who had a sore throat, diarrhea, and a 102-degree temperature. The nurse explained that the hospital could not give treatment because the baby was under a physician's care. The baby died of pneumonia several hours later. In affirming the trial court's denial of the hospital's motion for summary judgment, the court stressed the importance of the time lost in fruitless attempts to obtain medical aid.

Answer A is preferable because it gets to the point more quickly and clearly than Answer B. Answer A summarizes the absolute right of refusal cases to provide the context for a lengthy discussion of *Manlove*. The issue in this case is whether Wennerberg fits the exception, not whether she fits the rule. Because *Manlove* is the leading case on the exception to the rule, it deserves detailed consideration and the reader's focused attention. Answer B, however, describes in detail cases that do not need to be explained at this point, if at all. Writers who devote a paragraph to each of several cases in succession tend to ramble and fail to analyze the issues. Answer B also makes it hard for both the reader and the writer to understand what law is relevant. You can write more clearly and briefly by summarizing the relevant law when appropriate.

Similar principles apply to describing statutes. As stated earlier, you should quote the statutory provision at issue, but often it will be necessary to explain the statutory scheme, or part of the scheme, into which that provision fits. It is better to summarize this part of the law than to quote it. A summary is usually more direct than a quotation, fits into the flow of your discussion much better than a longer quotation, and lets the reader concentrate on the statutory text that will be used to resolve the issue.

◻ Consider the following descriptions of the entire citizen suit provision from the problem discussed earlier:

ANSWER A: Section 17 of the state Water Quality Act provides:

(a)   Authority to bring civil action—Any person may commence a civil action on his own behalf against any person who is alleged to be in violation of this Act or a regulation promulgated thereunder.

(b)   Notice—No action may be commenced under this section prior to sixty days after the plaintiff has given notice of the alleged violation to the person.

ANSWER B: Section 17 of the state Water Quality Act authorizes any person to bring a civil action against any other person for violating the act or regulations adopted under the Act. Subsection (b) provides: "No action may be commenced under this section prior to sixty days after the plaintiff has given notice of the alleged violation to the person."

Answer B summarizes part of the citizen suit provision and then quotes the notice language. The summary helps the reader understand the citizen suit provision, and the quotation focuses the reader's attention on the text that will be used to decide the question. Answer B is the better answer. By quoting the entire section, Answer A fails to focus attention on the specific language at issue.

5. Synthesize the law whenever necessary.

You will often find that several highly relevant cases support your position or that several cases need to be distinguished. You are then obliged to describe these cases together—to synthesize them. Synthesizing cases gives the reader a complete understanding of the entire law supporting or opposing your position on a particular issue or sub-issue. Synthesizing cases is also consistent with the guideline in Chapter 9 (Organization) which states that all of the law should be described before it is applied to or distinguished from the facts. Resist the temptation to describe a case, then show how it is applicable, describe another case, show how it is also applicable, and so forth. Such an approach leaves the reader with no clear understanding of the law.

Randall Byars recently signed a contract to purchase a house in the community to which he has been relocated. He has since discovered that at certain times of the year atmospheric conditions are such that the fumes from a nearby chemical plant become trapped at ground level. The fumes smell noxious and cause watery, burning eyes. Although this problem was not apparent when Byars was shown the house, the seller, Stephen Graham, was aware of the problem. This was the primary reason Graham sold the house, but he never mentioned the problem to Byars. Byars is your client and wants to know whether he can get out of this contract. The highest court in your state has decided these two cases:

Stewart v. Avery (1984)

The appellee, Jessica Avery, sued to rescind a contract for the purchase of a house. The appellee contends that the appellant deceived her by not disclosing that the house contained high levels of radon—odorless and colorless radioactive particles that can cause cancer. Normally, the rule of *caveat emptor* applies to the purchase of real estate, requiring the buyer to thoroughly inspect the property before agreeing to purchase it. Here, however, such an inspection would not have revealed the high levels of radon. Such a defect is a critical factor in the transaction, affecting the value of the property and its potential resale value. Thus, rescission is appropriate to relieve the appellee from the burden of this agreement, obtained through the appellant's silence on a matter he surely knew was material to the transaction. The decision of the trial court to rescind the contract is, therefore, affirmed.

Waters v. Morton (1991)

The appellee was granted rescission of a contract for the purchase of a house. The appellee did not discover until after the purchase that the septic tank and drain lines were inadequate. This deficiency resulted in the overflow of raw sewage into the front yard after every heavy rain. This condition was apparent only then.

Passive concealment of defective realty constitutes an exception to the rule of *caveat emptor.* This exception places a duty on the seller to disclose facts not apparent to the buyer that would probably affect his decision to purchase.

Here, even the most diligent of examinations would not have disclosed this defect, because the problem was apparent only after a heavy rain. The appellant knew of the deficiencies in the sewage system, yet he allowed the appellee to purchase the property without disclosing these facts. Such conduct constitutes fraud and warrants rescission of the contract. Affirmed.

Consider these descriptions of the law:

ANSWER A: Byars is entitled to rescind his purchase contract. Even a diligent inspection would not have revealed the problem with the toxic fumes, and Graham failed to disclose this problem to Byars before he signed the contract. Although the general rule in purchasing real property is *caveat emptor*, an exception exists when the defect is not discernible through a thorough inspection and the seller is aware of the defect yet fails to disclose it, knowing that such information is relevant to the buyer's decision to purchase. *Stewart v. Avery; Waters v. Morton.*

In both *Stewart* and *Waters* the sellers withheld material information regarding a defect in the property, even though they knew the purchasers could not discover the defect by inspecting the property. In *Stewart*, the seller of a house did not disclose that the house contained high levels of radon. In *Waters*, the seller did not disclose the inadequacy of the septic system, which caused the overflow of raw sewage into the front yard after every heavy rain. In both cases the sellers withheld information that the purchasers could not have discovered through a diligent inspection of the premises.

[Discussion analogizing cases to buyer's situation omitted.]

Further, in each of these cases, the information withheld was material to the purchaser's decision. The radon levels and the inadequacy of the septic system affect the value of the properties involved. The sellers in each case had a duty to disclose the facts regarding the defect in the property. In both *Stewart* and *Waters*, concealment of the defect constituted fraud and warranted rescission of the contract.

[Discussion analogizing cases to buyer's situation omitted.]

ANSWER B: Byars is entitled to rescind his purchase contract. Even a diligent inspection would not have revealed the problem with the toxic fumes, and Graham failed to disclose this problem to Byars before he signed the contract. Although the general rule in purchasing real property is *caveat emptor*, an exception exists when the defect is not discernible through a thorough inspection and the seller is aware of the defect yet fails to disclose it, knowing that such information is relevant to the buyer's decision to purchase. *Stewart v. Avery; Waters v. Morton.*

In *Stewart*, the court granted rescission of a contract for the purchase of a house when the seller had failed to disclose that the house had high levels of radon. The court found that this information affected the value of the property and, therefore, was relevant to the purchaser's decision to buy the house. Reasoning that even the most diligent inspection of the premises would not have revealed the radon levels, the court placed the burden of disclosing this fact on the seller.

[Discussion analogizing cases to buyer's situation omitted.]

In *Waters*, the court also granted a rescission of a sales contract because the seller failed to disclose a defect in the real estate. The seller had failed to disclose that the septic system was inadequate, causing an overflow of raw sewage into the front yard after any heavy rain. The condition was not apparent at any other time. The court reasoned that the seller's knowledge of this defect and the buyer's inability to discover it during a diligent inspection of the premises warranted rescission of the contract.

[Discussion analogizing cases to buyer's situation omitted.]

Answer A is better because it summarizes and synthesizes the *Stewart* and *Waters* cases according to the two sub-issues raised. Answer A explains the law of the two cases concerning failure to disclose and then explains the law concerning information that is material to the purchaser's decision. The discussion that follows each sub-issue likely will be focused and coherent.

Answer B, by contrast, summarizes the cases sequentially. Because the cases are not integrated or related to each other, the reader must pull together the law that the cases represent. Answer B is also confusing because it does not discuss the two sub-issues separately and would require the writer to analyze both sub-issues after each case summary.

The principles in this chapter address many of the most common and difficult problems you will encounter in describing the law. The following exercises will give you practice using these principles.

Exercise 10-A

Describe the law based on your answers to Exercise 5-A, pp. 61–64.

Exercise 10-B

Describe the law based on your answers to Exercise 5-B, pp. 64–67.

11

Explaining the Analysis

AFTER YOU DESCRIBE the law supporting your position, you will explain how the law actually supports your position. Similarly, after you describe the law that might support a counterargument, you will explain how the law fails to support that counterargument. This chapter builds on the lessons in Chapter 10 (Describing the Law). It identifies particular problems in analyzing the law and explains how to resolve them.

1. Be precise.

Effective communication is directly related to the care with which words are chosen and sentences and paragraphs are structured. The late T. M. Bernstein of *The New York Times* once said: "If writing must be a precise form of communication, it should be treated like a precision instrument. It should be sharpened, and it should not be used carelessly." Bernstein's statement is perhaps more true of legal writing than of journalistic writing. Legal conclusions depend on the application of specific cases, statutes, and constitutional provisions to specific situations. Your analysis will be strengthened by your precision in analyzing problems. Precision leads to clarity. It is also good discipline because it forces you to identify and correct weaknesses in your discussion.

☐ Consider the following approaches to analyzing the citizen suit problem in Chapter 10:

ANSWER A: The court does not have jurisdiction to hear Thorpe's citizen suit. Section 17(b) of the state Water Quality Act provides: "No action may be commenced under this section prior to sixty days after the plaintiff has given notice of the alleged violation to the person." In this case, Thorpe did not meet the requirement for sixty days' advance notice. Nor did he give specific notice of the alleged violation to the defendant. His notice was too general to let the defendant know what the violations are. His citizen suit therefore can be dismissed.

ANSWER B: The court does not have jurisdiction to hear Thorpe's citizen suit. Section 17(b) of the state Water Quality Act provides: "No action may be commenced under this section prior to sixty days after the plaintiff has given notice of the alleged violation to the person." In this case, Thorpe did not meet the requirement for sixty days' advance notice because he gave notice only twenty-eight days before he filed the suit. Nor did he give the necessary notice of the alleged violation to the defendant. The requirement to give "notice of the alleged violation" under the Water Quality Act was not met by a general threat against the defendant's "stinking operation." Because the requirement of sixty days' notice was intended to give potential defendants an opportunity to correct violations, and because of the great variety in potential violations of the Act, Thorpe should have identified the alleged violations more specifically. His citizen suit can therefore be dismissed.

Both answers begin with a thesis sentence and a description of the relevant law. Answer B is better because it explains precisely that the court does not have jurisdiction to hear Thorpe's citizen suit for two reasons: (1) The requirement of sixty days' notice is not met by twenty-eight days' notice, and (2) Thorpe's notice was not specific enough to satisfy the statutory requirement to give "notice of the alleged violation." The reader of Answer B knows why the writer reached this conclusion.

Answer A, on the other hand, contains no specific statements about the relationship between the statutory rule and the facts of this case. Instead, it contains general statements that the rule was not met. While it is sometimes possible for a reader to figure out these steps, you should leave nothing to chance.

2. Show every step in your analysis.

Because memos are written for lawyers, it is safe to assume that the reader will have a basic understanding of the law and the legal process. It is not safe, however, to assume that the reader will be able to see how the cited cases or statutes support your conclusion. It is not enough to state that a particular result will occur; you must identify the analytical steps leading to that result. If there are several "givens" and one issue, you should discuss the "givens" before you discuss the issue. A reader who is able to follow all the important steps of your thought process on paper will be able to evaluate the soundness of your conclusions and act accordingly. Failure to show all the steps of your analysis may give the reader an incomplete understanding of the issue or sub-issue you are discussing and thus little or no confidence in your conclusion.

In a way, writing a memorandum or brief is like giving directions to your home. You know how to get there, but the directions you give or the map you provide must be complete enough to enable someone else to get there. Each important feature or turn in your analytical map must be clearly identified, or your reader is likely to get lost. Your directions should include only what is necessary—no more, but also no less. Many writers understand their subject so well that they compress several analytical steps into one, make unexplained assumptions, fail to define important terms, and in many other ways obscure their thinking from the reader. Make sure your directions are clear and complete.

■ Your client, Carl Norbert, was recently injured when the jeep he was driving struck a deer and ran off the road. The jeep, which was owned by the state Fish and Game Department, was signed out to Stephanie Bennett, a field biologist for the Department. She allowed Norbert to drive it because he was considering a job with the Department. He was driving through state game land at the time. Norbert believes that Bennett was negligent in not accompanying him in the jeep and for not telling him about the numerous deer on state land. He would like to recover from the Department for his injuries. You have been asked to assume the Department's negligence and determine whether the state's Sovereign Immunity Act would bar an action for his injuries.

ANSWER A: The Sovereign Immunity Act does not bar an action against the Fish and Game Department because the Department had control of the vehicle. The Act, which generally prohibits suits against "state parties" for damages caused by negligent acts, is a statutory codification of the common law doctrine protecting the government or sovereign against suits for the government's alleged negligence. The Fish and Game Department is a "state party." Although the Act does not define the term, the courts have held other departments to be state parties. *E.g., Wold v. Department of Transp.* Under the doctrine of vicarious liability, state parties are liable for the acts of their employees. *Wold.*

The Department is liable for negligence because the statute contains an exception for the "operation of any motor vehicle in the possession or control of a state party." Bennett had control over the jeep because it was signed out to her and because she allowed Norbert to drive it without accompanying him. The only case interpreting this provision, *Hall v. Department of Banking,* is distinguishable. In *Hall,* the court held this provision inapplicable when a Department of Banking employee took a vehicle without permission and negligently ran Hall's car off the road. The court in *Hall* held that the Department did not have control or possession of the vehicle. Our case is different because Bennett had permission to take the jeep and because she then authorized Norbert to drive it.

ANSWER B: The Sovereign Immunity Act does not bar an action against the Fish and Game Department because the Department had control of the vehicle. The Act generally prohibits suits against "state parties" for damages caused by negligent acts.

The Department is liable for negligence because the statute contains an exception for the "operation of any motor vehicle in the possession or control of a state party." The only case interpreting this provision, *Hall v. Department of Banking*, is distinguishable. In *Hall*, the court held this provision inapplicable when a Department of Banking employee took a vehicle without permission and negligently ran Hall's car off the road. The court in *Hall* held that the Department did not have control or possession of the vehicle.

Answer A is better because it explains every step needed to show how the writer reached her conclusion. It explains the general rule in the statute and then explains that the statute codifies the common law sovereign immunity doctrine. This is a helpful step for readers who are unfamiliar with sovereign immunity or who understand sovereign immunity only as a common law doctrine. Answer A explains that the Department is a state party and would be liable for the acts of its employees. These are "givens" in this case, but the discussion would be incomplete without them. Answer A discusses the exception to sovereign immunity, showing why it is applicable, and then discusses *Hall*, a potential basis for a counterargument, showing why it is distinguishable.

Answer B is the same as Answer A except that several steps are missing. These missing steps seriously undermine Answer B's effectiveness and credibility. Answer B omits the following: an explanation that the statute codifies the common law rule, an explanation of how the Department is a state party and would be liable for the acts of its employees, an explanation of precisely how the Department had control over the jeep, and an analysis distinguishing *Hall*. These omissions leave gaps in the discussion. Some readers will see these gaps as evidence that the writer has not thought through the problem or is hiding something. Other readers will simply be confused. Still others will be able to fill in the blanks, but you shouldn't take any chances. Fill in the gaps. A writer who leaves gaps in her analysis hasn't justified the conclusion.

3. Describe every reasonable basis for your conclusion.

In many legal problems, several reasons or legal theories may lead to the same conclusion. A particular action may have violated several laws, for example. Because you want to convince your reader that you have reached the right conclusion, your discussion should reflect these reasons and theories. You should take care to include only the most persuasive or effective reasons or theories. A good test is whether each reason or theory could stand on its own without support from the others. If so, it is probably worth including. Using weak reasons or theories to support your conclusion hurts your credibility with the reader.

▢ Your client, Theresa Clare, owns Tess's Bed and Breakfast, an elegant Victorian house in which up to seven rooms are rented to overnight guests who are served breakfast in the morning. The house is located in a residential area in the city of Nekoosa. Several neighborhood teenagers have recently formed a band they call "Slow Death." They practice each night from 9 P.M. to 1 or 2 A.M. in a garage two doors away. The noise from the band has been recorded continuously at thirty to seventy decibels at the front door of your client's house. Her business has decreased dramatically since the band began practicing, and she has been unable to persuade the teenagers or their parents to control the noise. The City Council has not taken any relevant action. She wants to know what she can do.

There is one relevant case in your jurisdiction:

Hooke v. Allen (1982)

To save energy and reduce his electric bills, Raymond Allen erected a seventy-foot tower with a windmill at the top. Shortly after the windmill was erected, it began to make a loud and continuous noise. Pearl Hooke, his nearest neighbor in a residential area, filed suit, claiming that the windmill caused a private nuisance. The trial court ordered the windmill dismantled, and we affirm.

A private nuisance is an unreasonable interference with the use and enjoyment of land. Noise is an actionable private nuisance if the health and comfort of ordinary people in the vicinity are injured and if the injury is unreasonable under all the circumstances. The trial court found that the windmill's noise is louder, more constant, and more offensive than other noises in the vicinity. The noise occurs both during the day and at night when people are trying to sleep. The trial court also found that other windmill designs or locations would reduce the noise. Because of these findings, we have no reason to disturb the trial court's order.

Section 305.5(c) of the Nekoosa Municipal Code states:

Unless specifically authorized by the City Council, no person may cause any noise that exceeds fifty decibels. The City Council may order the cessation of any unauthorized activity under this subsection.

ANSWER A: The band's practice violates the city's municipal code and constitutes a private nuisance. It therefore can be stopped.

The band's noise level violates section 305.5(c) of the Nekoosa Municipal Code. Section 305.5(c) provides: "Unless specifically authorized by the City Council, no person may cause any noise that exceeds fifty decibels." Because the band's noise has been continuously recorded at thirty to seventy decibels in front of Clare's house, and because the City Council has not authorized the noise, the band violates the ordinance. Section 305.5(c) also provides that the "City Council may order the cessation of any unauthorized activity under this subsection." The City Council could therefore order the noise stopped.

The practice also constitutes a private nuisance because it unreasonably interferes with Clare's use and enjoyment of her land. In *Hooke v. Allen*, the court held that noise can constitute a private nuisance if it injures the health and safety of ordinary people in the vicinity and if the injury is unreasonable under all the circumstances. In that case, the court held that noise from a nearby windmill was injurious because of its loudness, duration, offensiveness, and occurrence at night. At thirty to seventy decibels, the band is often unreasonably loud. The Nekoosa Municipal Code generally limits noise from any person to fifty decibels, and this limit may be understood as a maximum reasonable level. Like the windmill noise in *Hooke*, the band noise occurs at night when people are trying to sleep. Although the band noise is not continuous, as was the noise from the windmill, it does last for four or five hours each night. That it is offensive is manifest by the dramatic decline in Clare's business since the band began practicing. The court in *Hooke* found the windmill noise unreasonable partly because moving the windmill or choosing another design would have reduced the noise. Here, the band could have avoided an unreasonable interference with Clare's use of her land by practicing at a different time of day or in a location more removed from the neighbors. The band practice is a private nuisance and may be enjoined.

ANSWER B: The band's practice constitutes a private nuisance because it unreasonably interferes with Clare's use and enjoyment of her land. In *Hooke v. Allen*, the court held that noise can constitute a private nuisance if it injures the health and safety of ordinary people in the vicinity and if the injury is unreasonable under all the circumstances. In that case, the court held that noise from a nearby windmill constituted a private nuisance because of its loudness, duration, offensiveness, and occurrence at night. Like the windmill noise in *Hooke*, much of the noise occurs at night when people are trying to sleep. That it is offensive is manifest by the dramatic decline in Clare's business since the band began practicing. The band is causing a private nuisance and may be enjoined.

Answer A is better. It discusses both grounds for proceeding against the band—private nuisance and violation of the municipal code. Answer A also discusses a complete range of relevant factual analogies between *Hooke* and this case. The completeness of the answer makes the writer's conclusion more persuasive.

Answer B justifies the writer's conclusion less completely and less persuasively. By ignoring the ordinance as an independent basis for action, the writer overlooks an option that his client or the court, if properly informed, might want to use. By ignoring several factual analogies, the writer makes the nuisance claim seem weaker than it really is. Describing every reasonable basis for your conclusion, in other words, is another way of ensuring that your analysis has been thorough and of communicating that analysis to the reader.

4. Explain the context.

When the importance of a legal issue or sub-issue to the resolution of a problem may not be apparent to the reader, you must explain how that issue or sub-issue fits into the factual situation and how it relates to the rights and responsibilities of those involved. When the problem involves a single subsection of a complicated statute, for example, you should at least outline the statute. Failure to describe the context may leave a reader guessing about the significance of an issue or sub-issue you raise.

☐ Ann White, an elderly woman, was detained by the clerk of a department store in which she was shopping because the clerk suspected that White had stolen several items from the store. The clerk grabbed White by the wrist as she was leaving the store and quietly said, "OK, come with me, lady." The clerk then led her by the wrist back to the manager's office, told her not to move, offered her a cup of coffee, and propped a chair against the outside of the door to prevent her escape while he looked for the manager. When the clerk and the manager returned a few minutes later, they found that she had not stolen anything, even though her physical description closely fit that of a woman who in previous weeks had taken several items from the store.

State Compiled Laws § 32.01 provides:

> A merchant's employee who has reasonable grounds to believe that goods have been unlawfully taken by a person may, for the purpose of attempting to effect a recovery of said goods, take the person into custody and detain him in a reasonable manner for a reasonable length of time. Such action does not render a merchant's employee civilly or criminally liable for false imprisonment.

Consider these two ways of discussing the liability of the store for false imprisonment:

ANSWER A: The store is liable for White's false imprisonment because it did not detain her in a reasonable manner. State Compiled Laws § 32.01 provides:

> A merchant's employee who has reasonable grounds to believe that goods have been unlawfully taken by a person may, for the purpose of attempting to effect a recovery of said goods, take the person into custody and detain him in a reasonable manner for a reasonable length of time. Such action does not render a merchant's employee civilly or criminally liable for false imprisonment.

The clerk in this case grabbed the wrist of an elderly woman who was leaving the store, led her by the wrist to the manager's office, and then physically restrained her there. The clerk's quiet voice and offer of a cup of coffee do not change his excessive use of force.

ANSWER B: The store falsely imprisoned White and is not relieved of liability by state statute because the store's clerk detained her in an unreasonable manner. A person is liable for false imprisonment whenever he intentionally restrains another person against that person's will. There was false imprisonment here because the clerk prevented White from leaving the store and put her in the manager's office, all against her will.

The statutory defense of State Compiled Laws § 32.01 does not absolve the store of liability. Section 32.01 provides:

> A merchant's employee who has reasonable grounds to believe that goods have been unlawfully taken by a person may, for the purpose of attempting to effect a recovery of said goods, take the person into custody and detain him in a reasonable manner for a reasonable length of time. Such action does not render a merchant's employee civilly or criminally liable for false imprisonment.

The clerk had reasonable grounds to suspect White because she matched the description of an elderly shoplifter. In addition, the detention period of two or three minutes is a reasonable length of time. The clerk nevertheless failed to detain White in a reasonable manner. He grabbed the wrist of an elderly woman who was leaving the store, led her by the wrist to the manager's office, and physically restrained her there. The clerk's quiet voice and offer of a cup of coffee do not diminish his excessive use of force.

Answer B is preferable because it describes the statute as a defense to the common law tort of false imprisonment, shows that false imprisonment has been committed here, and completely explains the application of each element of the statute—reasonable grounds, reasonable manner, and reasonable time—to White's situation. Answer A, however, incorrectly implies that unreasonable manner is necessary for false imprisonment. By focusing only on the issue supporting that conclusion, Answer A does not give the reader a complete and balanced picture. It seems to assume the reader will be able to fill in the gaps and fails to explain how each element of the statute applies to White's situation.

As you work through the following exercises, remember that your responsibility is to analyze the law accurately and completely.

Exercise 11-A

Explain your analysis of the issues and sub-issues raised in your description of the law in Exercise 10-A, p. 131.

Exercise 11-B

Explain your analysis of the issues and sub-issues raised in your description of the law in Exercise 10-B, p. 131.

12

Signposting

TELL YOUR READER where you are going, then clearly and carefully guide the reader as you go. This rule is especially important when you are discussing multiple issues, each of which may have several sub-issues. Thinking and writing about a legal problem is like hacking through a dense jungle: You often have little idea where you are or where you are going; you may backtrack, go in circles, or make long detours because you started in the wrong place or reached an impossible obstacle. While this process is necessary, the final product must be more direct. When you put your thoughts on paper, go straight to your conclusions. Take the reader only where necessary and erect clear signposts. Remember that you are far more familiar than the reader with the law and how it applies to the facts.

Signposting is especially important in legal writing because of the nature of your audience and the circumstances under which your document will be read. Your audience is likely to be lawyers, who read documents in a hurry, under pressure, and for a specific purpose. Good signposts can make the structure of your analysis so clear and transparent that even hurried and impatient readers can follow your logic and understand your conclusions. Poor signposts, on the other hand, can obscure the structure of the analysis and tax the patience of your readers.

This chapter sets out the basic principles of signposting. There are four types of signposts—thesis statements, paragraphs, topic sentences, and transitions.

1. Use thesis statements to state your conclusion for each issue and sub-issue.

A thesis is a sentence in the first or second paragraph of any formal paper that states the writer's conclusion. It gives the reader a foundation for reading and understanding the paper. Similarly, you should have a thesis stating your conclusion on each issue and sub-issue at the outset of the discussion. The reader wants to know right away what you are discussing and what position you are taking.

▢   Your client, Alice Woodford, is considering a lawsuit against a company that has threatened to stop delivering steel to her. Her state recognizes a cause of action for business or economic duress. One element in this cause of action is that the defendant must have threatened unlawful conduct. Which of the following introductions to the discussion is better?

ANSWER A: In *Porter v. Falk*, the court held that a defendant was not liable for business or economic duress when it threatened to take actions that it had a legal right to take.

ANSWER B: Woodford cannot recover civil damages for business or economic duress because the company with which she contracted for delivery of steel did not threaten her with unlawful conduct. In *Porter v. Falk*, the court held that a defendant was not liable for business or economic duress when it threatened to take actions that the defendant had a legal right to take.

Answer B is better because it begins with the writer's statement of the issue and its resolution. This statement provides the context for the rule that follows. Answer A, on the other hand, gives no direction as to why the rule matters or where the writer is going.

2. Use paragraphs to divide the discussion into manageable parts.

A paragraph is a group of sentences relating to one discrete idea or topic. The proper use of paragraphs helps to divide the discussion into parts that can be readily understood. Proper paragraphing is especially important in legal documents because of their complexity and the circumstances in which they are read. Improper paragraphing can mean that a reader misses or misunderstands your analysis.

Paragraphs are the building blocks of legal analysis. They are visual cues that the writer is moving to a new idea. Paragraphs also give the reader a mental pause. The reader expects legal writing to be divided into coherent paragraphs and is likely to become frustrated and impatient with solid pages of text.

As a building block, each paragraph contains only a part of the larger unit of information you are communicating to the reader. It is important not only that the reader is able to understand each paragraph as a unit but also that the reader is able to put all your paragraphs together to develop a complete picture. Each paragraph must play a significant role in the discussion and must clearly relate to both the paragraph before it and the paragraph after it. Therefore, you must put your ideas in logical order and tie them together.

The length of a paragraph depends primarily on how much information and reasoning you must include to develop a topic or idea fully. A typical paragraph contains four to eight sentences, including a thesis or topic sentence. A succession of two- or three-sentence paragraphs indicates one of two problems. Either you have not fully developed each idea, in which case your discussion will be superficial, or you have broken one discrete discussion into several parts, in which case your writing will seem fragmented.

To some extent, paragraph length is also a matter of discretion. An occasional short paragraph will capture the reader's attention and is an excellent device for emphasizing a point.

Paragraphs that are too long may present the biggest problem for readers. Long paragraphs may indicate that you have not sorted out your ideas, that you have included more than one topic in each paragraph, or that you need to tighten your sentence structure and eliminate unnecessary words. If you have a paragraph longer than a double-spaced page, try to find a logical place to divide it. Sometimes more than one paragraph is necessary to develop a single idea.

☐ Albert Sands owned an abandoned building in which he had stored highly flammable chemicals for several years. The drums in which the chemicals were stored had leaked and the floor had become saturated with them. After Sands removed the drums, several small fires occurred. The city fire department put out the fires. Last week, Sands's faulty wiring of an electrical circuit breaker caused another and larger fire. Sands called the fire department for help. Although Sands knew of the danger the saturated floor posed to firefighters, he did not warn the fire department. Paul Romano, a firefighter called to the scene, was injured when the saturated floor suddenly burst into flame and collapsed. He wants to know whether he can sue Sands for negligence. A potential obstacle is the "fireman's rule," under which emergency personnel injured in the line of duty cannot sue for negligence.

Compare the following discussions on the underlying policies for the rule:

ANSWER A: Jurisdictions recognizing the "fireman's rule" have enumerated several policies supporting the rule. The basic policies are fairness to the landowner and a desire to spread the cost of such injuries to the community through workers' compensation insurance.

Neither of these policies applies to this case. Fairness is not a factor here because Sands knew of the presence of the hazardous materials and because his failure to warn the firefighters responding to the call was directly responsible for our client's injuries. Some jurisdictions have upheld the fireman's rule to avoid penalizing landowners for seeking help from professionals trained and employed to handle emergencies.

These professionals are aware of and assume the normal risks involved in responding to dangerous situations, including fires resulting from landowners' negligence. Romano's claim, however, would not penalize Sands for the negligence that started the fire. Rather, it would be based on Sands's failure to warn the fire department of a risk that the department could not reasonably have foreseen. The desire to spread costs of such injuries to the community is also not a factor here.

The fireman's rule recognizes that firefighters will sometimes be injured in fighting negligently caused fires and that the community should pay workers' compensation claims for such injuries as part of the community's public safety effort. This policy does not apply when injuries occur because of a landowner's subsequent negligence.

Romano was injured not because of Sands's negligence in wiring the circuit breaker, but rather because of Sands's failure to warn of the chemically saturated floor. Sands, not the community, should pay for such injuries.

ANSWER B: Jurisdictions recognizing the fireman's rule have enumerated several policies supporting the rule. The basic policies are fairness to the landowner and a desire to spread the cost of such injuries to the community through workers' compensation insurance. Neither of these policies applies to this case.

Fairness is not a factor here because Sands knew of the presence of the hazardous materials and because his failure to warn the firefighters responding to the call was directly responsible for our client's injuries. Some jurisdictions have upheld the fireman's rule to avoid penalizing landowners for seeking help from professionals trained and employed to handle emergencies. These professionals are aware of and assume the normal risks involved in responding to dangerous situations, including fires resulting from landowners' negligence. Romano's claim, however, would not penalize Sands for the negligence that started the fire. Rather, it would be based on Sands's failure to warn the fire department of a risk that the department could not reasonably have foreseen.

The desire to spread costs of such injuries to the community is also not a factor here. The fireman's rule recognizes that firefighters will sometimes be injured in fighting negligently caused fires and that the community should pay workers' compensation claims for such injuries as part of the community's public safety effort. This policy does not apply when injuries occur because of a landowner's subsequent negligence. Romano was injured not because of Sands's negligence in wiring the circuit breaker, but rather because of Sands's failure to warn of the chemically saturated floor. Sands, not the community, should pay for such injuries.

Answer B is better because the structure of its three paragraphs is evident. The first paragraph identifies the two policies supporting the fireman's rule and states that these policies do not apply. The second paragraph describes the fairness policy and explains why that policy does not apply, and the last paragraph describes the cost-spreading policy and explains why it does not apply. Each paragraph contains a single basic point—no more and no less.

Answer A is much harder to read and understand. The first paragraph describes the policies underlying the fireman's rule, but it does not explain how the writer would apply these policies to the facts. The first paragraph thus is aimless. The second paragraph begins with the broad thesis that should have been in the first paragraph and wrongly implies that the second paragraph will discuss the reasons that neither policy applies. The second paragraph also has an incomplete discussion of the fairness policy. The third paragraph has incomplete discussions of both policies. The fourth and fifth paragraphs have a fragmented discussion of the cost-spreading policy. Each paragraph contains more or less than a single point, but none has just a single point. In short, Answer A doesn't make as much sense to the reader as Answer B.

3. Use topic sentences to define a purpose for each paragraph.

A topic sentence explains the basic point of a paragraph and thus provides a frame of reference for what is to follow. It is usually the first or second sentence of a paragraph. Because the paragraph is part of your discussion of a particular issue or sub-issue, the topic sentence should support your thesis (your conclusion on that issue or sub-issue). The topic sentence should also be connected to the previous paragraph. A topic sentence satisfies your reader's desire to know right away what a paragraph is about and enables a busy reader to skim through your analysis and see the key points. You can test the quality of your topic sentences by extracting them from your memo or brief and seeing whether they outline your analysis.

■   Your client, Cindy Ortez, was recently discharged from her job at Packey's Toys, Inc. for filing an antitrust complaint against her employer. As a general rule, an employer can discharge an at-will employee (one who is employed for an unspecified time period) at any time for any reason. There are certain exceptions to this rule, one of which occurs when the employee's discharge violates public policy. Several cases illustrate what types of discharges violate public policy. Consider the following excerpts from discussions of whether public policy has been violated in Ortez's case:

ANSWER A: . . . and was discharged when he refused to lie on the witness stand. The court held this to constitute a wrongful discharge because of the necessity of truthful testimony and because perjury is a criminal offense.

     Public policy can also be violated when an employer discharges an employee for exercising a statutorily conferred right. In *Frampton v. Central Indiana Gas Co.*, an employee filed a workers' compensation claim for injuries she received in the course of her employment. She was promptly fired. The court held this to be a wrongful discharge. In arriving at its conclusion, the court drew an analogy to retaliatory eviction under the state's landlord-tenant law. The court also determined that the discharge was contrary to the purposes of the workers' compensation statute. The court reasoned that public policy is violated when an employer discharges an employee for exercising a statutorily conferred right.

ANSWER B: . . . and was discharged when he refused to lie on the witness stand. The court held this to constitute a wrongful discharge because of the necessity of truthful testimony and because perjury is a criminal offense.

In *Frampton v. Central Indiana Gas Co.*, an employee filed a workers' compensation claim for injuries she received in the course of her employment. She was promptly fired. The court held this to be a wrongful discharge. In arriving at its conclusion, the court drew an analogy to retaliatory eviction under the state's landlord-tenant law. The court also determined that the discharge was contrary to the purposes of the workers' compensation statute. The court reasoned that public policy is violated when an employer discharges an employee for exercising a statutorily conferred right.

Both answers cover the same ground, but Answer A is clearer and more direct. The topic sentence in Answer A states the subject of the paragraph and connects the paragraph with the rest of the discussion before the description of the *Frampton* case begins. Answer A has a good topic sentence and guides the reader through the discussion.

Answer B is less direct. It begins the first full paragraph with a discussion of the *Frampton* case, without giving the reader any clue about the subject of the paragraph or why *Frampton* is being discussed. The analysis leading to the conclusion is harder to follow because it is less focused.

4. Use transitions to show the relationship between ideas.

Transitions are the directions the writer uses to guide the reader from one part of the discussion to another. Transitions signal to the reader that you have completed the discussion of one point and are proceeding to the next. A discussion that treats a second and separate point as a continuation of the first is confusing to the reader.

There is an important relationship between thesis statements and topic sentences on one hand and transitions on the other. The more clearly you have stated the thesis or topic sentence, the more obvious it will be to the reader when you move to the next point in your discussion.

To choose an effective transition, identify the precise relationship between the two ideas to be connected. For example, transitional words or phrases may be used to indicate the following:

- a similarity or difference between the previous point and the next one (similarly, also, in addition, furthermore, however, nevertheless, though, on the other hand);
- a simple enumeration of points (first, second, etc.);
- a causal relationship (consequently, therefore, thus, because);
- a temporal relationship (subsequently, previously, later, in the meantime, recently).

Transitions sometimes require more than a word or phrase—they may require a sentence or even a paragraph. Transitional sentences may appear at the end of one paragraph or at the beginning of the next. Transitional paragraphs generally are shorter than other types of paragraphs and should be used to explain a more complex relationship between paragraphs or ideas than could be explained in a word or sentence.

☐ Consider the following:

Answer A: Under traditional property law analysis, if two people own insured property as joint tenants and one co-owner destroys the property, the innocent co-insured cannot recover insurance proceeds. . . .

The modern approach allows the innocent co-insured to recover if that person's expectations of what the policy covered were reasonable. . . .

Answer B: Under traditional property law analysis, if two people own insured property as joint tenants and one co-owner destroys the property, the innocent co-insured cannot recover the insurance proceeds. . . .

Most courts today treat this issue as a contract dispute, regardless of how the insured property is owned. The modern approach allows the innocent co-insured to recover if that person's expectations of what the policy covered were reasonable. . . .

Answer B is better because it constructs a bridge between traditional property law analysis and the modern approach. That bridge—a transitional sentence—tells the reader that you are now switching from a property law analysis to a contract law analysis. Answer A, by contrast, leads the reader to believe that the second paragraph continues an analysis based on property law.

☐ Consider another illustration:

You work for the federal Equal Employment Opportunity Commission (EEOC). An employee for a company operating in Arizona has just filed a sex discrimination lawsuit in federal court against the company under Title VII of the Civil Rights Act of 1964. The case involves an interpretation of Title VII that could significantly affect the EEOC's implementation of the statute. Your client would like to intervene on behalf of the plaintiff to ensure that the EEOC's view of the law is brought to the court's attention. Rule 24 of the Federal Rules of Civil Procedure provides two methods of intervention. One method applies when a statute provides a conditional or unconditional right to intervene. Consider the following edited discussions:

ANSWER A: Rule 24(a) permits intervention of right when a federal statute confers an unconditional right to intervene. Title VII does not give the EEOC an unconditional right to intervene because intervention is based on the court's discretion when the EEOC certifies that "the case is of general public importance." The EEOC, therefore, may not intervene of right. Rule 24(b) allows permissive intervention when a federal statute grants a conditional right to intervene, as this one does. . . .

ANSWER B: Rule 24(a) permits intervention of right when a federal statute confers an unconditional right to intervene. Title VII does not give the EEOC an unconditional right to intervene because intervention is based on the court's discretion when the EEOC certifies that "the case is of general public importance." The EEOC, therefore, may not intervene of right. The EEOC should, however, be able to obtain permissive intervention. Rule 24(b) allows permissive intervention when a federal statute grants a conditional right to intervene, as this one does. . . .

The only difference between Answer A and Answer B is the sentence in Answer B: "The EEOC should, however, be able to obtain permissive intervention." This sentence alerts the reader that the writer has shifted to the discussion of permissive intervention. Because the sentence also draws a conclusion, it is a particularly concise transition. The absence of an effective transition in Answer A obscures its discussion of permissive intervention. The reader of Answer A could easily miss the shift.

These two examples illustrate that a transition need not be obvious to be effective. In the first example, a topic sentence at the beginning of the paragraph serves as the transition. In the second example, a thesis statement in mid-paragraph serves as the transition. If your thesis or topic sentence is precise and well placed, you may not need any other transitions from one point to the next.

The following exercises will help you practice using the guidelines described in this chapter.

Exercise 12-A

You represent Timothy McGraw, who has been arrested for robbing a coin shop. During the robbery, McGraw used a cane carved and painted to look like a shotgun. Swinging the cane around in a menacing manner during the robbery, McGraw told the shop owner he would "hurt [the shop owner] bad" if the shop owner did not cooperate. McGraw motioned with the cane for the shop owner to get into a closet. The shop owner complied, and McGraw then locked the closet. The shop owner, who was un-harmed, later told police he was afraid he would be shot or struck if he did not comply. McGraw has now been indicted for armed robbery.

Edit or rewrite the following discussion using the principles described in this chapter:

A person commits armed robbery when, with intent to commit theft, he takes the property of another by use of an "offensive weapon." State Code § 365(b). The courts have defined "offensive weapon" as including not only a weapon *per se*, but also anything used in a manner likely to cause death or great bodily injury. *Fann v. State; Meminger v. State.*

In both *Fann* and *Choate* the defendants used replicas of guns to commit robberies. The court held in both cases that the defendants could not be convicted of armed robbery because the legislature had specifically eliminated statutory language that would have brought replicas within the purview of the armed robbery statute. Like the defendants in *Fann* and *Choate*, McGraw cannot be convicted of armed robbery simply because he used something that looked like a gun.

In *Fann* there was no evidence that the defendant tried to strike the victim. In *Choate v. State*, the defendant was unable to do so, because the victim was seated in an enclosed booth. In both cases the court noted the lack of any evidence of an intent to harm the victim. Similarly, McGraw did not attempt to hit the owner, or show any intent to do so.

Unlike the defendant in *Fann*, who gave no indication of intent to strike the victim, McGraw did swing the weapon back and forth menacingly and did threaten to "hurt [the shop owner] bad" unless he cooperated. Further, the shop owner stated that he was fearful of being either shot or struck, indicating that the weapon's movement implied this threat. However, the court in *Fann* did not infer an intention to harm without substantive indication of such intent. The court is unlikely to find swinging the cane back and forth sufficient to establish McGraw's intent to strike the shop owner when McGraw made no attempt to do so. Therefore, because McGraw did not use the cane in a manner indicating an intent to harm the shop owner, he is not likely to be convicted of armed robbery.

In *Meminger* the defendant was convicted of armed robbery when he hit the victim in the head with a liquor bottle. The court held that because the bottle was used in a manner likely to cause harm, it was an offensive weapon. Unlike the defendant in *Meminger*, McGraw did not use the cane in a way indicating an intent to hit the shop owner, because he only swung the cane back and forth and did not swing it at the owner.

Exercise 12-B

Your client, Scott Spencer, was injured when he went on his first whitewater rafting trip. Before the trip he signed a rental agreement that included a paragraph releasing Rocky River Outfitters from liability for any damages arising from the trip. The release did not specifically mention "negligence." Your client thought it was merely a rental agreement and did not take the time to read it carefully before he signed. He is now considering a lawsuit against the company.

The issue is whether the word "negligence" must be included specifically in the release in order to bar an action for negligence. The intent of the parties, their relative bargaining position, and the specificity of the language of the release are all considered by the court in reaching this decision. The *Conner* and *Anders* cases are from your jurisdiction. The *Sommers* and *Cabel* cases are from other jurisdictions.

Edit or rewrite the following discussion using the principles discussed in this chapter:

The court in *Conner* held that a release was invalid and did not bar a cause of action arising from a motorcycle accident at a racetrack. The release purported to release the defendant from liability, but mentioned only "automobile racing" in a list of racing activities included. The court reasoned that motorcycle racing was not included under the commonly understood definition of automobile racing. In *Anders*, the court granted summary judgment to the defendant after the plaintiff sued for damages arising from the defendant's negligence in drilling oil and gas wells. The contract between the parties specifically absolved the defendant from liability arising from its negligence. The court based its decision on the equal bargaining positions of the parties and the unequivocal language of the contract. *Anders* did not address the specific issue presented here. The contract between Spencer and Rocky River Outfitters, however, did not contain the word "negligence." The decisions in *Sommers* and *Cabel* concluded that specific mention of the word "negligence" was not necessary if the intent of the parties was otherwise clearly expressed. The release in *Sommers* absolved a parachuting school from "any and all claims, demands, actions, . . . whatsoever, in any way resulting from personal injuries . . . arising from . . . parachute jumping." In *Cabel* the release covered "any and all losses, claims, actions, or proceedings of every kind and character . . . arising directly or indirectly from any activity . . . such as parachuting." Although not binding in this state, *Sommers* and *Cabel* held that the actions brought by students injured in parachute jumping were barred by the releases. In the release Spencer signed, he specifically absolved Rocky River Outfitters from liability for "any and all claims I have or may acquire against RRO for any personal injury or property damage I may sustain as a result of this rafting trip." Like the releases in *Sommers* and *Cabel*, this release specifically covered all claims that might arise from the specified activity in language that was obviously intended to be all-inclusive.

13

Drafting the Discussion

LEGAL WRITING DIFFERS from the kind of writing you probably did as an undergraduate in three ways: its purpose, the process, and the audience. Generally, the purpose of undergraduate papers is to allow students to develop their intellectual or creative talents within limits circumscribed by the assigned topic. The purpose of a legal memo or brief is much more practical and specific: to put in writing, in a way that is both credible and convincing, how the law applies to a client's particular legal problem. Whether you succeed or fail in this purpose can have serious consequences for your client. Although writing in law practice requires both intellect and creativity, it is never merely an intellectual or creative exercise.

The complexity of legal analysis makes the process of writing different from undergraduate writing, much of which is based on a linear approach. As the name suggests, the steps in the linear process go in a straight line from beginning to end with the tasks neatly divided into categories. You take them in that order, and you do not return to earlier steps. You perform the steps separately because they are independent of one another, and you perform them in a certain order because they build on one another. The theory is that nothing you learn along the way requires you to do additional work on earlier steps, and that the later steps may be taken only when earlier ones have been completed. The chart below illustrates this:

Linear Approach
Identify and narrow issues
Research
Analyze and organize
Write
Rewrite

Whatever the merits of the linear approach to some types of writing, it will not work for legal writing. If you try to follow a linear approach, you run the risk of oversimplifying the issues and overlooking important cases. Legal writing is too complex to be approached in a linear fashion and requires instead a recursive approach. In the recursive approach, you work on "later" steps while completing "earlier" steps, and then often return to later ones. The theory is that the later steps help you complete earlier ones and that what you learn along the way often requires you to revisit earlier steps.

The recursive approach includes the same five components that are used in the linear approach—identifying and narrowing issues, researching, analyzing and organizing, writing, and rewriting. When you receive an assignment, the first step is to identify tentative issues and begin the research. The steps after this tend to run together. The research will enable you to refine issues and may suggest others. When you are researching, you are not merely collecting sources, you are analyzing them to determine whether or how they are relevant to your client's case. During the research you begin writing your first, tentative analysis of each issue. This rough draft will likely reveal gaps in your research and may cause you to rethink the issues. Then you must do more research, analysis, and revision. This back-and-forth approach is not only normal but desirable.

The steps in the legal writing process can be compared to an inverted pyramid, as depicted below. The first step is understanding what questions you are required to answer and beginning the research. The last step is rewriting. This step may need to be repeated several times before the final draft is completed. Notice that two things occur as you proceed. You perform progressively fewer tasks, and your focus becomes clearer. The nature and number of steps that it takes to progress from the first step to the last will vary according to the nature of the problem. This chart illustrates a typical progression:

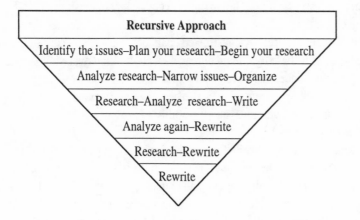

Recursive Approach

Identify the issues–Plan your research–Begin your research

Analyze research–Narrow issues–Organize

Research–Analyze research–Write

Analyze again–Rewrite

Research–Rewrite

Rewrite

Two ideas in the chart need to be emphasized. First, begin writing early, as soon as you have a grasp of what the law is and how it applies to your client's case. By writing early, you will keep your focus on the final product. Second, allow plenty of time for rewriting.

Writing as soon as possible is part of the process of continual definition and refinement of the issues and sub-issues; you will not know the parameters of the issues until you have researched them and written about them. The familiar saying that writing is thinking on paper is particularly applicable to the process of legal writing. During the early stages, sometimes called the pre-writing stage, write in any form that works best for you. Some writers brief cases, make charts, make notes on cards or looseleaf paper, write outlines, write pieces of the discussion, or use some combination. The worst thing you can do is to delay writing until you have digested every case you plan to use and analyzed every issue and sub-issue. By then you will be so familiar with the analysis you are apt to forget that your reader is not. Write early while you still have a fresh perspective. Think about a legal problem as a puzzle that you must solve for your reader by fitting the pieces together in the best possible configuration. Begin to construct the separate pieces as soon as you have a general idea of how the pieces will fit together. Then fit them together.

Allow plenty of time for rewriting because it may be the most difficult part of the process. During the pre-writing and writing stages, you concentrate on analyzing and structuring the problem, first in your own mind and then on paper. The rewriting stage requires a shift in perspective from writer to reader.

The final difference between legal writing and much undergraduate writing is the audience. The audience is usually another lawyer who is reading the document for a specific purpose—a judge or supervising attorney, for example, who needs to know how law and policy apply to a particular case. These lawyers, your readers, are a skeptical lot. They will not accept your conclusions on faith. Anticipate their skepticism about each argument you make and each conclusion you draw. They will expect a carefully constructed chain of logic without significant missing links. Write as if these hypothetical readers were looking over your shoulder.

Your audience will have other expectations of you as well. Among these expectations are an acceptable level of proficiency in your use of the English language and its conventions, and the ability to present complex material clearly and coherently.

Read your draft critically from the reader's perspective. Ask yourself whether a reader who does not have your knowledge of the law or the facts would find your analysis readable, credible, logical, and complete.

Learn to separate the intensely personal experience of producing a memo or brief from the product itself. After you have let the memo or brief rest, read it carefully. You will often find that the organizational scheme is not working the way you intended, that the discussion is unclear on some points, or that you have a sentence ten lines long. If you do not see any such problems, you are not looking at the paper critically enough. The development of your writing ability can be measured partially by the readiness with which you reorganize, delete, insert, or rewrite whole pages, paragraphs, or sentences.

This process, again, takes time. Those who indulge in the common undergraduate practice of cranking out an assignment the night before it is due will probably do poorly. The law demands precision and penalizes those whose work is rushed and sloppy.

This chapter pulls together the basic principles in Chapters 9, 10, 11, and 12 (Organization, Describing the Law, Explaining the Analysis, and Signposting). It shows, step by step, how to construct a discussion from the common law and statutory analysis explained in Chapters 6 and 7, as well as how to apply the principles for reaching a conclusion described in Chapter 8.

The organizational structure suggested in this chapter includes all the components of a complete discussion of each issue or sub-issue. It begins with your conclusion, then follows with a description of the rule or rules involved and an explanation of how those rules apply to a particular set of facts. If there is an apparently contrary position or counterargument, the structure requires several extra steps that parallel the main discussion: a statement that the counterargument is weaker (because, for example, it is based on distinguishable cases or illogical reasoning) or untenable (because there is no direct support for it), a description of the law or an interpretation of the law on which the counterargument would be based, and an explanation of why the law or its interpretation does not change your conclusion. Unless the discussion as a whole is short, the discussion of each issue should end with your conclusion. Use signposts throughout the Discussion to indicate its structure.

This structure ensures that you write everything you need to write for the reader to understand your analysis. It is logical and relatively easy to understand. It can be applied to both memoranda and briefs. Learning the basic steps of this structure at the outset will help you organize your ideas more efficiently and effectively. Not every discussion will fit this pattern, however. As you gain experience in legal writing, you will learn to recognize situations in which some deviation from the structure suggested here may result in a more cogent discussion.

1. For each issue, state your conclusion and briefly state the relevant law.

State your conclusion on any specific issue at the outset. Stating your conclusion first serves two purposes. First, it ensures that you have actually reached a conclusion. It is difficult, if not impossible, to begin writing a discussion of a legal issue until you have sorted out how the law applies to the relevant facts. Putting your conclusion first prevents you from writing a rambling discussion of law and facts that leaves the reader with only a set of considerations instead of a coherent legal analysis. If you cannot articulate your conclusion, you need to spend more time thinking. Second, putting the conclusion first enables the reader to follow your discussion more easily by pointing him in the right direction from the outset.

As explained in Chapter 12 (Signposting), your conclusion is a thesis that should be stated in terms of the issue. It should include both the relevant legal rule and the significant facts. Providing both of these important pieces of information at the outset ensures the reader's awareness of your basic premise. The introductory conclusion can often be stated in a single, well-written sentence, but complex issues may require two or three sentences.

Your conclusion should also state how relevant "givens" are resolved. Resolution of a particular issue may require discussion of three elements, for example, only one of which is an issue. A brief discussion of the two "givens" as part of the conclusion will help frame the discussion for the reader.

The examples in this chapter are based on the libel problem discussed in Chapter 6, as well as the charts used to analyze that problem.

◻ Consider the following introductory statements:

ANSWER A: Dooley did not commit libel because he did not intend his fliers containing false statements about Fremont to be read by others. In *Simmons v. Deluxe Plaza Hotel,* the court held that a person's reading of defamatory material does not necessarily show intentional publication. The fliers were published and subjected Fremont to the loss of social prestige.

ANSWER B: Dooley did not commit libel. Libel is the "intentional publication of false statements about a person that humiliate that person or subject him to the loss of social prestige." *White v. Ball.* Two elements of this rule have been satisfied. The fliers were published when they were released by accident. The fliers also subjected Fremont to the loss of social prestige because they accused him of having a criminal record. The intent element has not been met, however, because Dooley did not intend his fliers to be read by others.

ANSWER C: Dooley did not commit libel through the fliers he prepared. Libel is the "intentional publication of false statements about a person that humiliate that person or subject him to the loss of social prestige." *White v. Ball.*

Answer B is best because it states a conclusion on the issue, briefly describes the libel rule, and shows how the two "givens" are resolved. The writer concludes that Dooley did not commit libel because he did not intentionally publish the fliers, and then the writer quotes the basic libel rule. The writer addresses each "given" in sentences that identify the rule and the relevant facts and that state how the "given" is resolved. Answer B thus provides a good framework for the ensuing discussion.

Answer A shows the writer's conclusion on the libel issue. The description of the law, however, focuses only on the intent element. As a result, the reader has not been informed of the basic legal framework for the discussion that follows. The two "givens" are resolved, but it is impossible to know on what basis, because the significant facts are not identified.

Answer C states a conclusion but does not give the reader any indication of the legal or factual basis for that conclusion. Answer C thus does not focus the discussion for the reader. Although it does quote the libel rule, it does not show how any of the "givens" were resolved.

2. For each sub-issue, state your conclusion in terms of the rule.

This step requires you to state your conclusion for each sub-issue that arises under an issue. Like the first one, this step ensures that you have actually reached a conclusion and makes it easier for the reader to follow your discussion. Again, your conclusion should include both the relevant legal rule and the significant facts. You do not need to describe any law or analyze "givens"; merely state the thesis for the sub-issue.

This step and steps 3 through 7 specifically address sub-issues. If only one element of a rule is at issue, however, follow these steps for that single issue.

▨   Consider the following conclusions on intent to publish:

ANSWER A: Dooley did not intentionally publish the fliers because they were released by accident.

ANSWER B: Dooley did not intentionally publish the fliers.

ANSWER C: The first issue is whether Dooley intentionally published the fliers.

Answer A is best because it states the conclusion in terms of the rule and provides the reason, which helps the reader understand what will follow. Answer B states the conclusion in terms of the rule but does not provide the reason, making it harder for the reader to understand the rest of the discussion. Answer C states the issue but gives no conclusion and no reason. Sentences like this confuse the reader and often indicate that the writer has no idea where the discussion will go.

3. Describe the law that supports your conclusion for each sub-issue.

As Chapter 10 (Describing the Law) explains, the law at issue provides a structure for your discussion. Therefore, a description of the applicable law supporting your position should immediately follow your conclusion. This description must be accurate and complete. It may be as brief as a sentence or as long as several paragraphs, depending on the complexity of the problem and the strength of potential counterarguments.

For common law problems, state the general rule first, then describe cases supporting your conclusion that apply the rule. For statutory problems, quote or summarize the relevant provision first, then explain how any judicial decisions may have modified, extended, restricted, or defined the statute. Whether you are discussing a statutory or a common law issue, your description of a case should ordinarily require only a few sentences and should focus on the facts and reasoning relevant to the issue or sub-issue. Avoid the historical approach; instead, give the reader a concise view of the current state of the law.

◻ Consider the following descriptions of the law:

ANSWER A: Intent occurs when the defendant should reasonably be aware of the likelihood that the material may be read by others. *Simmons v. Deluxe Plaza Hotel.* In *Simmons*, the court held that a letter making false accusations against the plaintiff was not intentionally published even though it was read by the plaintiff's wife.

ANSWER B: In *Simmons v. Deluxe Plaza Hotel*, the court held that a letter making false accusations against the plaintiff was not intentionally published even though it was read by the plaintiff's wife. The letter had been addressed to the plaintiff personally and sent by certified mail. The court noted the precautions the defendant had taken to prevent the letter from being read by third persons, and reasoned that "a mere conceivable possibility or chance" that the letter would be read by others did not demonstrate intent.

ANSWER C: Intent occurs when the defendant should reasonably be aware of the likelihood that the material may be read by others. *Simmons v. Deluxe Plaza Hotel.* In *Simmons*, the court held that a letter making false accusations against the plaintiff was not intentionally published even though it was read by the plaintiff's wife. The letter had been addressed to the plaintiff personally and sent by certified mail. The court noted the precautions the defendant had taken to prevent the letter from being read by third persons, and reasoned that "a mere conceivable possibility or chance" that the letter would be read by others did not demonstrate intent.

Answer C is best because it summarizes the relevant law clearly and completely. It defines intentional publication—the element at issue here. It then describes the facts and reasoning of the *Simmons* case, thus providing a framework within which to compare the facts of Dooley's case.

Answer A summarizes the legal principles and states that *Simmons* is analogous, but it does not fully describe the facts in *Simmons* or the court's rationale. It will be difficult to describe fully the analogies between *Simmons* and Dooley's case on the basis of this summary. Answer A , unfortunately, represents a common error in legal writing.

Answer B explains the facts and rationale of *Simmons* but omits the basic legal principles. Without the legal principles, the reader will have difficulty discerning why the facts and rationale in *Simmons* are significant.

4. Explain why the law supports your conclusion for each sub-issue.

Once you have stated your conclusion and the relevant law, you must explain the reasons for your conclusion. This explanation is the most important part of your discussion and should include every step in your reasoning process as well as every reasonable basis for your conclusion.

In problems involving the common law, you will explain your reasoning by comparing or contrasting your facts with those of the relevant cases. First you should explain how the facts of the decided cases support your conclusion. Most of the time you will point out similarities between the facts of these cases and the facts of your case, although sometimes you will point out differences. In general, you should analogize cases with holdings consistent with your position and distinguish cases with holdings contrary to your position. Remember to base similarities and differences on the specific legal rule at issue. You will then explain how the reasons and policies of the decided cases support your conclusion. This explanation is part of the analytical method set out in Chapter 6 (Common Law Analysis).

☐   Possible explanations for your conclusion in the libel problem include the following. The sentence in italics is from Answer C in the previous example.

ANSWER A: *The court noted the precautions the defendant had taken to prevent the letter from being read by third persons and reasoned that "a mere conceivable possibility or chance" that the letter would be read by others did not constitute intent.* Similarly, Dooley did not intend for anyone to read the fliers when they were knocked out of his hands in an accident and read by third parties. Thus, the fliers were not published intentionally.

ANSWER B: *The court noted the precautions the defendant had taken to prevent the letter from being read by third persons and reasoned that "a mere conceivable possibility or chance" that the letter would be read by others did not constitute intent.* Similarly, Dooley did not intend for anyone to read the fliers when they were knocked out of his hands in an accident and read by third parties. Like the defendant in *Simmons*, Dooley could not reasonably have been expected to anticipate that publication would occur.

ANSWER C: *The court noted the precautions the defendant had taken to prevent the letter from being read by third persons and reasoned that "a mere conceivable possibility or chance" that the letter would be read by others did not constitute intent.* Like

the defendant in *Simmons*, Dooley could not reasonably have been expected to anticipate that his fliers would be read by third persons.

Answer B is best because it compares the facts in both cases. Words and
phrases such as "similarly" and "like the defendant in *Simmons*" alert the reader
that a comparison is being made. Answer B also explains how the underlying policy
in *Simmons*—to hold a defendant responsible only for harm he could reasonably
have anticipated—is reinforced by the writer's conclusion.

Answer A compares the facts of *Simmons* with those of Dooley's case but
says nothing about the underlying reasons or policies. The court's reasoning will
necessarily guide the discussion about factual similarities. Answer A is deficient
because it does not reveal why the factual similarities are important.

Answer C is a cryptic version of Answer B. It does not fully compare the
Simmons facts with those of Dooley's case, nor does it clearly explain how the
rationale in *Simmons* supports the writer's conclusion. The analysis is too brief to
be informative.

You should handle problems involving statutory analysis similarly. First
explain how the language of the statute and the facts of any cases interpreting that
statute support your conclusion. Next explain how the policies of the statute and
the policies of any cases interpreting the statute support your conclusion. These
statements are part of the method of analysis described in Chapter 7 (Statutory
Analysis).

5. Describe any reasonable counterargument for each sub-issue and state why it is unpersuasive.

As explained in Chapter 9 (Organization), you should state your reasons for rejecting an opposite conclusion only after you have explained the reasons for reaching
your conclusion. When you state your reasons for rejecting an opposite conclusion,
you begin your response to potential counterarguments and signal to the reader that
you are moving to a different part of the discussion. You should use a transition that
serves as the thesis of your counterargument. Your transition should also explain
or summarize the counterargument in terms of the sub-issue.

A counterargument is a plausible reason for arriving at a different conclusion. If no counterargument can be advanced against your conclusion, you can skip
this and the next two steps. If your opponent could advance one or more
counteraguments, this and the next two steps are intended to make sure you
address them.

Potential counterarguments can be made by either side, and you may or may
not know them in advance. If your conclusion favors your opponent, your client

may have a counterargument. If your conclusion favors your client, your opponent may have a counterargument. Sometimes, such as when your client is in litigation, you will know the counterarguments because your opponent will already have made them. More often, you will have to predict the counterarguments based on the law.

This and the next two steps follow a pattern similar to that provided in the second, third, and fourth steps. You should state your conclusion concerning the counterargument, explain the relevant law, and then explain why the relevant law and applicable facts support that conclusion. If more than one counterargument is possible, you should repeat these three steps for each.

◻ Consider the following thesis statements for the counterargument in the libel problem:

ANSWER A: *White v. Ball* is also relevant.

ANSWER B: Because Dooley did not intentionally publish the fliers, *White v. Ball* is inapplicable.

ANSWER C: *White v. Ball* is analogous to Dooley's case because the defendant in *White* intended a third party to read his letter when he prepared it.

ANSWER D: Fremont could argue, relying on *White v. Ball*, that Dooley intentionally published the fliers.

ANSWER E: Dooley could argue that because he did not intentionally publish the fliers, *White v. Ball* is inapplicable.

Answer B is best because it addresses the most logical counterargument, which is based on an analogy to *White v. Ball*. Answer B also explains why the counterargument will fail: Dooley did not intentionally publish the fliers. It serves as a thesis statement for the discussion that follows, as well as a transition from the previous part of the discussion.

Answer A is virtually useless because it does not explain whether the case supports the discussion or supports the counterargument. Nor does it explain why the *White* case is even relevant.

Answer C is confusing because it states the counterargument from the viewpoint of the lawyer making it. When you state the counterargument, however, you are not stating your position. You are stating an opposing position, and you need to help your reader understand that. Answer B addresses the counterargument simply by denying its validity—*White v. Ball* is inapplicable.

Answer D begins with the clause "Fremont could argue." Sentences that begin with such clauses are usually poor for two reasons: They often do nothing more than state the obvious, and they rarely state a thesis or specific position.

Answer D is poor for both reasons. It states the obvious (Fremont will argue that Dooley intentionally published the fliers) and does not introduce the discussion to follow.

Like Answer D, Answer E begins by stating the obvious—"Dooley could argue that." Unlike Answer D, it states a thesis and therefore is a better answer. Stylistically, however, it is inferior to Answer B. The prefatory clause "Dooley could argue that" adds length but no meaning to the sentence.

The counterargument in this problem is relatively simple. When the basis for the counterargument is more complex, you should state and respond to the counterargument in more precise terms: "Because the defendant's conduct was intentional, it was not privileged." This part of the discussion, again, needs to introduce the counterargument, state why it is unpersuasive, and serve as a transition.

6. Describe the law on which the counterargument for each sub-issue would be based.

To be even minimally credible, opposing arguments require some legal basis. Your discussion should summarize the relevant cases or statutory provisions supporting the counterargument.

Resist the temptation to automatically divide legal authority into "for" and "against" categories. Support for a counterargument most often will arise from similarities or differences in the same statutes or cases as those used in developing your conclusion, or from competing policies the court has emphasized in cases you have already described. In these situations you can simply refer to the statute or cases, describe only those parts of the law that have not already been described or, when appropriate, skip this step altogether. Sometimes, however, you will find separate cases or lines of cases resolving the same legal issue differently, or you will have a choice of statutes to be applied. In these situations, the adverse law will be new to your reader because you did not use it in describing the law supporting your conclusion. You must describe the different lines of authority completely and fairly. Only then can the reader appreciate the strength of your position and the weaknesses of the counterarguments.

◻ Consider these descriptions of the opposing law:

ANSWER A: In *White*, the defendant wrote a letter making allegedly false accusations against company employees. The court held that publication occurred. "It is receipt by a third person that makes the statements so damaging," the court reasoned.

ANSWER B: In *White*, the defendant wrote a third person, a company president, making allegedly false accusations against company employees. The court held that intentional publication occurred because the president received and read the letter.

ANSWER C: In *White*, the defendant wrote a third person, a company president, making allegedly false accusations against company employees. The court held that intentional publication occurred because the president received and read the letter. "It is receipt by a third person that makes the statements so damaging," the court reasoned.

Answer C is best because it describes the relevant facts and policy of the *White* case as well as the court's holding. It therefore provides a framework from which to distinguish the facts in Dooley's case. Although the court's reasoning seems more relevant to publication than intent to publish, it could provide the basis for a counterargument minimizing the importance of intent when publication has occurred.

Answer A, by contrast, contains such a brief summary of the facts in *White* that it is impossible to determine exactly what happened. The reader needs to know that the person to whom the accusations were addressed in *White* was the same person who read them. That fact helps distinguish *White* from Dooley's case. Because Answer A does not contain that information, the reader will not be able to easily understand the writer's subsequent analysis of *White*.

Answer B contains a good description of the facts but is silent about the court's rationale. Again, stating the court's rationale will help guide the discussion about factual differences. By not stating it, the writer will have a difficult time answering a counterargument based on the court's reasoning.

7. Explain why the counterargument does not change your conclusion for each sub-issue.

Once you have set out the law on which the counterargument would be based, you must explain why another conclusion is less convincing than your conclusion. This part of your discussion is second in importance only to your initial explanation of how the law supports your conclusion. Just as you did in your explanation of the law supporting your conclusion, you must include every reason and every step in your analysis. Be sure to address the strongest counterarguments. A writer gains credibility by acknowledging and refuting the most difficult counterarguments, not by constructing and rejecting weak or insupportable arguments. You and your reader need to understand the weaknesses in your position to ensure that your conclusion is indeed the most likely outcome. If you find that you cannot respond to the strongest or most persuasive counterarguments, you may want to change your conclusion.

For common law problems, you will first explain how the decided cases do not support the opposing argument. Many times, you will do this by explaining that the decided cases are distinguishable from your case. At other times, you will do this by drawing analogies to the decided cases. Again, factual contrasts or comparisons should be based on the law at issue. Next you will explain how the reasons and policies of the decided cases do not support the counterargument.

You should handle problems involving statutory analysis similarly. First explain how the statutory language and the facts of the decided cases do not support the counterargument. Then explain how the policies of the statute and any cases interpreting the statute fail to support the counterargument.

After you have answered the counterargument, restate your conclusion. This statement may be unnecessary if the discussion is relatively brief. Even in a longer discussion, this statement can often be short, but it is helpful to reiterate for the reader how your analysis supports your conclusion. Otherwise, your discussion may end abruptly with your last point and force the reader to pull the various steps of your analysis together.

◼ Here are several possible analyses of the counterarguments in the libel problem. The sentence in italics is taken from Answer C in the previous example.

ANSWER A: *"It is receipt by a third person that makes the statements so damaging," the court reasoned.* The defendant's planned and intentional distribution of the letter in *White*, however, is different from Dooley's release of the fliers. In addition, Dooley's fliers were read by passersby on the street, not the apartment tenants for whom he prepared the fliers. Although the court was concerned with the damaging effect of publication, libel occurs only when there is intent to publish. Dooley did not intentionally publish the fliers.

ANSWER B: *"It is receipt by a third person that makes the statements so damaging," the court reasoned.* The defendant's planned and intentional distribution of the letter in *White*, however, is different from Dooley's accidental release of the fliers after he had decided not to publish them. In addition, the company president to whom the letter was addressed in *White* was the same person who read the letter. In Dooley's case, by contrast, the fliers were read by passersby on the street, not the apartment tenants for whom he prepared the fliers. Although the court was concerned with the damaging effect of publication, libel occurs only if there is intent to publish at the time the documents are published. Dooley did not have that intent.

ANSWER C: *"It is receipt by a third person that makes the statements so damaging," the court reasoned.* The defendant's planned and intentional distribution of the letter in *White*, however, is different from Dooley's accidental release of the fliers after he had decided not to publish them. In addition, the company president to whom the letter was addressed in *White* was the same person who read the letter. In Dooley's case, by contrast, the fliers were read by passersby on the street, not the apartment tenants for whom he prepared the fliers.

Answer B is best because of its completeness. The writer includes several arguments. The first two show differences between the facts of *White* and the facts of Dooley's case. The third argument is of a different kind. It directly addresses the tension between the elements of publication and intent to publish. When two cases seem to stand for somewhat different conclusions, it is important to find credible ways to reconcile them.

Answer A ineffectively states the factual differences between *White* and Dooley's case. To be understandable, a discussion must show what is being compared or contrasted. A discussion that explains the facts of one case without describing the facts of the other is impossible to understand. When the writer makes assertions with no justification, those assertions simply are not credible.

Answer C compares the facts but leaves out any discussion of the court's reasoning in *White*. By not fully addressing the counterargument, Answer C gives it more credibility than it actually deserves. Failure to restate the conclusion compounds the problem.

8. Edit the discussion to include signposts.

The first seven steps in this chapter provide a structure for developing your discussion. The first, second, and fifth steps, in which you state your conclusion on the issue, your conclusion on the sub-issue, and your response to a potential counterargument, tell your reader where you are going. But these steps, by themselves, do not necessarily ensure that your reader will understand the discussion supporting your conclusion or your discussion of the counterargument. If the reader does not understand the discussion, your memo or brief is of little value. This last step is based on Chapter 12 (Signposting) and is included here to help you make your writing more understandable.

If you put the best answer for each of the first seven steps in a separate paragraph, your discussion so far would look like this (the paragraphs are numbered for reference only):

1. Dooley did not commit libel. Libel is the "intentional publication of false statements about a person that humiliate that person or subject him to the loss of social prestige." *White v. Ball.* Two elements of this rule have been satisfied. The fliers were published when they were released by accident. The fliers also subjected Fremont to a loss of social prestige because they accused him of having a criminal record. The intent element has not been met, however, because Dooley did not intend his fliers to be read by others.

2. Dooley did not intentionally publish the fliers because they were released by accident.

3. Intent occurs when the defendant should reasonably be aware of the likelihood that the material may be read by others. *Simmons v. Deluxe Plaza Hotel.* In

Simmons, the court held that a letter making false accusations against the plaintiff was not intentionally published even though it was read by the plaintiff's wife. The letter had been addressed to the plaintiff personally and sent by certified mail. The court noted the precautions the defendant had taken to prevent the letter from being read by third persons, and reasoned that "a mere conceivable possibility or chance" that the letter would be read by others did not demonstrate intent.

4. Similarly, Dooley did not intend for anyone to read the fliers when they were knocked out of his hands in an accident and read by third parties. Like the defendant in *Simmons*, he could not reasonably have been expected to anticipate that publication would occur.

5. Because Dooley did not intentionally publish the fliers, *White v. Ball* is inapplicable.

6. In *White*, the defendant wrote a third person, a company president, making allegedly false accusations against company employees. The court held that intentional publication occurred because the president received and read the letter. "It is receipt by a third person that makes the statements so damaging," the court reasoned.

7. The defendant's planned and intentional distribution of the letter in *White*, however, is different from Dooley's accidental release of the fliers after he had decided not to publish them. In addition, the company president to whom the letter was addressed in *White* was the same person who read the letter. In Dooley's case, by contrast, the fliers were read by passersby on the street, not the apartment tenants for whom he prepared the fliers. Although the court was concerned with the damaging effect of publication, libel occurs only if there is intent to publish at the time the documents are published. Dooley did not have that intent.

Although this discussion is reasonably complete, it is still rough. It contains two one-sentence paragraphs (paragraphs 2 and 5). Although one-sentence paragraphs may occasionally be appropriate to emphasize a particular point, they are not appropriate here. In addition, the point of several of the paragraphs, and the relationship between them, is not clear. Finally, the overall structure of the discussion is hard to see.

The lead paragraph focuses on the entire question of libel, while the other six paragraphs focus on one element of libel. This difference in focus is a signal that the first paragraph should not be combined with the other paragraphs. But should it be divided? It contains only four sentences—a thesis, a description of the overall legal rule, and a sentence for each of two "givens." It is unlikely that dividing this paragraph will improve the discussion. The first paragraph can thus be left unchanged.

Paragraphs 2, 3, and 4 discuss the conclusion on the intent-to-publish sub-issue, and paragraphs 5, 6, and 7 discuss the counterargument. The discussion of your conclusion and the discussion of the counterargument should generally be in separate paragraphs. These two parts of your discussion are so different that combining some of each in the same paragraph would confuse the reader.

Signposts for paragraphs 2, 3, and 4 should explain the relationship of these paragraphs. That relationship is not clear from the text. Paragraph 2 states a conclusion, and the first sentence in paragraph 3 helps explain that conclusion by describing the legal rule on which the conclusion is based. The discussion does not state why the holding and facts in *Simmons* are being explained, however. The reader, while likely to understand why you have stated the basic legal rule, will wonder why the case is being described in detail. Usually, cases are described in detail because the writer is using them to make analogies or distinctions. Before reading about *Simmons*, your reader will expect some type of signal, or signpost. Because the discussion analogizes *Simmons* to Dooley's case, you should state that it is analogous by editing this sentence:

> In *Simmons*, the court held that a letter making false accusations against the plaintiff was not intentionally published even though it was read by the plaintiff's wife.

It now reads:

> This case is analogous to *Simmons*, in which the court held that a letter making false accusations against the plaintiff was not intentionally published even though it was read by the plaintiff's wife.

This change tells the reader why *Simmons* is being explained. It also clarifies the relationship between paragraph 4 and the rest of paragraph 3.

As already suggested, paragraph 2 needs to be combined with another paragraph, which would have to be paragraph 3. Should those two paragraphs also be combined with paragraph 4? Because all three paragraphs state and describe the legal basis for the conclusion, a single paragraph would be coherent. Would it be too long? As noted in Chapter 12 (Signposting), a general rule is that paragraphs should contain between four and eight sentences. Seven sentences is not unduly long for a single paragraph.

Paragraphs 5, 6, and 7 need less editing. Paragraph 5 is plainly a transition sentence, and its relationship to paragraphs 6 and 7 is clearly stated.

These paragraphs do need to be consolidated, however. Because it is only a single sentence, paragraph 5 should be combined with paragraph 6. Paragraph 7 can stand by itself because it distinguishes the law described in paragraphs 5 and 6 from Dooley's situation.

The final discussion looks like this:

Dooley did not commit libel. Libel is the "intentional publication of false statements about a person that humiliate that person or subject him to the loss of social prestige." *White v. Ball.* Two elements of this rule have been satisfied. The fliers were published when they were released by accident. The fliers also subjected Fremont to a loss of social prestige because they accused him of having a criminal record. The intent element has not been met, however, because Dooley did not intend his fliers to be read by others.

Dooley did not intentionally publish the fliers because they were released by accident. Intent occurs when the defendant should reasonably be aware of the likelihood that the material may be read by others. *Simmons v. Deluxe Plaza Hotel.* This case is analogous to *Simmons,* in which the court held that a letter making false accusations against the plaintiff was not intentionally published even though it was read by the plaintiff's wife. The letter had been addressed to the plaintiff personally and sent by certified mail. The court noted the precautions the defendant had taken to prevent the letter from being read by third persons, and reasoned that "a mere conceivable possibility or chance" that the letter would be read by others did not demonstrate intent. Similarly, Dooley did not intend for anyone to read the fliers when they were knocked out of his hands in an accident and read by third parties. Like the defendant in *Simmons,* he could not reasonably have been expected to anticipate that publication would occur.

Because Dooley did not intentionally publish the fliers, *White v. Ball* is inapplicable. In *White,* the defendant wrote a third person, a company president, making allegedly false accusations against company employees. The court held that intentional publication occurred because the president received and read the letter. "It is receipt by a third person that makes the statements so damaging," the court reasoned.

The defendant's planned and intentional distribution of the letter in *White* is different from Dooley's accidental release of the fliers after he had decided not to publish them. In addition, the company president to whom the letter was addressed in *White* was the same person who read the letter. In Dooley's case, by contrast, the fliers were read by passersby on the street, not the apartment tenants for whom he prepared the fliers. Although the court was concerned with the damaging effect of publication, libel occurs only when there is intent to publish at the time the documents are published. Dooley did not have that intent.

This chapter has thus far focused on the intent-to-publish sub-issue from the Dooley case in Chapter 6. As you may recall, a second sub-issue is whether the fliers were false.

◼ Consider these discussions of that sub-issue:

ANSWER A: The fliers are false because Fremont has no record of criminal convictions. "A statement is false if the gist, the sting, of the matter is false." *White v. Ball.* The fliers accused Fremont of having a "long record of criminal convictions as a landlord." In fact, he has no criminal convictions at all. The gist of the fliers is thus false.

This case is different from cases in which the court held that statements with minor errors were substantially accurate. *Willow v. Orr; White v. Ball.* In *Willow*, a wife's allegation that her estranged husband had "kidnapped" their son was held to be substantially accurate. The husband took their son to another state for six weeks without her knowledge. Although he did not "kidnap" the child in a legal sense because he did not violate any judicial custody order, the court found that the allegation was substantially true because of the nontechnical way that "kidnap" is used in child custody cases. Similarly, in *White*, the court held that an accusation of theft against company employees was substantially accurate because an employee's friend took a watch after the employee allowed the friend on the defendant's premises.

Unlike the statements in *Willow* and *White,* the statement about Fremont in the fliers is not substantially accurate. An accusation that someone has a record of criminal convictions is generally understood as significantly different from an accusation that someone has a record of housing violations. Even though the violations were corrected only after a threatened court order, Fremont was not convicted or even charged with one criminal offense, and he certainly does not have "a long record of criminal convictions," as the fliers asserted. The fliers are false.

ANSWER B: The fliers are false because Fremont has no record of criminal convictions. "A statement is false if the gist, the sting, of the matter is false." *White v. Ball.* The fliers accused Fremont of having a "long record of criminal convictions as a landlord." In fact, he has no criminal convictions at all. This case is different from cases in which the court held that statements were substantially accurate. *Willow v. Orr; White v. Ball.*

In *Willow*, an ex-wife's allegation that her husband had "kidnapped" her child was held to be substantially accurate. Although he did not "kidnap" the son in a legal sense because he did not violate any judicial custody order, the court found that the allegation was substantially true because of the nontechnical way that "kidnap" is used in child custody cases. Similarly, in *White*, the court held that an accusation of theft against company employees was substantially accurate.

These cases are different from Dooley's case because the statement in the fliers is not substantially accurate. Although only technical differences exist between the public and legal understanding of kidnapping, substantial differences exist between criminal convictions and notices of housing violations.

Even though the violations were corrected only after a threatened court order, Fremont was not convicted or even charged with one criminal offense, and he certainly does not have "a long record of criminal convictions," as the fliers asserted. Nor is this a case like *White*.

ANSWER C: The other issue is whether the fliers are false. "A statement is false if the gist, the sting, of the matter is false." *White v. Ball.* The fliers accused Fremont of having a "long record of criminal convictions as a landlord." In fact, he has no criminal convictions at all.

Dooley could argue that the "gist" of the statement is accurate because Fremont received three notices of violation from the local housing commission for inadequate lighting and locks, and corrected them only after the commission threatened to seek a court order. He may say that he used the term "criminal" only as a way of expressing the seriousness of the violations. That argument is likely to be unpersuasive.

This case is different from *Willow v. Orr.* In *Willow*, an ex-wife's allegation that her husband had "kidnapped" her child was held to be substantially accurate. Although the husband did not "kidnap" the son in a legal sense because he did not violate any judicial custody order, the court found that the accusation was substantially true because of the nontechnical way that "kidnap" is used in child custody cases.

Although only technical differences exist between the public and legal understanding of kidnapping, substantial differences exist between criminal convictions and notices of housing violations. Even though the violations were corrected only after a threatened court order, Fremont was not convicted or even charged with one criminal offense, and he certainly does not have "a long record of criminal convictions," as the fliers asserted.

This case is also different from *White v. Ball.* In *White*, the court held that an accusation of theft against company employees was substantially accurate because an employee's friend took a watch after the employee allowed the friend on the defendant's premises. Again, a substantial difference exists between violations of the housing code and "a long record of criminal convictions as a landlord." The gist of the matter is that Fremont has no criminal convictions.

Answer A is best. It states a conclusion at the outset, describes the law on which the conclusion is based, and then shows how the law applies to Dooley's factual situation. There are no analogous cases, however, to support the conclusion. The writer concludes that the fliers are false, but both of the cases described involve factual situations in which the court held the statements to be true. Answer A thus uses the rule in *White v. Ball* and shows how the rule applies. Answer A then sets out the facts and holdings of both cases and distinguishes them. The cases are used together, or synthesized, because they have similar facts and the same holding.

Answer B is difficult to read and understand. The paragraph structure is choppy and hard to follow. For example, the last sentence in the first paragraph should be the first sentence of the second paragraph. Answer B also does a poor job of describing the facts of *White v. Ball.* The description of the holding in that case does not provide a full understanding of what happened. Nor does the bare statement that *White* is distinguishable explain why.

Answer C begins without giving the writer's conclusion. Readers of legal documents are confused and frustrated by such introductions. The writer adds to the reader's confusion by describing *Willow* and distinguishing it, and then describing and distinguishing *White*. Notice the repetition in the last two paragraphs of Answer C. When cases are this similar, discussing one at a time makes the discussion choppy and repetitious, and also gives the reader an incomplete understanding of the law. Discussing several similar cases together furthers the reader's understanding of the law. Similarly, distinguishing a group of cases together is better than distinguishing one at a time, particularly when the reasons for distinguishing them are the same.

What changes would you make if you combined the discussion of both sub-issues?

This chapter has shown how you might draft the discussion of both sub-issues in the libel problem. You should have noticed differences in the analysis of the two sub-issues. When drafting the discussion for other problems, you may notice additional differences. When you do, follow the steps outlined in this chapter and keep in mind their underlying purposes.

The following exercises should help you learn to use these steps.

Exercise 13-A

Ralph Watson, a hockey fan, hired Claude Deemer to work temporarily at Watson's grocery store. Deemer had just been suspended from his semiprofessional hockey team for unsportsmanlike conduct and violence. While working at the store, Deemer assaulted a customer named Allen Worthington. Worthington's family wants to know whether he can recover against Watson for his injuries. Which of the following discussions is best? Why?

ANSWER A: Watson is liable for hiring Deemer. In *Tyus v. Booth*, the court held that the plaintiff may recover only after showing that the employer knew or should have known that the employee had a propensity toward violence. In that case, the employee worked at a service station and assaulted a customer. The victim sued the employer, claiming that the employer was negligent in not finding out beforehand that the employee had previously been convicted of assault. The court held that the employer had no duty to learn of the employee's criminal record when the employer had not seen the employee behave in a manner indicating a propensity toward violence.

Tyus is different from our case because Watson knew that Deemer had a propensity toward violence. As an avid fan and season ticket holder of the hockey league in which Deemer played, Watson knew that Deemer had been suspended for twenty-one days for unsportsmanlike conduct and fighting. Watson knew that this suspension occurred in a league that is plagued with violence and unsportsmanlike conduct. Watson also knew that hockey, by itself, is a violent sport that attracts dangerous and frightening people like Deemer.

Watson may argue that violent hockey playing does not indicate a propensity toward violence off the hockey rink. The unusually violent nature of this particular hockey league, and the reason for Deemer's suspension, suggest that Watson likely will be unpersuasive. Hockey is not, after all, the Bolshoi ballet.

In *Hersh v. Kentfield Builders, Inc.*, the court held that an employer was not liable for an employee's assault on a salesman when the employer did not know the violent nature of the employee's criminal record and had not seen the employee behave in a manner indicating a propensity toward violence. Although the employer probably knew that the employee had a criminal record, he did not know that the employee had been convicted of manslaughter and carrying a concealed weapon. The court stated that the employer had no duty to investigate the employee's criminal record in the absence of evidence of the employee's propensity toward violence.

Hersh is different from our case because, again, Watson knew that Deemer had a propensity toward violence. Watson held season tickets to the hockey league in which Deemer played. He was there the night Deemer was suspended for twenty-one days for unsportsmanlike conduct and fighting. He knew that the league had a reputation for violence and unsportsmanlike conduct. As described above, Watson will not be able to argue successfully that violent hockey playing does not indicate a propensity toward violence off the hockey rink.

Knowing that Deemer was violent, Watson hired him to work in a public place. Deemer assaulted a customer in that public place—the produce department of Watson's store—as Deemer was cleaning vegetable trays. In fact, much of Deemer's work involved contact with customers. Watson should have expected that someone like Deemer would eventually have a violent altercation with a customer. The fact that Deemer's assault was provoked by three teenage boys shows Watson's negligence, because only an employee who is prone to violence would have reacted by chasing and beating one of the boys.

This case is thus different from *Hersh*, because the employer in that case did the right thing. He had the employee work in a location that was not usually open to the public. This employee, whom the employer probably knew to have a criminal record and to have been belligerent at times, was required to clean out model homes not open to the public. After the employee injured a salesman with a knife, the employer was held not liable for negligence in hiring this employee. Deemer, however, worked in a public place. It is reasonable to expect that customers in a grocery store will frequent the produce department, will come into contact with the employer's maintenance workers, and will sometimes be obnoxious. Every business owner knows that some customers will be obnoxious. Watson is liable for hiring Deemer.

ANSWER B: Watson is most likely responsible for Deemer's assault on a customer because he hired Deemer, knowing of his violent hockey playing, and then placed him in a position involving public contact. An employer is liable for the intentional torts of an employee committed on a customer at the workplace if (1) the employer knew or should have known beforehand of the employee's propensity toward violence and

(2) the employer had the employee work in a place open to the public. *Tyus v. Booth*; *Hersh v. Kentfield Builders, Inc.*

Watson satisfies the "propensity toward violence" requirement because he knew of Deemer's violent hockey playing before hiring him. In both *Tyus* and *Hersh*, the courts held that an employer was not liable for an employee's assault on a person at the workplace because the employer had no knowledge, and no reason to know, of the employee's prior conviction for a violent crime. In both cases, the employer had not seen the employee behave in a manner that suggested a propensity toward violence. In this case, however, Watson actually knew of Deemer's propensity toward violence. As an avid fan and season ticket holder of the hockey league in which Deemer played, he knew that Deemer had been suspended for twenty-one days for unsportsmanlike conduct and fighting. Watson also knew that this suspension occurred in a league that has a lot of violence and unsportsmanlike conduct.

Watson may argue that violent hockey playing does not indicate a propensity toward violence off the hockey rink. The unusually violent nature of this particular hockey league, and the reason for Deemer's suspension, suggest that Watson likely will be unpersuasive.

Deemer's lack of a criminal record does not change this conclusion. In *Tyus* and *Hersh*, the courts held that employers were not liable for the assaults committed by their employees in part because they had not seen evidence of violent behavior beforehand. Because the employers were unaware of their employees' violent criminal records, these records were irrelevant. Deemer's actual behavior before the assault—not the presence or absence of a criminal record—demonstrates Watson's negligence in hiring him.

Watson satisfies the "public place" requirement because he hired Deemer to work in areas open to the public. This case is analogous to *Tyus*, in which the employee worked in a service station and assaulted a customer, because Deemer's work also involved public contact. Deemer assaulted a customer in a public place—the produce department of Watson's grocery store—as Deemer was cleaning vegetable trays. The presence of three teenage boys in the produce department supports this conclusion.

Watson may argue that Deemer did not have regular customer contact in the same way as the employee in *Tyus*. Because Deemer did have some customer contact, however, this argument is not likely to prevail. This case is distinguishable from *Hersh*, in which the court held an employer not negligent for an employee's assault on a salesman because the employee worked in an area not usually open to the public. Unlike the employee in *Hersh*, Deemer was working in a public place—in the produce department of a grocery store, where public contact could reasonably have been expected—when the assault occurred. Although the assault was provoked by three obnoxious teenage boys, it occurred in a place open to the public. Watson likely will be held liable for Deemer's assault on Worthington.

ANSWER C: Watson most likely is responsible for Deemer's assault on a customer because he hired Deemer, knowing of his violent hockey playing, and then placed him in a position involving public contact. An employer is liable for the intentional torts of an employee committed on a customer at the workplace if (1) the employee has a propensity toward violence, (2) the employer knows or should know of that propensity, and (3) the employer had the employee work in a place open to the public. *Tyus v. Booth*; *Hersh v. Kentfield Builders, Inc.*

Deemer satisfies the "propensity toward violence" requirement because of his violent hockey playing. In *Tyus* and *Hersh*, a customer and a salesman each were assaulted by employees who previously had been convicted of violent crimes. The courts recognized that such crimes were evidence of a propensity toward violence. Similarly, Deemer's manner of playing hockey is evidence of his propensity toward violence. Deemer was suspended from his hockey team for twenty-one days for unsportsmanlike conduct and fighting. In addition, his hockey league is plagued with violence and unsportsmanlike conduct. The unusually violent nature of this particular hockey league, and the reason for Deemer's suspension, suggest that Deemer's propensity toward violence is not limited to the game of hockey.

Watson satisfies the "knowledge" requirement because he knew of Deemer's propensity toward violence when he hired Deemer. In both *Tyus* and *Hersh*, the court held that an employer was not liable for an employee's assault on a person at the workplace because the employer had no knowledge, and no reason to know, of the employee's prior conviction for a violent crime. In both cases, the employer had not seen the employee behave in a manner that suggested a propensity toward violence. In this case, however, Watson actually knew of Deemer's propensity toward violence because Watson, an avid fan and season ticket holder of the hockey league in which Deemer played, watched the game in which Deemer was suspended.

Even if Watson did not actually know of Deemer's propensity toward violence, he *should* have known of that propensity. His familiarity with Deemer, the team, and the league gives him constructive knowledge.

Deemer's lack of a criminal record does not change the conclusion that Watson had actual or constructive knowledge of Deemer's propensity toward violence. In *Tyus* and *Hersh*, the courts held that employers were not liable for the assaults committed by their employees in part because the employers had not seen evidence of violent behavior beforehand. Because the employers were unaware of their employees' violent criminal records, these records were irrelevant. Deemer's actual behavior before the assault—not the presence or absence of a criminal record—demonstrates Watson's negligence in hiring him.

Watson satisfies the "public place" requirement because he hired Deemer to work in areas open to the public. This case is analogous to *Tyus*, in which the employee worked in a service station and assaulted a customer, because Deemer also had public contact. Deemer assaulted a customer in a public place—the produce department of Watson's grocery store—as Deemer was cleaning vegetable trays. The presence of three teenage boys in the produce department supports this conclusion. Although Deemer probably did not have customer contact to the same extent as the employee in *Tyus*, customer contact was an inevitable part of his job.

This case is distinguishable from *Hersh*, in which the court held the employer not negligent for his employee's assault on a salesman because the employee worked in an area not usually open to the public. Unlike the employee in *Hersh*, Deemer was

working in a public place when the assault occurred. Although the assault was provoked by three obnoxious teenage boys, it occurred in a place open to the public.
Watson will likely be held liable for Deemer's assault on Worthington.

Exercise 13-B

1.   Draft the discussion for an office memorandum based on the facts and materials
      in Exercise 6-B, pp. 78–80.

2.   Draft the discussion for an office memorandum based on the facts and materials
      in Exercise 6-C, pp. 80–82.

Exercise 13-C

1.   Draft the discussion for an office memorandum based on the problem contained
      in the text of Chapter 7 and Exercise 7-A, pp. 85–93.

2.   Draft the discussion for an office memorandum based on the facts and materials
      in Exercise 7-D, pp. 94–95.

3.   Draft the discussion for an office memorandum based on the facts and materials
      in Exercise 7-E, pp. 95–97.

14

Revising and Editing

ALMOST EVERYTHING you need to know about writing can be summarized in one principle: Write to communicate. You will impress the reader more with good organization, thoughtful analysis, and clear writing than with rhetorical flourishes, knowledge of Latin, or extensive vocabulary. Anything you write that interferes with the reader's ability to understand—no matter how good it sounds—is wrong.

Although there is little about the law that cannot be explained to a lay person, most nonlawyers are mystified by legal writing. They believe—too often with good reason—that legal writing is a careful blend of the pompous and the dull, consisting of lengthy sentences, unintelligible phrases, and plenty of legal jargon. This style of writing results from misplaced professional pride, professional insecurity, sloppy thinking, the desire to impress clients, habit, and blind repetition of previous bad legal writing. Legal writing, however, does not have to be this way. The law is a literary profession; legal writing should and often does approach the level of good literature. Many judicial opinions, for example, are remembered not only for their ideas but also for the way in which they are expressed.

Revising and editing are essential to both the substance and appearance of your writing. By revising and editing, you can improve the substance of your analysis as well as the style of your writing by clarifying points and including analytical steps you had previously ignored. You can also improve your credibility. Lawyers who see revising and editing as fluff hurt themselves and their clients.

1. Be direct and precise.

As stated in Chapter 13 (Drafting the Discussion), letting your writing rest before editing allows you to take a fresh look at it. To make sure that your writing is as direct and precise as possible, review your draft paragraph by paragraph, word by word. In writing and editing, you should find that your thinking—and consequently your memo or brief—becomes increasingly clear and focused.

Lack of focus is the primary reason that so much legal writing is imprecise. If you are unclear about what you want to say, obviously you cannot say it clearly and precisely. Think some more about the exact idea you want to convey and then consider the most direct way to express that idea. If you cannot find the right words, perhaps it is because your concept of what you want to say is still fuzzy. There is an interplay between thoughts and words. On the one hand, clear thinking can help you find the right words to express your idea. On the other hand, the right words can help clarify your thinking.

Assume, for example, that your client's wells have been contaminated by a nearby impoundment containing liquid industrial waste. In *Branch v. Western Petroleum, Inc.*, the highest court of your state held that a company which disposed of toxic industrial waste on its property in close proximity to the plaintiff's wells was strictly liable for the contamination of these wells. You have written the following sentence in a draft:

> When addressing this issue, the supreme court's decision in *Branch v. Western Petroleum, Inc.* must be strongly considered.

The most basic question in editing your own writing is: What do I mean? If the sentence you have written does not clearly answer that question, revise it so that it does. Then review it again. Precise writing results from continual self-criticism as you go through your draft sentence by sentence. Early drafts often include vague expressions of imperfectly formed ideas. You have not made a mistake by including such language in a draft—that's what drafts are for—but you will make a mistake if you don't recognize and correct the problem.

The sentence in question indicates that there is binding precedent in your state on this issue, but is it dispositive? The phrase "must be strongly considered" doesn't answer this question. Suppose you decide that it is dispositive. The revised sentence might look like this:

> The supreme court's decision in *Branch v. Western Petroleum, Inc.* will likely govern the outcome of this case.

This sentence is more definite, but the thought is still incompletely expressed. Another important question in revising your writing is: Have I completed the thought? The sentence says that the *Branch* decision will likely govern the outcome, but it doesn't say why. The third draft completes the thought and forms a transition to the supporting sentence that follows:

> The supreme court's decision in *Branch v. Western Petroleum, Inc.* will likely govern the outcome of this case because the facts are virtually identical. In both cases, disposal of toxic waste contaminated wells on adjacent property.

Some writers are reluctant to take a clear position, fearing they may be wrong, and so resort to the kind of vague language that the first draft of this sentence illustrates—the supreme court's decision "must be strongly considered." This timidity defeats the whole purpose of a legal memo or brief. Remember that you have analyzed the problem, whereas your reader has not, and that your job as a writer is to express your analysis as precisely as you can.

2. Blend precision with simplicity.

As you strive for precision, be careful to state your ideas as simply as possible. Avoid jargon, legalese (said defendant, to-wit, heretofore), and Latin phrases, as well as long words, sentences, and paragraphs. Persons untrained in the law should be able to read and understand your writing.

Two equally precise statements of the same idea may vary considerably; one may be understandable to the reader, the other may be confusing. You should make the reader's job as easy as possible by stating your point as simply as the material allows.

◻ Consider these descriptions of a city ordinance:

ANSWER A: The ordinance forbids, *inter alia,* inhalation and exhalation of the fumes of a lighted *cannabis sativa* instrument.

ANSWER B: Among other things, the ordinance forbids marijuana smoking.

Answer B is better because it is simple and precise. Answer A has far more words, but it probably conveys less information to the average reader. The Latin name for marijuana may make the writer seem learned, but this impression is of no value if the reader does not know what is being said. Similarly, the wordy phrase that describes smoking in Answer A, while technically correct, does not convey anything more than the word "smoking." In addition, Answer A is less precise than Answer B because a "lighted *cannabis sativa* instrument" could arguably exclude a pipe used for smoking marijuana. Answer A is also obscured by legal jargon. The Latin phrase for "among other things," *inter alia,* is one of many you will encounter in the law; substitute an English translation whenever possible.

3. Use verbs whenever possible to make your writing forceful.

A. Prefer the active voice. Active voice—where the verb in a sentence states an action performed by the subject, rather than upon it, as in the passive voice—makes your writing clear and forceful. Active voice is immediate and direct, leaves no ambiguity about who is doing what, and often requires fewer words. Passive voice, by contrast, is detached and often ambiguous. Writers who use passive voice must either omit the actor or append it to the sentence with a prepositional phrase.

☐ Consider these statements:

ANSWER A: The department shall disclose all relevant information to the requesting party.

ANSWER B: All relevant information shall be disclosed to the requesting party.

Answer A is clearer and more forceful than Answer B because the verb (shall disclose) states an action to be performed by the subject (department). Answer A, unlike Answer B, states who will disclose the information. If Answer B is changed to read "All relevant information shall be disclosed to the requesting party by the department," it is still less forceful than Answer A and slightly longer. Although passive voice may be useful if you want to emphasize the object being acted upon or omit any reference to the actor, you should use it only for good reason.

B. Avoid excessive nominalizing. To nominalize is to express the key action with a noun instead of a verb. Nouns are static; they only state what is. Verbs are dynamic because they state what happened. Therefore, using a verb (e.g., operate) instead of the noun form of that verb (e.g., perform an operation) makes your writing more dynamic.

☐ Compare these two sentences:

Answer A: Disruption of the school board meeting by a group of angry parents resulted in a reconsideration of the board's plan to close three high schools.

Answer B: A group of angry parents disrupted the school board meeting and forced the board to reconsider its plan to close three high schools.

Answer B is better because it uses verbs or verb forms—"disrupted" and "forced . . . to reconsider"—to describe the main ideas, whereas Answer A uses nouns—"disruption" and "reconsideration." Note the weak phrase "resulted in" in Answer A. Such verbs often signal that a nominalization will follow: resulted in a modification of (modified), resulted in a solution to (solved), resulted in a settlement of (settled).

Below are a few phrases that lawyers commonly use and the verbs that should replace them:

bring about a resolution	resolve
make a determination	determine
make an assumption	assume
make a proposition or proposal	propose
take under consideration	consider
state by implication	imply
reach an agreement	agree

Lawyers use other nominalizations as well. You should avoid them and use action verbs whenever possible.

4. Be concise.

One of Professor Strunk's favorite maxims, according to E. B. White, was "Omit needless words." Strunk wrote, "This requires not that the writer make all his sentences short, or that he avoid all detail and treat his subjects only in outline, but that every word tell."[1] Every part of your memo, every word in every sentence, should be there for a reason. If not, delete it; excess language clouds your thinking and the reader's understanding. Needless words result from repetition, fuzzy thinking, use of a long phrase when a short phrase or single word will do, and poorly structured clauses, among other things.

 A. Avoid wordy phrases. Some phrases are inherently wordy and should be replaced with a single word.

Compare these two statements:

ANSWER A: Due to the fact that the defendant had a history of driving while drunk, the judge imposed the maximum penalty.

ANSWER B: Because the defendant had a history of drunk driving, the judge imposed the maximum penalty.

Answer B substitutes one word, "because," for the phrase "due to the fact that," resulting in a shorter, more direct sentence. Answer B also substitutes "drunk driving" for "driving while drunk." Here are some other wordy phrases and suggested substitutes:

despite the fact that	although
in accordance with	under
subsequent to	after

---

[1] WILLIAM STRUNK JR. & E. B. WHITE, THE ELEMENTS OF STYLE 23 (3d ed. 1979).

at such time as	when
until such time as	when
at the present time	now
in regard to	about
in relation to	about
due to the fact that	because

B. Avoid tautological phrases. Certain phrases are often used when a single word would suffice, simply because we are accustomed to using them. Legal writers, especially, are loyal to traditional phrases. For example, "cease" is almost always followed by "desist," and "aid" by "abet." Many of these word pairings were originally formed in early England by combining the same words from different languages (Anglo-Saxon, Norman, Latin) because lawyers then had a choice of languages or needed more than one word to communicate clearly. This is obviously no longer necessary, yet many legal writers continue to use traditional phrases such as "null and void," "devise and bequeath," "fraud and deceit," and "false and untrue." Scrutinize word pairings to determine whether both parts are necessary or, if not, which of the two more clearly expresses your meaning.

Some other tautological phrases are:

unexpected surprise	basic fundamentals
next subsequent	false misrepresentation
continue to remain	true facts
consensus of opinion	sufficient enough
positive benefits	actual fact
it is possible that he may	final result

C. Avoid unnecessary modifiers. Unnecessary modifiers divert the reader's attention from the words they modify and make your writing less forceful.

☐ Compare these two sentences:

ANSWER A: A well-drafted complaint basically should set out the facts clearly establishing that the plaintiff is entitled to the relief sought.

ANSWER B: A well-drafted complaint should set out the facts establishing that the plaintiff is entitled to the relief sought.

The two sentences are identical except for the modifiers "basically" and "clearly." These words are distracting and are not necessary to explain what a well-drafted complaint should do. It is not incorrect to use such adverbs as modifiers, but you should ask yourself whether each one is necessary or contributes anything to your meaning. Some commonly overused modifiers are: basically, very, extremely, truly, clearly, completely, generally, virtually, obviously, and surely.

D. Scrutinize sentences beginning with "there" or "it." The following sentences are normal in English syntax:

> It is raining.
> There is no room for doubt.

But do not start a sentence with "it" or "there" if it would lengthen the sentence unnecessarily or impede the reader's understanding.

 Compare these two sentences:

ANSWER A: There was a large bush overhanging the intersection, and it was this obstruction that blocked the driver's view of oncoming traffic.

ANSWER B: A large bush overhanging the intersection blocked the driver's view of oncoming traffic.

"There was" and "it was" in Answer A add nothing except length and impede the reader's understanding of the main ideas. Answer B is shorter and more direct.

Sentences that begin with "it" or "there" are often doubly repetitive. They tend to include phrases such as "the type of," "the case that," "in the nature of," and "of the sort," which add nothing to a sentence except length.

 Consider the following:

ANSWER A: The courts rarely grant summary judgment.

ANSWER B: It is rarely the case that the courts grant summary judgment.

Answer A is shorter and more concise than Answer B. Using extraneous words requires your reader to work harder to understand your point. Streamline your writing by including only what is necessary.

5. Eliminate unnecessary information and repetition.

A. Avoid redundancies. A word, phrase, or concept may be repeated to provide a transition from one thought to another. Repeating a word, phrase, or concept may lead the reader smoothly to the next point. Repetition should be purposeful, however, and not merely redundant.

☐   Compare the following:

ANSWER A: The primary problem with rejecting improperly filed documents is the injustice of being unfair to the client, who had no control over how the case was handled.

ANSWER B: The primary problem with rejecting improperly filed documents is unfairness to the client, who had no control over how the case was handled.

Answer A is repetitive because it states that the problem is the "injustice of being unfair." Answer B is better because it simply uses "unfairness."

B. Avoid extraneous facts. Including unnecessary information makes your writing less concise and more difficult to understand. Think carefully about the point you wish to make; omit any definitions, details, or commentary the reader does not need to understand your point.

☐   Consider the following two discussions:

ANSWER A: This jurisdiction has previously recognized the rescue doctrine to assure the rescuer that any slight negligence on his part would not bar recovery for his damages. In *Garber v. Radic*, the plaintiff sued both the railroad and the negligent driver for injuries the plaintiff sustained trying to save a victim trapped in a car stalled on railroad tracks. At trial, the jury found that the railroad had not been negligent and that the plaintiff had been contributorily negligent, thus barring his recovery. The plaintiff appealed and the appellate court reversed, adopting the rescue doctrine in order to encourage rescuers to extend aid to those in peril.

ANSWER B: This jurisdiction has previously recognized the rescue doctrine to assure the rescuer that any slight negligence on his part would not bar recovery for his damages. In *Garber v. Radic*, the plaintiff sued a negligent driver for injuries he sustained while trying to save a victim trapped in a car. The appellate court allowed the negligent plaintiff to recover and adopted the rescue doctrine to encourage rescuers to extend aid to those in peril.

Answer B is better because it says only what needs to be said. Answer A burdens the reader with unnecessary information about the railroad and the location of the stalled car. It also includes unnecessary procedural information. As you edit, focus on what the reader needs to know to understand your point.

6. Edit intrusive or misplaced words and phrases.

A reader expects the verb to follow the subject in most sentences. Do not make the reader wait for important information by inserting a phrase or clause between the subject and the verb. This delay is irritating and possibly confusing enough to require a second or third reading of the sentence.

▢ Compare the following:

ANSWER A: No document, that is, no contract, invoice, receipt, bill of lading, or other similar item regarding the transaction between the parties, specified the date of delivery.

ANSWER B: No document specified the date of delivery. The date was not in any contracts, invoices, receipts, bills of lading, or other similar items regarding the transaction between the parties.

Answer A separates the subject (document) from the verb (specified) with the long phrase defining "document." This long interruption delays the reader's understanding of what is significant about these documents. Answer B is better because it does not burden the main sentence with the definition of "documents." Instead, it tells the reader the important information first, then follows with the qualifying definition.

Modifying words and phrases should generally be as close as possible to the word or phrase they modify. The more words that come between these elements, the greater the risk that the sentence will not say what you intend. Confusion can also result when a word or phrase may modify more than one other element in a sentence. Consider the following:

The officer served the warrant for illegal dumping at the defendant's place of business.

It is impossible to determine whether the illegal dumping occurred at the defendant's place of business, or whether the warrant for this offense was merely served on the defendant at his place of business. The sentence could be rewritten to convey either meaning:

The officer served the defendant with a warrant charging him with illegal dumping at his place of business.

At the defendant's place of business, the officer served the defendant with a warrant for illegal dumping.

7. Use correct grammar, punctuation, and spelling.

Errors in grammar, punctuation, and spelling suggest that the writer is sloppy and careless—qualities that people do not want in a lawyer. Minor errors distract the reader from the message to be conveyed. Major errors may distort the message or make it unintelligible. In either case, the communication between writer and reader is interrupted.

Always proofread your sentences to make sure they are technically correct, even if you begin by using spell-checking programs on your computer or word processor. These programs will not catch incorrectly used, but correctly spelled, words such as "to" for "too" or "he" for "the." These programs will also not flag omitted words or catch legal terms whose spelling is peculiar to the law.

Any lawyer's bookshelf should include at least one good reference book on grammar and another on style. Appendix G lists selected books that address these topics.

Exercise 14-A

Edit the following for wordiness and imprecision:

1. Canon 9 requires a lawyer to avoid even the appearance of impropriety. Despite the fact that this requirement has led several courts to disqualify attorneys even though no actual impropriety existed, clearly the appearance of impropriety is not always sufficient. For example, in *Blumenfeld v. Fusco*, the court held that the fact of the marriage of two attorneys employed by different firms did not create an appearance of impropriety sufficient to warrant disqualification of the wife in a case in which the propounder had been represented by the wife's firm at some point in the past. The case involved a challenge to a will, in which an associate in the firm representing the propounder was married to a partner in the firm retained to represent the *caveator* in the trial *de novo* following the trial in probate court. It was the court's finding that no actual impropriety existed since the husband worked in the real estate department and had no contact with the attorneys who were actually representing the *caveator*. In reversing the trial court's disqualification of the wife, the appellate court balanced the need to avoid the appearance of impropriety with the plaintiff's right to employ the counsel of his choice. In *Blumenfeld v. Fusco*, considerations relevant to the latter outweighed the former, given the improbability that any impropriety had actually occurred.

2. It is interesting to note that no court which has addressed the question of recognizing fraud in the context of an adoption has refused to do so where there was some kind of evidence of active concealment. For example, in *In re Baby J.*, the court found fraudulent concealment of the truth where the adoption agency told the parents that the birth mother was an eighteen-year-old unwed mother who could not care for the baby. The truth in this case, which the agency was clearly aware of, was that the mother was a thirty-five-year-old patient in a mental institution and the father was presumed to be another patient. The truth was discovered only by the adoptive parents after their thirteen-year-old adopted son was diagnosed as having an inherited mental disorder. Similarly, in *Roe*, the court awarded damages due to the fact that the adoption agency placed three school-aged children for adoption, telling the prospective parents that the children were normal, healthy children. The agency clearly knew that this was not

the truth because it had test results and psychological evaluations showing that the children had a history of dangerously violent behavior and other behavior disorders. In both cases the court placed its emphasis on the agencies' actual knowledge and active concealment of the truth.

Exercise 14-B

Edit or rewrite the sentences below as needed:

1. Due to the fact that medical malpractice lawsuits are of the type that can be lengthy and expensive, plaintiffs and their attorneys should carefully weigh the chances of a successful outcome before proceeding to file a complaint.

2. The defendant's reprehensible conduct clearly falls in the category of fraud and deceit and should be punished to the fullest extent of the law by the maximum fine allowed under the statute.

3. Being immaterial, irrelevant, and a product of hearsay, the attorney strenuously objected to the witness' testimony.

4. A view generally held by most jurisdictions is that the "fireman's rule" acts as a bar to any recovery by emergency personnel for certain injuries suffered as a result of the peril such personnel have been summoned to handle.

5. Because the deadline for answering had passed, the attorney filed a motion correctly attempting to open the default.

6. The plaintiff's allegation was that the warning given by the manufacturer in relation to the hazardous nature of the product was not sufficient enough to inform the public about the dangers involved.

7. It was the discrepancy in the testimony of the defendant that persuaded the jury of her guilt as to all the charges.

8. It was essentially the plaintiff's contention that basic, fundamental fairness required he be given another chance to prove his case, in view of the unethical nature of the conduct on the part of the defendant's attorney.

9. Until such time as the witness makes the decision to disclose the information required by the court, he will be held in contempt of court.

10. In weighing the benefits of a recreational camp versus possible injury to the lake, it cannot be concluded that the former will compensate for the latter.

Part D

THE
OFFICE MEMORANDUM

15

Elements of an
Office Memorandum

A LAWYER'S MOST important job is advising a client how to approach a particular situation in light of the relevant law. Sound legal advice may permit a client to benefit from some situations and avoid exposure to liability in others. When a client seeks advice too late, proper counseling can minimize the damage. Even if litigation occurs—for whatever reason—good legal advice can help bring about a fruitful conclusion. For every case that goes to court, however, there are dozens of others that were never litigated, and did not have to be, because someone followed a lawyer's advice.

Legal advice to a client is often based on a formal memorandum of law, which is a basic document of legal writing. It is usually written by a clerk or junior attorney for a more experienced attorney to predict what effect application of the relevant law will have on the client's situation. Senior attorneys use memoranda to determine what advice to give a client. Three fundamental principles should guide you in researching, drafting, and writing an office memorandum:

Be objective. The hallmark of a memo is objectivity. Scrupulously examine your own arguments as well as those you anticipate from your opponent. Only then can you honestly assess the strengths and weaknesses of your client's case. Above all else, you must be honest about what the law permits and what it does not; you cannot afford to mislead the senior attorney or your client with wishful thinking or advocacy.

Be thorough. Office memos form the basis for major decisions people make. Consequently, you should make every effort to ensure that these decisions can be made on the basis of sound analysis. You can do this only if your knowledge of the relevant law is solid and your thinking is clear.

Communicate. The memo must be organized and written so that your thoughts are clearly presented and precisely stated. All of your effort is for nothing unless the reader understands what you are saying. People do not usually read legal writing for fun, so make the reader's job as easy as you can. Remember, too, that your reader may not be familiar with the relevant law.

The memorandum is composed of several distinct but related sections. Label each section (except the heading) by underlining or capitalizing its name on a separate line immediately preceding that section. Although there are many variations, the following format for preparing a legal memorandum is widely used. Appendixes A and D are sample memoranda using this format, which you should read in conjunction with this chapter.

1. Heading

The Heading is the part of the memorandum that tells who wrote it, to whom it is written, what it is about, and the date. It should look like this:

MEMORANDUM

To:	Cheryl Scott
From:	Eli Blackburn
Re:	Possible abuse of discretion by trial judge in enjoining landfill operation, Department of Environmental Resources v. Fredericks, file no. 93-104
Date:	October 3, 1993

The explanation of the subject not only identifies the client and the file number but also briefly describes the general legal question. This description helps separate the memo from other memos in the same file and also provides a means of locating the memo later if a similar issue arises concerning different parties.

2. Questions Presented

This section should contain balanced and understandable statements of the legal questions you will answer in the memo. When there is more than one question, indicate each by a symbol (for example, "I," "II," or "A," "B"). Each Question must describe the relevant legal rule and summarize the legally significant facts. How to formulate these questions is discussed in Chapter 18 (Questions Presented).

3. Brief Answer (optional)

This section provides a short answer to each of the questions presented in the previous section. The Brief Answer is a conclusion and a brief explanation of the reasons for that conclusion. It is useful because it provides immediate answers to the questions. This section is optional because it serves essentially the same purpose as the Conclusion section of the memo, although it differs from the Conclusion in length and form.

Because the Brief Answer section immediately follows the Questions Presented section, it should begin with a direct response to each of the questions, such as "yes," "no," "probably," or "probably not." Each answer should be self-contained and should be identified by the same symbol as the question to which it pertains. The answers should not include citations to cases, regulations, or statutes except when citations are so determinative of the issue that it would be senseless to exclude them.

◼ A judge has enjoined your client, Al Fredericks, from operating a landfill on his property because it causes odors and groundwater contamination. The Question Presented in your memo is whether the judge abused her discretion in granting the injunction. Consider these Brief Answers:

ANSWER A: No. The judge's ruling was well within her reasonable discretion. Her conclusion that the damage to nearby landowners from odors and groundwater pollution outweighs the harm caused to the defendant by the injunction is amply supported by the record.

ANSWER B: Injunctive relief is proper only when the damage being enjoined outweighs the harm to the defendant caused by the injunction. A trial court's injunction can be reversed on appeal only if the judge abused her discretion. The findings of the trial judge indicate that she did not abuse her discretion.

Answer A is better because it answers the question in a single word, "no," and then succinctly explains this conclusion by applying the legal rule to the summarized facts. Answer B fails to answer the question immediately and directly. Though it gives a bare statement of the legal rules involved, it fails to explain the conclusion. Answer A directly answers the question and explains the answer. Answer B does neither.

4. Statement of Facts

The Statement of Facts is a formal and objective description of the relevant facts in the problem. It must be accurate and complete. This section of the office memo is addressed in Chapter 17 (Statement of Facts for an Office Memorandum).

5. Discussion

The Discussion is the heart of the memo and draws on lessons from many of the chapters in this book, particularly Part C (Basic Concepts of Legal Writing). The Discussion is divided into segments according to the issues and sub-issues presented by the problem. Each segment may be headed by a restatement of the Question Presented. The Discussion must also be objective. Objectivity in an office memo is addressed in Chapter 16 (The Discussion).

6. Conclusion

The Conclusion section is a somewhat longer and slightly different version of the Brief Answer. The Conclusion is longer because it contains a more thorough description of the reasoning supporting the ultimate conclusion. For each issue, it briefly describes the relevant law and explains how the law does or does not apply to the facts in this case. The theory is that a busy reader will read the Brief Answer, a reader who has a little more time will read the Conclusion section, and a reader who has enough time will read the entire memo. The Conclusion also differs from the Brief Answer in that it is not segmented by issues. As with the Brief Answer, the Conclusion section should not include citations except in rare instances.

☐   Consider these possible Conclusion sections for a memo on the landfill injunction problem:

ANSWER A: Injunctive relief is proper when the damage being enjoined outweighs the harm to the defendant caused by the injunction. The judge found that the injunction would deprive the defendant of his only source of income, but it would substantially reduce odor and groundwater contamination problems for neighboring landowners.

ANSWER B: The judge did not abuse her discretion in granting the injunction because she carefully followed the *Redding v. Stone River Flour Co.* standards for equitable relief. The judge found that an injunction would deprive the defendant of his only source of income, and that he and his wife would have severe trouble continuing to make payments for their house and car. The court also found, however, that eighteen neighboring landowners became nauseated from the site's odors and that the wells from which they pumped household water were contaminated with a variety of harmful chemicals. There is sufficient evidence to show she did not abuse her discretion.

ANSWER C: The judge did not abuse her discretion in granting an injunction because she reasonably concluded that the damage being enjoined outweighed the harm to the defendant caused by the injunction. The judge found that the injunction would deprive the defendant of his only source of income but that it would substantially reduce odors and groundwater contamination for neighboring landowners. Although her conclusion may be debated, it has ample support in the record.

All three answers cover the same ground, but Answer C is the best. Answer C states a conclusion and then summarizes the applicable law and the relevant facts to show how they justify that conclusion. The answer is brief and to the point.

Answer A, in contrast, is not an answer at all. It describes the relevant law and the facts, but it does not draw any explicit conclusion from them. Because the purpose of a memo is to predict the likely outcome of a legal dispute, Answer A is useless.

Answer B offers a conclusion but is much too long and detailed. Only essential facts belong in the Conclusion section; other facts belong in the Discussion. In addition, Answer B is deficient because of its reference to the *Redding* rule. Bare case citations communicate little because the reader likely will have no idea of the significance of a particular case. Remember, the Conclusion section must be self-contained.

The parts of the memorandum used as examples in this chapter illustrate the most fundamental rule of memorandum writing: Be objective. Because the memorandum concludes that the trial judge did not abuse her discretion by issuing the injunction, it does not tell the client what he wants to hear. This unfavorable conclusion indicates that an appeal in this case would mean a great deal of time and trouble with little likelihood of success. The lawyer should try to resolve the client's problem in some other way. Being a good lawyer means looking for every possible way to help a client and being completely honest—even when the findings are unfavorable.

16

The Discussion

THE DISCUSSION in a memorandum will be based mostly on lessons described earlier, especially in Parts B and C. This chapter identifies additional principles concerning objectivity that are important in a memorandum.

1. State your conclusion on each issue or sub-issue objectively and candidly.

Legal memos are written to predict outcomes. Clients rely on memos to make choices about their lives and businesses. Senior lawyers rely on memos to advise clients and make decisions concerning strategy or procedure. Just as your description of the law and your analysis must be scrupulously objective, so must your prediction of the outcome of the issue under consideration.

Your prediction is reflected in your conclusion. Properly stating your conclusion requires you to balance adverse interests. On one hand, you must take a position. Clients and senior attorneys do not want a set of competing considerations. They want you to tell them how the issue will likely be resolved. They want you to make a judgment, to predict the outcome. They do not want waffling statements such as "our client might prevail" or "our client has a chance of successfully defending the claim."

On the other hand, your obligation to be objective requires you to point out the weaknesses in your client's position. Accordingly, statements such as "our client will prevail" or "our client definitely will lose," while stating a position, might be misleading in their confidence. Some legal positions are sufficiently one-sided to merit such confidence. If they are, such as when you have one or a series of "givens," you should make an unequivocal statement. Often, however, your analysis will lead you to conclude that your client's chances of success are best measured in degrees of probability, rather than absolutes. Your task then is to frame your conclusion candidly to reflect these degrees of probability.

Each case is different, and the possible ways to describe your conclusion are limited only by your creativity. Strong conclusions can be expressed as "most likely," somewhat certain conclusions can be expressed as "probably," even less certain conclusions can begin with "on balance," and so forth. The point is that you must balance competing considerations in your statement.

■ You represent Herbert Pearson, the owner of a 52-foot sports fishing yacht that was transported by ship from Florida to Columbo, Sri Lanka. As the yacht was being unloaded at Columbo, the ship's crane malfunctioned, causing the yacht to fall into the water and sink. The yacht, worth $750,000, is now a total loss. Pearson wants to sue the shipowner for damages, and you have been asked to write a memo on his chances of success.

The United States Carriage of Goods by Sea Act ordinarily would limit Pearson's recoverable damages to $500. Your research has revealed, however, cases holding that the shipowner would not be entitled to limit its liability if it failed to advise Pearson properly in the bill of lading that the limitation was applicable and that the limitation could be avoided by paying a greater freight rate. The language in the bill of lading issued to Pearson is ambiguous. You nonetheless believe that the reasoning of the authorities supports Pearson's position, that a decision in Pearson's favor would be fair, and that the arguments supporting Pearson's position are significantly stronger than opposing arguments. Consider the following statements of your conclusion:

ANSWER A: Pearson will prevail in recovering full damages for loss of his yacht.

ANSWER B: Pearson may prevail in recovering full damages for loss of his yacht, but there are strong arguments to the contrary.

ANSWER C: Pearson will most likely prevail in recovering full damages for loss of his yacht.

Answer C is best because it honestly and candidly conveys the writer's views on Pearson's chances of success. It gives the writer's best judgment while letting the reader know that there is some room for doubt.

Answer A is too bold; it leads the reader to believe that there is no chance that a court will decide the case in favor of Pearson. Answer A is not objective.

Answer B gives the reader a mixed message. It says that Pearson may succeed but, then again, he may not. This is not a prediction; it is merely a statement that the case could go either way. Conclusions such as this are confusing and do not satisfy the writer's obligation to assess the client's chances of success candidly and objectively.

2. Describe the law objectively.

Although there are many legitimate ways to describe the law, you must describe it objectively. Avoid the temptation to oversimplify or slant your explanation so that it favors your client's position. Objectivity in describing the applicable law is essential to your credibility. In any subsequent litigation, your client will not want to learn for the first time that there is a case or statutory provision hostile to her position. Because memos predict likely outcomes in actual or potential legal disputes, the importance of maintaining objectivity in describing the law cannot be overemphasized.

Objectivity may differ from accuracy. It is possible to explain the supportive cases or statutory provisions accurately but fail to explain other cases or provisions that are relevant but damaging. Sometimes these omissions are stark, but they can also be subtle.

☐ The new state Recycling Act requires each municipality with more than 5,000 people to set up a recycling program. Your client, the village of Elk Crossing, is interested in obtaining a grant to finance a recycling program for its population of 700. The village seeks your opinion on whether it can obtain a grant under the Act to pay for its recycling program. The Elk Crossing recycling program is one of the oldest and most successful in the state and has been featured in several national magazines. Consider these descriptions of the Act's grant provision:

ANSWER A: Section 902 of the Recycling Act provides that "the Department of Environmental Quality shall award grants for the development and implementation of municipal recycling programs, upon application from any municipality."

ANSWER B: Section 902 of the Recycling Act provides that "the Department of Environmental Quality shall award grants for the development and implementation of municipal recycling programs, upon application from any municipality. In awarding these grants, the Department shall give priority to municipalities that are required to establish a recycling program under this Act."

Answer B is better because it contains both the good news and the bad news. The good news is that grants are available to municipalities that are not required to set up a recycling program. The bad news is that these municipalities are given a lower priority than other municipalities. A description like this gives your client a much better sense of its chances than Answer A. By stating only the good news, Answer A sets up your client to learn the bad news later—probably after a lot of wasted time and expense.

3. Explain the analysis objectively.

Objectivity in memorandum writing is important because the weaknesses of your position will come to light sooner or later, and it is better for that to happen sooner. An objective analysis is one that a reasonable attorney, reading dispassionately, would find to be an accurate and fair explanation of the strengths and weaknesses of your position. Even if your description of the law is objective, that does not necessarily mean your analysis will be objective. You must avoid putting a "spin" on your analysis to favor your client's position.

☐   Consider these analyses of the recycling grant problem:

ANSWER A: The village will be able to obtain a grant only if funds remain after the Department has awarded grants to municipalities required to establish a recycling program. Section 902 of the Recycling Act provides that "the Department of Environmental Quality shall award grants for the development and implementation of municipal recycling programs, upon application from any municipality. In awarding these grants, the Department shall give priority to municipalities that are required to establish a recycling program under this Act." The village of Elk Crossing qualifies for a grant because "any municipality" may be awarded a grant under section 902. Municipalities required to implement recycling programs are given first priority for this grant, and Elk Crossing is not one of those municipalities. Therefore, it will be able to obtain a grant only if funds remain after the other grants have been awarded.

ANSWER B: The village will be able to obtain a grant. Section 902 of the Recycling Act provides that "the Department of Environmental Quality shall award grants for the development and implementation of municipal recycling programs, upon application from any municipality. In awarding these grants, the Department shall give priority to municipalities that are required to establish a recycling program under this Act." The village of Elk Crossing qualifies for a grant because "any municipality" may be awarded a grant under section 902. The Department will ensure the availability of funds for Elk Crossing because it is required to encourage recycling under the Act. It would be absurd and inappropriate for the Department to award grants only to larger municipalities and deny a grant to a nationally prominent program with a long and successful history.

ANSWER C: The village will be able to obtain a grant only if funds remain after the Department has awarded grants to municipalities required to establish a recycling program. Section 902 of the Recycling Act provides that "the Department of Environmental Quality shall award grants for the development and implementation of municipal recycling programs, upon application from any municipality. In awarding these grants, the Department shall give priority to municipalities that are required to establish a recycling program under this Act." The village of Elk Crossing qualifies for a grant because "any municipality" may be awarded a grant under section 902. Municipalities required to implement recycling programs are given first priority for this grant, and Elk Crossing is not one of those municipalities. Therefore, it will be able to obtain a grant only if funds remain after the other grants have been awarded. The national prominence of the Elk Crossing recycling program, however, coupled with its long and successful history, may make it difficult for the Department to deny the village a grant.

Answer C is best. Answer C concludes that Elk Crossing may be able to obtain a grant if funds are available after the high-priority municipalities have received their grants. Answer C then states that the national prominence and success of the Elk Crossing program may make it difficult for the Department to deny a grant. The Department may award larger municipalities slightly smaller grants, ensuring there is enough money for Elk Crossing, for example, or it may give Elk Crossing high priority among the smaller municipalities. Answer C explains the law and the facts and then discusses the possible effect of the program's success in objective terms.

Answer B is wrong because it is not objective. First, it omits the legal analysis showing that Elk Crossing is a low-priority municipality. Second, it indulges in editorial commentary that effectively contradicts part of the statute. Answer B provides much the same basic legal analysis as Answer A but then adds several sentences to show why the grant will be awarded. Answer B states that the Act requires the Department to encourage recycling and then, using that premise, states that money will be available to smaller municipalities. The statute, however, specifically gives priority to larger municipalities. The writer is advocating when she ought to be assessing her client's chances of success.

Answer A is wrong for a different reason. Although it concludes that the Department may be able to award Elk Crossing a grant, it does not discuss factors that may affect how the Department exercises its discretion. The national prominence and success of the Elk Crossing program are surely among these factors. Simply ignoring these factors makes it seem as if Elk Crossing is just another small municipality. By being "too objective," in other words, Answer A is biased against the village.

The following exercises are intended to help you apply these principles.

Exercise 16-A

Using your answers to Exercise 9-A, pp. 117–18, draft the discussion as if you were preparing an office memorandum.

Exercise 16-B

Using your answers to Exercise 9-B, pp. 119–20, draft the discussion as if you were preparing an office memorandum.

17

Statement of Facts for a Memorandum

AN OFFICE MEMO structured according to the traditional pattern has a separate section for the Statement of Facts. This statement gives the reader a context for the legal problem at issue and shows what facts are important to its resolution.

Every legal problem involves the interplay of numerous facts, only some of which are relevant to its analysis. Whether you acquire these facts from interviews with clients or witnesses, from examination of documents, or from a senior attorney, you will invariably accumulate more facts than necessary. These facts also tend to be disorganized and scattered through different interview notes and documents. You must set aside extraneous facts and work with only those necessary to understand and resolve the legal issues. You must then present these remaining facts intelligibly, accurately, and coherently. The basic principles for selecting and appropriately stating the facts of a case are best understood in the context of a specific problem.

☐ You represent Clara Finch in a land dispute. An interview with her and a subsequent investigation have revealed the following facts, stated in the order you learned them:

In 1941, George Brauzakas purchased a forty-acre tract of land on the north side of County Highway Q, which runs east and west. Finch purchased five acres of this tract from Brauzakas in 1973 and built her home on this parcel. Finch's primary means of access to her home is by a dirt road running from the highway through William Amodio's (formerly Brauzakas's) property. Brauzakas sold the remainder of his land (thirty-five acres) to Amodio in 1975. Amodio has recently felled several large trees across the road through his property to prevent Finch from using the road. Finch's lot adjoins the Amodio property on its north side. There is no reference to Finch's use of the road in Amodio's deed to the property, and there is no recorded easement. Finch is an eighty-year-old widow living on a small pension. Finch has another access to her house by a dirt road leading from another highway, but that route takes her thirty miles and forty-five minutes out of her way. Amodio is a wealthy banker who bought the Brauzakas property on speculation that land prices would continue to increase. Amodio has stated several times that he blocked the road because he does not like Finch. Brauzakas and Finch had only an oral agreement that she could use his road as long as he owned the land.

There are two relevant appellate decisions in your state:

Carson v. Dow (1934)

[handwritten: RIGHT OF ONE OWNER TO USE ANOTHER'S LAND TO DRIVE THROUGH]

The appellant, Carl Carson, brought this action for injunctive relief against Edward Dow, claiming that he had an express easement to run a natural gas pipeline across Dow's property, and that Dow refused him access. There is no recorded easement. The trial court held that there was no express easement because of the absence of any mention of the alleged easement in Dow's deed to the property or in any other written agreement. We agree. Absent some written contractual agreement, there can be no express easement.

Watzke v. Lovett (1954)

Andrew Watzke purchased a tract of land from Peter Lovett. The tract is located on the shore of a lake and is surrounded on the remaining sides by property owned by Lovett. The only means of access to Watzke's property is by a road that crosses Lovett's property and connects to a public highway. Lovett has recently blocked the road, claiming that Watzke has no right to use it. Watzke conceded to the trial court that there is no written agreement creating an easement across Lovett's property, but argued that the court should imply an easement out of necessity. The trial court refused. We reverse.

When a parcel of land is owned by one person, and that person transfers part of that parcel to another person, access to the transferred part cannot be denied if the only means of access is through the remaining part of the original parcel. A showing of strict necessity is required before an easement will be implied. The landlocked nature of Watzke's property satisfies that requirement in this case. Watzke has an implied easement to use the road over Lovett's property.

Certain facts have special significance in light of these two cases. The following is a procedure for selecting and stating them.

1. Identify the legally significant facts.

The legally significant facts are those that will affect the legal outcome of your client's case. As explained in Chapter 3 (Case Analysis and Case Briefs), some facts of a judicial opinion are more important than others. The most important facts are those the court used to determine whether to apply particular legal rules to the case it was deciding. Writing a legal memo reverses this perspective. Instead of looking backward to determine what facts a court thought were important, you must look forward to predict what facts in your client's case a court is likely to find significant. You can determine these facts only after you have identified the relevant rules and the corresponding issues.

Isolating the legally significant facts is a process of eliminating extraneous facts until only those necessary to resolve the legal issues remain. This process allows a clearer understanding and analysis of the problem because it focuses the reader's and writer's attention exclusively on the facts that matter. Identify all significant facts, regardless of whether they help or hurt your client's position.

When the legal rules are clear and unmistakable, you will need to identify relatively few significant facts. The ambiguity or vagueness of many legal rules, however, means that the legal significance of some facts will depend on how the rule is interpreted. These borderline facts should be included if the interpretation requiring them is plausible.

Emotional facts should be included if those facts have independent legal significance or are likely to influence the outcome by appealing to a judge's sympathy and sense of justice. When the law is straightforward and applies to your problem so clearly that there is little doubt concerning the outcome, emotional facts have little or no significance and should be omitted. When the law is not straightforward or the outcome is uncertain, however, emotional facts take on greater significance. Many exceptions to general rules have been made or expanded to reach a just result in light of the facts. Nonetheless, the value of emotional facts is speculative because a court may ignore them. Because a court cannot ignore legally significant facts, such facts give the best indication of the likely outcome.

The *Carson* and *Watzke* cases indicate that Finch could raise two possible legal objections. She could claim that she has an express easement or that she has an implied easement by necessity. The *Carson* court held that an express easement must be created either in a written agreement or in the deed to the property across which the easement runs. It is thus legally significant that there is no provision in Amodio's deed permitting Finch to use the road across Amodio's property and that there is no recorded easement. These facts will make it difficult for Finch to claim an express easement, but they must nonetheless be included in the Statement of Facts.

The claim that Finch has an implied easement by necessity involves a somewhat different set of legally significant facts. The court in *Watzke* held that when the only means of access to a person's property is through the property of the person who originally transferred the land, the person seeking access is entitled to an implied easement by necessity. In Finch's case, it is legally significant that there is a road across the Amodio property which Finch uses to get to her home, that there is another route to Finch's house, and that Brauzakas sold part of his property to Finch and the remainder to Amodio.

Although the significance of many facts will be immediately apparent, the significance of others will depend on how the legal rules are interpreted. For example, the *Watzke* court indicated that an easement will be implied only out of strict necessity. As a result, the existence of the second road may work to Finch's disadvantage. It may thus be significant that Finch is eighty years old and that the other road would take her thirty miles and forty-five minutes out of her way (facts which may have appeared at first to be emotional ones) because these facts tend to show that Finch's use of Amodio's road is more of necessity than convenience. These facts should be included in a Statement of Facts because they may have a bearing on the strict-necessity rule, even though there was no other access in *Watzke*.

Finch's problem involves a number of emotionally significant facts you should exclude from analysis—particularly those that make it appear that the wealthy banker Amodio is spitefully imposing a hardship on the poor widow Finch. Although these facts might greatly influence how a judge would perceive the fairness of the situation, they have nothing to do with either of the legal rules concerning easements. Similarly, it is not significant that Amodio bought the property on speculation. Identify only the facts that are relevant to the possible application of a legal rule.

2. Identify key background facts.

Legally significant facts tell part of the story, but these facts alone may not tell the whole story. Background facts are often needed to make the factual situation understandable and to put the legally significant facts in context. Include as many background facts as the reader needs to understand the problem, but no more.

In Finch's case, for example, it probably would help the reader to state that Brauzakas's tract was forty acres, that Finch's parcel is five acres, and that Amodio's is thirty-five acres. This information provides background for the implied-easement question by clarifying Brauzakas's original ownership and subsequent division of the property. The dates on which Finch and Amodio bought their property from Brauzakas may be helpful, although the date on which Brauzakas purchased the land is not. In addition, it is useful to state that Brauzakas and Finch had an oral agreement, because this fact highlights the absence of a written agreement. The name of the highway, however, is probably not useful here. Nor is it helpful to state that Amodio blocked the access by felling several trees; the statement that he blocked the access will do.

3. Organize the facts intelligibly.

The statement of legally significant and key background facts should tell your client's story completely and coherently. The most sensible and convenient method of organization is to relate the facts in chronological order. Chronological order is easy for the reader to understand because it is the usual way a story is told; it is convenient for the writer because the facts are stated as they occurred. Although you may organize facts in a number of ways, you should never organize them according to issues, even though you separately analyze the issues in the Discussion. Such segmentation invariably results in repetitious and disjointed factual statements.

In writing a Statement of Facts for this problem, you should begin with Finch's purchase of the property from Brauzakas and their oral agreement permitting her to use the dirt road across his tract. This chronological beginning of the problem sets the stage for the events that follow. You should then state that Brauzakas sold the rest of his land to Amodio. Amodio's deed for the property contains no reference to Finch's use of the road, and there is no recorded easement. Recently, you would continue, Amodio has blocked the road to prevent Finch from using it. You should then add that Finch is eighty and that, while there is another access to her house, this alternative route takes her thirty miles and forty-five minutes out of her way. This last statement is difficult to place chronologically, but it fits here because it suggests the possible consequences of the blocked access. The reader would easily understand a statement drafted along these lines.

4. Describe the facts accurately and objectively.

Describe legally significant facts precisely, for they are crucial to the outcome. It is improper and misleading, for example, to say simply that Brauzakas and Finch had an agreement concerning her use of the dirt road, because it matters whether that agreement was oral or written. It is also improper to say simply that Finch has another access to her property, because her age and the circuitous route are relevant to the legal rule concerning implied easements by necessity. These are legally significant facts, and you must describe them precisely. You may summarize background facts, but only if you do so accurately.

Be careful to describe the facts rather than evaluate, analyze, characterize, or argue with them. It is one thing to say that Amodio blocked the road, but it is quite another to say that Amodio wrongfully blocked the road. The latter is an evaluative statement that belongs only in the Discussion or Conclusion. Similarly, it is one thing to say that the alternate route takes her thirty miles and forty-five minutes out of her way, but another to conclude that the other route is impossibly difficult for a person of her age. State the facts objectively in the Statement of Facts; you can argue and analyze in the Discussion.

☐ Consider these factual statements:

ANSWER A: Clara Finch is an eighty-year-old widow living on a meager pension. She has a house on a small tract separated from the highway by property owned by William Amodio, a wealthy banker, who bought the land from the previous owner on speculation that prices would rise. The previous owner had long permitted Finch to use the dirt road through the property, but Amodio has refused access out of dislike for Finch. Although there is another road that Finch could use, it takes her thirty miles and forty-five minutes out of her way.

ANSWER B: Clara Finch's land is separated from the highway by William Amodio's land. Finch had a deal with the previous owner that she could use an old road through the tract for access to her five-acre lot. Amodio, whose property is thirty-five acres in size, has blocked Finch's access to her property. There was no mention of Finch's easement in the agreement, and the easement is not recorded.

There is another road Finch could use, but that route takes her a considerable distance out of her way, and she is eighty years old. Both Amodio and Finch bought their land from the same person. She bought five of his forty acres in 1973; Amodio bought the remaining thirty-five acres in 1975.

ANSWER C: George Brauzakas, who owned a forty-acre tract, sold Clara Finch five acres of that tract in 1973. Finch then built her home on this land. They agreed orally that Finch could use an old road through his property for access to her home because her lot was separated from the highway by the remaining part of his tract. In 1975, Brauzakas sold this thirty-five acre tract to William Amodio. There is no reference to Finch's use of the road in Amodio's deed to the property, and there is no recorded easement. Amodio has now blocked the dirt road across his property. Finch, who is eighty, has access to her house through a dirt road leading from another highway. That route takes her thirty miles and forty-five minutes out of her way.

Answer C is best because it is a neutral and accurate description of the facts, stated in chronological order. Answer C includes the legally significant facts and just enough background facts for the reader to understand the problem.

Answer A is biased. The income or motives of the parties involved are not legally relevant. Answer A also omits such legally significant facts as the absence of a written agreement, a separate recorded easement, or a reference to an easement in Amodio's deed.

There are three problems with Answer B. First, it tries to describe separately the facts pertaining to two closely related issues. The result is repetitious and disjointed. Second, it uses vague terms such as "land," "deal," and "considerable distance" instead of more precise terms, thus raising unnecessary questions and perhaps changing the meaning of the statement. Third, it draws a legal conclusion by describing the road as an easement. Legal conclusions belong in the Discussion, not in the Statement of Facts.

The following exercises will give you practice with the Statement of Facts in particular problems.

Exercise 17-A

Stephen Farley, tired of country life and wanting to get a fresh start, recently moved to a large city from his parents' melon farm, where he had lived for twenty-two years. When Farley arrived in the city, he spent several days trying to find an apartment that suited his needs. Living in hotels was quickly consuming his meager savings. Finally, Farley saw an ad in the paper:

> New, beautiful, spacious, one-bedroom apartment; recently redecorated; extremely clean; nice neighborhood; walking distance to university; immed. occupancy; no pets. $95 per mo. Resistance Realty Co. 591-1001.

Farley called the number and talked to a rental agent who confirmed all the statements in the ad and told Farley the place was perfect for his needs. The agent further told Farley that several people were interested in the apartment and that Farley should sign the lease at the realty office and then go see the apartment. Taking the agent at his word, Farley went to the realty company, paid a $500 security deposit, and signed the lease. Farley then went to look at his new apartment and received the shock of his life. The neighborhood was the worst one in town. Two winos were asleep on his front steps and several of the apartment windows were broken. The toilet did not work and there was no hot water. Two rats were sitting on the sofa, roaches were hiding everywhere, and there were large holes in some of the walls. The floors and walls were grimy. Farley went out to his car to leave and found that all of his hubcaps had been stolen. He went back to the realty office and demanded that the agent tear up the lease and refund his money. The agent refused, saying "A deal is a deal."

Rule of Law: Every sale of a leasehold estate carries with it an implied covenant that the leased property is fit for human habitation. A lease is unenforceable if the covenant is breached.

Issue: Whether the leased apartment was so unfit for human habitation that the realty office breached the covenant of habitability.

Assume the above rule of law and issue are the only ones that apply to Farley's case.

1.   List the legally significant facts.

2.   Does it matter that Farley's hubcaps were stolen? Explain.

3.   List any key background facts.

4.   Draft a Statement of Facts based on your answers to the previous questions. Is it objective and understandable?

Exercise 17-B

This exercise is based on the facts and cases from Exercise 9-B, pp. 119–20.

1.   List the legally significant facts for this problem.

2.   List any key background facts.

3.   Draft a Statement of Facts for this memorandum based on your answers to 1 and 2. Is it objective and understandable?

18

Questions Presented

A BASIC PRINCIPLE of legal education and legal practice is that you receive answers only to the questions you ask. The exactness of the question determines the precision and usefulness of the answer.

An office memorandum usually begins with a section stating the questions presented by the problem. This section alerts the reader to the specific issues addressed. It is, therefore, important to frame the questions in this section as precisely as possible. A question that is too broad or too narrow misrepresents the scope or focus of your analysis and makes your discussion less effective.

Properly framing a legal question is a two-step process requiring you to combine the lessons from Chapters 5 and 17. First, you must identify precisely the legal rules that might apply to your problem. Second, you must identify the legally significant facts—the facts that determine whether a particular rule applies to the situation.

The formula for framing a question is simple: Does the relevant law apply to the significant facts? Both the law and the facts should be included in a succinct, one-sentence question.[1] The question should be precise and complete. Generally, the legal rule should precede the facts.

When you have formulated a question by combining the relevant law with the significant facts, check to be sure that it conforms to the following principles:

---

[1] The Questions Presented section has its origins in the beginning of your research and analysis. As you work through a problem, your understanding of the rules and the legally significant facts will become more refined and complete. The Questions Presented section, therefore, is the link between your initial work and the final product.

1. Be understandable.

A question should be as precise and complete as possible without being so complex that your reader cannot understand it. When a problem involves so many facts relevant to a single issue that including them in the question would make it too long and awkward, you should examine the significant facts and choose only the most relevant. You may be able to summarize or condense closely related facts, but you should do so only with great care. Whenever you generalize about the facts, you risk distorting them or making the issue seem broader than it really is. When in doubt, err on the side of being specific and awkward.

When a legal issue has several sub-issues, you should have a separate question for each. To make sure your reader understands that they are sub-issues, you may want to use a brief introductory question to identify the broad issue and set the sub-issues in context. The Questions Presented in Appendix A serve as an example.

2. Be objective.

Remember, an office memo should predict what a court is likely to do with a particular problem. Therefore, you must avoid advocating or anticipating a certain result. Include the significant facts favoring each side of the case. If you paraphrase facts to make the question more readable, do so objectively. You should also state the law objectively and not take a partisan approach. If the legal rule has several reasonable interpretations, state the rule so that you can discuss all of these interpretations. When the interpretations differ greatly, present separate questions for each.

☐   Your client, Eric Vosberg, is a frail, chronically ill, thirteen-year-old boy. Deborah Starsky is a seventeen-year-old girl Vosberg and others know to be a neighborhood bully. She has been known to pick fights and has been found guilty of several misdemeanors in juvenile court. Two weeks ago, Starsky confronted Vosberg while he was on his way to a violin recital. She told Vosberg to put his nose against a nearby telephone pole. Vosberg complied. Starsky instructed Vosberg not to move until she gave him permission and then walked away. At no point did Starsky explicitly threaten Vosberg, touch him, or prevent him from continuing down the sidewalk. Vosberg remained at the pole for two hours and then ran home. He missed the recital and has suffered severe emotional problems as a result of the incident. Vosberg's parents want to know whether they can sue Starsky.

Your research has revealed only one relevant case:

Palmer v. Woodward (1960)

After making several purchases in Schwenson's Department Store, the appellant, Roger Palmer, left. He began to walk down the sidewalk when the appellee, Troy Woodward, a store detective, ran from the store and yelled, "Stop!" Palmer stopped.

Woodward approached Palmer, stood in his way, and put his hand on Palmer's chest. After telling Palmer he had to go back and see the store manager, Woodward gently grasped Palmer's elbow and led him back into the store. Palmer, sixty-eight, has failing health and a heart condition. He did not resist. As a result of the incident, Palmer suffered a mild heart attack and severe emotional distress.

Palmer filed suit for false imprisonment. The trial court dismissed Palmer's complaint, holding that restraint, a necessary element of false imprisonment, had not occurred. The trial court reasoned that Palmer voluntarily complied with Woodward's demands because he did not resist or make any attempt to free himself. We disagree.

The trial court correctly stated that false imprisonment requires the defendant to actually confine or restrain the plaintiff. The restraint must be obvious, and the plaintiff must be aware that he is being restrained. But the restraint does not have to be forceful; threats, express or implied, can be sufficient. In this case, the appellant is a frail, elderly man. The appellee is a six-foot, five-inch, 220-pound, semiprofessional football player who works part time as a store detective. Blocking another person's way is restraint when the aggressive person is obviously stronger, as he was here. In addition, the appellee touched the appellant by taking his arm and guiding him into the store. We hold that under the facts of this case, particularly the great disparity of physical strength, there was sufficient restraint. Reversed.

Consider the following attempts to state the question:

ANSWER A: Whether Vosberg can recover damages for false imprisonment.

ANSWER B: Whether Vosberg was sufficiently restrained to support a cause of action for false imprisonment.

ANSWER C: Whether the apparent strength of Vosberg and Starsky was so unequal that Vosberg can recover damages for emotional distress.

ANSWER D: Whether sufficient restraint to support an action for false imprisonment exists when a seventeen-year-old juvenile delinquent with a police record and a reputation of being a bully instructs a frail, chronically ill, thirteen-year-old boy who plays violin to remain in one place.

ANSWER E: Whether the fact that a seventeen-year-old female delinquent, who has been convicted several times and who has a reputation of being a bully and a fighter, gave instructions to a frail, thirteen-year-old boy, on his way to a violin recital, to put his nose against a phone pole and stay there until told otherwise, but never touched the boy or blocked his path and walked away immediately after the boy complied with the instructions, though the boy did not move from the pole for two hours, constitutes sufficient restraint to support an action for false imprisonment, when the boy missed the recital and suffered severe emotional problems as a result.

ANSWER F: Whether restraint sufficient to support an action for false imprisonment exists when a seventeen-year-old girl known as a juvenile delinquent and bully instructs a frail thirteen-year-old boy to remain in one place, and he does so for two hours after she has walked away, even though the girl neither touched him nor blocked his path.

The *Palmer* case indicates that your problem concerns what type of force, if any, is required to satisfy the restraint element of false imprisonment. Answer F is the best way of stating that question. Answer F correctly identifies the relevant law, includes the facts of the problem that a court is likely to find legally significant, and states the law before the facts. The question in Answer F is neither unduly narrow nor overly broad. It is readable and objectively stated. Answer F clearly identifies the precise legal question presented.

Answer A, by contrast, is useless. The question is too broad and makes no attempt to pinpoint the legal rule or the legally significant facts. The writer might just as well have stated the question: "Whether the law has been violated."

Answer B does pinpoint the legal question of restraint, but it fails to place that question in context because it omits the facts that will provide the basis for its resolution. A question framed this way is too unfocused to be of any value.

Unlike Answers A and B, which are too broad, Answer C is too narrow. By limiting the legal question to whether the strength of the parties is unequal, it fails to consider other factors that contribute to restraint. In addition, the mention of damages for emotional distress mistakes the real issue. Whether the plaintiff can recover damages for emotional distress is a different question from whether there has been restraint. In this respect, Answer C illustrates an important reason to ask the right question; if you ask the wrong question, you are likely to get the wrong answer. Even if your discussion covers the right issue, you have seriously misled the reader about the direction of the memo. Finally, Answer C, like Answers A and B, omits the significant facts of the case.

Answer D is not objective. The question exaggerates the strength of the client's case because the facts included are relevant to only one side of the question. Answer D fails to note that Starsky did not touch Vosberg or block his path. Whenever you state a question, you must include those facts that hurt your case as well as those that help it. Answer D also includes some irrelevant facts, such as Vosberg's being a violinist.

Answer E is complete enough. It includes all the significant facts and properly states the issue of law. It is so complete, however, that it is awkward and unreadable. Answer E does not sort out the most relevant facts. Answer E also includes several facts that are not legally significant, such as those concerning the violin recital and telephone pole. While you may want to include some background facts in the Statement of Facts, do not include them in the Questions Presented.

As you complete the following exercises, remember that your questions must combine the relevant law with the significant facts. They form the basis for the rest of the memorandum, and you should focus them as sharply as possible.

Exercise 18-A

Flower Hughes, a twenty-two-year-old law student who also holds a graduate degree in business and accounting, recently inherited $200,000 from a rich uncle. To celebrate her good fortune, Hughes decided to have a few drinks at the Blue Goose Inn, a local tavern. Hughes arrived at noon and had several drinks during the course of the afternoon. Soon after her arrival (about three drinks later), she explained to Ron Zoeller, the bartender and sole owner of the Inn, that she wanted to invest her inheritance in some enterprise that would yield a high return.

Zoeller began telling her what a fine business he had in the Blue Goose, and how he was getting old and would like to sell it. He told Hughes that the net worth of the Goose was $200,000 and that she could expect to make a $20,000 net profit each year. He admitted that he had only made $12,000 each year for the three years he had owned the place, but assured Hughes that revitalization of the inner city and proposed construction would probably double or triple the Inn's profits in no time. The net worth of the Goose was really only $160,000. Zoeller went to the back room and produced a ledger book that he said contained his business records. The entries in the book had obviously been altered to reflect the figures he had quoted to Hughes. (He had altered them originally for tax and insurance purposes). Hughes examined the book briefly and expressed some concern about the validity of the figures. Zoeller replied: "Sure there might be some mistakes; I'm not very good with figures." He added, "What good are figures anyway? A good businessman trusts his instincts above all else." Zoeller then offered to sell Hughes the tavern for $190,000. Hughes smiled and said she would think it over.

At about 5 P.M., several of Hughes's friends joined her at the tavern. Hughes continued drinking until 1 A.M., when Zoeller leaned over the bar and said, "Tell you what, because you're such a nice kid, I'll sell you the whole place for $175,000. It's a real steal." Hughes, who was intoxicated by this time, could not hear Zoeller over the noise in the tavern, and asked him to write his statement down. Zoeller then wrote his exact statement on one of the bar's napkins, which had "Blue Goose Inn" printed on it. It said, "Ron Zoeller offers to sell the Blue Goose Inn to Flower Hughes for $175,000." Hughes laughed and said, "Sure, why not? It'll be a good time."

The next day Hughes remembered the conversation and went to Zoeller and said she hoped he was only joking around. Zoeller said he was serious and that he intended to hold Hughes to the contract. He also told Hughes that a customer who had been sitting next to Hughes at the bar was toying with his new tape recorder at the time. The customer had accidentally recorded the entire conversation, Zoeller said, and was willing to lend him the tape. He also named several other witnesses who heard the conversation and who would confirm the agreement if necessary.

Hughes has come to you for assistance. After some research and thought on the matter, you have discovered the following statute and cases from your state:

State Rev. Laws § 60.1(4) *Statute of Frauds*

No action shall be brought against any person . . . (4) upon any contract for the sale of lands, tenements, or hereditaments, or any other interest concerning them . . . unless the agreement upon which said action shall be brought, or some memorandum or note thereof, shall be in writing and signed by the person to be charged therewith, or by some other person thereunto by him lawfully authorized.

Treacher v. Plums (1932)

The appellant, Ivan Treacher, entered into an oral contract with the appellee, Roy Plums, whereby Treacher purported to sell Plums a ten-acre tract of farm land for Plums's son. Treacher proposed the deal at 10 A.M. and Plums immediately agreed. They did not put the agreement in writing because Plums was illiterate. Instead, they immediately proceeded to the church, and they both stated the terms of the agreement in front of the minister and two witnesses. Later that day, Plums wanted out of the deal. Treacher refused and filed suit. The trial court found that the state Statute of Frauds rendered the agreement of no effect. We agree.

The original Statute of Frauds was enacted in England in the seventeenth century. The statute in our state, which is modeled on the English Statute of Frauds, has been interpreted extensively by the courts. Case law has now clearly established that the statute requires contracts for the sale of land to be in writing. The writing must state with reasonable certainty and accuracy (1) the parties to the contract, (2) the subject matter to which the contract relates, and (3) the terms and conditions of all promises constituting the contract and by whom and to whom the promises are made.

In this case, there is no question that the terms of the contract, the subject matter, and the parties were all described with the requisite certainty. The exact location and size of the property, the purchase price, the conditions of payment, and the names of both parties were all stated. The fact remains, however, that they were not stated in writing. We have recognized two purposes served by the statute. One is evidentiary—putting the agreement in writing ensures that there will be proof of the agreement. The second is cautionary—reducing the agreement to writing requires the parties to think through the proposed transaction carefully and make sure they are serious about going through with the deal. Even if we were at liberty to disregard the statute, in this case we find that the second purpose was not fulfilled. Affirmed.

Divine v. Zarwakov (1964)

The appellant, Carla Divine, brought suit seeking rescission of her contract with Zarwakov's School of Ballet. Divine, who has a sixth-grade education and is twenty-five years old, always dreamed of becoming a great dancer. She began taking lessons in classical ballet at Zarwakov's dance school in response to a special introductory offer of ten lessons for thirty dollars. During this time she was repeatedly told that she was a natural dancer and that she had exceptional rhythm, grace, and poise. The school told her that with minimal training she would be assured of a spot as a principal dancer in one of the national dance companies. On the basis of this encouragement, Divine entered into a series of written contracts in which she agreed to pay $10,000 over the next five years for private dance lessons. In reality, Divine is extremely uncoordinated and has no natural aptitude for dance. The trial court held that she was bound by the terms of the contract and dismissed her suit. We disagree.

Courts in this state will not enforce an agreement when there has been a misrepresentation in the inducement to contract. The party seeking to be relieved of the bargain must establish six things: (1) false representations, (2) of material facts, (3) that the defendant knew were false, (4) that the defendant intended the plaintiff to rely on, (5) that the plaintiff was justified in relying on, and (6) the plaintiff suffered damages as a result of this reliance. There is no doubt that there were false representations, that the defendant knew they were false, that the defendant intended the plaintiff to rely on them, that the plaintiff relied on them, and that she was damaged as a result. The only questions here are whether they were material facts and whether the plaintiff was justified in relying on the representations of those facts.

We hold that while these representations were not material facts in the strict legal sense, they were sufficient to satisfy the requirement. Ordinarily, a representation is material if it would induce a reasonable person to change his or her position. When there has been some artifice or trick by the representor, or when the parties do not in general deal at arm's length, or when the representee does not have equal opportunity to become apprised of the truth or falsity of the fact represented, material facts in the strict sense are not required.

The same reasoning applies to the justifiable reliance element. The dance school held itself out to be an expert. Given the plaintiff's lack of knowledge and education, not to mention her lifelong dream, she can properly be said to have been justified in relying on the dance school's representation of the material facts. Misrepresentation in the inducement to contract is especially reprehensible in cases such as this, which smack of undue influence, falsehood, suppression of the truth, and lack of free exercise of rational judgment. Reversed.

1. Identify the relevant legal rules, as well as the elements of those rules. What issues and sub-issues are presented?

2. What are the legally significant facts, both favorable and unfavorable to Hughes, for each issue and sub-issue?

3.   Draft the Questions Presented for an office memorandum based on your answers to 1 and 2. Are they objective and readable?

Exercise 18-B

This exercise is based on the facts and cases from Exercise 9-B, pp. 119–20.

1.   Identify the relevant legal rules, as well as the elements of those rules. What issues and sub-issues are presented?

2.   What are the legally significant facts for each issue and sub-issue?

3.   Draft the Questions Presented for this memorandum based on your answers to 1 and 2. Are they objective and readable?

Part E

BRIEFS

19

Elements of a Brief

THE LAWYER AS ADVOCATE is the counterpart of the lawyer as counselor. To the client, the lawyer is a counselor; to the outside world, the lawyer is an advocate. As an advocate, the lawyer exercises persuasion in a variety of ways to achieve results favorable to the client. Many times, a lawyer will help a client avoid a lawsuit by convincing a potential adversary that the client's position is solid. At other times, a lawyer may convince a government agency to adopt a more favorable attitude toward the client's position. While effective advocacy can help keep a dispute out of court, it can also increase the likelihood of success if litigation is necessary.

The brief is the formal document a lawyer uses both to convince a court that the client's position is sound and to persuade a court to adopt that position. Briefs are similar to office memos in many respects, and many of the principles that apply to memos also apply to briefs. Both must honestly state the law, the facts of the case, and the reasons for their conclusions clearly and concisely. The advice in a memo, of course, is worthless if it cannot be defended in litigation.

Briefs differ from memos, however, in two important respects. The first difference is the tone of the documents: briefs argue; memos discuss. The writer of a memo is developing a legal strategy with other attorneys; the writer of a brief is submitting a legal argument to opposing counsel and a judge or panel of judges, all of whom will scrutinize it. Open and honest assessment of the client's position, required for memos, is absolutely wrong for briefs. The brief writer must make the client's position seem as strong as possible, emphasizing favorable arguments and minimizing the force of opposing arguments. It is not enough that the client's position appear logical or even desirable; it must seem compelling.

The second difference is the thinking process used in drafting the documents. The brief writer knows the basic conclusions in advance and searches for arguments and materials supporting those conclusions and showing that his client's position is stronger and should prevail. The memorandum writer, by contrast, is concerned with objectively determining whose position is most sound and usually will not come to a conclusion until relatively late in the process of research and analysis.

There are two kinds of briefs. A brief to a trial court (sometimes called a memorandum of law or memorandum of points and authorities) is the document presented to a trial court in support of, or in opposition to, various motions, or to convince the court to decide the merits in a particular way. A brief to an appellate court is the document presented to a reviewing court challenging or defending a trial court's decision in a case.

Appellate and trial court briefs differ in several ways. Appellate briefs focus more on broad policy because appellate courts are more concerned with establishing and applying rules that will work in many situations. Trial court briefs tend to focus more on the facts of an individual case because trial courts are closer to the parties and more concerned with deciding cases according to established precedent than with establishing new law. Appellate briefs are usually accompanied by an edited transcript of the record from the lower court. Appellate briefs also have more elements and tend to be more formal than trial court briefs. These differences are described in more detail in Chapters 23 (Briefs to a Trial Court) and 24 (Briefs to an Appellate Court).

Following is a generally accepted format for both the brief to an appellate court and the brief to a trial court:

Brief to an Appellate Court	**Brief to a Trial Court**
Title Page	Caption
Index	
Authorities Cited	
Opinion(s) Below	
Jurisdiction	
Constitutional Provisions, Statutes, Regulations, and Rules Involved	
Standard of Review (required by some courts)	
Questions Presented	Questions Presented (optional)
Statement of Facts	Statement of Facts
Summary of Argument	
Argument	Argument
Conclusion	Conclusion
Appendix(es)	

The name of each section (except the Title Page and Caption) should be underlined or capitalized and placed immediately above that section.

When drafting a brief you should be aware of three things. First, trial and appellate courts usually have specific rules concerning the format and content of briefs. These rules ensure some uniformity and make it easier to compare arguments made in opposing briefs. Specific court rules control when they vary from the general rules given here. Second, the importance of many of the elements of an appellate brief may seem obscure at first, and many of the court rules will concern seemingly minor items such as length, page size, and citation form. Although some of these elements and rules may seem tedious and overly technical, you should take them seriously. Many courts reject incorrectly presented briefs. Third, briefs are rarely drafted in the order these elements appear. You will usually write the Argument, Summary of Argument, Statement of Facts, and Questions Presented before you write the other elements.

The following is a description of each element of a brief. The discussion focuses primarily on appellate briefs because they have more elements than trial court briefs. The Discussion also explains when an element in a trial court brief differs from its counterpart in an appellate court brief. Examine Appendixes E and F (sample appellate court briefs) and Appendixes B and C (sample trial court briefs) in conjunction with this chapter.

1. Title Page or Caption

The Title Page of an appellate brief identifies the court, the docket number, the name of the case, the side represented, and the names and addresses of counsel. The Title Page of briefs filed in the highest state appellate court or the Supreme Court of the United States also identifies the term of the court and the court from which the appeal is taken. The Title Page distinguishes the brief from many others received by the court and ensures that the brief will be placed in the proper file. Appendixes E and F show a standard Title Page for appellate briefs, though there can be minor stylistic variations.

The first page of the brief to a trial court has a Caption, which looks like this:

UNITED STATES DISTRICT COURT
FOR THE DISTRICT OF SUPERIOR

WESTBROOK NEIGHBORHOOD ASSOCIATION, Plaintiff, vs. ELLISON RECYCLING, INC., Defendant.	Civ. Docket No. CZ-8071-93 Hon. F. A. Hollender

MEMORANDUM OF LAW
IN SUPPORT OF DEFENDANT'S MOTION TO DISMISS

The Caption substitutes for the Title Page; it identifies the court, the name of the case, the docket number, the motion or other matter under consideration, the judge, and the side represented. Appendixes B and C illustrate another type of caption for a trial court brief, based on somewhat different court rules.

2. Index

The Index is a table of contents for the appellate brief and is sometimes labeled as such. It lists each element of the brief and the page on which that element begins. In addition, the point headings used in the Argument should be stated in full in the order they appear, with page numbers corresponding to their locations. The point headings, described in detail in Chapter 21, are specialized thesis sentences that introduce parts of your argument. This outline of the point headings gives the reader a concise and easily understood summary of your argument. The briefs in Appendixes E and F show a basic format for the Index.

3. Authorities Cited

This section, also called Table of Authorities or Citations, lists all of the legal and other materials used to support the Argument in an appellate brief and shows every page on which those materials are cited. This list of authorities permits a judge or opposing counsel to determine quickly where you examined specific cases, statutes, or other materials. It also provides a quick reference for complete citations to any materials used in the brief.

The Authorities Cited section is usually divided into several basic categories, including cases, constitutional provisions, statutes, and miscellaneous materials. Each of these categories can be subdivided. Subdividing is for the reader's benefit. It will often be helpful to have a separate section for cases decided by the court to which the brief is addressed. For example, you might list cases under the headings "Michigan Cases" and "Other Cases," or you might list them under "United States Supreme Court Decisions," "Sixth Circuit Court of Appeals Decisions," and "Other Federal Decisions." You might also create categories to emphasize specific statutes, administrative rules, secondary authorities, or the legislative history of a particular act. Avoid cluttering the brief, however, with numerous subcategories that have only a few citations.

Cases, secondary authorities, and other materials should be listed in alphabetical order in each category. Statutory sections, constitutional provisions, and other materials that cannot be listed alphabetically should be listed in numerical order. The briefs in Appendixes E and F show how to list Authorities Cited.

4. Opinions Below

This section of an appellate brief indicates where the decisions of the lower courts or government agencies that have decided this case can be located, in case the reviewing court wants to read them. Provide a citation for these previous decisions if they have been reported; if they have not yet been reported, say so and show their location in the record. For example:

> The opinion of the Court of Appeals for the District of Columbia Circuit is unreported and is reprinted at pages 1a-2a of the appendix to the petition for certiorari (Pet. App.). The opinion invalidated a rulemaking order of the Federal Communications Commission. The Commission's rulemaking order is reported at 7 F.C.C.R. 8072 (1992) and is reprinted at Pet. App. 3a-36a.

5. Jurisdiction

This section of an appellate brief, also called a Jurisdictional Statement or Statement of Jurisdiction, provides a short statement of the jurisdictional basis for the appeal. Because jurisdiction itself is often an issue in trial courts and is also asserted in the complaint, this section is unnecessary for briefs to a trial court. Some state appellate courts require a Jurisdictional Statement only in limited circumstances. The Jurisdiction section should briefly inform the court of the factual circumstances, court rules, or statutory provisions on which appellate jurisdiction is based. Thus:

> The judgment of the United States Court of Appeals for the Seventh Circuit affirming the decision of the United States District Court was entered on September 7, 1990. The petition for a writ of certiorari was filed on November 27, 1990, and this Court granted certiorari on February 19, 1991. The jurisdiction of this Court is invoked under 28 U.S.C. § 1254(1).

6. Constitutional Provisions, Statutes, Regulations, and Rules Involved

This section tells the court what codified provisions are relevant to the determination of the case and where in your brief the judge can scrutinize the exact language of these provisions. The name of this section varies according to the materials included. When you have one or two provisions that are relatively short, you should state the exact language in full. When you have many provisions or the provisions are lengthy, you should provide the name and citation in this section and indicate that the provisions are stated in full in one or more appendixes at the end of your brief.

Thus:

Section 29 of the Mobile Home Commission Act, Mich. Comp. Laws Ann. § 125.2329 (West Supp. 1993), provides as follows:

> A utility company shall notify the department ten days before shutoff of service for nonpayment, including sewer, water, gas, or electric service, when the service is being supplied to the licensed owner or operator of a mobile home park or seasonal mobile home park for the use and benefit of the park's tenants.

Or:

The texts of the following statutes relevant to the determination of the present case are set forth in the Appendix: Sections 3(c)(2)(6) and 10(b) of the Federal Insecticide, Fungicide, and Rodenticide Act, 7 U.S.C. §§ 136a(c)(2)(6), 136h(b)(Supp. III 1991); Tucker Act, 28 U.S.C. § 1491 (1988 & Supp. IV 1992).

7. Standard of Review

This section contains a concise statement of the appropriate standard of review to be exercised by the appellate court, with citations to authority supporting the applicability of that standard. The location of the standard of review within the brief may be specified by court rules. The appellate court's standard of review will vary, depending on the legal issues involved and the procedural posture of the determination being appealed. The various standards of review are generally not contained in the court rules, but are developed in case law. They are discussed in greater detail in Chapter 24 (Briefs to an Appellate Court). A typical standard of review section reads as follows:

> The issue before this Court is whether the trial court erred in dismissing the complaint for lack of personal jurisdiction. The court's review of the grant of a motion to dismiss is *de novo*. *Larkin v. Smith Realty Co.*

If a dispute exists over the applicable standard, your discussion will be more detailed. You will have to demonstrate why your position on the appropriate standard is correct and why your opponent's is wrong.

8. Questions Presented

This section states the legal issues involved in a brief and tells the court the matters you intend to address. The Questions Presented in a brief are similar to those in a memorandum. Both must include the legal rule and a summary of significant facts, and both must be precise and understandable.

Unlike the Questions Presented in an office memorandum, though, the questions in a brief should be slanted toward your client's position and should reflect your interpretation of the law. If you are using that interpretation to emphasize certain facts in your Argument, your questions should contain these facts. In addition, the questions should be stated so that they prompt an affirmative answer. As Chapter 20 (The Argument) describes in detail, your brief should project a positive tone; it should argue for a particular conclusion rather than simply against the contrary conclusion. If you are appealing an unfavorable trial court decision, for example, your questions might begin: "Whether the trial court erred. . . ." Your opponent, appealing the same decision, might begin: "Whether the trial court properly held. . . ." Both questions suggest an affirmative answer.

There are two styles of presenting the questions in a brief, and these styles differ principally in their argumentative tone and completeness. The better style, which you should use, is to state the question so completely and so persuasively that it answers itself:

> Whether the trial court deprived the defendant of his right to due process of law under the Fourteenth Amendment by admitting into evidence a confession that was extracted from the defendant after twenty-two consecutive hours of interrogation by rotating teams of detectives.

This way of presenting the question combines the relevant legal rule and the significant facts so that the only reasonable answer seems to be "yes." This style is very effective, although you should not risk your credibility by overstating or distorting your position. The other style states questions in their barest form:

> Whether admission into evidence of the defendant's confession violated his right to due process under the Fourteenth Amendment.

This question does not provide significant facts, nor does it make the answer obvious, although it does frame the issue in a way that would be acceptable to both sides.

Many briefs to a trial court are so short or straightforward that the Questions Presented section is unnecessary. The section is necessary, however, in long or complex trial court briefs, which often contain multiple issues.

9. Statement of Facts

The Statement of Facts in a brief, also known as Statement of the Case or simply Statement, is a descriptive account of the facts from your client's point of view. Although this statement cannot omit any damaging facts, you should write it to promote the court's understanding of and sympathy for your client's situation. Many lawyers and judges believe that the Statement of Facts, which is discussed in detail in Chapter 22, is the most important section of any brief.

10. Summary of Argument

This section is a concise statement of your major conclusions and the most important reasons supporting them. It conveys to a judge the essence of your argument and is particularly useful when a judge has not had time to read the entire brief before oral argument. For this reason, make sure that your summary is specific to the case under review and not merely a list of general legal principles. The Summary of Argument should be self-contained; the reader should not have to look elsewhere to understand the argument. Like the Conclusion in an office memorandum, the Summary of Argument should contain no citations to cases, statutes, or regu-lations unless the authority is well known or absolutely essential to the reader's understanding. Each major conclusion should be in a single paragraph. The briefs in Appendixes E and F show examples of the Summary of Argument.

11. Argument

The Argument is the foundation on which the rest of the brief is constructed. Like the Discussion in an office memorandum, it is the heart of the document. Although the Statement of Facts and Summary of Argument are important, and sometimes decisive, your client generally wins or loses on the quality and substance of what you say in the Argument. An effective Argument in a brief is developed using the basic concepts of legal writing described in Part C. The Argument should be clear and compelling; it should reflect a sound understanding and thoughtful analysis of the relevant law. Although the Argument is similar to the Discussion, it is different from the Discussion in two important ways.

First, this section of the brief should be an argument rather than an objective discussion of the law. You should state, in forceful and affirmative language, your strongest arguments and issues first and present your client's position on each issue or sub-issue before you refute the position of your opponent. These and other principles of advocacy presented in Chapter 20 (The Argument) will help you present your case more convincingly.

Second, the Argument should contain point headings. Point headings are conspicuous thesis statements that preface each logical segment of your Argument. Because they are capitalized, underlined, or formatted in a prominent way, point headings make it easier for the reader to understand the structure and content of your Argument. Point headings are always included in appellate briefs, but their use in trial court briefs is optional. As with Questions Presented, point headings should be included in trial court briefs that are lengthy or complex. Point headings are discussed in detail in Chapter 21. The guidelines given in previous chapters, combined with those concerning advocacy and point headings, should help you prepare an effective Argument. Appendixes E and F show sample Arguments for appellate briefs, while Appendixes B and C show sample Arguments for trial court briefs.

12. Conclusion

This section describes what you want the court to do. It precisely states what relief you are requesting from the court—particularly if the relief you seek is more complicated than affirming or reversing the lower court's judgment. The request for relief is usually one sentence in length. In trial briefs with complex arguments, you may include a brief summary of the arguments supporting your conclusion. Immediately following, you should include the address, phone number, and signature of at least one of the attorneys who prepared the brief. You should also include the date. The Conclusion section in an appellate brief should look like this:

> For all the foregoing reasons, the judgment of the Ingham County Circuit Court should be reversed and the case remanded for a new trial.
>
> Respectfully submitted,
>
> _____
>
> Charles McGrady
> Attorney for Appellants
>
> Smith, Dunmore & Coffin
> 420 Brookshire Commons
> Greensboro, N.C. 27402
> (919) 423-0706

March 1, 1994

The Conclusion section in a trial court brief is presented in the same form but requests different relief from the court. For example:

> For the foregoing reasons, the plaintiffs respectfully request that the defendant's motion for summary judgment be denied.
>
> Respectfully submitted,
>
> _____
>
> Charles McGrady
> Attorney for Plaintiffs
>
> Smith, Dunmore & Coffin
> 420 Brookshire Commons
> Greensboro, N.C. 27402
> (919) 423-0706

March 1, 1994

13. Appendixes

This section contains the quoted statutes from the section of your brief called Constitutional Provisions, Statutes, Regulations, and Rules Involved. There can be a separate Appendix for each major category of statutes in the brief. There should also be an Appendix for any diagrams or charts you include. If you use more than one Appendix, give each a short descriptive title. Each of the sample briefs in Appendixes E and F contains its own Appendix showing the relevant statutes.

This chapter has identified and described each component of a brief. Although assembling a brief may seem complicated, everything in a brief is for the court's convenience or for the purpose of presenting your client's position as persuasively as possible.

20

The Argument

ADVOCACY IS THE CRAFT of persuasion. It is the means by which an attorney persuades a court to adopt her client's position as its own. An effective advocate will show a court that deciding for one side would be logical and desirable, and that deciding for the other side would not. Courts in an adversary system depend on advocates to illuminate the strengths and weaknesses of competing positions. An advocate thus assists the court in deciding a case. Many times, the arguments, cases, and even the language of the winning brief will appear in the court's opinion. For better or worse, the skill and resources of counsel are often as important to a decision as the relevant law.

Coherence and credibility are essential to effective advocacy. The analytical, writing, and organizational principles from Parts B and C apply to the Argument. The advocate's research must be complete, her analysis sound, and her conclusions sensible. Clear organization, thoughtful analysis, and a logical progression are essential. A writer who is not understandable is not effective.

Honesty about the law and the facts is also essential to effective advocacy. A brief should rely on shading, emphasis, and overall strength of argument for its persuasive value, rather than on omission or distortion of the relevant law or misstatement of facts. The subtlety of this distinction in certain cases makes it no less important.

The Model Rules of Professional Conduct, which have been adopted in most jurisdictions, prohibit an attorney from knowingly making "a false statement of material fact or law to a tribunal." They also prohibit an attorney from knowingly failing "to disclose to the tribunal legal authority in the controlling jurisdiction known to the lawyer to be directly adverse to the position of the client and not disclosed by opposing counsel."[1]

---

[1] MODEL RULES OF PROFESSIONAL CONDUCT, Rule 3.3(a)(1) & (3) (1992).

The Model Rules of Professional Conduct and the Federal Rules of Civil Procedure also establish a minimum standard for the kind of argument an attorney can make. The Model Rules state that a lawyer may not "bring or defend a proceeding or assert or controvert an issue therein, unless there is a basis for doing so that is not frivolous, which includes a good faith argument for an extension, modification or reversal of existing law."[2] This ethical rule is reinforced by Rule 11 of the Federal Rules of Civil Procedure and parallel rules that exist in many states. Rule 11 is intended to ensure that briefs, motions, and other papers filed in court have a reasonable factual and legal basis. Under Rule 11, a lawyer implicitly certifies that a paper has a reasonable basis by filing or otherwise presenting it to a court. Rule 11(b) provides:

> By presenting to the court (whether by signing, filing, submitting, or later advocating) a pleading, written motion, or other paper, an attorney or unrepresented party is certifying that to the best of the person's knowledge, information, and belief, formed after an inquiry reasonable under the circumstances,—
>
> (1) it is not being presented for any improper purpose, such as to harass or to cause unnecessary delay or needless increase in the cost of litigation;
> (2) the claims, defenses, and other legal contentions therein are warranted by existing law or by a nonfrivolous argument for the extension, modification, or reversal of existing law or the establishment of new law;
> (3) the allegations and other factual contentions have evidentiary support or, if specifically so identified, are likely to have evidentiary support after a reasonable opportunity for further investigation or discovery; and
> (4) the denials of factual contentions are warranted on the evidence or, if specifically so identified, are reasonably based on a lack of information or belief.

Rule 11 allows a court to impose sanctions against lawyers who violate the rule. Formal sanctions include reasonable expenses incurred by the opposing party because of the filing of the paper and reasonable attorney fees. Informal sanctions include embarrassment as well as loss of confidence by clients and potential clients.

The importance of honesty to your professional future cannot be overstated. Federal Judge Lynn N. Hughes puts it plainly:

> *Honesty* in fact and law determines not only the outcome of the case but also your future as a lawyer. If you appear before me well prepared and if you present your case with integrity and class, I will forget you by dinner. But if you misrepresent your facts or law or if you try cute evasions, I will remember you after you have turned gray. Do not sell off your integrity for any client. No matter how smart you may be, if I cannot approach your presentation with trust, you are but half heard at best.

---

[2] MODEL RULES OF PROFESSIONAL CONDUCT, Rule 3.1 (1992).

The following principles will help you present the Argument forcefully, persuasively, and honestly.

1. Present your strongest issues, sub-issues, and arguments first.

When your client's case involves several independent issues, present the strongest issue first, followed by the next strongest issue, and the next, and conclude with the weakest. Similarly, when several arguments support your client's position on an issue or sub-issue, present them in descending order of strength. The "strongest" issues, sub-issues, or arguments are those most likely to persuade a judge to rule in favor of your client.

If you apply this principle, your brief will be more persuasive for several reasons. First, to capture the court's full attention, you must demonstrate that your client's legal position is impressive. The beginning of the Argument sets the tone for what follows. Because the strongest issues or arguments are necessarily the most compelling ones, beginning with them enhances your credibility. Second, the less persuasive issues and arguments are more compelling when you use them to buttress stronger issues and arguments than when you present them strictly on their own merits. Conversely, stronger issues and arguments seem less compelling when you present them after weaker issues and arguments. Third, crowded dockets— even at the appellate level—often mean that a brief will not necessarily be read in its entirety by all the judges or clerks. If you present the strongest issues and arguments first, they are much more likely to be read.

A corollary to this guideline is this: Omit weak arguments and issues. In pre-writing and drafting briefs, think of as many arguments and issues as possible. Some of these arguments will be weak because there is scant authority to support them or because the rule in question has never been applied to the facts before the court. Sometimes, of course, you will have to include such arguments in your brief because you have nothing stronger. When you do have stronger arguments, however, you should omit the weak ones because weak arguments undermine your credibility and divert attention from more persuasive arguments.

If you have arguments of nearly equal strength, consider which arguments will have the strongest appeal to the court to which you are submitting your brief. If you are writing to an appellate court, look for examples in which the court has treated a similar issue or a case with similar policy considerations. If you are writing to a trial court, consider the court's function. It is bound by decisions of the appellate courts within its jurisdiction. As previously noted, a trial court is more likely to base a decision on settled law than on unsettled law. Thus, in most cases it would be the better strategy to base your first argument on settled law within the jurisdiction.

◻ Consider the following situation:

On November 5, Paula Jennings was elected to her first term as Justice of the Peace for Monroe County, a position that enabled her to perform civil weddings and hear small claims cases. Immediately after her election, she reversed her previous support for a highly controversial court reform proposal—one that was an issue in many of the election races, including hers. After she took office on January 2, a group of citizens circulated petitions for her recall. The petitions, filed with the appropriate county official on March 15, included a statement that the basis for the recall was her "opposition to the court reorganization plan." Section 5 of the State Elections Act provides:

> The petition or petitions, which shall clearly state the reason or reasons for the recall, shall not be filed against an officer until the officer has actually performed the duties of that office to which he or she has been elected for a period of six months during the current term of that officer.

After filing a suit to prevent Jennings's recall, her attorney filed a motion for summary judgment. Relying on section 5, he prepared two outlines of a brief in support of that motion:

ANSWER A: The petitions are invalid under the Elections Act because they do not meet the section 5 requirement of a clear statement of the reasons for recall. The statement on the petitions that Jennings opposes the court reorganization plan does not clearly inform voters whether it is her position, her change of position, or both, that motivates the recall.

The petitions are also invalid because, contrary to section 5, they were submitted before Jennings had been in office for six months. Because the petitions were submitted on March 15, less than two-and-one-half months after Jennings took office on January 2, the six-month requirement was not fulfilled.

ANSWER B: The petitions are invalid under the Elections Act because, contrary to section 5, they were submitted before Jennings had been in office for six months. Because the petitions were submitted on March 15, less than two-and-a-half months after Jennings took office on January 2, the six-month requirement was not fulfilled.

The petitions are also invalid because they do not meet the section 5 requirement of a clear statement of the reasons for recall. The statement on the petitions that Jennings opposes the court reorganization plan does not clearly inform voters whether it is her position, her change of position, or both, that motivates the recall.

Answer B is better because the six-months argument is stronger than the clear-statement argument. The six-months argument addresses an unmistakable error; section 5 is explicit and leaves little doubt about what is required. The clear-statement argument addresses a more debatable issue. In the absence of any relevant case law, "opposition to the court reorganization plan" may or may not be reasonably understood as a clear statement. Beginning with that argument, as Answer A does, is a less forceful way of presenting the case.

2. When issues are equal in strength, present the most significant issues first.

The most significant issues are not necessarily the strongest ones. The most significant issues are those that, if resolved favorably, would help your client most. In a criminal case involving two equally strong issues, for example, you should first discuss the issue that would exonerate the defendant, and then discuss the issue that would merely win the defendant a new trial.

This principle is subordinate to the first principle because a strong but less significant argument is more persuasive than a weak but more significant argument. Likelihood of success should be your main consideration. Assume, for example, that a convicted pickpocket could raise two issues on appeal. He could argue with strong precedent that the judge erred in permitting him to be convicted solely on the basis of hearsay, and he could argue with tenuous support that the statute under which he was convicted was unconstitutionally vague. The hearsay issue should be presented first, even though it is less significant than the constitutional question, simply because it is more likely to succeed. If, however, the vagueness issue were at least as strong as the hearsay issue, it should be presented first. Winning on the vagueness issue would result in his release rather than just a new trial.

Presenting the most significant issues first is important for the same basic reasons as presenting the strongest issues first. If you present a serious issue first, the court is more likely to take the entire brief seriously than if you begin the brief with an issue concerning a technical violation of an obscure law. In addition, less significant issues seem more compelling when you use them to buttress important issues than when you use them to introduce an argument.

▢ Consider again the Jennings example:

The petition drive against Paula Jennings garnered 7,850 signatures. In the last election, 32,000 people in Monroe County voted for a candidate for governor. The State Elections Act further provides:

Sec. 2. Every elective officer in the state except a judicial officer is subject to recall by the voters of the electoral district in which the officer is elected.

Sec. 6. The petitions shall be signed by a number of qualified and registered voters equal to not less than 25% of the number of votes cast for candidates for the office of governor at the last preceding general election in the electoral district of the officer sought to be recalled. The person or organization sponsoring such recall shall have ten days to file additional signatures after any determination that the petitions submitted contain an insufficient number of qualified and registered voters.

Jennings's attorney has prepared two outlines of a brief to the trial court concerning these sections:

ANSWER A: The petitions are invalid because they challenge an officer specifically exempted from recall by the Elections Act. Section 2 expressly excepts "a judicial officer" from the Act, a term that necessarily includes a justice of the peace performing such judicial activities as deciding small claims cases.

Even if there were no such exemption, the petitions would still be invalid because, contrary to section 6, they do not contain signatures equal to 25% of the votes for governor in Jennings's electoral district in the last election. Because the petitions have only 7,850 signatures and 32,000 people in the district voted for a candidate for governor in the last election, they are 150 signatures short of the section 6 requirement.

ANSWER B: The petitions are invalid because, contrary to section 6 of the Elections Act, they do not contain signatures equal to 25% of the votes for governor in Jennings's district in the last election. Because the petitions have only 7,850 signatures and 32,000 people in the district voted for a candidate for governor in the district in the last election, they are 150 signatures short of the section 6 requirement.

Even if there were enough signatures, the petitions would still be invalid because they challenge an office specifically exempted from recall by the Elections Act. Section 2 expressly excepts "a judicial officer" from the Act, a term that necessarily includes a justice of the peace performing such judicial activities as deciding small claims cases.

Answer A is better because it places the issue of the substantive validity of the petitions before the issue of sufficient signatures, even though both issues are very strong. A favorable decision on the exempt-officer issue would foreclose the recall effort altogether, but the sufficient-signature issue may only delay the recall because section 6 allows ten days for the filing of additional signatures. Answer A emphasizes the more significant issue, and gives the less significant issue more strength by discussing it after, and therefore in light of, the more significant issue. Answer B, by contrast, emphasizes the less significant issue and obscures the more significant issue.

Answer A also shows a more logical progression of thought than does Answer B. Answer A states, in effect, that the Elections Act does not apply, and even if it does apply, the requirements of the Act were not met. Each issue is independent of the other. Answer B, on the other hand, illogically states that the requirements of the Elections Act were not met, and even if they were, the Act does not apply. Answer B assumes that the Elections Act applies to this situation when discussing the first issue but not when discussing the second. Answer A is better because it arranges the issues both logically and in order of significance.

How should the arguments and issues for sections 2, 5, and 6 of the Elections Act be combined? Explain.

3. Present your client's position on each issue or sub-issue before answering counterarguments.

This principle is a slight modification of the rule in Chapter 9 (Organization) requiring you to state the reasons *for* a conclusion before responding to reasons *against* it. In a memo your conclusion may support your client or it may support your opponent. But in a brief, your Conclusion must not only convince the court to decide *for* your client, it must also convince the court to decide *against* your opponent. Your client's position should define the order and tone of argument on any given issue or sub-issue. You can make that position much clearer by stating and justifying it before answering counterarguments. If you attack your opponent's arguments before advancing your own, you face two potential problems. One, you risk not stating your position intelligibly, or worse yet, not having your main argument read at all. Two, you sound defensive and imply that your opponent's point of view is more interesting or important to the court.

If there are several arguments opposing your client's position on an issue or sub-issue, present the strongest ones immediately after you have explained your client's position. Your opponent's strongest counterarguments are likely to be the most interesting to the court, and you gain credibility by promptly confronting them.

☐ Ian LeVasseur was convicted of second degree murder on the basis of a voice-print identification made possible because the victim had been operating a tape recorder just before the crime occurred. LeVasseur has appealed on the ground that voiceprint identification is inherently unreliable. Although courts in his state have not decided this issue, courts in two neighboring states with identical rules of evidence have decided the following cases:

State v. Decker (1963)

Alan Decker was convicted of arson on the basis of a voiceprint identification from the recording of a wiretapped telephone conversation. The sole issue on appeal is the propriety of the trial judge's ruling that permitted the voiceprint to be admitted into evidence. Our law does not permit evidence of a scientific test to be admitted unless its scientific basis and reliability are generally recognized by competent authorities. Voiceprint analysis, however, is not so recognized; there is little literature on the subject and great disagreement among experts as to its accuracy. For that reason, we reverse and remand for a new trial.

State v. Manning (1973)

Margerita Manning was convicted of second degree murder in connection with the bombing of an office building that led to the death of a secretary employed there. Some twelve minutes before the explosion, local police received a phone call warning that the building should be evacuated. That call was taped and was used in a subsequent voiceprint identification that formed the evidentiary basis for Manning's conviction. Her appeal challenges the reliability of voiceprint identification. We affirm.

The record before this court indicates that voiceprint analysis is a widely accepted and scientifically accurate method of identification that has the support of many experts. Because its scientific basis and reliability are generally recognized, the trial judge committed no error in admitting the voiceprint identification into evidence.

The prosecutor's brief on appeal might be organized in either of the following ways:

ANSWER A: The voiceprint analysis was properly admitted into evidence. In this state, scientific tests are admissible when their reliability and scientific basis are generally recognized by competent authorities. *People v. Greene.* Although this state's courts have not addressed the admissibility of voiceprints under this rule, other states' courts have. In *State v. Decker*, the court held that a voiceprint analysis was improperly admitted because of the lack of scientific literature and disagreement among experts as to its accuracy. *Decker* is distinguishable because it was decided in 1963 when voiceprint analysis was at an early stage of development. In the 1973 case of *State v. Manning*, however, the court held that a voiceprint was properly admitted into evidence, because by that time the reliability and scientific basis for voiceprint analysis were widely recognized by experts. *Manning* reflects significant developments in the field over ten years and underscores the correctness of the trial judge's ruling in this case.

ANSWER B: The voiceprint analysis was properly admitted into evidence. In this state, scientific tests are admissible when their reliability and scientific basis are generally recognized by competent authorities. *People v. Greene.* Although this state's courts have not addressed the admissibility of voiceprints under this rule, other states' courts have. In a 1973 case, *State v. Manning*, the court held that the reliability and scientific basis for voiceprint analysis are widely recognized by experts and, hence, that voiceprints can be admitted into evidence. *Manning* reflects significant developments in this field and underscores the correctness of the trial judge's ruling in this case. Although a 1963 case, *State v. Decker*, held to the contrary, it was decided before voiceprint analysis had become a widely accepted and scientifically reliable identification technique.

Answer B is preferable because it describes the favorable case before it responds to the unfavorable case, rather than the other way around. Answer B states that voiceprint analysis is widely accepted and was thus proper in this case, and then distinguishes *Decker* as out of date. This response to *Decker* is consistent with the prior analysis of *Manning*, and is persuasive in that context. Answer A is less clear because the older case is distinguished before the affirmative argument is even stated. Even when *Manning* is discussed, the analysis is not as sharply focused as it is in Answer B. In addition, Answer A is defensive, and gives greater weight to the counterargument.

4. Use forceful and affirmative language.

Word choice is as important as structure in an argument. Words can make an argument seem confident or defensive, bold or halting, credible or dubious. They can also make a position seem conservative or radical. Words cannot substitute for a good argument, but they can greatly enhance it. The lawyer whose arguments are stated with authority and confidence is the most convincing to a court. The following guidelines are illustrative.

A. Present arguments from your client's point of view. The tone of your argument should be positive rather than negative or defensive. Thus, you should frame both your arguments and your rebuttal of counterarguments in terms of why your client should win rather than why the opponent should lose. By presenting arguments from your client's point of view, you show control over the issues and write a more persuasive brief.

The plaintiffs brought an action under the federal Noise Control Act of 1972, alleging section 1337 of the Judicial Code as the sole basis of jurisdiction. The defendant has filed a motion to dismiss on the ground that the plaintiffs did not allege an amount in controversy of $50,000 or more. The plaintiffs' argument to the federal district court might be stated in either of the following ways:

ANSWER A: The defendant incorrectly contends that the plaintiffs' failure to allege $50,000 as an amount in controversy deprives the court of jurisdiction. Section 1337 of the Judicial Code provides original jurisdiction to the federal courts of "any civil action or proceeding arising under any Act of Congress regulating commerce," but it does not require an allegation of an amount in controversy. Because the federal Noise Control Act, under which the plaintiffs brought this action, is a congressional regulation of commerce, the defendant's contention is untrue. Section 1332 requires an allegation of an amount in controversy for federal jurisdiction, but the plaintiffs do not rely on section 1332.

ANSWER B: This Court has jurisdiction to hear this case. Section 1337 of the Judicial Code provides original jurisdiction to the federal courts of "any civil action or proceeding arising under any Act of Congress regulating commerce," but it does not require an allegation of an amount in controversy. The plaintiffs have alleged jurisdiction under the federal Noise Control Act, a congressional regulation of commerce. The defendant's claim that an amount in controversy was not alleged is thus irrelevant. Because the plaintiffs do not rely on section 1332, which requires an allegation of amount in controversy for federal jurisdiction, this Court has jurisdiction.

Both answers cover the same ground, but they convey different messages. Answer B says the plaintiffs have jurisdiction; Answer A says the defendant's claim is untrue, but it never clearly says the federal district court has jurisdiction. Answer B is better because it is more positive and lucid. Answer B turns the defendant's denial of jurisdiction into an affirmative argument that the court has jurisdiction. It demonstrates control over the direction and tone of the argument. Answer A, which is dominated by the defendant's viewpoint, does not.

B. Present the law from your client's point of view. Balanced descriptions of the law belong in office memos but not in legal briefs. The law should be characterized to favor, and be consistent with, the client's position. The legal rules and principles, of course, determine what arguments can be made. But they should also be an integral part of the Argument, stated with the same forcefulness and tone as the application of the law to the facts. The description of the law would otherwise disrupt the flow and direction of the Argument.

☐ Consider this illustration:

Mary Elston brought an action against Juan Guerrero, the driver of a car that struck her van from the rear, causing Elston a serious back injury. At trial, Guerrero's attorney attempted to introduce evidence to show that Elston's van had seat belts and that most, if not all, of Elston's injuries could have been avoided had she been wearing a seat belt. The trial judge refused to admit that evidence. The state's appellate courts have not addressed this question. The case was tried under the state's comparative negligence rule, and Guerrero's attorney was attempting to mitigate damages. The jury returned a verdict for Elston and awarded $225,000 in damages. On appeal, Guerrero's attorney might characterize the relevant law from other states in two ways:

ANSWER A: When seat belts are available to the plaintiff in an auto negligence action and the plaintiff's failure to use them caused or contributed to her injuries, the defendant in some states is entitled to have the damage award reduced accordingly. *E.g., Bentzler v. Braun.* This rule is based on the reasonable view that the use of seat belts reduces serious injuries and fatalities from automobile accidents and that those riding in cars should know of this additional safety factor. *Braun.* Cases to the contrary are based on the questionable premises that the duty to fasten seat belts arises only if the plaintiff anticipates the accident, that not all vehicles have seat belts, and that not all people use them. *E.g., Kopischke v. First Continental Corp.* When seat belts are available, though, it is manifestly unfair to penalize a defendant for the plaintiff's failure to exercise a simple precaution that is surely in the plaintiff's best interest.

ANSWER B: The courts of other states are divided on whether a defendant in an auto negligence action is entitled to have the damage award reduced when seat belts are available to the plaintiff and the plaintiff's failure to use them caused or contributed to her injuries. Most courts, however, deny mitigation. A minority of the courts have held that the use of seat belts reduces serious injuries and fatalities from auto accidents, and that those riding in cars should know of this additional safety factor. *E.g., Bentzler v. Braun.* The majority of cases are premised on the view that that the duty to fasten seat belts arises only if the plaintiff anticipates the accident, that not all vehicles have seat belts, and that not all people use them. *E.g., Kopischke v. First Continental Corp.* The issue is which party should bear the cost of the plaintiff's failure to use seat belts. *Braun* probably represents the better reasoned view because the use of seat belts reduces injuries.

Answer A is better because it is confident, forceful, and presents the law in the light most favorable to Guerrero. Answer B, by contrast, is passive and balanced in tone. The writer does not sound convinced and thus is not convincing. Answer A shows the court how to decide in Guerrero's favor; it states the position favoring mitigation, presents that position as if it were clearly better, and encourages the court to select *Braun* as preferable policy. Unlike Answer B, it de-emphasizes the division of the courts and the minority position of the *Braun* case by merely implying these facts. Answer A, in short, describes the law in a way that advances the Argument.

C. Make your client's position seem objective. Because courts generally do not like to innovate, your client's position should appear to reflect the existing law. Even when a decision in your client's favor would break new legal ground, you must make it seem that a favorable decision is required by law, justice, and common sense. Whenever possible, avoid wordy references to your client's position, suggestions that your client's position is merely an interpretation of the law, and explicit indications that it diverges from the law. Conversely, you should characterize the opposition's case as distant from the existing law or as mere interpretation. You should, however, avoid a sarcastic or insulting tone.

☐ Consider the following:

A complaint filed with the State Bar Association charged Leon Gibbon, an attorney, with depositing in his personal checking account the funds of several estates for which he was doing probate work and converting $147,000 of these funds to his personal use. A hearing panel of the State Bar Association agreed with the complaint after an evidentiary hearing and voted to suspend Gibbon from the practice of law for five years. Gibbon appealed to the State Bar Grievance Board, which affirmed the panel's findings and increased the suspension to a lifetime disbarment. Gibbon appealed the Board's disbarment decision to the state's highest appellate court. The State Bar Association's attorney might characterize its position on appeal in either of these ways:

ANSWER A: The State Bar Association interprets the State Bar Grievance Rules to provide the Grievance Board with discretionary authority to increase a five-year suspension to a disbarment. The State Bar Association agrees with the Grievance Board's conclusion, after reviewing the detailed records, that "the uncontradicted evidence of serious violations of the state Rules of Professional Conduct warrants disbarment." The Board's failure to make a detailed statement of the reasons for disbarment is therefore irrelevant, notwithstanding the obvious importance of this matter to Gibbon.

ANSWER B: The State Bar Grievance Board has discretionary authority to increase a five-year suspension to disbarment. After reviewing the detailed record, the Board concluded that "the uncontradicted evidence of serious violations of the state Rules of Professional Conduct warrants disbarment." In light of that conclusion, a more detailed statement of reasons would serve no useful purpose.

Answer A emphasizes the State Bar Association's position, but Answer B emphasizes the correctness of the Grievance Board's decision. Answer B is better because it sounds more objective than Answer A. Answer A is also verbose and less forceful because it begins with "The State Bar Association interprets . . . ." Finally, it suggests more weakness in the State Bar Association's position than necessary ("Board's failure," "obvious importance of this matter to Gibbon," and "interprets the . . . Rules"). The difference between the two answers is one of emphasis; the skillful use of emphasis makes a more persuasive argument.

5. Fully argue your client's position.

Because the brief is a statement of reasons for adopting a certain position, these reasons should be stated as completely as possible. The principle in Chapter 11 (Explaining the Analysis) requiring an explicit statement of all the analytical steps needed to reach a conclusion takes on a new dimension in advocacy. Here are two guidelines:

A. Make effective use of the facts. As Chapter 22 (Statement of Facts for a Brief) shows in more detail, the facts have both logical and emotional value. The application of law to facts is the essence of legal reasoning, but the facts may also be used to gain empathy for the client. By marshaling and emphasizing the appropriate facts, you can often overcome a weak legal position and make a court see the desired outcome as compelling. Similarly, you can minimize the strength of your opponent's position by de-emphasizing damaging facts—explaining them, summarizing them, or describing them blandly. Always use the facts to your client's advantage—in briefs to both trial and appellate courts.

◼   Edgar Brown was convicted of first degree murder. Defense counsel has two drafts of the brief on appeal:

ANSWER A: The trial judge erred by not charging the jury with the lesser included offense of voluntary manslaughter. A defendant is entitled to a jury charge for manslaughter whenever there are enough facts to convince a reasonable person that the homicide was committed under the influence of an irresistible passion caused by an insult or provocation sufficient to excite a reasonable person. *People v. Valentine.* The defendant in that case was convicted of first degree murder for killing a man who repeatedly insulted the defendant during a quarrel by calling him a window peeper and a liar, among other things. The court held that these facts would justify a verdict of voluntary manslaughter and that the trial court erred by giving jury instructions that precluded conviction for that crime.

Brown's case is similar to *Valentine* because the record shows that Brown committed the homicide after being taunted about a sensitive personal matter. Brown described the decedent as "my best friend from army days," even though the decedent had broken Brown's nose in a fight the previous year. Brown was depressed and unemployed, and the killing occurred during a weekly poker game after the decedent called him a "welfare bum" and a "loser." Any reasonable person in Brown's position would have been similarly provoked.

ANSWER B: The trial judge erred by not charging the jury with the lesser included offense of voluntary manslaughter. A defendant is entitled to a jury charge for manslaughter whenever there are enough facts to convince a reasonable person that the homicide was committed under the influence of an irresistible passion caused by an insult or provocation sufficient to excite a reasonable person. *People v. Valentine.* The defendant in that case was convicted of first degree murder for killing a man who repeatedly insulted the defendant during a quarrel by calling him a window peeper and a liar, among other things. The court held that these facts would justify a verdict of voluntary manslaughter and that the trial court erred by giving jury instructions that precluded conviction for that crime.

Brown's case is similar to *Valentine* because the record shows that Brown committed the homicide after being taunted about a sensitive personal matter. Brown was extremely depressed after his layoff from an auto plant, where he had worked for seventeen years. He had been unable to find other work because of the local high unemployment rate. Both he and his wife testified that he had trouble concentrating after he was laid off, that he frequently forgot things, and that their marriage was strained. The homicide was committed during a weekly poker game with friends. Like the decedent in *Valentine* who repeatedly insulted the defendant, the decedent in this case, Brown's "best friend from army days," began to taunt Brown about being a "loser," a "welfare bum," and a "social parasite." Although Brown and the decedent had engaged in a brief fistfight a year earlier, several persons, including the decedent's wife, testified they had long since made up. After the decedent ignored repeated warnings to quit, Brown suddenly lunged at him with a paring knife used to make sandwiches. Brown later could remember nothing of the homicide except experiencing blind rage. A reasonable person in Brown's position would have been similarly provoked.

Answer B is better because its vivid detail forces the court to see the issue from Brown's viewpoint. The additional facts not only place the incident within the manslaughter rule but they also paint a sympathetic portrait of a harassed man pushed to the breaking point. The facts are set out in chronological order, showing Brown's growing frustration and unhappiness. Answer A's analysis of the facts, by contrast, is poorly organized, omits important facts, and does not describe precisely what happened. Answer A mentions the fistfight in a damaging way, while Answer B carefully excuses and blends this point into the argument. Answer A is unpersuasive because it does not provide insight or foster empathy for Brown's situation. To be an effective advocate, you must learn to recognize the most valuable facts and weave them strategically into your legal argument.

B. Make effective use of legal policies. In writing briefs, the relationship between rules and policies is important. Policies define the reasons for the legal rules in question. The result you advocate must be significant from a policy standpoint; technical infractions of the law, therefore, are usually not enough. Policy arguments are also important when the legal rules or the facts do not provide you with a strong position, particularly at the appellate level. As discussed in Chapters 23 and 24 (Briefs to a Trial Court and Briefs to an Appellate Court), policy arguments are generally more important in appellate briefs than in briefs to trial courts.

☐   Section 8 of the Township Rural Zoning Act requires a public referendum on the "adoption of a zoning ordinance" when 8% of the registered voters in the township sign petitions requesting a referendum. Seymour Township adopted its zoning ordinance in 1962. Several weeks ago, the Township Board rezoned an eighty-acre tract from agricultural to residential. Township residents gathered sufficient signatures to request a referendum, but a trial court ruled that section 8 applied to the initial decision to zone, not to subsequent zoning amendments. The citizens' brief to the court of appeals could be summarized in the following ways:

ANSWER A: Section 8 of the Township Rural Zoning Act requires the requested referendum. Section 8 applies to the "adoption of a zoning ordinance," a term that includes not only the initial decision to zone but also subsequent amendments. Because such amendments obviously become part of the ordinance, they should be treated in the same manner.

ANSWER B: Section 8 of the Township Rural Zoning Act requires the requested referendum. Section 8 applies to the "adoption of a zoning ordinance," a term that includes not only the initial decision to zone but also subsequent amendments. Because such amendments obviously become part of the ordinance, they should be treated in the same manner.
     This conclusion is important to the underlying purpose of section 8—ensuring that the ordinance is acceptable to a majority of those living in the township. Because zoning amendments might make the ordinance unacceptable to those citizens, the

referendum requirement should apply equally to zoning amendments and the original ordinance. Zoning amendments, moreover, significantly affect the quality of life of township residents by prescribing the existence, location, and density of new developments. The public ought to be able to vote on these important decisions. Finally, because the right to vote is a fundamental one, any perceived ambiguities about the scope of a legislative grant ought to be resolved in favor of that fundamental right.

Answer B's completeness makes it far more compelling than Answer A. Answer A is merely an argument about the meaning of the language in section 8, an argument that sounds uninspired and lame because it does not make effective use of the underlying policies. Answer B reaches the same conclusion, but it relies far more on the underlying policy of majority approval for zoning decisions than on the meaning of the words. It states that the legislative intent requires that section 8 be applied to zoning amendments, regardless of the ambiguous language of the law.

The exercises that follow provide an opportunity to apply these principles.

Exercise 20-A

Arnold Jones, the driver of a fuel oil truck, was convicted of driving on the left side of a two-lane highway. He said that he did so to avoid a large and unexpected patch of ice. It was rush hour. No one was forced off the road.

State Law § 117.01 provides:

It shall be a misdemeanor for any person to drive in the left lane of a two-lane highway.

The following four cases from the state court of appeals interpret this statute:

Cain v. State (1969)

The defendant was convicted for driving on the wrong side of the road. The defendant was joyriding with friends and was intoxicated. Two cars were forced off the road. We reject his appeal. Traffic safety is of paramount concern. There can be no exceptions, for exceptions would undermine any confidence the reasonable person would have in highway safety.

McKinney v. State (1975)

The defendant was convicted for driving on the wrong side of a two-lane highway when he swerved to avoid hitting a child. There was little traffic, and the incident occurred during the day. We reverse. Although every reasonable person has a right to expect other cars to stay in their appropriate lanes, it would be intolerable for the law to put a driver in this kind of dilemma.

Shoop v. State (1981)

The defendant was convicted for driving on the wrong side of a two-lane highway when he swerved to avoid hitting a pothole. The defendant is a mechanic, and he testified that the pothole was clearly visible. He also testified that the pothole was likely to have irreparably damaged a tire and bent the tie rod on his car. The road was generally rough, and there was light traffic. We affirm. Financial self-interest is not enough to outweigh highway safety.

Gordon v. State (1991)

The defendant, a volunteer fireman driving to a fire station for an emergency call, was convicted of violating State Law § 117.01. He was not using flashing lights or a siren, and there was nothing about his car to distinguish it as an emergency vehicle. The defendant was passing long lines of cars to get to the station. We affirm the conviction. An exception to § 117.01 would be permissible when there is a clear public necessity, but this is not the proper case for such an exception.

The attorney for Jones has filed a motion with the trial court to dismiss the charge.

1.   Using the statute and cases, how would you make the most effective argument for Jones?

2.   Using the statute and cases, how would you make the most effective argument for the state?

Exercise 20-B

Yvonne Hardy, an employee of Tri-State Fuel Co., was driving a fuel tanker truck loaded with an expensive and highly flammable grade of oil. She had been following a pickup truck filled with pumpkins for several miles on a two-lane highway when the latch on the back of that truck suddenly came loose, spilling pumpkins on the right side of the highway. The driver of the pickup immediately pulled over. Hardy swerved into the left lane to avoid the pumpkins, forcing a car driven by Ted Hansen off the road. Hansen, who was coming from the opposite direction in the correct lane, suffered severe injuries.

Hansen sued Tri-State for negligence and claimed that Hardy (and thus Tri-State) was negligent *per se* under State Code § 98.01. Hardy testified at trial that she had driven fuel trucks for eight years. She stated that she did not think she could maintain control of the truck if she struck the pumpkins and that she did not have time to stop. She also testified that there was an extremely narrow shoulder on the right side of the highway and that it dropped off sharply into a small river valley. She said she had reason to believe the truck would explode if she went off the road or lost control, and that she did not see Hansen's car until just before he drove off the road. The driver of the pickup truck testified that he recovered eleven pumpkins, ranging from fifteen to twenty pounds in size, from the road. Other pumpkins shattered when they struck the road, he said, and several cars ran over unbroken pumpkins after the incident. The trial court found Tri-State negligent *per se* and awarded Hansen $175,000 for his injuries. Tri-State has appealed.

State Code § 98.01(c) provides:

Upon all roadways of sufficient width, a vehicle shall be driven upon the right half of the roadway except as follows:

. . . .

    (c) When an obstruction exists making it necessary to drive on the left half of the roadway.

The highest appellate court in the state has decided the following cases:

Meekhof v. Golden (1939)

Meekhof brought an action against Golden for injuries Meekhof sustained when the automobile Golden was driving forced Meekhof off the road. Golden, who was intoxicated, was in the left lane of a two-lane highway at the time. The trial court awarded Meekhof $6,100 in damages, and we affirm. State Code § 98.01 requires all vehicles to be driven on the right side of the roadway except in specifically defined situations. The obvious purpose of this statute is to protect persons and property on the left side of the roadway. Golden's violation of the statute constitutes negligence *per se*, and the trial judge so instructed the jury. None of the exceptions stated in the statute is applicable here.

Yerrick v. Boughton (1956)

The appellee, Cecelia Boughton, was seriously injured when Bruce Yerrick's Model T automobile, which was fast approaching hers in the same lane, forced her off the road to avoid an accident. Boughton brought an action for negligence to recover for her injuries and argued that Yerrick's violation of State Code § 98.01 constituted negligence *per se*. The trial court agreed and awarded judgment to Boughton. Although Yerrick admitted that he was driving in the left lane of the highway, he argued pursuant to subsection (c) that an obstruction made it necessary for him to drive in the left lane. The obstruction was a bumpy and somewhat uneven forty-yard stretch of the right lane, which Yerrick told the trial court "might have severely damaged my antique car." We agree with the trial court.

    The purpose of § 98.01, as we said in *Meekhof v. Golden* (1939), is protection of persons and property on the left side of the roadway. There is no obstruction within the meaning of § 98.01(c) unless there is an obstacle that prevents, or is likely to prevent, the driver's safe passage on the right side of the roadway. In any case, it is not intended simply for the convenience of drivers who claim for financial or other reasons that their vehicle is somehow special. A bumpy and uneven road in itself does not meet that test. Affirmed.

James v. Strange (1964)

Alton Strange was driving about twenty miles per hour on a two-lane street in a residential neighborhood when a child suddenly ran in front of him, chasing a ball.

Knowing he did not have time to stop, Strange swerved suddenly and sharply into the left lane. In so doing, he crashed into Kristine James's vehicle, which was traveling in the opposite direction. Neither the child nor James was injured. James sued Strange for damages to her vehicle, arguing that Strange was negligent *per se* under State Code § 98.01. Strange admitted that he did not see the other car until he struck it. The trial court dismissed the suit.

This court has often stated that § 98.01 is designed to protect persons and property on the left side of the roadway. *E.g., Yerrick v. Boughton* (1956). Drivers have a right to believe that the statute will be observed. At the same time, it would offend the conscience to force a driver to choose between killing a child and subjecting himself to a negligence lawsuit. Section 98.01(c), which permits travel on the left side of the road when an obstruction makes such travel necessary, encompasses small children who run into the roadway. There is no negligence *per se* here. Affirmed.

1.   Assume you are representing Tri-State:

      (a)   Will your argument emphasize the general rule in the statute or the exception? Explain.
      (b)   Affirmatively state your client's position in one sentence.
      (c)   What argument(s) will you use to support that position?
      (d)   How will you synthesize the cases supporting each argument? Why?
      (e)   What facts will you emphasize and why?
      (f)   What policies will you emphasize and why?
      (g)   Identify and refute the strongest argument against your client's position.
      (h)   Draft the argument for Tri-State based on your answers to these questions.

2.   Assume you are representing Hansen:

      (a)   Will your argument emphasize the general rule in the statute or the exception? Explain.
      (b)   Affirmatively state your client's position in one sentence.
      (c)   What argument(s) will you use to support that position?
      (d)   How will you synthesize the cases supporting each argument? Why?
      (e)   What facts will you emphasize and why?
      (f)   What policies will you emphasize and why?
      (g)   Identify and refute the strongest argument against your client's position.
      (h)   Draft the argument for Hansen based on your answers to these questions.

Exercise 20-C

Read the following selections from the transcript of the record in *Lee v. PlayChem Corporation*:

Excerpt from Complaint of Susan Lee

(Page 4 of the record)

      1.   The plaintiff, Susan Lee, is a resident of the City of Clear Lake, County of Clear Lake, State of East Carolina. The plaintiff is a minor of the age of 5 years.

2. On October 16, 1992, on application duly made on her behalf, Thomas Lee, the plaintiff's natural father, was, by an order of court duly given and made, appointed guardian *ad litem* of the plaintiff for purposes of this action.

3. The defendant, PlayChem Corporation (PlayChem), is a corporation organized and existing under the laws of Delaware and is engaged in the business of manufacturing and distributing chemistry sets for educational and other purposes, with its principal place of business in the City of Muskegon, Michigan.

(Page 5 of the record)

6. On May 30, 1992, Thomas Lee purchased a Chem VIII chemistry set from the defendant. This particular set contained no instructions for its use, contrary to the custom and practice of PlayChem.

7. On September 21, 1992, the plaintiff mixed three chemicals in the set (crushed charcoal, powdered sulfur, and potassium nitrate), forming gunpowder. Not knowing the danger of this mixture, she heated it, causing an explosion that seriously injured her, blinding her in the left eye and severely disabling her right hand.

8. The plaintiff's injuries were proximately caused by the defendant's failure to observe reasonable care in the manufacture and distribution of the particular chemistry set in question in the following respects:

   (a) in not including instructions for the use of the set;
   (b) in not inspecting each set to determine whether instructions were included; and
   (c) in failing to respond to Thomas Lee's request for instructions for the set.

9. As a proximate result of the negligence of the defendant, the plaintiff will be permanently restricted to monocular vision and will never again be able to engage in activities that require binocular vision. Furthermore, the plaintiff will never be able to engage in activities that require two hands, which will severely restrict a highly promising career in almost any field she could have chosen. Finally, the plaintiff has endured, and will in the future continue to endure, great pain and suffering, all to her damage of $2,500,000.

Answer of Defendant PlayChem Corporation

(Page 11 of the record)

The facts alleged in Paragraphs 1–7 of the plaintiff's complaint are admitted, excepting those concerning the plaintiff's alleged injuries. The defendant specifically denies each and every allegation in Paragraphs 8–9 of the plaintiff's complaint.

AFFIRMATIVE DEFENSE

At the time in question, the plaintiff's parents, Thomas and Ann Lee, were guilty of negligence because of their failure to use the degree of care that would have been used by an ordinarily reasonable and prudent person under the same or similar circumstances. They were negligent for the following reasons:

1. They gave a highly complicated and dangerous chemistry set to their five-year-old child;
2. They failed to provide any supervision over the child's use of the set; and
3. They failed to prevent the child from using the set after discovering that it did not contain the necessary instructions for use.

Such negligence on their part caused, or contributed to, the matters in the plaintiff's Complaint.

Affidavit of Ronald York

(Page 33 of the record)

My name is Ronald York and I am the manager of the sales division of the PlayChem Corporation, Muskegon, Michigan. PlayChem manufactures and sells chemistry sets, primarily for educational purposes, and has done so since 1936. Our advertising literature states truthfully that dozens of college professors, Nobel Prize nominees, and corporate chemists got their start with a PlayChem chemistry set.

The Chem VIII chemistry set contains seventy-eight different kinds of chemical elements and compounds, a Bunsen burner, and a variety of laboratory equipment. Detailed instructions are included with each set. These are complicated chemistry sets, and we sell relatively few of them.

On June 2, 1992, I received a telephone call from a Mr. Thomas Lee of Clear Lake, East Carolina. He said that he had just purchased a Chem VIII set for his daughter, but that the set did not contain instructions. We sent the instructions immediately after he called, but the envelope came back. We apparently had not gotten his proper address, and I did not know how to reach him.

Deposition of Thomas Lee by Defendant's Attorney

(Page 51 of the record)

Q: When was your daughter Susan born?

A: Susan was born on June 1, 1987.

Q: Could you tell me about Susan's special abilities?

A: Well, Susan began to speak when she was six months old. She could read and write by her second birthday, which was right after we moved to Clear Lake. A neighbor in our apartment building told us there were some child development experts at the state university who could help us, so we made an appointment to see them. They tested Susan. They said she has a genius-level IQ. We then enrolled her in a special learning program for gifted children at the university.

(Page 55 of the record)

Q: Could you tell me about why you bought Susan a chemistry set?

A: She was very good at science. She had also been taught some chemistry in her special program.

Q: Is that why you bought her an advanced chemistry set?

A: Well, yes. She was able to learn very quickly, if you know what I mean.

Q: Why did you buy her a Chem VIII set? That was about the most advanced set, was it not?

A: As I just said, she was very good at science. The Chem VIII set is designed for sixteen- to eighteen-year-old children. I asked her teacher if he thought Susan could handle such an advanced set. He said he thought so, so I bought it for her fifth birthday and gave it to her.

Q: Had Susan done any experimentation with chemicals in school?

A: No.

Q: Had Susan ever used another chemistry set?

A: No, but the teacher was confident she could follow the instructions.

(Page 61 of the record)

Q: What happened just before the accident?

A: I was finishing with the dishes after dinner when Susan said she was going downstairs to play with the chemistry set. I said OK. Everything was quiet for about two hours, and then there was an explosion. It was horrible, really. I would rather not go into the details.

Q: I appreciate that, Mr. Lee. Could you tell me how often she had used the set before this incident?

A: It is hard to say, but perhaps a dozen times.

Q: Did you ever assist her or watch her when she played with the set?

A: Not really. I asked her questions about what she was doing, but I did not oversee her in any sense.

Q: Was anyone else with her at the time?

A: No.

(Page 62 of the record)

Q: This chemistry set was not part of her formal study or homework at the university, was it?

A: No, it was not. It helped her a lot, though, and the teachers said she made some very good contributions in class because of her use of the set.

Q: Let me come back to that special program for gifted children for just a minute. That program was optional, right?

A: Yes. Susan started in the program when she was four, though she wasn't required to attend school until she was six. But everyone we spoke to recommended it highly and said it would help her a great deal.

(Page 69 of the record)

Q: When did you first notice that there were no instructions in the chemistry set?

A: When Susan played with it the first time, she said there weren't any instructions for it.

Q: Did you seek to procure a set of instructions for the set?

A: I did. I called the company and asked for them.

Q: Did you get an answer?

A: No.

Q: Did you try to stop Susan from playing with the set until you got an answer?

A: No.

Excerpt from the Opinion of Judge Gleit

(Page 78 of the record)

The principal legal issue here is whether the plaintiff's parents were contributorily negligent in permitting her to use the chemistry set alone and without instructions. The law in this state does not permit a minor child to be charged with contributory negligence, so the defendant has attempted to pin that charge on her parents. Counsel for the Lees argues that the doctrine of parental immunity for negligent torts applies here, and I must reluctantly agree. The doctrine is a useless and counterproductive bit of legal baggage, but it is the law in this state. *Lanir v. Lanir* (1929). The doctrine bars the contributory negligence claim. The plaintiff's motion for partial summary judgment on the issues of parental immunity and contributory negligence is hereby granted. A trial for determination of the defendant's negligence will be scheduled shortly.

Excerpt from the Order of Judge Gleit

(Page 180 of the record)

In summary, I find that the allegations concerning the plaintiff's injuries as specified in Paragraph 9 of the complaint are true, and that the defendant's negligence caused those injuries. I hereby find and adjudge the defendant to be liable for the sum of $800,000 for the damages caused to the plaintiff. So ordered.

The following case is the only relevant decision by the Supreme Court of East Carolina:

Lanir v. Lanir (1929)

Jacob Lanir was injured when the 20-gauge shotgun he was using to hunt deer accidentally discharged into his foot. He brought an action against his father for negligently instructing him in the use of the gun. The trial court sustained the father's demurrer, and we affirm. A proper respect for the role of the family in our society counsels us to conclude that the courts are no place to air grievances between a father and son.

Each of the following three cases is from a different state:

Kates v. DeSantis (1968)

Six-year-old Emily Kates completed her first day of school by getting off the school bus, waiting for the bus to drive away, and then being struck and injured by a car driven by Richard DeSantis as Emily attempted to cross the highway to get home. The child's parents sued DeSantis for negligence. DeSantis in turn claimed that they were contributorily negligent in failing to properly instruct her on how to leave a school bus and cross a highway. The trial court disagreed with DeSantis because of the rule we established in *Geller v. Geller* and then awarded damages for the child's injuries. We affirm.

This case involves the interplay between parental immunity and contributory negligence. When parental immunity is applicable, it bars contributory negligence claims for injuries caused by third parties to their children.

In *Geller v. Geller*, we set aside the traditional rule making parents immune from personal injury actions for negligence brought by their children except in two areas: (1) the exercise of parental authority or discipline over the child, and (2) the provision of food, clothing, housing, medical care, and other care. The phrase, "other care," must be narrowly understood or it will swallow these exceptions and re-establish complete parental immunity. "Other care" does, however, extend to actions dealing with a child's education. These and other actions relating to the provision of food, clothing, housing, and medical care deal with basic necessities of health, morals, and well-being for which society imposes a legal obligation upon the parents. The state requires parents to provide for a child's education, and for this reason the *Geller* exception applies.

Peterson v. Peterson (1971)

We are asked to reconsider our long-established doctrine that parents are immune from negligence actions brought by their children. We replace that doctrine with one that makes parents liable only if they do or fail to do what an ordinary and reasonably prudent parent would do in similar circumstances.

Ernest Peterson and his twelve-year-old son, Fritz, were riding home from a fishing trip when the elder Peterson stopped on the highway. The father believed that a tire on the boat trailer he was towing had gone flat and asked Fritz to go out on the road to inspect it. While doing so, Fritz was struck and injured by another vehicle. Fritz sued his father for negligence. His father filed a motion to dismiss, and the trial court dismissed the suit. We reverse.

Parental immunity is a useless doctrine based on reasons that are no longer persuasive. The argument that tort immunity prevents the disruption of family harmony is unsound because there is no such immunity for property disputes within a family. In addition, there should be less disruption for tort actions because adverse judgments will normally be paid by the defendant's insurance company rather than, as in property actions, out of the defendant's pocket. The rationale that immunity prevents collusive lawsuits actually applies to any kind of lawsuit and should not be a basis for denying one kind of lawsuit. The threat to parental authority and discipline is the only plausible rationale for preserving any part of the doctrine. Surely a parent should be able to spank a child or order a child to stay in his room without being sued for battery or false imprisonment.

In *Geller v. Geller*, the supreme court of another state abolished parental immunity except in regard to "(1) the exercise of parental authority or discipline over the child, and (2) the provision of food, clothing, housing, medical care, and other care." We reject that approach because it makes arbitrary distinctions about different kinds of parental behavior for purposes of immunity. We also believe it wrong that a parent could shield negligent behavior under the umbrella of the exceptions stated.

For these reasons, we adopt a "reasonable parent" rule similar to that which applies to other areas of negligence. We reverse and remand for further proceedings on the merits.

Wilkes v. Torkko (1980)

Nine-year-old Sarah Wilkes was at Lake Winnebago, floating on an old automobile inner tube, when she was struck and seriously injured by a speed boat operated by Amos Torkko. She had come to the lake with her mother, Martha Wilkes, who was sitting on the shore at the time. Sarah Wilkes brought an action against Torkko for negligence. Torkko sought to join her mother for contribution because, he alleged, she was negligent in failing to properly supervise her daughter. Martha moved for summary judgment on the basis of parental immunity, and the trial court granted the motion. We affirm.

This case involves both contributory negligence and parental immunity. The record provides good reason to believe that Martha Wilkes was contributorily negligent in the injury of her daughter. There was testimony that many speedboats were cruising the lake that day, that many of them were cruising near the shore, and that Sarah Wilkes had never been on a lake in an inner tube before. The record also shows that Martha Wilkes was reading a novel rather than watching her daughter. Although Martha was contributorily negligent, parental immunity bars that defense in this case.

This state has long shielded parents from negligence actions by their children, and for good reason. The integrity of the family unit is essential to the growth and development of our society. We are unwilling to permit judges and juries to intrude on the difficult and sensitive problems of raising children. In that regard, we disagree with the approach taken by another state in *Peterson v. Peterson*, which would permit recovery by children when parents "do or fail to do what an ordinary and reasonably prudent parent would do in similar circumstances." The people of our state are too diverse to be judged by a common standard. We do not believe, for example, that the same standard could apply to suburban parents in a major city and rural parents in the smallest hamlet.

Finally, we reject the notion that third parties can recover from immune parents. Allowing recovery would put a strain on the family relationship. In addition, allowing recovery by a non-parent defendant from a negligent parent would affect the child's recovery because parent and child are considered a single economic unit.

1.   What issues are involved in this problem?

2.   Assume you are representing the Lees on appeal:
     (a)   What is your client's strongest issue?
     (b)   What is your client's most significant issue? Is it the same as your client's strongest issue? Explain.
     (c)   State your client's position on each issue in the order you would present these issues. Outline the arguments you would use to support your position on each issue. State the arguments PlayChem would use in response and your answers to them.
     (d)   Draft the argument for the Lees on appeal. Make effective use of the facts of this case and the policies of the decided cases to support your position.

3.   Assume you are representing PlayChem on appeal:
     (a)   What is your client's strongest issue?
     (b)   What is your client's most significant issue? Is it the same as your client's strongest issue? Explain.
     (c)   State your client's position on each issue in the order you would present these issues. Outline the arguments you would use to support your position on each issue. State the arguments the Lees would use in response and your answers to them.
     (d)   Draft the argument for PlayChem on appeal. Make effective use of the facts of your case and the policies of the decided cases to support your position.

21

Point Headings

POINT HEADINGS ARE statements of the legal conclusions the advocate is asking the court to adopt. They correspond to the issues, sub-issues, and other salient points in the brief, and are usually capitalized or underlined to stand out from the rest of the text. Point headings serve two important purposes; one relates to organization and the other to advocacy.

Point headings serve a useful organizational purpose because they help a court understand the direction and content of the brief. They are located within the body of the Argument and are also listed in the Index. In the Argument, point headings serve as conspicuous thesis statements for the different sections of the brief. In the Index, they provide the court with a complete and concise summary of the Argument. A judge interested in reading only about a particular point can scan the Index and then turn to the appropriate page. In addition to assisting the court, point headings assist the advocate in drafting the brief, because they magnify organizational flaws and provide a useful way of checking on the content of the argument under each heading.

Point headings are also an important part of advocacy because they are basic statements of the advocate's contentions and, as such, they make the Argument more understandable to the court. Because judges are required to decide a variety of complicated matters, they are more likely to be persuaded by briefs that are easily understood. In addition, the special placement of point headings in the Index, coupled with their special treatment in the Argument, impresses the structure of your argument more sharply in the reader's mind.

The logic of the argument in the brief unfolds in the point headings. You should arrange point headings in outline form from the most general to the most specific. State your primary arguments in capitalized point headings known as major headings, and preface major headings with Roman numerals. State the significant points supporting each primary contention in minor headings. Preface minor headings with capital letters. (Some advocates underline minor headings to distinguish them from subheadings). Finally, state the significant points supporting a minor heading in subheadings. Preface subheadings with Arabic numerals. Only rarely will you need to provide headings for the arguments supporting a subheading.

The basic rules of outlining apply to point headings. Never use minor headings or subheadings under a heading unless you use two or more of them. If you have only one minor heading or subheading under a broader heading, consolidate it with the broader heading.

Thus:

I. FIRST MAJOR HEADING.
    A. First minor heading.
    B. Second minor heading.
       1. First subheading.
       2. Second subheading.
       3. Third subheading.

II. SECOND MAJOR HEADING.

The basic principles for formulating and placing point headings are as follows:

1. State your legal conclusions and the basic reasons for these conclusions.

Point headings should be an integral part of the Argument section. They should be confident, forceful sentences cast in terms most favorable to your client. Because they are thesis statements for parts of your Argument, each point heading should indicate the issue being discussed (including the relevant legal rule), your position on this issue, and the basic reasons for that position. When lesser headings are used under a larger heading, however, the larger heading need contain only your position concerning the application of a particular legal rule because the lesser headings will provide the reasons for that position. A major heading, for example, may draw a general legal conclusion whose underlying rationale is provided by several minor headings. Each minor heading, then, will contain a legal rule, a conclusion concerning its application to your case, and your basic reasons for that conclusion. Case or statutory citations should not be used as a shorthand reference to the applicable legal principle because the reader is usually not afforded any direction by a bare citation.

▢ Consider the following situation:

The Williams Act is a federal statute that specifies disclosure requirements and imposes restrictions concerning tender offers. A tender offer is the term used to describe an offer by an individual or group of individuals to purchase a certain percentage of the outstanding stock of a corporation. The State of Huron has enacted a similar statute regulating tender offers that has more stringent requirements than the Williams Act. You represent a client seeking to make a tender offer who would like to avoid the requirements of the Huron statute. Your research indicates that state statutes sometimes can be declared unconstitutional if a federal statute governs the same subject. The supremacy clause makes the federal Constitution or statutes "the supreme law of the land." This "preemption doctrine" may be invoked when the congressional purpose in enacting the federal law is frustrated by the operation of the state statute. You might frame a major point heading on this issue in any of these ways:

ANSWER A: THE PREEMPTION DOCTRINE REQUIRES THAT A STATE LAW NOT FRUSTRATE THE PURPOSE OF CONGRESS.

ANSWER B: THIS CASE IS GOVERNED BY *HINES V. DAVIDOWITZ, PEREZ V. CAMPBELL, KEWANEE OIL CO. V. BICRON CORP.,* AND THEIR PROGENY.

ANSWER C: THE HURON STATUTE IS PREEMPTED UNDER THE SUPREMACY CLAUSE BECAUSE IT CONFLICTS WITH THE OBJECTIVES OF THE WILLIAMS ACT, THEREBY FRUSTRATING THE PURPOSES OF CONGRESS.

Answer C is best because it is an assertive and positive statement of your client's position. It states a legal conclusion and provides a reason for that conclusion, thus introducing the court to the argument that follows. It also incorporates the basic legal rule.

Answer A is merely a statement of a legal principle without any explanation of how that principle applies to the present case. The heading draws no conclusions and provides no reasons supporting the client's position. Although a conclusion might be implied from the argument that follows, the writer of Answer A has wasted an opportunity to advance the client's position.

Answer B is worse because it does not even describe the basic legal principle involved. If the reader is not familiar with the cases cited, the point heading is useless. Even if the reader is familiar with the cases, the point heading provides no more than the applicable legal rule. To this extent, Answer B is simply another way of stating Answer A.

2. Structure point headings so that they are both specific and readable.

Point headings must relate legal rules to specific factual situations. The more specifically these rules and facts are stated, the more persuasive the point headings will be. There is a limit, however, to how much information you can compress into a single sentence without making a heading incomprehensible. Framing a point heading is essentially a balancing act. When deciding how general or specific you should be, remember that point headings must both adequately summarize your argument and be readable.

☐ The state Environmental Protection Act provides in part that any person may bring a lawsuit for injunctive relief against any other person whose actions are "likely to pollute, impair, or destroy the air, water, or other natural resources, or the public trust therein." A sportsmen's club brought a lawsuit under that Act to prevent oil drilling in a state forest. After a bench trial, the court granted judgment for the defendants. Counsel for the plaintiff might use one of these point headings on appeal:

ANSWER A: The plaintiff presented uncontradicted evidence of likely pollution, impairment, or destruction of the air, water, or other natural resources, or the public trust therein because the plaintiff showed that oil development activities at the proposed sites, including seismic survey work, exploratory drilling, new roads, and other activities would substantially diminish elk populations in the forest by diminishing their habitat and would also adversely impact bear and bobcat populations, and that it would take these species at least forty to fifty years to recover from these effects.

ANSWER B: The plaintiff presented uncontradicted evidence of likely pollution, impairment, or destruction of natural resources by showing that oil drilling activities would have a substantial and prolonged impact on elk, bear, and bobcat populations in the forest.

ANSWER C: The plaintiff presented uncontradicted evidence that oil drilling activities would adversely affect the forest.

Answer B is best because it states and applies the statutory rule, summarizes the relevant facts, draws a conclusion, and is readable. It is a persuasive introduction to the argument that will support and develop the conclusion stated in the point heading. Answer A is almost useless as a persuasive or organizational tool because it is too detailed. It gives a more complete statement of the applicable law and the relevant facts, but it is difficult to read and understand. The additional details contribute nothing significant. Answer C represents the other extreme; it is easy to read but too vague to be of much use. It does not state the statutory rule concerning the likelihood of pollution, impairment, or destruction of the environment, nor does it state how the forest is likely to be adversely affected. Answer B reconciles the two extremes.

3. Place headings at logical points in your brief.

Point headings must reflect your organizational scheme. You should outline your brief before drafting it, and the headings you eventually formulate for the Argument should correspond to the specific points in your outline. Generally, you should include a separate point heading for each issue and sub-issue. If necessary, you should add another level of headings for the major points under each issue or sub-issue. In addition to point headings that make the Argument more specific, you may need point headings to divide your issues or sub-issues into categories. For example, when you have two or more broad categories of issues, such as several objections to the constitutionality of a statute and several jurisdictional issues, you should include a separate point heading for each category.

Placement of headings is a matter of balance and good judgment. As a rule, point headings should provide logical breaks in your Argument. A well-written brief carries the reader smoothly from one point to another. Having too few point headings may make your brief more difficult to understand and lead to a long-winded, poorly organized Argument. Having too many point headings can cause your brief to lose momentum and persuasive force. They can interrupt an Argument inappropriately, make the organizational scheme confusingly complex, and draw excessive attention to relatively insignificant points. In some cases, although it may be logical to divide the arguments under a heading into subheadings, it may not be prudent. You can often strengthen several weak arguments by combining them rather than by presenting them individually. Each will lend support to the others and give the appearance of a stronger overall Argument.

☐ The State Radiation Control Act provides for the licensing of persons and medical establishments using X-rays and other sources of ionizing radiation. It also provides that a court "may grant temporary and permanent equitable relief" against persons who have violated the Act. Your client, Health Scan Associates, specialized in providing X-rays. A trial court has enjoined your client from providing X-rays until its equipment and technicians are licensed under the Act, even though they meet nearly all of the safety and training requirements of the Act. The licensing process could take six months or more. The trial court has held that "an injunction is automatically required when the Act is being violated." Traditionally, injunctions are issued only when the harm they will prevent outweighs the harm they will cause to the defendant. In addition, injunctions may be issued automatically, with no balancing of interests, when there are repeated or continuing violations of the statute. You are drafting a brief supporting your motion for a stay of the injunction pending appeal and plan to argue that the injunction was wrong under both theories. Your point headings might be drafted in the following ways:

ANSWER A:

II.   THE TRIAL COURT ERRED IN ENJOINING HEALTH SCAN FROM PROVIDING X-RAYS UNTIL IT COMPLIES WITH THE TECHNICAL REQUIREMENTS OF THE RADIATION CONTROL ACT.

    A.   The Act requires the automatic issuance of an injunction only for significant and continuing violations, not for minor violations such as those committed by Health Scan.

    B.   The harm to Health Scan from its loss of income while awaiting proper licensing, its possible bankruptcy, and the dismissal of its thirty-four trained workers outweighs the state's interest in technical compliance with the Act.

ANSWER B:

II.   THE TRIAL COURT ERRED IN ENJOINING HEALTH SCAN FROM PROVIDING X-RAYS UNTIL IT COMPLIES WITH THE TECHNICAL REQUIREMENTS OF THE RADIATION CONTROL ACT.

    A.   The injunction should not have been issued automatically because the appellant did not commit significant and continuing violations of the Act.

    B.   Even if the Act purported to make injunctive relief mandatory, it could not do so because such relief is always within the trial court's discretion.

    C.   The injunction should not have been issued because the Act makes such relief discretionary rather than mandatory.

    D.   The injunction should not have been issued because the harm to the appellant far outweighs the state's interest.

        1.   The injunction will greatly injure the appellant by causing a total loss of income for six or more months, possible bankruptcy, and unemployment of thirty-four workers.

        2.   The injunction will only slightly accelerate the time by which the appellant technically complies with the Act.

ANSWER C:

II.   THE TRIAL COURT ERRED IN GRANTING THE INJUNCTION BECAUSE THE INJUNCTION WAS NOT MANDATORY UNDER THE RADIATION CONTROL ACT AND BECAUSE THE BALANCE OF EQUITIES FAVORS THE APPELLANT.

Answer A provides a straightforward yet complete outline of the client's position and is the best of the three answers. The organizational scheme is smooth and understandable. Each of the client's basic contentions is summarized in a single minor heading.

Answer B is too choppy to be effective. It has too many headings and thus obscures the basic thrust of the Argument. The second minor heading (B) should be incorporated with the first minor heading (A) because the two points are closely related and because they are more forceful when made together. Similarly, the third and fourth minor headings (C and D) should be combined, as in Answer A. Moreover, subheadings 1 and 2 after the fourth heading (D) add little to the single heading on that issue in Answer A. Finally, Answer B refers to Health Scan as "the appellant," which makes it harder for the reader to understand which party is involved. It is often better to use the proper name, a descriptive label (e.g., licensee), or the trial court designation (e.g., defendant).

Answer C represents the other extreme by omitting the minor headings. The organizational scheme of the Argument is not explained and its persuasive value is diminished accordingly.

Working through the following exercises should improve your understanding of these concepts.

Exercise 21-A

Edward Hinkle is appealing an order of the State Industrial Commission denying his claim for worker's compensation benefits. Hinkle was employed by the Goff Medical Supply Co. to deliver medical supplies to clinics, doctors, and hospitals. The boxes containing the supplies were secured by rubber bands about twelve inches long and one-half inch wide. There was testimony before an administrative law judge that Hinkle and several other Goff employees engaged in rubber band "fights" at least two or three times a week. Hinkle's supervisor said he observed such fights several times each month and discouraged them on at least one occasion.

One day, when Hinkle was loading supplies in his truck as part of his regular work, two other employees flipped rubber bands at him. Hinkle immediately flipped a rubber band back at them. One of these employees then found an eighteen-inch sliver of wood and stepped toward Hinkle, brandishing it like a sword. Hinkle took the wood from her and used a rubber band to shoot the wood through the air at the employee. The other employee batted the sliver with a trash can lid she had been using as a shield, and the deflected sliver struck Hinkle in the face, blinding him in the right eye. The entire episode lasted about two minutes. Section 45 of the State Worker's Compensation Act provides for compensation of injuries that are not self-inflicted to "every employee who is injured by accident arising out of or in the course of his employment." There is one pertinent appellate decision:

Sperry v. Industrial Commission (**1989**)

The petitioner asks this Court to review an order of the State Industrial Commission denying him worker's compensation benefits for serious injuries he sustained when he fell from a truck that a co-worker was driving around the parking lot at the warehouse where they worked. The petitioner testified that the incident occurred during regular working hours, that they were using the truck to make "figure eights" in the light snow that had just fallen, and that they had never done this before. The petitioner and his co-worker worked in the shipping department at the warehouse, and neither drove nor loaded trucks as part of their regular work. We affirm the Commission's order and we hereby adopt the following four factors for determining whether a particular act of horseplay arises "out of or in the course of" employment and thus is compensable under section 45 of the Worker's Compensation Act.

1. Extent and seriousness of the deviation. We fully recognize the value of a little nonsense in any employment situation, and we understand that workers cannot be expected to attend strictly to their jobs every minute. The injury here, however, resulted from a lengthy and serious departure from the petitioner's job.

2. Completeness of the deviation. It is one thing for an employee to engage in a bit of horseplay as part of the performance of his duty. It is another to completely abandon the employment and concentrate one's energies on something unrelated to one's job, as occurred here.

3. Extent to which horseplay has become a part of the employment situation. The act of horseplay here occurred only once. It was not a custom in the warehouse.

4. Extent to which the nature of employment may be expected to include some horseplay. Relevant considerations here include the existence of things in the work environment that are readily usable for horseplay and the presence of lulls in the work. We do not believe that, given petitioner's work environment, a truck especially lends itself to horseplay.

For all of these reasons, the Commission's order is affirmed.

1. Assume you are representing Hinkle:
   (a) What is the basic outline of your Argument?
   (b) Draft point headings to correspond to each point in your outline. Do these headings serve as thesis statements for the text you would draft under them? Do they incorporate the rule of law and relevant facts? Are they specific and readable?

2. Assume you are representing the Industrial Commission:
   (a) What is the basic outline of your Argument?
   (b) Draft point headings to correspond to each point in your outline. Do these headings serve as thesis statements for the text you would draft under them? Do they incorporate the rule of law and the relevant facts? Are they specific and readable?

Exercise 21-B

This exercise is based on the Arguments drafted in response to the advocacy questions from Exercise 20-C, pp. 242–49.

1.   Assume you are representing the Lees:
    (a)   What is the basic outline of your Argument?
    (b)   Draft point headings to correspond to each major point in your outline. Do these headings serve as thesis statements for the text under them? Do they incorporate the rule of law and the relevant facts? Are they specific and readable?

2.   Assume you are representing PlayChem:
    (a)   What is the basic outline of your Argument?
    (b)   Draft point headings to correspond to each major point in your outline. Do these headings serve as thesis statements for the text under them? Do they incorporate the rule of law and the relevant facts? Are they specific and readable?

Statement of Facts
for a Brief

THE STATEMENT OF FACTS in an office memorandum relates the facts necessary to understand and resolve the legal issues presented. The Statement of Facts in a brief does that and more; it subtly persuades the court that fairness requires a decision in your client's favor. Many advocates believe that the Statement of Facts is the most significant part of a brief because it defines the setting in which the case will be decided. Whether it is or not, it does have substantial persuasive value.

Factual statements in office memos and briefs are similar in many respects and, therefore, many of the basic rules are the same. The Statement of Facts must be an honest and accurate description of the events that gave rise to the litigation. All legally significant facts must be included and stated precisely, whether they are favorable to the client or not. Key background facts should be included, but distracting details should not. The facts must be stated logically and understandably.

Although similar to the Statement of Facts in an office memo, the Statement of Facts in a brief contains two additional kinds of information. First, it contains emotionally significant facts. These facts, which are omitted from an office memo unless they are also legally significant, should be included in a brief because they can have a substantial effect on a court's decision-making process by appealing to its sympathies and sense of justice. The strongest cases are both emotionally appealing and soundly based on the relevant law. Cases that are weak on the law can often be strengthened by a factual situation that arouses sympathy. Second, the factual statement in a brief describes the procedural background of the case—including the major events that led to this point in the litigation, the decisions of any lower courts that heard the case, and brief explanations of their decisions. These procedural facts give both trial and appellate courts a better understanding of the case and what relief the advocate requests.

Appellate briefs, unlike trial briefs, are accompanied by a transcript of the record. The transcript includes the pleadings, affidavits, exhibits, and other documents submitted to lower courts, and the decisions of those courts. The record also includes the transcribed oral proceedings before the courts, such as arguments on motions or the testimony at trial. The transcript of the record thus provides the complete factual and procedural background of the proceedings in the lower courts. The Statement of Facts in a brief should show the pages in the record where the stated facts can be found. For example: "The police found the pistol under Anderson's pillow. (R. at 33.)" This citation shows the source of this fact to be on page 33 of the record. Generally, a single fact or group of related facts should be followed immediately by a citation. When you are paraphrasing or summarizing facts spread throughout several pages in the record, such as pages 13, 14, 15, and 16, you can group them together and cite them as follows: (R. at 13–16.) At other times, you will need to mention several separate pages: (R. at 11, 28, 30.) Once you have provided a citation to the record in your Statement of Facts, you no longer need to refer to the record when using those facts.

☐ The basic principles for persuasively stating the facts are best set forth in the context of a hypothetical problem.

You represent Iris Monge in a sex discrimination case. The trial court dismissed her complaint, and she is appealing that decision. The following excerpts are taken from the transcript of the record in *Monge v. Shannon Development Co.*:

Excerpt from Complaint of Iris Monge

(Page 6 of the record)

III.

The plaintiff was employed by the defendant from August 1991 to January 30, 1993, when she resigned her position.

IV.

During her employment the plaintiff advanced from a Class IV secretary to a Class II secretary and consistently received excellent job evaluations.

V.

From September 1992 to the time of her resignation, the plaintiff was subjected to severe, excessive, and inexcusable sexual harassment by her supervisor, Clarence Dudley. Specific instances of this sexual harassment include making obscene jokes to other male employees in the plaintiff's presence, making loud remarks about personal parts of her anatomy, suggesting to other employees that he had engaged in sexual relations with her, asking her to have sexual relations with him during lunch hour, placing his hands on her, and calling her "my little girl."

(Page 8 of the record)

VIII.

The plaintiff is thirty years of age, divorced, and the sole provider for her two young children. The plaintiff has exhausted her savings, and the defendant has refused to reinstate her to her former position.

IX.

On January 15, 1993, the plaintiff filed a sexual discrimination charge with the Equal Employment Opportunity Commission (EEOC). As of the date of this complaint, the EEOC has taken no action except to inform the plaintiff that it would be unable to process her charge until November 1993.

WHEREFORE, the plaintiff prays that this Court grant a preliminary injunction requiring the defendant to reinstate the plaintiff to her former position pending the EEOC investigation of her charge.

Excerpt from Affidavit of Earl Shannon

(Page 20 of the record)

I am Earl Shannon, and I am the sole owner and manager of Shannon Development Company. My company has branch offices in four states and employs more than 150 persons. Clarence Dudley was a supervisor in my design department for six years, and he had always performed satisfactorily. I was unaware of the situation between Monge and Dudley until February 20, 1993, when Monge informed me of the true reasons for her resignation. At that point I questioned Dudley and promptly fired him when he confirmed Monge's story. My purpose in firing Dudley was to make an example of him. I refuse to tolerate such immoral activity in my company.

(Page 21 of the record)

Since her discharge I have written a letter to Monge informing her of my deep regret over the incident and her treatment by Dudley. Also, when Monge approached me and informed me of her hardships, at two consecutive times, I offered to rehire her, but she would have had to start at a lower position than her previous one. I cannot reinstate her to her previous position because that position has been filled by a new employee, and it would be unfair to discharge that employee.

Excerpt from Deposition of Clarence Dudley

(Page 42 of the record)

Q: Do you admit that you committed the acts of harassment that the plaintiff enumerated in Paragraph 5 of her complaint?

A: I don't think it was harassment but I did them, yes.

Q: If it was not harassment, how would you classify such actions?

A: Mostly, I was just joking around and sometimes I was honestly showing my appreciation. For example, when I touched her and called her "my little girl," it happened like this: She would do a good job for me on something. I would pat her on the shoulder to show my appreciation for her good work. And I did call her "my little girl," but it was just another way of showing my appreciation.

Q: Did you always treat her like this?

A: No.

Q: Why did you treat her like this after September of 1992?

A: I guess I was just hurt and angry.

Q: Why? Could you explain further?

A: Well, when Monge came to work we really hit it off, if you know what I mean. We started dating and things got serious between us. We became very intimate and we even talked of marriage. I was going to divorce my wife, of course, when all this was going on. Then all of a sudden, in September, she told me she wanted to break off the relationship. I felt hurt and used.

Trial Court Order

(Page 50 of the record)

This action was heard on the defendant's motion to dismiss for want of subject-matter jurisdiction. The parties filed documents in support of and in opposition to the motion.

The court being fully advised, it is

ORDERED that the motion be granted, and that the plaintiff's complaint be and hereby is dismissed.

Excerpt from Trial Court Memorandum Opinion

(Page 52 of the record)

A litigant filing suit based on Title VII must first follow certain procedures. Specifically, the litigant must present a "right to sue" letter to the court or satisfy the court that 180 days have expired since the filing of the charge with the Equal Employment Opportunity Commission. A federal district court lacks subject-matter jurisdiction unless one of these prerequisites is satisfied. The plaintiff has shown neither in this case. The waiting period was imposed by Congress and serves the beneficial function of resolving many claims of discrimination outside of court. This conciliation process must be protected. Therefore, this court refuses to allow a litigant to circumvent the statutory requirements.

The following federal court of appeals opinion is from this circuit:

Knowles v. Armond Tool & Die Co. (1978)

The appellant, Sheila Knowles, worked as a press operator in the appellee's plant for more than five years. Since she began her employment in January 1972, she was continually paid one dollar less per hour than the male employees with the same seniority who were doing the same work. She complained several times to the management that she should be paid the same wage, and these complaints eventually led to her discharge on April 18, 1977. She filed a sex discrimination complaint pursuant to Title VII of the Civil Rights Act of 1964 with the Equal Employment Opportunity Commission (EEOC) on April 30, 1977. On May 30, she wrote the EEOC inquiring about the status of her complaint. The Commission informed her that because it was backlogged it could not process her claim for at least six months. The company refused to reinstate her to her former position or give her any job at all, saying that she was a "liberal and a troublemaker" and that "we don't want this kind of person working for us." She is married and is the only source of support for her husband, who has been unemployed for two years. The appellant filed suit on June 9, 1977, seeking an injunction reinstating her to her former position. The district court dismissed the case for lack of subject-matter jurisdiction. We reverse.

Title VII of the Civil Rights Act of 1964 forbids employers to discriminate against employees on the basis of sex. A Title VII plaintiff normally must satisfy the procedural provisions of the Act to be heard in federal court. First, the person must file a charge with the EEOC. Second, the complainant must receive a "right to sue" letter from the EEOC or permit 180 days to elapse from the filing of the charge. Although the congressional purpose of encouraging conciliation must be respected, it makes little sense to force a complainant to wait 180 days when the EEOC has indicated it will not attempt conciliation prior to the expiration of that period. This is especially true when, as here, it appears unlikely that the parties will voluntarily resolve their differences. In such situations, no congressional policy will be undermined by allowing the suit to proceed. In fact, a valuable congressional purpose—elimination of invidious discrimination based on sex—will be preserved. In this case, the company refused to attempt negotiation or other resolution of the problem. A district court has implied jurisdiction in such situations to issue a preliminary injunction ordering reinstatement of the plaintiff and preserving the *status quo* pending the EEOC investigation of the matter. Reversed.

The following principles should help you draft the Statement of Facts for a brief.

1. Describe the facts from your client's point of view.

The old adage that there are two sides to every story assumes a new meaning in advocacy. Show the court how your client saw the events unfold and describe them in a way that arouses sympathy for your client's position. This does not mean that you omit all facts except those that favor your client, but rather that you should help the court to see the situation from your client's point of view. You should, of course, never omit or distort legally significant facts, whether they help or hurt your position.

In the Monge case, your Statement of Facts should emphasize the injustice of her situation and her innocence in the matter. This characterization will make it easier for the court to decide the case in her favor. You might start by highlighting her early promotions with the company and then describe how intolerable her working conditions became, placing the supervisor and the company in as poor a light as possible. After showing that Monge was forced to resign because of her supervisor's behavior, you should show that she is suffering extreme hardship as a result of the company's actions. You should state that she has unsuccessfully tried to find other work, has exhausted her savings, and has two small children to support. Your statement should also convey the idea that it would be insulting for her to accept a lesser position with the same company. This is the way Monge sees it, and this is how the court should see it.

2. Vividly describe favorable emotional facts and neutralize your opponent's emotional facts.

Facts that are emotionally favorable to your client are valuable persuasive tools when used effectively. The more vividly you describe these facts, the more likely it is that a court will be sympathetic to your client. At the same time, however, you cannot ignore unfavorable emotional facts without undermining your credibility, because the other side is sure to raise them. In addition, by raising unfavorable facts in your statement, you can blunt their force. You can bleach hostile facts of their color by summarizing, explaining, paraphrasing, or otherwise minimizing them.

In Monge's case, you should describe all the facts relating to Monge's suffering and the conditions that prompted her resignation exactly as they occurred. Be as detailed and graphic as space will allow. Summarizing favorable facts will make your statement less persuasive. On the other hand, matter-of-factly summarizing the facts regarding Shannon's reasons for firing Dudley and Monge's relationship with Dudley will make your argument more persuasive. You should be honest and state, for example, that Monge and Dudley had a social relationship, but you need not and should not provide the details. While you have an obligation to raise unfavorable emotional facts, you have no obligation to make your opponent's emotional appeals.

3. Organize your statement to emphasize favorable facts and de-emphasize unfavorable facts.

Emphasize, de-emphasize, and shade legally and emotionally significant facts by artfully arranging them in the Statement of Facts. This principle differs from the previous ones in that it concerns location rather than description of specific facts, and it is particularly important when your case involves few emotionally favorable facts.

You should begin and end the Statement of Facts with favorable facts, burying unfavorable facts in the middle. The most helpful facts are often those that tend to show how wrong the other party's actions were, how right your client's actions were, and the significant consequences of these actions to your client. Placing these facts at the beginning will immediately invoke the court's sympathy toward your client. Placing facts that explain, mitigate, or justify your client's actions at the end of the statement is often, but not always, appropriate. This method of organization minimizes the force of unfavorable facts and ends the statement on a favorable note. Placing unfavorable facts in the middle makes them less likely to attract the reader's attention. Other ways to minimize unfavorable facts are to place them next to facts that favor or explain your client's position, or to hide them in a group of favorable facts. When possible, background facts should be placed where they will enhance the persuasiveness of your factual statement, but never where they would detract from its persuasiveness.

In your zeal to give facts the appropriate emphasis, be careful not to make your statement nonsensical or hard to follow. Your first priority is to tell a story the reader can understand.

In Monge's case, you should begin with facts that show the degree of sexual harassment to which she was subjected. By showing how severe and inexcusable the harassment was, you place her supervisor and her employer in as poor a light as possible. Only then should you say that Monge had been involved with her supervisor in a nonprofessional capacity. By placing the facts of the discrimination first, you minimize any importance the court might give the fact that she had had an affair with her supervisor. In the same way, you should emphasize that Monge had sought and been denied a reinstatement to her former position before you state that Shannon had investigated the discriminatory treatment, fired Dudley, written Monge an apology, and twice offered her another position. All of these facts are legally relevant, according to the federal court of appeals' opinion in the *Knowles* case, because they tend to show that Monge and Shannon might have reconciled their differences. These facts also tend to put Shannon in a favorable light, and you should make sure that the court sees these facts only in the shadow of the company's refusal to reinstate Monge.

You should include the necessary background facts about the Shannon Company after you have described Shannon's refusal to reinstate Monge. You can further minimize Shannon's honest-appearing intentions by showing that Monge is the sole supporter of two children, that she has been unable to find other work, and that she has exhausted her savings. This will end your statement on a note of sympathy for Monge and minimize Shannon's conciliatory actions by hiding them between two blocks of favorable facts.

By arranging the facts in this way you highlight the unfair treatment and helplessness of Monge and place the company and Dudley in an unfavorable light. A persuasive factual statement is especially important in Monge's case because of the questionable strength of her legal position on the conciliation issue. In *Knowles*, the lack of effort to resolve the matter was much greater than it has been here.

☐ Now that you have seen the techniques for drafting a persuasive Statement of Facts, examine the following:

ANSWER A: The appellant, Iris Monge, accepted a position with the appellee, Shannon Development Company, in August 1991. On January 30, 1993, she was forced to resign because of sexual harassment by her supervisor, Clarence Dudley. (R. at 6.) Dudley made obscene jokes and crude comments about personal parts of Monge's anatomy to other male employees in Monge's presence. In addition, he often implied or suggested to others that he had engaged in sexual relations with Monge, frequently touched Monge, and called Monge "my little girl." He also repeatedly asked her to have sexual relations with him during the lunch hour. This behavior, which was prompted by Monge's refusal to continue seeing her supervisor socially, led to her resignation. (R. at 6, 42.) Monge's work had always been satisfactory; in one year she had advanced from a Class IV to a Class II Secretary. (R. at 6.)

On January 15, 1993, Monge filed a complaint with the Equal Employment Opportunity Commission (EEOC) alleging a violation of Title VII of the Civil Rights Act of 1964 due to her supervisor's sexual harassment of her at her job. On March 1, 1993, Monge contacted the EEOC and was informed that her charge would not be processed until November 1993. (R. at 8.) Monge twice asked the appellee to reinstate her to her former position. The appellee refused to reinstate her, although Earl Shannon, the company's sole owner, apologized for Dudley's actions. The appellee claimed that Monge's former position was filled and offered Monge a lower position at a lower rate of pay, which she refused. (R. at 8, 20–21.) Shannon Development Company has offices in four states and employs more than 150 people. Dudley was fired after Shannon learned of his activities. (R. at 20.)

Monge, who is divorced and the sole provider for two children, is in dire financial straits. She has been unable to find work, has tried unsuccessfully to obtain credit, and has exhausted her meager savings. (R. at 8.) She filed suit in federal district court on March 15, 1993, alleging a violation of Title VII and seeking a preliminary injunction ordering Shannon to reinstate her to her former position pending the EEOC determination of her charge. (R. at 8.) The court held that it lacked jurisdiction and dismissed the case. (R. at 50.) Monge appealed to this Court.

ANSWER B: The appellant, Iris Monge, accepted a position with the Shannon Development Company in August 1991. Her supervisor was consistently satisfied with her work, and she advanced from a Class IV to a Class II secretary in a very short period of time. Shannon Development Company has offices in four states and employs more than 150 people. Earl Shannon is the sole owner of the company. Monge filed a complaint on January 15, 1993, with the Equal Opportunity Employment Commission (EEOC), alleging sexual harassment on the part of her employer. She resigned from her job on January 30, 1993, because she could no longer tolerate the situation. Her supervisor was subjecting her to verbal and physical abuse. Monge is currently in a precarious position. She twice requested reinstatement to her former position and both times Shannon refused her request. He offered her a lesser position, but she refused. After learning of Dudley's harassment of Monge, Shannon fired him to make an example of him because Shannon stated he would not tolerate such immoral activity in his company. He also wrote a letter of apology to the appellant expressing his sympathies for Dudley's abuse of the appellant.

Monge filed suit in federal district court on March 15, 1993, alleging a violation of Title VII and seeking a preliminary injunction ordering Shannon to reinstate her to her former position pending the EEOC determination of her complaint. The court held that it lacked jurisdiction and dismissed the case.

Answer A is better. It relates Monge's story from her perspective in a concise and understandable way, and it shows where the facts are located in the record. Answer A highlights the sexual harassment by vividly describing how Monge was treated and closes on a sympathetic note by describing Monge's desperate financial position. In addition, it neutralizes the legally significant and emotional facts that favor Shannon by placing them in the middle of the statement—after the facts concerning the harassment and Shannon's refusal to reinstate Monge and before the facts of Monge's financial condition. The emotional facts favoring Shannon's position—such as Monge's relationship with Dudley—are mitigated by the bland description. Shannon's desire to eliminate immoral activity in the company and his reasons for firing Dudley are not detailed. Answer A, in short, has applied the three principles of perspective, description, and organization to make a forceful and persuasive factual statement.

Answer B, on the other hand, is not persuasive at all. Several introductory sentences include unimportant background facts instead of facts that advance Monge's position. In addition, Answer B concludes by showing the sincerity of Shannon's efforts to correct the problem. Facts showing the severity of sexual harassment and Monge's financial condition are summarized and, therefore, used ineffectively. On the other hand, the facts showing Shannon's willingness to remedy the problem are described in detail, tending to place Shannon in a more favorable light. In addition, Answer B includes no citations to the record and fails to include all the procedural facts.

The following exercises should help you learn to write a persuasive Statement of Facts for a brief.

Exercise 22-A

Ellen Brummer is appealing a trial court decision refusing to declare void a release and settlement agreement executed between her and Ivan Pearce. The following information is extracted from the transcript of the record.

Direct Examination of Ellen Brummer

(Page 41 of the record)

Q: Could you refresh the court's memory about how this matter started?

A: Sure. About two years ago, now, April 14, 1992, my daughter, Nancy, was hurt in a car accident. She was twelve at the time and already a very good violin player. Her tutor said that with normal development she might be able to play for a major symphony orchestra. Mr. Pearce's car collided with the one I was driving and Nancy was thrown against the back of the front seat. She was sitting in the back seat. Her face was severely lacerated, and the doctor said there was a chip fracture in her nasal bones. Well, we were able to settle with Mr. Pearce and his insurance company shortly after we filed a lawsuit. The agreement was for about $7,500, which we thought would cover the extent of her injuries.

Q: Then what happened?

A: We settled on August 18, 1992. Then in October, on the 14th, we had another doctor, Dr. Dion, perform an electroencephalogram on her. He said she had severe brain damage. We didn't know that when we signed the agreement.

Cross-Examination of Ellen Brummer

(Page 45 of the record)

Q: Did you read the settlement before you signed it?

A: Yes.

Q: You read it so that you would know what you were signing, is that correct?

A: Yes.

Q: Did you think you understood the settlement when you signed it?

A: Well, I thought so at the time, but I didn't think much about it.

Direct Examination of Dr. Francis Dion

(Pages 56–57 of the record)

Q: Could you describe what you found from your tests?

A: Well, to summarize, Nancy is suffering from a post traumatic seizure disorder. Her brain was physically damaged in the accident. I will probably be able to control the disorder, but there is no question in my mind that she will require the care of a physician for seizures her entire life. I might add that she has impaired reading and hand-eye coordination and will require special help for her education.

Cross-Examination of Dr. Francis Dion

(Page 63 of the record)

Q: An electroencephalogram taken immediately after the accident would have disclosed this abnormality, would it not?

A: I think there is a reasonable medical probability of that, yes.

Release and Settlement Agreement between Ellen Brummer and Ivan Pearce

(Page 88 of the record)

FOR THE SOLE CONSIDERATION of Seven Thousand Five Hundred and 00/100 Dollars ($7,500.00), the receipt and sufficiency whereof is hereby acknowledged, the undersigned, Ellen Brummer, individually and as a parent and natural guardian of Nancy Brummer, a minor, hereby releases and forever discharges Ivan Pearce and Ajax Insurance Company, their heirs, executors, administrators, agents and assigns, and all other persons, firms or corporations liable or who might be liable, none of whom admit liability but all expressly deny any liability, from any and all claims, demands, damages, actions, causes of action, or suits of whatsoever kind or nature, and particularly on account of loss or damage to the property and on account of bodily injuries, known and unknown, and which have resulted or may in the future develop, sustained by Nancy Brummer, a minor, or arising out of damage or loss, direct or indirect, sustained by the undersigned in consequence of an automobile accident occurring on April 14, 1992.

Oral Opinion of Judge Miles Maloney

(Page 92 of the record)

Well, I think I've heard enough to decide this matter. The briefs of counsel and the testimony of the witnesses paint the picture pretty well. Because there is no controlling law in this state, I find the case of *Nokovich v. Myles Insurance Exchange* persuasive. That case says, in essence, that the words of a settlement agreement mean what they say. The agreement the parties signed is airtight, as near as I can tell. I sympathize with Ms. Brummer, but she signed the agreement. The defendant's motion for a directed verdict is granted.

The following cases are from different states:

Nokovich v. Myles Insurance Exchange (1962)

Helen Nokovich signed a settlement relieving Myles Insurance Exchange of "any and all claims" that "have resulted or may in the future develop" from injuries Nokovich sustained when she was struck by an automobile whose driver was insured with Myles. She now claims that she intended to release only her claim under the liability section of the insurance policy and not her claim under the section concerning medical payments. The trial court disagreed with her, and we affirm.

Settlement agreements are contracts and are governed by the law of contracts. When the language is clear and unambiguous, the test is not what the parties intended the contract to mean, but what a reasonable person would have thought the language meant. The language of the settlement here plainly bars all subsequent claims, and we so hold.

Brooks v. Pingel (1941)

Theodore Brooks learned of a severe brain injury suffered by his eight-year-old son several months after he had signed a settlement agreement with Keith Pingel holding Pingel "forever harmless" of any further claims arising from a fight between his son and Pingel's son. This injury is so severe that Brooks's son is now permanently paralyzed on his right side. The trial court refused to void the contract on the ground of mistake, but we reverse.

Settlements for personal injury claims are much different from normal contract matters. Brooks has shown here that neither party to the release knew about the hidden injury. This is not a case in which there is lack of knowledge of unexpected consequences of a known but apparently negligible injury. The parties knew that Brooks's son had been struck on the head and back, but they did not know about the brain injury. The release clause is therefore inapplicable.

1. What are the legally significant facts of this case?

2. What other facts are emotionally favorable to Brummer?

3. What other facts are emotionally favorable to Pearce?

4. What are the important procedural facts of this case?

5. Draft a Statement of Facts for Brummer on appeal. How do you begin the statement? How do you end it? How do you emphasize facts favorable to Bruinmer and de-emphasize those favorable to Pearce?

6.   Draft a Statement of Facts for Pearce on appeal. How do you begin the statement? How do you end it? How do you emphasize facts favorable to Pearce and de-emphasize facts favorable to Brummer?

Exercise 22-B

This exercise is based on the facts and cases from Exercise 20-C, pp. 242–49.

1.   What are the legally significant facts in this problem?

2.   What other facts are emotionally favorable to the Lees?

3.   What other facts are emotionally favorable to PlayChem Corporation?

4.   What are the important procedural facts of this case?

5.   Draft a Statement of Facts for the Lees on appeal. How do you begin the statement? How do you end it? How do you emphasize facts favorable to the Lees and de-emphasize facts favorable to PlayChem Corporation?

6.   Draft a Statement of Facts for PlayChem on appeal. How do you begin the statement? How do you end it? How do you emphasize facts favorable to PlayChem and de-emphasize facts favorable to the Lees?

23

Briefs to a Trial Court

LAWYERS SUBMIT BRIEFS to a trial court to persuade the court to decide some aspect of litigation in their client's favor. They write briefs in a variety of contexts and at many stages of litigation. These briefs all have one thing in common, however: Their audience is the trial judge.

The principles for good legal writing set forth in Part C and the advocacy principles in Chapter 20 (The Argument) apply to all briefs filed with a trial court. The following tactical considerations apply specifically to briefs written to a trial court. Although the examples in this chapter involve civil cases, the principles described here also apply to criminal cases.

Briefs to a trial court fall into four categories:

Briefs submitted in support of or in opposition to motions that are dispositive of some or all of the issues in the case without a trial. These briefs are generally filed either before or after discovery. Civil cases begin when the plaintiff files a complaint alleging that the defendant has done or is about to do something illegal and requesting relief. If the defendant believes that the complaint is not based on a valid legal theory, that the court lacks personal jurisdiction, or that there is some other fundamental defect on the face of the complaint, it will probably file a motion to dismiss based on Rule 12(b) of the Federal Rules of Civil Procedure or the parallel state rule. The defendant will attach a "memorandum of law in support of motion to dismiss," which is a brief explaining why the motion should be granted. (A brief to a trial court, particularly one that supports or opposes a motion, is often called a "memorandum of law" or "memorandum of points and authorities.") The plaintiff will file a brief opposing the motion. The trial court will then decide whether to grant the motion.

If the case is not dismissed, it proceeds to discovery. During this period, the Federal Rules of Civil Procedure and their counterpart state rules allow each side to learn more about the facts surrounding the case. After discovery is complete, either side may file a motion for summary judgment (or partial summary judgment) under Rule 56 of the Federal Rules or the parallel state rule. A party filing a summary judgment motion claims that the material facts are not in dispute and that she is entitled to judgment as a matter of law. Again, each party will file a brief with the trial court supporting its position, and the judge will decide whether to grant the motion.

Briefs submitted in connection with discovery disputes. The basic methods of discovery are written questions to opposing parties or potential witnesses (interrogatories), written requests to the other side to admit certain facts (requests for admission), written requests for the production of documents, and oral questions to potential witnesses (depositions). The trial courts expect that discovery will ordinarily be conducted in a fair and responsible manner. Occasionally, however, a party will claim that the other side is asking for privileged information, is making an overly burdensome request for the production of documents, is not responding to proper discovery requests, or in some other way is violating the rules governing discovery. When that happens, a party will often file a motion for some type of relief with the trial court and a brief in support of its motion, and the other party will file an opposing brief.

Briefs submitted in connection with evidentiary or procedural disputes. Before or during trial, disputes often arise about whether a particular piece of evidence should be admitted, or how the case should proceed. When that happens, a party is likely to file a motion with the trial court to exclude the evidence in question or for other appropriate relief. The other side will then file a reply brief, and the judge will decide how to proceed.

Briefs submitted on the substantive issues in the case before and after trial. The trial is the main event in litigation. The plaintiff must present evidence to establish all of the facts necessary to prove its claims. The defendant must present evidence to rebut the plaintiff's proof or establish the facts necessary to support any affirmative defenses. The evidence presented generally consists of witnesses' testimony and documents. Some trials are finished in a few hours. Others continue for months. After all evidence has been received, the judge or jury (depending on the case) renders a decision.

Briefs may be submitted at the commencement and at the conclusion of trials to provide the court with each party's view of the facts and how the issues should be resolved. A pre-trial brief defines the issues for the judge and demonstrates how the law applies to facts a party hopes to establish. In nonjury cases, a post-trial brief ties all of the evidence together (with citations to the record) and urges the court to reach certain conclusions based on the application of the law to that evidence. In cases decided by juries, a post-trial brief may present legal arguments supporting or opposing a motion for judgment notwithstanding the verdict or a motion for a new trial.

Each type of brief has different requirements. Pre-trial and post-trial briefs in non-jury cases are generally the longest because they contain a full rendition of the relevant facts and complete discussion of the issues. Briefs written on discovery, procedural, or evidentiary issues, on the other hand, are usually short and generally include only an abbreviated discussion of the facts and law. Briefs on dispositive motions fall in the middle. They tend to be longer and more detailed than briefs on procedural or evidentiary issues, but shorter than pre-trial or post-trial briefs. The legal analysis, however, is frequently as detailed as a pre-trial or post-trial brief, primarily because of the importance of these motions. Of course, the existence of a clear legal bar to the claim or defense should be conveyed to the court in one or two pages.

■ The following problem will help illustrate the basic tactical considerations that apply to briefs filed with trial courts:

Peter Miller was a passenger in a small private plane that crashed in a swamp in the state of West Florida. The plane was owned by the pilot, Dennis Chisolm, who was Miller's friend. The crash was caused by a defective fuel pump which, because of Chisolm's neglect in maintaining the plane, was not corrected. Chisolm, who is 67 years old and retired, escaped with minor injuries. Miller suffered serious injuries, including permanent spinal damage that has left him confined to a wheelchair. Since the crash Chisolm has become extremely depressed from guilt for having injured his friend. Psychiatric counseling has not helped.

Your firm represents Chisolm. Shortly after the crash Miller settled with Chisolm for $1.5 million, the limit of Chisolm's insurance policy plus one-half of Chisolm's life savings. He decided to settle based on your firm's advice that the settlement would end the matter as far as he was concerned and that he would have no further liability arising from the accident. Chisolm is living off the balance of his savings of $500,000. He has no other source of income.

Miller has recently commenced suit against Aaron Industries, the manufacturer of the engine and fuel pump, seeking $10 million in damages. Aaron has filed a third-party complaint against Chisolm, seeking contribution for any liability Aaron may have to Miller. Miller has offered to accept the same settlement from Aaron of $1.5 million, but Aaron has refused to discuss settlement at any figure. You have been requested to prepare a brief in support of a motion for summary judgment against Aaron's third-party complaint on the grounds of the "settlement-bar" rule.

Your research has revealed these West Florida cases:

Sarasota Pools v. Buccaneer Resorts (W. Fla. 1989)

Paula Jensen, a guest at the defendant's resort, was injured when the pool's diving board cracked, causing Jensen to strike the side of the swimming pool. The diving board had been improperly installed by the pool contractor, Sarasota Pools, and then improperly maintained by the resort. Jensen settled with Buccaneer for $75,000 and filed suit against Sarasota. She obtained a judgment of $50,000. Sarasota has brought this suit against the resort for contribution. The trial judge dismissed the complaint. The district court of appeals affirmed. We affirm.

Much disagreement exists in the various states and among the lower courts in this state concerning the rights of contribution between joint tortfeasors when the plaintiff has settled with one or more of them. Two leading views have emerged. Under the first, all tortfeasors may recover against one another for each one's percentage of fault regardless of the settlement, but the settling tortfeasors receive credit against their liability for settlement funds paid to the plaintiff. Under the second, settling tortfeasors cannot recover from non-settling tortfeasors for contribution; neither can non-settling tortfeasors sue settling tortfeasors. The second view is called the "settlement-bar" rule. A settling tortfeasor has literally "bought his peace" by settling and is entitled to freedom from any further litigation arising out of the incident. The plaintiff's claim against the non-settling tortfeasors is reduced to reflect the settlement proceeds received.

After much consideration we are persuaded that the settlement-bar rule is the better alternative. We find this rule to be much easier to enforce and fairer because it provides more predictability so parties can know the consequences of their conduct in advance. We also find that the settlement-bar rule has the salutary effect of encouraging settlements and avoiding litigation, which is much needed relief, given the congestion in our courts. Accordingly, we adopt the settlement-bar rule for all contribution actions in this state.

Raseen v. Harrison Construction Co. (W. Fla. Dist. Ct. App. 1993)

Ahmad Raseen's house in Silver Lake, West Florida, collapsed during Hurricane Andrew. He sued Harrison Construction Co., the contractors that built the house, claiming that they were negligent in construction, and Designs for Living, the architects, claiming negligent design. Harrison and Designs cross-claimed against each other. After commencement of the trial, Raseen settled with Designs for $30,000. Designs then moved to dismiss Harrison's cross-claim against it. The trial court granted the motion on the basis of the court's decision in *Sarasota Pools v. Buccaneer Resorts*. The jury subsequently returned a $150,000 verdict against Harrison. Harrison appealed, claiming that the trial court erred in dismissing Designs. We agree.

Designs' settlement in this case appears grossly disproportionate to the liabilities involved. The record suggests that Designs is primarily liable for the collapse of the plaintiff's house. The court should hear the evidence, determine the percentage of liability each should bear for Raseen's damages, and enter judgment accordingly. The settlement-bar rule thus far has been applied in this state only to personal injury cases, which present special difficulties in proving damages and assessing fault. We see no reason to extend it to a case such as that before us now involving only property damage. In addition, it is difficult to understand how any public policy of reducing litigation would be served because the trial had commenced when the settlement with Designs occurred. Reversed.

Sunshine Health Care, Inc. v. Rollins (W. Fla. Dist. Ct. App. 1991)

Dr. Alfred Rollins is licensed to practice medicine in this state. Sunshine is a health maintenance organization that employed the doctor. The genesis of this case was Rollins's treatment of Ina Rivkind at the Sunshine Clinic for a dog bite. There is little question that Dr. Rollins was negligent in treating the wound, which caused the bite to become infected. Ms. Rivkind subsequently was required to have a serious operation to cure the infection, which has left her with permanent disfiguring marks on her arm. Ms. Rivkind threatened to sue Dr. Rollins for malpractice and the clinic for negligence in hiring the doctor because there is serious question about the doctor's credentials. In separate negotiations before any suit was filed, Ms. Rivkind agreed to a $90,000 settlement with the clinic and a $5,000 settlement with the doctor. The clinic brought this action against the doctor for contribution arising out of the settlement. The trial court dismissed. We affirm.

There is a strong policy in this state of upholding settlements and holding parties to the terms of their bargain. *Sarasota Pools v. Buccaneer Resorts.* This policy is especially strong where, as here, both wrongdoers have settled with the plaintiff. It makes no difference that each party had not known how much the other was settling for. They both received the benefit of their respective bargains—the end of litigation. The settlement-bar rule precludes either of them from now reopening the dispute in an attempt to redistribute the liability.

You have also located a pertinent law review article, portions of which appear below:

Elizabeth B. Burns, *The Settlement-Bar Rule: Tough Choices, Tough Answers,* 89 Tallahassee L. Rev. 135 (1993)

Perhaps one of the greatest areas of philosophical disagreement in modern law concerns the problem of contribution among joint tortfeasors when the plaintiff has settled with one or more of them. The question most often arises in cases of personal injury, but not exclusively so. Many instances of property damage occur in which two or more potential defendants share responsibility, making the rule just as applicable as in personal injury cases. In addition, many property damage cases involve personal injury or are cases in which an injury just as easily could have occurred. Although some cases have drawn a distinction between personal injury and property damage, applying certain rules of contribution in the former and not in the latter, there is no rational basis for doing so. The problem is highlighted in a case involving both personal injury and property damage. Is there any logic to applying two different rules to such a case? The answer is no.

. . . .

Each of four different views on the contribution question has merit. Each also requires courts to make tough choices among competing considerations. In *Sarasota Pools v. Buccaneer Resorts,* the West Florida Supreme Court selected the settlement-bar rule as the law in West Florida. Under this rule a settling tortfeasor literally buys his peace with the world. He cannot be sued by anyone who may also be liable to the plaintiff but neither can he sue anyone. The incident and the litigation are over as far as a settling tortfeasor is concerned.

The settlement-bar rule has much to commend it and serves many valuable policy goals. First, it is easy to enforce. The only legitimate question is whether there has been a *bona fide* settlement. If the settlement is collusive or a sham, the court can disregard it and rule on the contribution claim as if no settlement occurred. Second, the settlement-bar rule is fairer to the settling tortfeasor in that it gives him the benefit of his bargain. Any settling tortfeasor certainly believes that once he settles with the plaintiff, his obligations with respect to the incident are at an end. The settlement-bar rule enforces that expectation. Third, the settlement-bar rule provides predictability and certainty in this troublesome area of the law. A defendant knows that he can either litigate or settle. If he chooses the latter he can do so with confidence that he will not later be drawn into any subsequent litigation arising out of the incident. Finally, and perhaps most importantly, the settlement-bar rule encourages settlements, thus reducing litigation. This is perhaps the greatest policy consideration supporting the rule. The cost of litigation today is enormous and is a social cost that we all share. Significant resources are conserved every time a dispute is settled short of litigation. Because encouraging settlements is the primary policy underpinning the rule, there would seem to be no justification for applying the rule when that policy is not served.

. . . .

The settlement-bar rule does not come without cost. The major cost is potential unfairness to other non-settling defendants. The plaintiff is permitted to proceed against them for the full amount of the plaintiff's claim, less what the plaintiff received from the settling tortfeasor. The non-settling tortfeasor who is barred from contribution, therefore, may be held to a greater share of liability than he should legitimately have to bear. For example, if the plaintiff's damages are $100,000 and the plaintiff settles with Defendant A for $10,000, Defendant B would be fully liable for the balance of $90,000, even if Defendant B's share of responsibility for the plaintiff's damages may only be 20%.

The short answer to this dilemma, however, is that the non-settling tortfeasor could have settled but chose not to do so and instead risked litigating the claim. Presumably, the non-settling tortfeasor did this knowing he had no contribution rights. One would imagine that the lack of contribution rights would be a significant incentive for a non-settling tortfeasor to settle.

------

1. Focus more on the applicability of legal rules than on policy.

Trial judges are more concerned with deciding cases in accordance with the applicable legal rules than with the effect of their decisions on subsequent cases or on the policies underlying the rules. Trial judges favor a straightforward application of the law to the facts before them.

Briefs to trial courts therefore should focus more on the applicable legal rules contained in statutes and cases than on the policies supporting them. Include the text of any relevant statute and the rules from cases on point, and explain their importance. If a judge believes a rule or a statute covers a particular issue, he will be less inclined to make the effort to follow an argument that policy considerations compel a different conclusion. Focusing on the legal rules is especially important in procedural, discovery, and evidentiary disputes, because these areas are comprehensively governed by codifications. This is not to say that policy has no place in a brief to a trial court. Policy is important to trial judges—especially when the law is unclear or in transition. But given a trial judge's caseload, policy generally takes a back seat to the hard legal rules.

◻ Consider these drafts from the brief in support of the motion for summary judgment:

ANSWER A: The settlement-bar rule precludes Aaron's contribution action against Chisolm. *See Sarasota Pools v. Buccaneer Resorts.* The facts in *Sarasota* are virtually identical to those presented here. In *Sarasota,* the plaintiff settled with one tortfeasor and then brought suit against the non-settlor and obtained a judgment. The non-settling tortfeasor then sued the settling tortfeasor for contribution. The supreme court, holding that a joint tortfeasor who settles is insulated from further liability, affirmed the trial court's dismissal of the non-settling tortfeasor's action. Similarly, this Court should dismiss Aaron's contribution action because Aaron, a non-settling tortfeasor, is seeking contribution from Chisolm, a settling tortfeasor. The *Sarasota* court reasoned that precluding these actions would encourage settlements, and that reasoning applies to this case.

ANSWER B: Aaron's third-party action against Chisolm should be precluded under *Sarasota Pools v. Buccaneer Resorts,* in which the court held that the settlement-bar rule applied in a suit virtually identical to that presented here. Barring such an action in this case would serve the social good by encouraging settlements. It would also fulfill the parties' expectations that the amounts they have settled for represent their total liability. Finally, it would ease the burden of congestion in our courts. In *Sarasota,* the court recognized all of these policies.

Answer A is better. Answer A emphasizes the applicable rule and straightforwardly applies the rule to the facts. Answer A focuses primarily on the similarities between *Sarasota Pools* and our case, and only incidentally on policy.

Answer B provides only the barest explanation of the rule and how it applies to this case. The otherwise compelling effect of the case is therefore substantially diminished. The policy discussion, moreover, is much more extensive than the discussion concerning the applicability of *Sarasota Pools*. The applicability of the case will be of more interest to the trial judge than the underlying policies.

2. Emphasize that fairness requires a decision in your client's favor.

Some cases should not be filed at all, and some legal arguments have no plausible answer. In situations like this, when the law is clear and the trial court has no discretion, a brief based on the legal rules alone should be sufficient to prevail. The "issues" in such cases are actually "givens," which are described in Chapter 5 (Identifying and Selecting Issues for Analysis). But when the adversary system is working properly, each party has a plausible legal basis for its position. The facts then assume great importance.

You should generally focus on the justice of a decision in your client's favor. You must try to convince the trial judge that your client has behaved prudently and fairly, that the other party has behaved imprudently or unfairly, and that to decide the issue for your client would work justice. You can accomplish this in a number of ways. One way is to show that your client is innocent of any wrongdoing or overreaching. Another is to demonstrate that your opponent took advantage of your client or otherwise engaged in some deceptive practice. A third is simply to point out the unfair negative consequences that a decision adverse to your client would have without an appropriate benefit to the winner.

Trial judges are close to the litigants, at least much closer than judges sitting on courts of appeals. Most people bring genuine disputes into the courtrooms, and many are very complex. Trial judges are acutely aware that each decision they make has real world consequences and can drastically affect people's lives. Within the confines of the applicable legal rules, therefore, trial judges tend to strive for just or fair results. This principle should sound familiar to you; it is discussed as an important consideration in Chapter 8 (Reaching a Conclusion).

Using facts to your advantage requires subtlety. You must bring the facts to the court's attention without giving the impression that you are trying only to play on the judge's sympathy. Simply arguing that a result would be unjust, without legal grounds to support a decision in your client's favor, is likely to fail. The best approach is to weave facts favorable to your client into your legal argument.

 Consider the following:

ANSWER A: Aaron's suit against Chisolm should be dismissed. Chisolm settled shortly after the incident for the limits of his insurance policy plus one-half of his retirement savings, acknowledging his responsibility and doing what he could to make the plaintiff whole. Aaron, however, has refused to discuss settlement with Miller, choosing instead to gamble by litigating a case it might lose and exposing itself to greater liability. Aaron should not now be permitted to involve Chisolm in such a gamble and risk eventually undoing Chisolm's settlement—particularly because Chisolm's insurance limits are exhausted, and his savings would be required to pay any judgment in favor of Aaron, which would leave Chisolm destitute. This is the very hardship the settlement-bar rule was intended to remedy.

ANSWER B: Aaron's suit against Chisolm should be dismissed. The law precludes contribution from a settling tortfeasor. *Sarasota Pools v. Buccaneer Resorts.* Chisolm has settled. Aaron has not. Chisolm has "bought his peace" and is insulated from further liability.

ANSWER C: Aaron's suit against Chisolm should be dismissed. Chisolm is retired. The settlement with Miller exhausted the limits of Chisolm's insurance and consumed one-half of his life savings. Chisolm would be left destitute if he were now required to pay a judgment in favor of Aaron. Chisolm has suffered enough for injuring his friend. Allowing the suit to proceed would be grossly unfair and unjust because Chisolm may be required to pay twice, thereby penalizing Chisolm for settling his dispute with Miller.

Answer A is best because it emphasizes the facts favorable to Chisolm, and because it demonstrates to the court that justice would not be served by a decision in Aaron's favor. Answer A also weaves the facts into the legal context of the settlement-bar rule to demonstrate that the rule was intended to address the very situation presented here.

Answer B makes no use of the facts favorable to Chisolm and is thus lifeless. It correctly states the legal rule but fails to animate it by placing the rule in the context of the human situation. Answer B also does not indicate how a decision in Chisolm's favor would work justice.

Answer C, while using many favorable facts, does so ineffectively. It does not artfully blend the facts with the legal principles. Answer C also goes too far in describing Chisolm's grief, which by itself is not compelling because it has no bearing on the legal rules. Chances are you have already lost if you must throw yourself upon the mercy of the court.

3. Be brief.

Trial judges usually have large caseloads, and trial courts are overwhelmed by the sheer volume of paper filed in connection with motions and trials. Most trial judges and their clerks therefore do not have the luxury of time to read, much less appreciate, extended arguments—no matter how sophisticated, well reasoned, or compelling they may be. Short, focused, and cogent briefs that make only the points necessary to prevail are more likely to be read, and the arguments in them more often understood and appreciated, than longer briefs that attempt to cover all points in great detail. Although trial courts generally place page limitations on briefs—frequently between fifteen and twenty-five pages—you should resist the temptation to fill the number of pages permitted unless absolutely necessary. Your "brief" should be as brief as possible.

This principle requires you to make important judgments about what is important enough to include in the brief. Several considerations assist in exercising this judgment. First, if you have cases directly on point, discuss only those. A discussion of other cases that may be analogous is unnecessary and tends to muddle an otherwise clear presentation. Second, avoid extended discussions of policy. If the policy supporting a decision in your client's favor cannot be stated in one or two sentences, then it is probably too complex to be included in the brief. Third, keep your argument and analysis as straightforward and simple as possible. Try to include only arguments that compel the conclusion you seek, not ones that simply support it. Fourth, spend as little time as possible distinguishing the authority relied on by your opponent. This does not mean that you should ignore it. Rather, you should tell the court in the fewest possible words why it is inapplicable and then not discuss it again. Similarly, address one or two major flaws in your opponent's argument rather than every one. A trial court is more interested in understanding your position and learning your basic reasons for not accepting your opponent's position than it is in reading your conclusive refutation of every argument advanced by your opponent.

☐ Consider the following:

ANSWER A: Aaron's third-party complaint against Chisolm should be dismissed. In *Sarasota Pools v. Buccaneer Resorts*, the West Florida Supreme Court adopted the settlement-bar rule, which precludes any non-settling tortfeasor from recovering contribution from a settling tortfeasor. *Sarasota* is directly on point. In that case, the injured party settled with the resort and filed suit against the non-settling pool contractor. The court held that the settlement-bar rule precluded such a suit. The court reasoned that the policy of encouraging settlements and providing settling wrongdoers with the benefit of a bargain would be furthered by such a ruling. Other decisions are in accord. *E.g., Sunshine Health Care, Inc. v. Rollins.*

The facts of the present case are virtually identical. Chisolm settled with the plaintiff shortly after the incident. The plaintiff then sued Aaron, and Aaron brought this claim against Chisolm. The settlement-bar rule should preclude Aaron's suit just as it did the claim against *Sarasota Pools*. The policy articulated in *Sarasota Pools* of encouraging settlements would be served by such a ruling.

Any reliance by Aaron on *Raseen v. Harrison Construction Co.* is misplaced. In *Raseen*, the non-settling tortfeasor and the settling tortfeasor were both sued at the same time and cross-claimed against each other. Raseen settled with one defendant, and during trial the court dismissed the second defendant's cross-claim against the first. The court of appeals reversed, holding that the settlement-bar rule did not require dismissal. *Raseen* is contrary to the West Florida Supreme Court's holding in *Sarasota Pools* and was therefore incorrectly decided. Moreover, *Raseen* is distinguishable because it did not involve personal injury and the settlement did not occur until after the trial had commenced. Accordingly, the public policy articulated in *Sarasota* of avoiding litigation through settlements would not be served.

ANSWER B: Aaron's third-party complaint against Chisolm should be dismissed. In *Sarasota Pools v. Buccaneer Resorts,* the injured plaintiff settled with one tortfeasor, then brought suit against the other. The court considered the competing rules concerning contribution among joint tortfeasors and concluded that it would adopt the settlement-bar rule, which precludes an action for contribution against a settling tortfeasor. The court articulated several policies favoring this rule. The court observed that the rule was easier to enforce, fairer, and provided more predictability, allowing the parties to know the consequences of their conduct in advance. The court also held that the settlement-bar rule has the salutary effect of encouraging settlements and avoiding litigation, providing much-needed relief from the congestion in our court system.

The court in *Sunshine Health Care, Inc. v. Rollins* reached a similar result. In that case an injured plaintiff settled with the medical clinic where she was negligently treated, as well as with the doctor. Both defendants settled prior to suit being filed. The clinic, which paid a much greater amount in settlement than the doctor, subsequently brought an action against the doctor for contribution. The court dismissed the action based on *Sarasota,* citing the strong policy of encouraging settlements and holding parties to the terms of their bargain.

The applicability of the settlement-bar rule as the law in this state was recently recognized in a well-written article on contribution, Elizabeth B. Burns, *The Settlement Bar Rule: Tough Choices, Tough Answers,* 89 Tallahassee L. Rev. 135 (1993). The writer acknowledged the policies served by application of the rule, observing that the most important policy fostered by the rule is that of encouraging settlements.

The present case is analogous to *Sarasota* and *Rollins.* The plaintiff settled with Chisolm and then brought suit against Aaron. Aaron now attempts to seek contribution from Chisolm. The settlement-bar rule as expressed in *Sarasota* and *Rollins* expressly precludes such an action.

Any attempt by Aaron to rely on *Raseen v. Harrison Construction Co.* is misplaced. In that case the plaintiff sued both the construction company and the architect, Designs for Living, for the collapse of the plaintiff's house as a result of Hurricane Andrew. Harrison and Designs cross-claimed against each other. The plaintiff settled with Designs for $30,000. Judgment was eventually obtained against Harrison Construction Co. in the amount of $150,000. The court of appeals reversed the trial court's dismissal of Designs, holding that the settlement-bar rule did not preclude Harrison from continuing to litigate its cross-claim against Designs. The court held that the settlement-bar rule applied only in personal injury cases and saw no reason to extend the doctrine to cases involving only property damage. The *Harrison* case directly conflicts with *Sarasota Pools* and therefore was incorrectly decided by the court. In any event, *Harrison* is distinguishable because it involved property damage only. Moreover, in *Harrison* both parties were named defendants and the trial was proceeding when one party settled. Accordingly, the policies of discouraging litigation and relieving congestion in the court system would not have been served.

Answer A is better because it says everything that needs to be said, and in fewer words. Answer A states the rule, tells the court that there is a case from the West Florida Supreme Court directly on point, summarizes the policy in one sentence, and concisely disposes of the opposing authority.

Answer B, while a complete and well-reasoned answer, is simply too long for a brief to a trial court. It needlessly discusses all of the cases in detail and thereby extends the discussion without adding force. This extended discussion actually detracts from the inherent forcefulness of the leading case on point. Similarly, the discussion of the law review article is unnecessary, especially because cases directly support Chisolm's position. References to law review articles in a brief to a trial court are unnecessary except when the law is unclear or no analogous authority can be found. Legal periodicals, however, are often cited in appellate briefs. Answer B also spends too much time discussing the policy considerations supporting the settlement-bar rule and distinguishing the one case that tends to support Aaron's position. In short, although Answer B has the makings of a good appellate brief, it is simply too detailed for a brief to a trial court.

4. Write for the court.

Writing for the court involves two considerations—the local court rules and the temperament of the judge. Most federal district courts and many state trial courts have rules that dictate how briefs should be filed. They often state the form and content of these briefs as well as the maximum page length. As stated in Chapter 19 (Elements of a Brief), you must know and follow these rules. Many courts simply refuse to read briefs that do not follow the local rules.

Writing for the court also means tailoring your writing to the temperament of the judge who will decide whether your client wins or loses. Judges strive to be impartial and to decide cases based on the applicable law and the relevant facts. Trial judges nonetheless have individual judicial philosophies and attitudes, which can influence their decisions.

A judge can become known as strict, lenient, a stickler, or a policy-oriented judge. You can learn about a particular judge's philosophies and attitudes from reading legal journals or other publications, from discussions with other attorneys, or from the judge's published opinions.

When you know the identity of the judge, you should tailor your brief to his or her particular leanings. For example, you would concentrate more on the wording of court rules for the stickler and focus more on policy for the policy-oriented judge. If a judge has personally written an opinion on or close to the issue, you should read that opinion, and consider referring to it. You should, of course, determine whether an appellate court has affirmed or reversed that opinion.

Any brief, however, even a brief written with an individual judge in mind, should be able to stand on its own merits. You should always, therefore, follow the basic principles of advocacy, writing, and analysis described in this book. Sometimes another judge is assigned to the case at the last minute and sometimes, particularly in busy courts, the judge's law clerk (not the judge) reads the briefs and recommends a decision. Judges can also become annoyed at being perceived in a certain way, or can decide cases in ways that are inconsistent with their reputation. In addition, an appellate court can reverse the trial judge's decision if the decision has an inadequate factual or legal basis. If you know who the judge is, however, you can nonetheless shade your brief in ways that enhance the likelihood that your client will prevail.

■ Assume that the trial judge assigned to the case is an outspoken advocate of reducing congestion in the courts and is known to exert considerable pressure on litigants to settle. Consider the following:

ANSWER A: Aaron's third-party complaint against Chisolm should be dismissed. In *Sarasota Pools v. Buccaneer Resorts,* the West Florida Supreme Court squarely held that a non-settling tortfeasor is precluded from asserting a claim for contribution against a settling tortfeasor. *Sarasota* is controlling here. Chisolm settled with the plaintiff and therefore is not liable to Aaron, the non-settling tortfeasor, for contribution.

Raseen v. Harrison Construction Co. is contrary to the holding in *Sarasota* and therefore should be disregarded as wrongly decided. In any event, *Raseen* is a different case because the plaintiff there sued both wrongdoers and it was only after trial commenced that the plaintiff settled with one wrongdoer.

ANSWER B: Aaron's third-party complaint against Chisolm should be dismissed. In *Sarasota Pools v. Buccaneer Resorts,* the court held that a non-settling tortfeasor is precluded from recovering contribution from a settling tortfeasor because of the settlement-bar rule. The court held that the settlement-bar rule served the laudable public policy purpose of encouraging settlements, thereby easing congestion in the court system. The policy underlying the settlement-bar rule fully supports its application here. Chisolm settled soon after the incident. If he had believed that a settlement would not insulate him from further liability, he might not have settled. Moreover, enforcing the settlement-bar rule would preclude the additional action that Aaron, the non-settling tortfeasor, now seeks to bring against Chisolm.

Raseen v. Harrison Construction Co. is a very different case. In *Raseen* the plaintiff sued both wrongdoers, and it was only after trial commenced that the plaintiff settled with one. The policy of encouraging settlements and thereby avoiding litigation would not be served by imposing the settlement-bar rule under those circumstances.

Answer B is better because it is tailored to the judge's disposition. Answer B emphasizes that application of the settlement-bar rule would encourage settlements and help relieve court congestion, arguments to which the judge is known to be receptive. Answer A misses this opportunity to appeal to the judicial philosophy of the judge and is therefore inferior. Answer A would be appropriate if the judge were known for deciding cases strictly in accordance with the letter of the law, but it is not as persuasive to a judge who has already expressed a view on the policies underlying the relevant rule. Both answers communicate Chisolm's argument, and both are persuasive. Answer B, however, is more likely to impress the judge who has been assigned to this case.

The following exercises should help you apply the principles outlined in this chapter.

Exercise 23-A

Assume you are the lawyer representing Aaron Industries. Prepare the argument for the brief in opposition to the motion for summary judgment.

Exercise 23-B

This exercise is based on the facts and cases in Exercise 6-B, pp. 78–80. Mary Quale has sued Dr. Farmer for the negligent death of her son. All of the facts in Exercise 6-B were brought out during discovery, and they are not in dispute. There is no dispute that Farmer was negligent. Farmer's lawyer has filed a motion for summary judgment with the trial court, claiming that Farmer's negligence did not proximately cause her son's death.

1. Write the argument portion of Farmer's brief supporting the motion for summary judgment.

2. Write the argument portion of Quale's brief opposing the motion for summary judgment.

3. Which is stronger? Explain. Is this conclusion consistent with your response to question 5 in Exercise 6-B? With the principles in Chapter 8?

Exercise 23-C

This exercise is based on the facts and cases in Exercise 7-D, pp. 94–95. The Metropolitan Social Welfare League filed a motion to intervene in the lawsuit brought by the Swift Land Development Corporation.

1.   Write the argument portion of the League's brief supporting its motion to intervene.

2.   Write the argument portion of Swift's brief opposing the motion to intervene.

3.   Write the argument portion of the city's brief opposing the motion to intervene.

4.   Which is stronger? Explain. Is this conclusion consistent with your response to question 7 in Exercise 7-D? With the principles in Chapter 8?

24

Briefs to an Appellate Court

ONCE THE TRIAL COURT enters a judgment, whether it is a judgment of dismissal, summary judgment, or judgment on the merits after a trial, the case is finished unless the losing party appeals. To appeal a case, the losing party (the appellant) must allege that the trial court committed a specific reversible error. For example, the appellant may assert that the trial court erred by failing to admit certain evidence, by misinterpreting or failing to follow a rule of procedure, by not applying the proper legal rule, by incorrectly interpreting the rule, or by failing to properly instruct the jury. If there is conflicting evidence at trial, the appellant may also challenge the trial court's findings of fact—the determination of which version of the facts is correct. Appeals challenging factual findings, however, are rarely successful.

Generally, a party may appeal only from a final judgment. The final judgment rule is designed to prevent piecemeal appeals until a matter has finally been resolved by the trial court. Sometimes, however, and under very limited circumstances, appeals are permitted from orders entered by the trial court prior to the entry of final judgment. These are known as interlocutory appeals. In federal courts some interlocutory appeals are brought as of right, but most are heard only if the trial court, in its discretion, certifies the order for interlocutory appeal and the appellate court, in its discretion, decides to hear the appeal. Rules governing interlocutory appeals in state courts vary significantly. State rules of appellate procedure should always be consulted.

Losing litigants have a right of appeal from final judgments to an intermediate appellate court in the federal system and in most state systems. The losing party in the intermediate appellate court has a right in some instances and some states to appeal to the highest state court or, in the federal system, to the United States Supreme Court. In the overwhelming majority of appeals, however, the highest court has discretion whether to hear the case. If the court declines to hear the case, the decision of the intermediate appellate court is final.

A losing litigant appeals by filing a notice of appeal in the appellate court having jurisdiction over the matter. Each party then submits briefs to the appellate court explaining why the trial court did or did not commit reversible error. Appellate briefs are subject to extensive rules concerning content, length, and style. Each appellate court requires litigants to follow its rules. Appellate briefs also tend to be longer and more formal than briefs to trial courts. The rules for style and advocacy, however, remain the same. Several tactical considerations should be kept in mind when preparing appellate briefs.

1. Focus on the claimed errors of the lower court.

An unsuccessful litigant cannot appeal simply because he does not like the trial court's decision. Nor can he prevail on appeal simply by demonstrating that the trial court made a mistake. An appellant must convince the appellate court that the trial court erred and that the error adversely affected the outcome. The appellee, on the other hand, must attempt to persuade the appellate court that the trial court ruled correctly on all points claimed to be error and that, even if any rulings were erroneous, they were harmless because they did not affect the outcome of the trial.

Because an appellate court is interested only in correcting mistakes made by the trial court, you should frame your argument in terms of the error you claim the trial court made or on the error your opponent alleges. The appellate court from the outset must fully appreciate the nature of the error and the procedural context in which it occurred.

Consider this principle in the context of the Miller v. Aaron Industries case from the previous chapter. You were unsuccessful in obtaining summary judgment in Chisolm's favor. The trial judge denied Chisolm's motion with the following opinion and order:

> Third-party defendant Chisolm has filed a motion for summary judgment with this Court, requesting an order of dismissal based on the settlement-bar rule. Chisolm, relying on the decisions in *Sarasota Pools v. Buccaneer Resorts* and *Sunshine Health Care, Inc. v. Rollins,* contends that he is entitled to dismissal because he settled with Miller, the plaintiff in this case.
>
> The Court disagrees. *Sarasota* is a very different case and not controlling. In *Sarasota,* the plaintiff settled with one tortfeasor, Buccaneer Resorts, and then litigated against the other, Sarasota Pools, obtaining a judgment. Sarasota afterward brought suit against Buccaneer for contribution. The court concluded that the settlement-bar rule should apply and affirmed the lower court's dismissal of the suit.

The decision in *Raseen v. Harrison Construction Co.*, relied on by Aaron Industries, is more instructive. The court there refused to dismiss for two reasons. The first was that the trial had already commenced when the settlement with one tortfeasor occurred and that tortfeasor sought dismissal. Although the court attempted to distinguish *Sarasota* for the second reason—that *Raseen* did not involve personal injury—the real distinction is in the timing.

That brings us to Chisolm's case. Suit is now pending between Miller and Aaron. The case appears unlikely to be settled. Granting Chisolm's motion will not conserve judicial resources or encourage settlements. This Court is not convinced that the rule even persuaded Chisolm to settle. The present case therefore is not the same as the wholly independent second trial sought by the non-settling tortfeasor in *Sarasota*. It is more like the situation in *Raseen*. IT IS THEREFORE ORDERED that third-party defendant Chisolm's motion for summary judgment is hereby DENIED.

The trial judge subsequently certified his order for an immediate interlocutory appeal, and the court of appeals accepted the appeal. You are handling the appeal. Consider the following:

ANSWER A: The trial court should have dismissed Aaron's third-party complaint. In *Sarasota Pools v. Buccaneer Resorts*, the West Florida Supreme Court held that a settling tortfeasor is not liable to a non-settling tortfeasor in contribution. The *Sarasota* case is controlling here.

ANSWER B: The trial court erred in denying Chisolm's motion for summary judgment. The West Florida Supreme Court held in *Sarasota Pools v. Buccaneer Resorts* that a settling tortfeasor is not liable in contribution to a non-settling tortfeasor. The *Sarasota* case is controlling, and the court's failure to follow the clear mandate of the supreme court is reversible error.

Answer B is better. Answer B clearly focuses the appellate court on the mistake made by the trial court that Chisolm claims is reversible error. Answer B also correctly describes the procedural setting of the trial court's decision and thus provides a framework for the remainder of the argument.

Answer A has a thesis sentence and properly states the law, but it does not do so in terms of the alleged trial court error. Answer A is too abstract and thus lacks the persuasiveness of Answer B.

2. Base your argument on the appropriate standard of review.

Appellate courts exercise different standards of review, depending on the nature of the case and the case's procedural posture when the trial court's decision was issued. The standard of review determines the latitude afforded to the appellate court to substitute its judgment for that of the trial court. Generally, appellate courts exercise plenary review, which is a *de novo* review, of all legal conclusions. This means they are free to substitute their judgment for that of the trial court on legal conclusions without giving any deference to the trial court's decision or reasoning. Appellate courts, however, are usually limited to a clearly erroneous or similarly restricted standard for review of the trial court's findings of fact. This restricted standard of review is a reflection of the great deference given to trial judges, who observe the witnesses first hand, in determining credibility when conflicting versions of the same event are introduced into evidence. In jury trials, it is also a reflection of the jury's role as the finder of fact.

Appellate courts generally exercise *de novo* review of summary judgments and dismissals granted on the pleadings. The standard of review for such decisions varies from state to state, however, and you should always check the law in your jurisdiction to determine the appropriate standard of review.

Always frame your argument to an appellate court in terms of the appropriate standard of review. You should state the standard of review at the beginning of the brief and, if it furthers your argument, periodically remind the court of the appropriate standard. The rules of many appellate courts require a statement of the applicable standard of review to be included in the opening sections of the brief. Even when such a statement is not required, always draft your main arguments with the applicable standard of review in mind.

◻ Consider the following examples:

ANSWER A: The trial court erred in denying Chisolm's motion for summary judgment. The scope of review of a grant or denial of summary judgment is *de novo*. This court therefore is not bound by the trial court's conclusions.

[Sections of argument omitted.]

The trial court incorrectly concluded that applying the settlement-bar rule in this case would not conserve judicial resources or encourage settlements. To the contrary, Chisolm's dismissal from the case would constitute a significant savings of judicial energy. If Chisolm's action is not dismissed, the court must consider issues of Chisolm's negligence in order to apportion the liability between Chisolm and Aaron. The issue of Chisolm's negligence will inevitably extend the trial and consume greater resources than if it were not in question. Moreover, enforcement of the settlement-bar rule may encourage Aaron to settle, because Aaron will know that if it loses, it must bear full responsibility for the plaintiff's damages without recourse against Chisolm. In any event, the policy is to encourage settlements in the first instance. Chisolm was encouraged to settle in the first instance on the belief that he would have no further liability. This Court is free to and should reject the trial court's erroneous conclusions to the contrary.

ANSWER B: The trial court erred in denying Chisolm's motion for summary judgment.
[Sections of argument omitted.]

The trial court was wrong in concluding that no judicial savings would accrue by applying the settlement-bar rule. Judicial economy would be served by trying only the issue of whether Aaron was negligent as opposed to the issues of whether Aaron and Chisolm were both negligent and the percentage of fault each should bear for Miller's damages. The court was also wrong in concluding that application of the settlement-bar rule would not encourage settlements. The court's focus is too narrow. Enforcement of the policy encourages settlements generally even if it does not encourage Aaron to settle in the present case. Chisolm certainly was encouraged to settle based on the belief that he would have no further liability.

Answer A is better. Answer A states the standard of review at the outset and again during the argument when the trial court's findings are discussed. Answer A thus reminds the appellate court that it is considering a denial of a motion for summary judgment and that it may therefore freely substitute its judgment for that of the trial court.

Answer B, on the other hand, does not remind the court that its scope of review is *de novo*. Even though appellate judges are presumed to know the scope of review, the failure to expressly remind the court of its scope of review risks the appellate court's inadvertently or subconsciously giving undue weight to the trial court's conclusions.

3. Emphasize that a decision in your client's favor would further the policies underlying the law.

As explained in Chapters 8 (Reaching a Conclusion) and 20 (The Argument), an argument that incorporates policy is stronger than one based solely on the law. Appellate briefs should contain a more extensive discussion of policy than trial court briefs. Appellate courts are responsible for providing guidance to the trial courts and for determining the direction of the law within their jurisdictions. Appellate judges, therefore, are very interested in understanding the policies supporting the applicable legal rules and determining whether those policies would be served by applying the rules to the case before them. This is especially true of the highest appellate court in a jurisdiction. A good appellate brief should clearly articulate the policies underlying the key legal rules and demonstrate how a decision in your client's favor would or would not further those policies.

 Consider the following:

ANSWER A: The trial court erred in denying Chisolm's motion for summary judgment. In *Sarasota Pools v. Buccaneer Resorts*, the West Florida Supreme Court adopted the settlement-bar rule, which precludes any action for contribution by or against a settling tortfeasor. *Sarasota* is controlling. In that case, the injured party settled with the resort. She afterward filed suit against the non-settling pool contractor and obtained a judgment. The pool contractor then commenced an action for contribution against the resort. The court held that the settlement-bar rule precluded such a suit. The court reasoned that the policy of encouraging settlements and providing parties who settle with the benefit of their bargain would be furthered by such a ruling. Other decisions are in accord. *E.g., Sunshine Health Care, Inc. v. Rollins.*

The facts of the present case are virtually identical. Chisolm settled with the plaintiff shortly after the incident. The plaintiff then sued Aaron, and Aaron brought this claim against Chisolm. The settlement-bar rule should preclude Aaron's suit just as it did the claim in *Sarasota Pools.* The policy articulated in *Sarasota Pools* of encouraging settlements would be served by such a ruling.

ANSWER B: The trial court erred in denying Chisolm's motion for summary judgment. In *Sarasota Pools v. Buccaneer Resorts,* the West Florida Supreme Court adopted the settlement-bar rule, which precludes any action for contribution by or against a settling tortfeasor. *Sarasota* is controlling. In that case, the injured party settled with the resort and filed suit against the non-settling pool contractor, obtaining a judgment. The pool contractor then commenced an action for contribution against the resort. The court held that the settlement-bar rule precluded such a suit. Other decisions are in accord. *E.g., Sunshine Health Care, Inc. v. Rollins.*

The court in *Sarasota* articulated several policies fostered by the settlement-bar rule. The court stated that the rule was much easier to enforce and much fairer than the alternatives. The court further observed that the rule provided more predictability, allowing the parties to know the consequences of their conduct in advance. The court also said that the settlement-bar rule had the salutary effect of encouraging settlements and providing much-needed relief for the congestion in our court system. Legal commentators have agreed. In her article, *The Settlement Bar Rule: Tough Choices, Tough Answers,* 89 Tallahassee L. Rev. 135 (1993), Elizabeth B. Burns pointed to the rule's tendency to encourage settlements as its single most beneficial policy.

The facts of the present case are virtually identical to those in *Sarasota.* Chisolm settled with the plaintiff shortly after the incident. The plaintiff then sued Aaron, and Aaron brought this claim against Chisolm. The settlement-bar rule should preclude Aaron's suit just as it did the claim against *Sarasota Pools.*

The policies underlying the settlement-bar rule would be well served by its application to this case. Chisolm would not have settled but for the belief that doing so would end his liability. The trial court's conclusion that the rule did not encourage Chisolm's settlement is simply wrong. This Court exercises plenary review in this manner and should disregard the trial court's erroneous determination. Moreover, to look at the current situation and determine whether the policy of encouraging settlements would be served is myopic. The proper question is whether the settlement-bar rule encourages settlements generally, not whether the rule should be disregarded after one tortfeasor settles if the remaining tortfeasors refuse to settle. The policy of conserving judicial resources would also be served by applying the settlement-bar rule to this case. The difficult issue of apportionment of fault between Aaron and Chisolm would be removed from the case, leaving for trial only the issue of Aaron's negligence.

Answer B is better. It effectively explains the key policies underlying the rule and demonstrates that the supreme court and a legal commentator have recognized the rule. Answer B then demonstrates how application of the rule to Chisolm's case would further the policies underlying the rule. It fleshes out the bare legal rules, making the argument much more compelling and significant to an appellate judge.

Answer A should look familiar to you. It is similiar to the better answer under the third principle in Chapter 23 (Briefs to a Trial Court). The answer is good for a trial brief but deficient for an appellate brief because it includes no extended discussion of policy. While Answer A correctly states the rules of law and mentions the supporting policy, it does not explain the underlying policy considerations and demonstrate how they would be served by applying the settlement-bar rule.

4. Explain how a decision in your client's favor would foster harmony or consistency in the law.

Appellate courts are concerned with the orderly development of the law. They want to ensure not only that the policies supporting the rules are being served but also that their decision will not create disharmony in the law or set bad precedent. You must therefore strive to convince the appellate court that a decision in your client's favor is consistent with previous decisions and that it would foster, rather than discourage, a rational development of the law.

☐ Consider the following:

ANSWER A: The West Florida Supreme Court's decision in *Sarasota Pools v. Buccaneer Resorts* is controlling.
[Argument on law and policy.]
The trial court's decision therefore should be reversed. Its decision is contrary to *Sarasota* and *Rollins*. For the reasons given, *Raseen* was incorrectly decided and should be disregarded.

ANSWER B: The West Florida Supreme Court's decision in *Sarasota Pools v. Buccaneer Resorts* is controlling.
[Argument on law and policy.]
A decision reversing the trial court would therefore be in complete accord with *Sarasota* and *Rollins*. To the extent that *Raseen* was correctly decided, it is not to the contrary. The trial in *Raseen* had already commenced when the settlement was reached.

The public policies of encouraging settlements and conserving judicial resources would not have been furthered by application of the settlement-bar rule in that case.

Answer B is preferable because it clearly articulates how a decision in Chisolm's favor would be consistent with the uniformity or harmony in this area of the law. Even the troublesome *Raseen* decision is harmonized. Answer A is little more than a summary. It fails to demonstrate how a decision in Chisolm's favor would contribute to the orderly development of the law. It does not attempt to harmonize the *Raseen* decision, leaving the court with two divergent lines of authority from which to choose. Answer A therefore is less persuasive than Answer B.

The following exercises should help you learn to apply these principles.

Exercise 24-A

Assume you are the lawyer representing Aaron Industries. Prepare the argument for the appellate brief supporting the trial court's decision on the motion for summary judgment.

Exercise 24-B

This exercise is based on the facts and cases in Exercise 6-C, pp. 80–82. Bradley Greenleaf brought a nuisance action against Peter Elliot. The case was tried before Judge Claudia Shea. All of the facts stated in the exercise are included in the record of the trial. Afterwards, Judge Shea delivered an opinion from the bench. The transcript of that opinion is as follows:

> I find that Greenleaf was damaged sufficiently for a nuisance action, but that his case has one fatal flaw. The law in this state does not give Greenleaf a legal right to the free flow of light. Without such a right, I must decide this case in favor of Peter Elliot.

1.   Assume you are Greenleaf's attorney. Would you appeal the entire decision?

2.   Assume you are Elliot's attorney. If Greenleaf appeals, would you cross-appeal any part of this decision?

3.   Draft the argument portion of Greenleaf's brief on appeal.

4.   Draft the argument portion of Elliot's brief on appeal.

5.   Which argument do you think is stronger? Explain.

Appendixes

MEMORANDUM

TO: Maria Hernandez
FROM: Loren Taylor _LT_
DATE: September 10, 1993
RE: Tyler's fraud claim against Eastern
         Pacific University, file no. P93-37

QUESTIONS PRESENTED

I. Whether, in an action for fraud, the elements of
lack of a reasonable basis for misrepresentation as well
as reasonable reliance on the misrepresentation have
been satisfied:

   A. Whether a university recruiter lacked a reasonable basis for a false representation to a student that
there was a preferential admissions policy for a graduate
program, when the recruiter believed there was such a
policy only because he knew that five of the university's
twenty-three other graduate programs had one.

   B. Whether the student's reliance on the misrepresentation was reasonable when the university recruiter
who made the false statement was acting in his official
capacity, but the student did not investigate the statement and heard nothing else to confirm or deny it.

II. Whether an action for fraud is allowed under the
three-year statute of limitations, which begins to run
when the plaintiff should reasonably have discovered the
fraud, when the misrepresentation concerning a graduate
program's admissions policy occurred about five years
ago, but the student learned of the misrepresentation
only six months ago even though he performed clerical
work for that program for the past four years.

BRIEF ANSWERS

I. A. Yes. The recruiter misrepresented the university's policy without any specific factual basis for
believing that the program had such a policy. His

personal belief that such a policy existed because other programs had that policy does not provide a reasonable basis for the statement.

    B.   Probably yes. The student was reasonable in relying on the recruiter's statement because a university recruiter can be expected to know about the school's graduate program. Although the student did not investigate the statement, he heard nothing that contradicted it.

II. Probably yes. The student did not discover the fraud until six months ago, when he was denied admission to the graduate school. Because he was never put on notice that the policy might not exist, even when he performed clerical work for the graduate program, he had no reason to discover the fraud earlier.

STATEMENT OF FACTS

    When Timothy Tyler began his senior year of high school in September 1988, he was trying to decide whether to attend Eastern Pacific University or Yosemite College. He had spoken to representatives of Eastern Pacific University's small and prestigious Global Policy Studies (GPS) program, which he wanted to attend after obtaining a college degree. The representatives had told Tyler that he would need excellent credentials to be admitted and pointed out that many of their students were honor graduates of major universities. There was no discussion about whether Eastern Pacific graduates received priority in admissions to the GPS program. The financial assistance office at Eastern Pacific told him no scholarships were available. A short time afterward, he accepted a full four-year athletic scholarship to attend and play soccer at Yosemite College. He planned to graduate from Yosemite College and then pursue a graduate degree from the College's International Environmental Protection program.

Several weeks later, Richard Cramer, a recruiter from Eastern Pacific University, approached Tyler about attending Eastern Pacific. Tyler asked about Eastern Pacific's GPS program and told Cramer he was interested in being admitted. Cramer told Tyler that Eastern Pacific gave its graduates priority in admission to the GPS program. "I'm telling you this," Cramer said at the time, "because I want you to play soccer at Eastern Pacific." No such policy exists. In fact, no Eastern Pacific graduates have been admitted to the GPS program since 1983. Cramer later said he believed Eastern Pacific had such a policy because he had recruited students for five of Eastern Pacific's twenty-three other graduate programs. Because these five programs had preferential admissions policies, Cramer said he thought it likely that the GPS program did too. No one told him that the GPS program had such a policy. Cramer never investigated the existence of this policy or the admission requirements for Eastern Pacific's GPS program.

Tyler gave up his scholarship at Yosemite to enroll at Eastern Pacific University. Because he received no scholarship at Eastern Pacific, he incurred substantial debt to pay his educational and living expenses. While an undergraduate, he worked part time in the GPS department. He assisted the admissions secretary during his freshman year by performing clerical work such as handling routine inquiries for applications and mailing letters. He was not involved with admissions decisions, and the priority admissions policy was never discussed.

In October 1992, when Tyler was a senior at Eastern, he applied for admission to the GPS program. In March 1993, Eastern Pacific denied the application, telling Tyler for the first time that Eastern Pacific graduates received no priority admission to the GPS program. Tyler has since applied to several other graduate programs and reapplied to Yosemite. He has not been admitted to any of these programs.

3

Tyler is considering a lawsuit against Eastern Pacific because of Cramer's statements and would like to know whether he has a claim for fraud.

DISCUSSION

I. Cramer's statement to Tyler that there is a priority admission policy for the Global Policy Studies (GPS) program probably constitutes fraud. Damages for fraud are recoverable under Cal. Civ. Code § 1709 (West 1985): "One who willfully deceives another with intent to induce him to alter his position to his injury or risk is liable for any damage which he thereby suffers." Deceit is defined to include the "assertion, as a fact, of that which is not true, by one who has no reasonable ground for believing it to be true." Cal. Civ. Code § 1710(2) (West 1985). As construed by the courts, fraud occurs when (1) a material representation has been made, (2) the representation is false, (3) the defendant knew the representation to be false or did not have sufficient knowledge to warrant a belief that it was true, (4) the defendant made the representation intending to induce the plaintiff to rely on it, (5) the plaintiff reasonably believed the representation to be true, (6) the plaintiff relied on it, and (7) the plaintiff consequently suffered damages. If one element is missing, there is no fraud. Nathanson v. Murphy, 282 P.2d 174, 177 (Cal. Ct. App. 1955).

These elements apply to both contract and non-contract cases, even though there is a separate statute for fraud relating to a contract. Cal. Civ. Code § 1572 (West 1982). The courts frequently cite both sections 1572 and 1710 regardless of the context. E.g., Carroll v. Gava, 159 Cal. Rptr. 778 (Ct. App. 1980) (misrepresentation in sale of real estate); Continental Airlines, Inc. v. McDonnell Douglas Corp., 264 Cal. Rptr. 779 (Ct. App. 1989) (alleged misrepresentation in brochure).

In the Tyler case, five elements of fraud are easily
established. First, Cramer's assertion about the priority
admission policy was material. A representation is
material if it is important enough to induce the plaintiff to act or refrain from acting. Ashburn v. Miller,
326 P.2d 229, 234 (Cal. Ct. App. 1958). Cramer's statement induced Tyler to attend Eastern Pacific University
instead of Yosemite College. Second, the statement was
false; there was no priority admissions policy. Third,
Cramer freely admitted when he made the statement that
he intended to induce Tyler to enroll at Eastern Pacific.
Therefore, the element regarding intent to induce action
has been satisfied. Fourth, Tyler relied on the statement because he gave up his scholarship at Yosemite
College to attend Eastern Pacific University. Finally,
Tyler suffered damages because he paid Eastern Pacific
University's tuition out of his own pocket and because he
was not admitted to Eastern Pacific's GPS program.
The only remaining questions are whether Cramer lacked
reasonable grounds for believing his statement to be
true and whether Tyler's reliance on the representation
was reasonable.

A.   Cramer had no reasonable grounds for making the
statement. Under the statute, as already noted, fraud
occurs when the person making the assertion "has no
reasonable grounds for believing it to be true." Cal.
Civ. Code § 1710(2). Because Cramer had no specific
information about the GPS admissions policy and based his
statement only on the likelihood that GPS would give
priority to Eastern Pacific graduates, he had no reasonable basis for making the statement.

The courts have required persons making such representations to have a reasonable factual basis for them,
generally grounded in personal inspection or investigation. In Wilbur v. Wilson, 2 Cal. Rptr. 770 (Ct. App.
1960), for example, the court held that the seller of a

5

79-acre farm was unreasonable in telling the purchaser
that the farm had 94 acres when the seller based his
representation solely on statements from the previous
owner. It was also unreasonable for the seller of a 765-
acre ranch to represent that it had 960 acres without
any factual basis or survey. Nathanson v. Murphy, 282
P.2d at 178. Similarly, it was unreasonable for the
seller of a lot containing substantial fill to tell the
purchaser that the lot was solid when he had no factual
basis for the statement, even though neither the seller
nor the previous owner had put fill on the lot. Ashburn
v. Miller, 326 P.2d at 237-38.

    Cramer's representation is similarly unreasonable.
Like the defendants in Wilbur, Nathanson, and Ashburn,
Cramer did not personally investigate the factual basis
for what he represented. Like the defendant in Ashburn,
who wrongly assumed that the lot had not been filled,
Cramer wrongly assumed that the GPS program had a priority admissions policy. Cramer's misrepresentation may
be more egregious than the misrepresentation in Wilbur
because the defendant in that case based his representation about the size of the property on a statement by
the previous owner. In Tyler's case, no one told Cramer
that GPS had a priority admissions policy.

    The fact that all five of the other graduate programs
Cramer knew about had priority admissions policies does
not make his belief reasonable. Cramer had no information
about the GPS admissions policy, and he knew that he had
no information about it. The lack of such information
about the admissions policy in the GPS and eighteen
other graduate programs means that his representation
was unreasonable.

    B. The court will probably conclude that Tyler's
reliance on Cramer's statement was reasonable. The
courts evaluate the reasonableness of a plaintiff's
reliance "in light of his own intelligence and infor-

mation." <u>Seeger v. Odell</u>, 115 P.2d 977, 980-81 (Cal. 1941). The plaintiff may recover for damages based on a reasonable-sounding representation even if he did not conduct his own investigation. <u>Ashburn</u>, 326 P.2d at 234-35. In <u>Ashburn</u>, for instance, the court found that the plaintiffs' reliance was justified because they trusted the defendant's assertions that the lot they were buying had no fill, and therefore did not investigate further. The court reasoned that a defendant may not mislead another and then benefit by asserting that the plaintiff should not have trusted him. <u>Ashburn</u>, 326 P.2d at 235. Tyler's case is analogous because he trusted Cramer and therefore did not investigate Cramer's representations.

When the plaintiff has not conducted his own investigation, the courts consider two factors in determining the reasonableness of the plaintiff's reliance: the position or experience of the person making the representation and the existence of facts that should make the plaintiff suspect the truth of the representation. <u>See</u> <u>Carroll</u>, 159 Cal. Rptr. at 780-81. Cramer's position as a representative of Eastern Pacific University and recruiter for its athletic program, and the absence of any facts contradicting his representation, justify Tyler's reliance.

When the person making the representation holds himself out as an expert on the subject of the representation, the courts have held that the plaintiff has acted reasonably in relying on the representation. In <u>Carroll</u>, for example, the court held that it was reasonable for the buyers of a mobile home park to rely on the seller's statement concerning zoning because the seller had experience with real estate generally and mobile home parks specifically. <u>Carroll</u>, 159 Cal. Rptr. at 780-81. Similarly, in <u>Gagne v. Bertran</u>, 275 P.2d 15 (Cal. 1954), the defendant held himself out as an expert in soil

7

testing for fill, and the court held that the plaintiffs were justified in believing his false representations about fill on the property they purchased.

Like the real estate expert in Carroll and the soil testing expert in Gagne, Cramer held himself out as an expert. His job requires him to provide prospective students with information about Eastern Pacific University. Tyler justifiably relied on Cramer's position and experience.

In addition, Tyler was told nothing that should have made him suspect the truth of Cramer's representation. The reasonableness of the plaintiff's reliance is questionable only when the plaintiff is given information that contradicts the representation. In Harper v. Silver, 19 Cal. Rptr. 78 (Ct. App. 1962), the seller of a boat told the buyer that the boat had matching 275 horsepower engines when in fact it had one 250 and one 275 horsepower engine, causing the boat to run erratically. Prior to the sale, the buyer talked to the mechanic who had replaced one of the original engines. Because the buyer never asked about the horsepower of the new engine, however, he did not discover any information that contradicted the original misrepresentation. As a result, the court held that the buyer's reliance on the original misrepresentation was reasonable. Id. at 81.

Similarly, nothing in Tyler's earlier conversations with GPS personnel contradicted Cramer's representation about the priority admission policy. His reliance on Cramer's representation was therefore reasonable. As a result, Cramer probably committed fraud.

II. Tyler's claim probably will not be time-barred for failure to comply with the statute of limitations even though Tyler's suit would be brought more than three years after the misrepresentation. The statute requires an "action for relief on the ground of fraud" to be

brought "[w]ithin three years" after all of the elements
of fraud have been met. Cal. Civ. Proc. Code § 338(d)
(West 1985 & Supp. 1993); Remus Films, Ltd. v. William
Morris Agency, 53 Cal. Rptr. 784 (Ct. App. 1968).   The
statute also contains an exception: "The cause of action
in that case is not to be deemed to have accrued until
the discovery, by the aggrieved party, of the facts
constituting the fraud."   Cal. Civ. Proc. Code § 338(d)
(West 1985 & Supp. 1993).   The plaintiff can toll the
statute only if he can show that he did not discover the
fraud until later and that, with reasonable diligence, he
could not have discovered it earlier. National Auto. &
Casualty Ins. Co. v. Payne, 67 Cal. Rptr. 784, 788 (Ct.
App. 1968).   Because Tyler discovered the fraud only six
months ago, and a court would likely conclude that he
could not reasonably have been expected to discover it
earlier, the statute of limitations will probably not bar
the claim.

Tyler did not have information sufficient to make
him suspicious of fraud until six months ago, which is
well within the three-year period.   This case is analogous to Seeger, in which the court did not bar an elderly
couple's fraud claim regarding their sale of a lot, even
though they failed to discover the fraud within the
statute's three-year limit. The couple said that they
were not put on notice of possible fraud within the
three-year period because of their age, the significant
distance between the place where the records were kept
and their home, and the lack of any occasion to investigate the truth of the representation.   115 P.2d at 982.

Similarly, nothing put Tyler on notice that he may
have been defrauded.   Tyler was not put on notice following
his discussion with Cramer that there was any question
regarding the priority admissions policy, and he did not
have information sufficient to make him suspicious of
fraud until his application was denied six months ago.

This is not a case in which the plaintiff had actual notice of possible fraud more than three years before filing suit, as in Bedolla v. Logan & Frazer, 125 Cal. Rptr. 59 (Ct. App. 1975). In Bedolla, the court denied a claim brought by the limited partners of a business against the general partners. The limited partners knew of some financial mismanagement by the general partners during the three years following the fraud. The court held that this financial mismanagement should have alerted them, as reasonably prudent men, to suspect the other wrongdoing that constituted the fraud and there-fore to discover the fraud earlier than they did.   Id. at 69-70.

Tyler's case is different, however, because the priority admissions policy was never mentioned during his employment and Tyler did not investigate the policy after he began working in the GPS program. Because he does not appear to have discovered any inconsistent information about the existence of the policy earlier, the court most likely would not hold him responsible for failing to investigate the policy earlier.

Nor did Tyler's part-time job in the GPS program put him in a position where he should have discovered the fraud.   In Payne, the court held that an action regard-ing the fraudulent sale of stock options was barred when the plaintiff corporation had two representatives on the defendant corporation's board of directors for eight years before filing the action. The court held that their duties on the board of directors, as well as their access to records, were sufficient to show that the plaintiff should have discovered the fraud earlier.   67 Cal. Rptr. at 789.   In this case, however, Tyler's job responsibilities in the GPS program did not involve admissions policy or admissions decisions. He did not have access to admissions files. He merely assisted the admissions secretary by performing such clerical work as

10

mailing letters and responding to requests for application forms. The court therefore probably would not bar
his claim under the statute of limitations.

CONCLUSION

Tyler can probably sustain a fraud claim against
Eastern Pacific University because Cramer's representation that Eastern Pacific's GPS program gives priority
admission to Eastern Pacific graduates satisfies all the
elements of fraud. The only elements likely to be con-
tested are whether Cramer lacked reasonable grounds for
believing his statement to be true and whether Tyler's
reliance on the statement was reasonable. Both are
probably met in this case.

Cramer had no reasonable grounds for believing his
statement to be true because he had no factual information that directly supported it. Although he knew that
at least five of Eastern Pacific's twenty-three other
graduate programs had priority admissions policies, he
did not know whether the GPS program had such a policy.

Tyler's reliance on Cramer's misrepresentation was
justifiable in light of Tyler's own intelligence and information. Cramer's position and experience in providing
students with information about the university, as well
as Tyler's lack of information that would contradict the
misrepresentation, made it reasonable for Tyler to believe
Cramer's statement. Because Tyler had no obvious reason
to suspect the falsity of the statement, he had no duty
to verify it.

Although Tyler would bring his claim approximately
five years after the fraud occurred, the court probably
would not dismiss a suit based on the three-year statute
of limitations. The statute begins running when a reasonably prudent person would have discovered the fraud.
Tyler received no information that contradicted Cramer's
original misrepresentation until his application to the
GPS program was denied six months ago.

Julia P. Chan, State Bar No. 71038
SAMUEL, PARKS & RIORDAN
485 Battery Street, 8th Floor
San Francisco, California 94111
Telephone: (415) 722-5454

Attorneys for Defendant EASTERN PACIFIC UNIVERSITY

SUPERIOR COURT OF THE STATE OF CALIFORNIA

IN AND FOR THE COUNTY OF SAN FRANCISCO

TIMOTHY TYLER,)	CASE NO. 1121-a
)	
Plaintiff,)	MEMORANDUM OF POINTS AND
)	AUTHORITIES IN SUPPORT OF
)	EASTERN PACIFIC UNIVERSITY'S
vs.)	MOTION FOR SUMMARY JUDGMENT
)	
)	
EASTERN PACIFIC UNIVERSITY,)	
)	
Defendant.)	
)	

Hearing Date: April 15, 1994
            Time: 9:30 a.m.
            Dept: 10

I. INTRODUCTION

Defendant, Eastern Pacific University (Eastern),
submits this memorandum in support of its motion for
summary judgment dismissing Plaintiff Timothy Tyler's
fraud action as barred by the three-year statute of
limitations. The alleged fraud occurred five years ago,
in 1988. Tyler did not file this suit until 1993.
Tyler should have discovered the alleged fraud in 1988
or 1989 but did not do so because he failed to act
diligently. Tyler's action therefore is time-barred.

II. STATEMENT OF FACTS

Eastern is a university in San Francisco. In October 1988, Eastern recruited Timothy Tyler, a high school senior residing in Wisconsin, to play soccer for the university. (Joint Stipulation of Facts ¶ 4.) Tyler matriculated at Eastern in September of 1989 and worked part time as a work-study student in the Global Policy Studies (GPS) program while he completed his under-graduate education. During his freshman year, Tyler assisted the GPS admissions secretary. His duties included sending packets containing the program's hand-book and application to prospective graduate students and assisting in sending out letters either accepting or rejecting applicants to the program. (Joint Stip. ¶¶ 5-6.) In October 1992, Tyler, who was then a senior at Eastern, applied for admission to the GPS graduate program. He was denied admission in March 1993. (Joint Stip. ¶ 11.)

After he was denied admission, Tyler asserted that he had been misled in October of 1987 about an alleged policy of Eastern to give priority to its own graduates for admission to its GPS program. Richard Cramer, the recruiter who approached Tyler about playing soccer for Eastern, admits telling Tyler about such a policy. (Joint Stip. ¶ 9.) Tyler, however, had been told by university representatives during his own investigation of the GPS graduate program that excellent credentials were required for admission and that many of the GPS graduate students were honor graduates of major univer-sities. No one in the GPS program has ever mentioned the priority admissions policy, since no such policy has ever existed. During the four years that Tyler was employed by the GPS program, 1989-1993, no Eastern graduate was admitted to the GPS program. In fact, no Eastern graduate has been admitted to the program since 1983. (Joint Stip. ¶¶ 10, 13-14.)

2

In October 1993, Tyler filed this suit against
Eastern, alleging that he had been fraudulently induced
to attend Eastern by Cramer's statement regarding the
priority admissions policy. Tyler asserts that he
declined a scholarship at another college to attend
Eastern and that, as a result, he has incurred substantial debt to pay tuition.

III. ARGUMENT

TYLER'S CLAIM IS BARRED BY THE STATUTE OF LIMITATIONS
BECAUSE HE FILED HIS COMPLAINT MORE THAN THREE YEARS
AFTER HE KNEW OR SHOULD HAVE KNOWN THAT THE RECRUITER'S
STATEMENT REGARDING THE PRIORITY ADMISSIONS POLICY WAS
INCORRECT.

The statute of limitations for fraud requires that
an action be brought within three years after all the
elements of fraud have been met. Cal. Civ. Proc. Code
§ 338(d) (West 1985 & Supp. 1994); Remus Films, Ltd. v.
William Morris Agency, 244 Cal. App. 2d 763, 53 Cal.
Rptr. 529 (1966). The statute further provides that the
limitation period is tolled until "after discovery, by
the aggrieved party, of the facts constituting the fraud
or mistake." Cal. Civ. Proc. Code § 338(d). A plaintiff seeking to rely on the "discovery" exception of
section 338(d) must prove that with reasonable diligence
he could not have discovered the fraud earlier. See
National Auto. & Casualty Ins. Co. v. Payne, 261 Cal.
App. 2d 403, 67 Cal. Rptr. 784 (1968).

The alleged fraud here occurred in 1988, when Tyler
declined the scholarship to another college and decided
to attend Eastern at his own expense. The statute of
limitations on the plaintiff's claim therefore expired
in 1991.

Tyler cannot rely on section 338(d) to extend the
limitations period because he failed to act with reasonable diligence in discovering the fraud earlier. The
test for determining whether a plaintiff's delay in

3

discovering the fraud was reasonable is an objective
one. The limitation period begins to run when the
plaintiff has information "sufficient to make a reasonably prudent person suspicious of fraud, thus putting
him on inquiry." Payne, 261 Cal. App. 2d at 410, 67 Cal.
Rptr. at 788; accord Bedolla v. Logan & Frazer, 52 Cal.
App. 3d 118, 125 Cal. Rptr. 59 (1975). In Payne, the
court held that an action regarding the fraudulent sale
of stock options was barred when the plaintiff corporation had two representatives on the board of directors
of the defendant corporation for eight years prior to
the filing of the action. The court found that the
directors' participation in the management of the
defendant corporation and their access to the books that
disclosed the truth about the options were sufficient to
make a reasonably prudent person suspicious of fraud
earlier.

Similarly, in Bedolla, the court held that a fraud
claim against an accounting firm was barred by the statute
of limitations when, in the three years following the
alleged fraud, the plaintiff general partners knew there
were irregularities in the way the defendants had been
keeping the financial records for several limited
partnerships. The court explained that this financial
mismanagement should have alerted the general partners,
as reasonable men, to suspect other wrongdoing. It held
that the statute began to run when the plaintiffs received
information sufficient to put them on inquiry. 52 Cal.
App. 3d at 125, 125 Cal. Rptr. at 64.

Tyler's lack of reasonable diligence here is even
more egregious than that of the plaintiffs in Payne and
Bedolla. Tyler should have realized in 1988 that the
recruiter's statement was inconsistent with the information he had already learned during his own investigation.
He knew that excellent credentials were required for
admission and that many of the students in the program

were honor graduates from major universities. He also
knew that no one he had spoken with previously had mentioned anything regarding a priority admissions policy.

Even if Tyler was not put on inquiry in 1988, he
was in 1989, when he actually worked in the admissions
office of the GPS program, assisting the admissions
secretary in handling inquiries and sending out letters
accepting and rejecting applicants. During this entire
time, no one ever mentioned the priority admissions
policy. These facts were sufficient to make a reasonably prudent person suspicious and placed Tyler under a
duty to inquire further. Tyler's failure to do so
precludes him from relying on section 338(d) to extend
the limitations period. A simple question would have
revealed the truth. Tyler's failure to ask that simple
question, given his access to the truth, establishes a
lack of reasonable diligence. The statutory period thus
expired by 1992.

Tyler's situation is far removed from those cases
in which the defrauded parties had no easy access to
the correct information and no reason to suspect fraud
before the three-year period expired. In Hobart v.
Hobart Estate Co., 26 Cal. 2d 412, 159 P.2d 958 (1945),
the plaintiff brought an action for a fraudulent stock
sale five years after the sale occurred. The court held
that the plaintiff was not barred by the statute of
limitations because he had no notice until five years
after the sale that the seller had misrepresented the
value of the stock, and because the seller, an attorney
who stood in a fiduciary relationship to the plaintiff,
actively discouraged the plaintiff from conducting an
independent investigation. 26 Cal. 2d at 439, 159 P.2d
at 973.

Similarly, in Seeger v. Odell, 18 Cal. 2d 409, 115
P.2d 977 (1941), the court allowed an elderly couple to
bring an action more than three years after the fraudu-

lent sale of their real estate. As in Hobart, the means
of discovery were not easily accessible and the plaintiffs had no reason to suspect wrongdoing. The court
held that it was not reasonable to expect the couple to
discover the fraud when the pertinent records were some
distance from their home, they had had no previous
chance to inspect the records, and they had no reason to
suspect fraud during the three-year period. 18 Cal. 2d
at 417, 115 P.2d at 982.

Tyler's case differs from Hobart and Seeger in two
important respects. First, the plaintiffs in Hobart
and Seeger had no reason to suspect a misrepresentation.
Tyler, on the other hand, surely knew that no graduate
from Eastern received preferential treatment during his
tenure as an employee in the admissions office. This
fact would have aroused suspicion in the mind of any
reasonable person. Second, the plaintiffs in Hobart
and Seeger could not reasonably have been expected to
investigate. In Hobart, the sellers discouraged him from
doing so, and in Seeger, the buyers lived some distance
away. Unlike those plaintiffs, Tyler had the information at his fingertips. No one actively concealed the
true admissions policy or discouraged him from investigating. All he had to do was ask.

The law requires plaintiffs in a fraud action to
exercise diligence in finding out the truth once they
have been put on notice that further inquiry is needed.
Tyler's failure to make even the simplest inquiry once
he had notice of the GPS program's true admissions
policy precludes him from relying on section 338(d) to
toll the statute of limitations. Therefore, the three-
year period for bringing a complaint expired no later
than 1992. Tyler's complaint, filed in 1993, is barred
by the statute of limitations and should be dismissed.

IV. <u>CONCLUSION</u>

For the reasons stated herein, Tyler's claim is time-barred, and Defendant's motion for summary judgment should be granted.

Dated: March 12, 1994

SAMUEL, PARKS & RIORDAN

By___*Julia P. Chan*___
       Julia P. Chan

Attorneys for Defendant
Eastern Pacific University

Maria Hernandez, State Bar No. 68223
HERNANDEZ & CRUZ
334 Mission Street
San Francisco, California 94133
Telephone: (415) 429-6848

Attorneys for Plaintiff TIMOTHY TYLER

SUPERIOR COURT OF THE STATE OF CALIFORNIA
IN AND FOR THE COUNTY OF SAN FRANCISCO

TIMOTHY TYLER,	)	CASE NO. 1121-a
	)	
Plaintiff,	)	MEMORANDUM OF POINTS AND
	)	AUTHORITIES IN OPPOSITION TO
	)	EASTERN PACIFIC UNIVERSITY'S
vs.	)	MOTION FOR SUMMARY JUDGMENT
	)	
	)	
EASTERN PACIFIC UNIVERSITY,	)	
	)	
Defendant.	)	
	)	

Hearing Date: April 15, 1994
Time: 9:30 a.m.
Dept: 10

I. INTRODUCTION

Plaintiff, Timothy Tyler, submits this memorandum in
opposition to Defendant Eastern Pacific University's
motion for summary judgment. The statute of limitations
was tolled in this action because Tyler had no reason to
suspect fraud or to inquire further until he discovered
the fraud in March 1993. This action therefore has been
timely filed and is not barred.

II. <u>STATEMENT OF FACTS</u>

Timothy Tyler was a member of his high school's varsity soccer team and was named to the state's All Star team. (Joint Stipulation of Facts ¶ 2.) In 1988, during the fall of his senior year, Tyler was recruited to play soccer for Eastern Pacific University (Eastern) by Richard Cramer, a recruiter for Eastern. Tyler had already accepted a full athletic scholarship to attend Yosemite College after graduation. (Joint Stip. ¶¶ 3, 5.)

In the course of their discussion, Cramer learned of Tyler's desire to obtain a graduate degree from the Global Policy Studies (GPS) program at Eastern. Cramer told Tyler that Eastern had a policy of giving priority to its own graduates in admission to the GPS program. Cramer admits that he had no idea whether the GPS program had such a policy and made this statement only to induce Tyler to play soccer for Eastern. (Joint Stip. ¶ 9.) Tyler had previously spoken with the staff of the GPS program and no such policy had been mentioned. That discussion with GPS staff had concerned the excellence of the program and the high caliber of student the program was able to attract. (Joint Stip. ¶ 10.)

Tyler subsequently declined the scholarship to Yosemite College and enrolled at Eastern. Since no scholarships were available, he financed his education by working part time and taking out substantial loans. Tyler was able to obtain a position as a student assistant in the GPS program. (Joint Stip. ¶ 5.) Although he assisted the admissions secretary during his freshman year, his responsibilities were primarily clerical—handling routine inquiries for applications and mailing letters as he was instructed by the secretary. Tyler was not involved in admissions decisions or aware of how they were made. The priority admissions policy was never mentioned during the course of his employment. (Joint Stip. ¶ 6.)

2

In October 1992, Tyler applied for admission to the GPS program. When his application was denied in March 1993, Tyler discovered for the first time that Cramer had deceived him regarding the admissions policy. (Joint Stip. ¶ 11.) Tyler promptly filed this action in October of 1993 to recover the damages incurred as a result of Cramer's deception.

III. ARGUMENT

TYLER'S ACTION FOR FRAUD WAS FILED WITHIN THE THREE-YEAR PERIOD ALLOWED BY THE STATUTE OF LIMITATIONS BECAUSE HE DID NOT DISCOVER UNTIL MARCH 1993 THAT HE HAD BEEN MISLED AND COULD NOT REASONABLY HAVE DISCOVERED THE FRAUD EARLIER.

The statute of limitations for fraud does not begin to run until "the discovery, by the aggrieved party, of the facts constituting fraud." Cal. Civ. Proc. Code § 338(d) (West 1985 & Supp. 1994). Discovery occurs when the plaintiff obtains information "sufficient to make a reasonably prudent person suspicious of fraud, thus putting him on inquiry." National Auto. & Casualty Ins. Co. v. Payne, 261 Cal. App. 2d 403, 409, 67 Cal. Rptr. 784, 788 (1968). When a plaintiff has no reason to suspect fraud, however, the statute of limitations does not begin to run. Seeger v. Odell, 18 Cal. 2d 409, 115 P.2d 977 (1941); Hobart v. Hobart Estate Co., 26 Cal. 2d 412, 159 P.2d 958 (1945).

Seeger and Hobart are controlling here. In Seeger, an elderly couple was misled about an execution sale of their real estate by the defendants' attorney, who assured them that, as an attorney, he knew all the pertinent facts about the sale. 18 Cal. 2d at 412, 115 P.2d at 979. Similarly, in Hobart, the plaintiff was misled about the market value of his stock by the attorney who had represented his family's business for a long time. In both cases, the plaintiffs had no reason to suspect that they had been misled. And in both cases, the court

3

held that the statute was tolled until the plaintiffs obtained information indicating that the attorneys had lied. <u>Hobart</u>, 26 Cal. 2d at 441, 159 P.2d at 974; <u>Seeger</u>, 18 Cal. 2d at 418, 115 P.2d at 982.

Tyler was similarly misled by someone who held himself out to be an expert. Tyler, a high school senior, had no reason to suspect that a recruiter employed by Eastern would lie to him about its admissions policy, just as the plaintiffs in <u>Seeger</u> and <u>Hobart</u> had no reason to suspect that the attorneys would lie to them. Thus, the statute did not begin to run until Tyler discovered Cramer's fraud in March of 1993.

Eastern's reliance on <u>Bedolla v. Logan & Frazer</u>, 52 Cal. App. 3d 118, 125 Cal. Rptr. 59 (1975), and <u>National Automobile & Casualty Insurance Co. v. Payne</u> is misplaced. In these cases, the plaintiffs were either aware of other wrongdoing by the defendants that should have aroused suspicion or were in a position to know the information that disclosed the fraud. In <u>Bedolla</u>, the court held that the plaintiff general partners should have suspected more wrongdoing on the part of the defendant accounting firm when the partners were already aware of other discrepancies in the books kept by the firm. 52 Cal. App. 3d at 130, 125 Cal. Rptr. at 68. And in <u>Payne</u>, the court held that members of a board of directors had a duty to discover a fraudulent sale of stock options that was contained in the corporate books. 261 Cal. App. 2d at 414, 67 Cal. Rptr. at 791.

Tyler, on the other hand, had no reason to suspect that Cramer had lied to him. His previous discussion with the staff of the GPS program had disclosed only that many of its students were honor graduates from major universities. There was no discussion regarding the preferential admissions policy. Unlike the defendants in <u>Bedolla</u>, Tyler had no information that should have led him to suspect fraud.

Tyler's situation is also very different from that of the directors in <u>Payne</u>, who had a fiduciary responsibility to know the contents of the corporation's books. Tyler, a part-time student worker, had no responsibility to learn how admissions decisions were being made. His job was to complete the various clerical tasks assigned to him by the secretary in the GPS program.

Tyler has been harmed by the deliberate deception Cramer used to induce him to attend Eastern for the benefit of its soccer team. He should not be barred from recovering for the damages he has incurred because it took four years for the truth to come to light. As observed by the court in <u>Twining v. Thompson</u>, 68 Cal. App. 2d 104, 113, 156 P.2d 29, 34 (1945):

> The courts do not lightly seize upon small circumstances in order to deny an award to an innocent victim of a fraud upon the ground that he did not discover the fraud sooner.

Since Tyler had no reason to suspect the lack of a priority admissions policy before his application was rejected, the statute of limitations began to run only in March 1993. This action therefore is timely.

IV. CONCLUSION

For the reasons stated herein, Eastern's motion for summary judgment should be denied.

Dated: March 17, 1994

HERNANDEZ & CRUZ

By *Maria Hernandez*
Maria Hernandez

Attorneys for Plaintiff
Timothy Tyler

5

MEMORANDUM

To: Sheldon Light

From: Lynn Wright LW

Re: Possible objection to federal jurisdiction in
         Westbrook Neighborhood Association v. Ellison
         Recycling, Inc., file no. 1417.

Date: July 7, 1980

QUESTIONS PRESENTED

I. Whether the plaintiff can assert citizen suit
jurisdiction for violation of the federal Clean Air Act,
which requires that sixty days' advance notice be given
to the defendant before a suit may be filed, when the
plaintiff filed suit after providing only thirty-seven
days' notice and when the defendant took some corrective
action but indicated that further corrective action was
unlikely until after the notice period expired.

II. Whether the plaintiff can assert federal question
jurisdiction for violation of the federal Clean Air Act
when the plaintiff has met all the requirements for
federal question jurisdiction and the Act states that it
does not restrict any right a person may have under any
statute or common law, even though permitting such
jurisdiction allows the plaintiff to avoid the sixty-
day notice requirement of the Act.

BRIEF ANSWERS

I.   No. The plaintiff's failure to comply with the
sixty-day notice requirement is fatal to citizen suit
jurisdiction. An exception to this rule, permitting
jurisdiction when the defendant says it will take no
corrective action, is inapplicable because the defendant
indicated it was taking corrective action.

II. Probably yes. The plaintiff has satisfied the
statutory requirements for federal question jurisdiction,
and the citizen suit provision expressly permits the

assertion of other jurisdictional bases for citizen enforcement suits.

STATEMENT OF FACTS

Ellison Recycling, Inc. (Ellison) began operating its oil recycling plant on the outskirts of Westbrook, Superior, on April 14, 1980. The next day, a number of local residents began complaining of intermittent but strong odors from the plant. Many of these people are members of the Westbrook Neighborhood Association, an organization of residents and landowners in the Westbrook area. On the same day, the Association wrote Ellison and the Superior Air Resources Board asking that corrective measures be taken.

The Board responded to the Association's request by stating that emissions from the plant were not regulated by the Superior State Implementation Plan (SIP) under the federal Clean Air Act except for the opacity limitation in section 33.1301 of the State Administrative Code. That section prohibits the discharge of visible atmospheric contaminants with a density of more than 20% opacity for more than three minutes in any twenty-four hour period. Opacity measures the darkness of smoke or emissions from a polluting source. Ellison did not respond to the Association's letter.

On May 20, 1980, the Association notified Ellison, the Board, and the United States Environmental Protection Agency (EPA) that it intended to file suit against Ellison within sixty days (July 19) unless Ellison complied with the opacity limitation. On June 22, Ellison wrote the Association, stating that it had recently hired a consultant to conduct a national search of air pollution control technologies available to oil recycling plants. Ellison said the consultant was scheduled to report back to the company on July 15 and it would know better how to proceed after that date.

Ellison also said that air pollution from the plant had
diminished to some extent because of adjustments made in
the shakedown process for the new plant, and that it hoped
the consultant's information would help it improve to
the degree of control required by the opacity regulation.

The Association filed suit in federal district court
on June 26, 1980, seeking declaratory and injunctive
relief against Ellison for violations of the opacity
regulation. The Association alleged twenty-eight
violations of the regulation in April, seventeen in May,
and twelve in June (up to the date suit was filed) and
claimed that several of its members were damaged in
excess of $10,000 each by emissions from the plant.
The Association bases jurisdiction on the citizen suit
provision of the federal Clean Air Act and on federal
question jurisdiction.

DISCUSSION

I.   Whether the plaintiff can assert citizen suit
jurisdiction for violation of the federal Clean Air Act,
which requires that sixty days' advance notice be given
to the defendant before a suit may be filed, when the
plaintiff filed suit after providing only thirty-seven
days' notice and when the defendant took some corrective
action but indicated that further corrective action was
unlikely until after the notice period expired.

The plaintiff does not have jurisdiction under the
citizen suit provision of the Clean Air Act because it
failed to provide the defendant with the required sixty
days' notice before filing suit. An alternative theory
used by several courts, which permits less than sixty
days' notice in citizen suits against defendants who
refuse to act during the notice period, is inapplicable
here because the plaintiff filed suit while the defendant
was working to correct the problem.

The Clean Air Act, 42 U.S.C. §§ 7401-7626 (Supp. III
1979), was the first comprehensive attempt by Congress
to prevent and control air pollution. Section 304(a) of

3

the Act, 42 U.S.C. § 7604(a)(1) (Supp. III 1979), permits citizens to bring actions against industrial sources and others in violation of emission standards or limitations under the Act to obtain court-ordered compliance. Jurisdiction is proper "without regard to the amount in controversy or the citizenship of the parties." 42 U.S.C. § 7604(a). Section 304(b)(1), however, limits this right by providing that "no action may be commenced" under section 304(a)(1)

> prior to 60 days after the plaintiff has given notice of the violation (i) to the [EPA] administrator, (ii) to the State in which the violation occurs, and (iii) to any alleged violator of the standard, limitation, or order.

42 U.S.C. § 7604(b)(1)(A).

A federal district court thus lacks subject matter jurisdiction unless a plaintiff provides the state, the EPA, and the defendant with sixty days' advance notice before filing suit. Strict compliance with the sixty-day notice provision is mandatory because statutes must be understood in terms of their plain meaning. E.g., Tennessee Valley Auth. v. Hill, 437 U.S. 153 (1978).

The legislative history also supports this interpretation. The conference report for the 1970 Clean Air Act Amendments, in which section 304 was added to the Act, states that a citizen suit plaintiff "must have provided the violator, the Administrator and the State with sixty days' notice" before filing suit. H.R. Rep. No. 1783, 91st Cong., 2d Sess. 56 (1970) (emphasis added).

A number of courts have required strict compliance with the sixty-day notice requirement. The leading case is City of Highland Park v. Train, 519 F.2d 681 (7th Cir. 1975), cert. denied, 424 U.S. 927 (1976). In Highland Park, the plaintiffs sought to have the EPA promulgate indirect source and significant deterioration regulations under the Clean Air Act in an attempt to prevent construction of a shopping mall and attendant road

expansion. The district court dismissed the plaintiff's
section 304 jurisdictional claim because the plaintiffs
had provided the defendant with no notice whatsoever.
The court of appeals affirmed, reasoning that Congress's
intent in enacting section 304 would be frustrated if
the notice requirement were ignored.

Similarly, the court in Loveladies Property Owners
Ass'n v. Raab, 430 F. Supp. 276 (D.N.J. 1975), aff'd,
547 F.2d 1162 (3d Cir. 1976), cert. denied, 432 U.S. 906
(1977), required strict compliance with the sixty-day
notice provision in the Federal Water Pollution Control
Act (FWPCA), 33 U.S.C. §§ 1251-1376 (1976 & Supp. III
1979). (The FWPCA citizen suit provision is similar in
all material respects to the one in the Clean Air Act.)
In that case, property owners sued Raab and the United
States to prevent landfilling by Raab on the edge of a
bay. The plaintiffs later amended their complaint by
naming EPA and certain EPA officials, among other persons,
as additional defendants. Although the plaintiffs notified the EPA regional administrator more than sixty days
before filing this amended complaint, the court held
that their failure to provide notice before filing suit
was fatal to the citizen suit claim. The court reasoned
that since courts are not free to ignore statutory
language, jurisdiction depends on strict adherence to
the notice provision. 430 F. Supp. at 281.

Although the courts in these and similar cases
requiring strict compliance emphasized the need to abide
by statutory language, they based their decisions on
several important policy considerations. First, the
full notice period provides an opportunity for out-of-
court settlements of disputes and thus lessens the likelihood of lawsuits that will add to the burden imposed
on the courts. City of Highland Park v. Train, 519 F.2d
at 690-91. Second, the notice period allows government
lawyers to better integrate the concerns identified in

5

the lawsuit into their overall enforcement efforts.
Id. at 690.   Third, jurisdictional provisions permitting
suits against the government abrogate the traditional
doctrine of sovereign immunity and should be strictly
construed.   West Penn Power Co. v. Train, 378 F. Supp.
941, 944 (W.D. Penn. 1974).

Although the factual pattern and policies relevant
to Westbrook's case differ somewhat from the cases cited,
there is ample support for requiring strict compliance
with the sixty-day notice provision here.   The Association
sent its notice of intent to sue on May 20, 1980, but
brought suit only thirty-seven days later, on June 26,
1980. The policy of encouraging out-of-court settlements
is a compelling reason to deny citizen suit jurisdiction.
By bringing an early suit, the Association precluded any
possibility of resolving the problem without litigation.
The other policy concerns of integrating citizen enforcement suits into the government enforcement scheme and of
sovereign immunity, however, are inapplicable to the
present case because those concerns are applicable only
to governmental defendants and Ellison is a private
party.

In response to the perceived rigidity of the strict
compliance approach, several courts have considered citizen
suit jurisdiction when the plaintiff has "substantially
complied" with the sixty-day notice requirement.   These
courts have reasoned that there is no point in waiting
the full sixty days when defendants respond prior to the
end of the period that they plan to take no action on the
notice.   Natural Resources Defense Council v. Callaway,
524 F.2d 79 (2d Cir. 1975);   Massachusetts v. United
States Veterans Admin., 541 F.2d 119 (1st Cir. 1976).
Although the reasoning by these courts is inconsistent
with the strict compliance approach, their insistence
that section 304 must be interpreted in light of its

6

remedial purposes may have great force, particularly for
a citizens' organization claiming exposure to pollution.
The substantial-compliance approach, however, is inapplicable to Westbrook's situation.

The court in Veterans Administration denied
jurisdiction because the plaintiff had not stated a
"prima facie claim of futility" sufficient to justify
jurisdiction after only forty days' notice.   541 F.2d
at 121-22.   That case is analogous to Westbrook's
situation. The plaintiff in Veterans Administration
alleged that a veterans hospital had violated the FWPCA
by failing to comply with a timetable for tying into a
municipal sewage system.   Although the plaintiff claimed
that notice would not cure past violations, the court of
appeals affirmed the dismissal of the citizen suit.
The court reasoned that "even conceding that no administrative action could cure the failure of the VA to meet
past deadlines for planning and construction of the
sewer tie-in, increased administrative action could
still expedite completion of the project."   Id. at 121.
The court suggested that the substantial compliance
theory is inapplicable if it is possible that some
administrative action "could" correct the problem.   Id.

The Westbrook Association did not substantially
comply with the sixty-day notice requirement because
Ellison was taking corrective action and so informed the
Association prior to the end of the notice period. This
case is thus similar to Veterans Administration because
"increased administrative attention" seems to be resolving
the problem. The plaintiff's complaint alleged a
significant but diminishing number of opacity violations
following the start-up of the plant--twenty-eight in
April, seventeen in May, and only twelve in the first
twenty-five days of June. The defendant's consultant
was to examine different control technologies and report

7

back by July 15, four days before the end of the notice period. Although significant work remained after that period, and it is not clear whether anything would be done, Ellison said it was correcting the problem. Even if that response can be considered ambiguous, the Veterans Administration case precludes substantial compliance when there is a possibility of further corrective measures.

Because Ellison said it was taking corrective measures, Callaway is distinguishable. In Callaway, the plaintiffs brought a citizen suit to enjoin the use of an ocean disposal site for dredge materials. The district court dismissed the suit because the plaintiffs had provided only forty-eight days' notice. The court of appeals reversed, holding that strict compliance was not required when the EPA and other agencies are given notice of the alleged violations and the defendant informs the plaintiff prior to the commencement of the suit that no action will be taken. The court reasoned that the purpose of the notice provision had been served because waiting longer would have been futile. 524 F.2d at 84 n.4. See also Conservation Soc'y v. Secretary of Transp., 508 F.2d 927, 938 n.62 (2d Cir. 1974), vacated on other grounds, 423 U.S. 809 (1975) (dicta concerning the district court's strict and therefore "crabbed construction" of the sixty-day notice provision). Westbrook's situation is far different from the "no action" reply considered in Callaway because Ellison documented its progress and indicated its plans to abate the problem.

The most compelling argument for applying the substantial compliance approach in Westbrook's case focuses on the defendant's continuing violations and the injunctive relief the plaintiff seeks. This argument, however, does not change the conclusion that there is no legitimate claim of futility here. In Callaway, where the court found substantial compliance, the plaintiffs sought to enjoin the use of certain ocean dump sites. In Veterans

8

Administration, by contrast, where the court found no
substantial compliance, the plaintiff sought fines
for a past failure to comply with the law rather than
injunctive relief against continuing violations.   But
because section 304 conditions a citizen's ability to
obtain court-ordered compliance on adherence to the
notice procedure, the absence of futility is controlling.

A third theory for jurisdiction under section 304,
"constructive compliance," can be discredited but not
distinguished from Westbrook's case.   Although the cases
use the terms "constructive compliance" and "substantial
compliance" interchangeably, constructive compliance
here refers to an approach permitting jurisdiction if
sixty days pass between the time notice is given and the
time of the court's first hearing on the lawsuit.

The only case that has used constructive compliance
is City of Riverside v. Ruckleshaus, 4 Env't Rep. Cas.
(BNA) 1728 (C.D. Cal. 1972).   In that case the plaintiffs filed suit to force the EPA to promulgate an air
pollution control plan for part of California.   The
plaintiffs provided no advance notice under section 304.
The court refused to dismiss the case since sixty days
had passed between the date that suit was filed and the
date that the court completed its hearing on the plaintiff's request for an injunction.   The court reasoned
that the lapse of these sixty days was sufficient for
purposes of section 304 because the EPA had the beneficial effect of the sixty-day notice provision during
that period.   4 Env't Rep. Cas. at 1731.

Constructive compliance would, if applied, permit
jurisdiction in Westbrook's case since in all likelihood
more than sixty days will have elapsed between the May
20 notice and the court's first hearing.   The court is
unlikely to apply this theory, however, because of its
weak legal basis.   Constructive compliance abrogates
the language in section 304(b) that "no action may be

9

commenced" before the plaintiff has provided sixty days'
notice. It also removes the notice provision from the
Act, since almost any imaginative plaintiff would obtain
sixty days of notice before the court's first hearing.
Constructive compliance, therefore, is not a valid basis
for citizen suit jurisdiction.

II. Whether the plaintiff can assert federal question
jurisdiction for violation of the federal Clean Air Act
when the plaintiff has met all the requirements for
federal question jurisdiction and the Act states that it
does not restrict any right a person may have under any
statute or common law, even though permitting such jurisdiction allows the plaintiff to avoid the sixty-day
notice requirement of the Act.

The court probably has federal question jurisdiction
over Westbrook's case. The plaintiff has met the statutory requirements for federal question jurisdiction, and
the Clean Air Act and the better reasoned cases permit
the assertion of such jurisdiction, although there is
significant authority to the contrary.

Section 1331(a) of the Judicial Code, 28 U.S.C.
§ 1331(a) (1976), provides that the federal district
courts have jurisdiction over civil actions against
private parties when the matter in controversy exceeds
$10,000 and the action arises under federal law. The
plaintiff has satisfied both requirements. Specific
members of the plaintiff Association have alleged damages
in excess of $10,000 each from the defendant's emissions.
The matter also arises under federal law because the
Clean Air Act requires SIPs to be federally approved and
enforceable. Citizens Ass'n v. Washington, 383 F. Supp.
136 (D.D.C. 1974).

The savings clause of the citizen suit provision,
section 304(e) of the Clean Air Act, 42 U.S.C. § 7604(e)
(Supp. III 1979), expressly permits citizen suit plaintiffs to allege other bases of jurisdiction:

Nothing in this section shall restrict any right
which any person (or class of persons) may have
under any statute or common law to seek enforcement
of any emission standard or limitation or to seek
any other relief (including relief against the
Administrator or a state agency).

The court in Natural Resources Defense Council v.
Train, 510 F.2d 692 (D.C. Cir. 1975), construed a
comparable savings provision in the FWPCA to permit
jurisdiction under section 1331(a) even when the plaintiffs had provided no advance notice of the suit.   In
Train, the plaintiffs filed suit against the EPA to
force it to publish effluent guidelines for specific
categories and classes of point sources. Jurisdiction
was based on section 1331(a). The EPA argued that the
court lacked jurisdiction because suits to compel the
EPA to perform a nondiscretionary duty can be brought
only under the citizen suit provision of the FWPCA. The
court rejected this argument and permitted jurisdiction,
reasoning that the citizen suit provision does not
restrict federal court jurisdiction over actions that
could have been maintained even in the absence of that
special authorization. 510 F.2d at 702. The court
viewed the savings clause as confirming that interpretation.

The court in National Sea Clammers Ass'n v. City of
New York, 616 F.2d 1222 (3d Cir. 1980), similarly concluded that the citizen suit provision of the FWPCA was
intended to expand rather than restrict the rights of
injured parties to bring actions. The plaintiffs in
that case, who made their living harvesting fish and
shellfish, sought injunctive and other relief against
the discharge of untreated sewage and toxic wastes.
The district court dismissed the plaintiffs' FWPCA claim
because they had not provided adequate notice under the
citizen suit provision of that Act. The court of appeals
reversed, holding that the plaintiffs could proceed under
section 1331(a). Id. at 1228. The court reasoned that

11

the citizen suit provision was particularly intended for persons who could not meet the existing jurisdictional requirements but who still had legitimate grounds for an enforcement action. The court concluded that persons who could previously bring an action under section 1331(a) now have the option of suing under section 304, but persons who could not previously obtain jurisdiction may sue only under section 304. Id. at 1227.

In Westbrook's case, similarly, the court probably has federal question jurisdiction even if it does not have jurisdiction under section 304. Like the FWPCA citizen suit provision in Train and Sea Clammers, section 304 was intended to expand the possible jurisdictional bases for citizen lawsuits to enforce the Act while leaving existing jurisdictional bases intact. The plaintiff's failure to provide adequate notice is thus relevant only to the section 304 claim. The plaintiff, therefore, should be able to proceed under section 1331(a).

Although there is significant authority to support the contrary position that the plaintiff's failure to provide adequate notice precludes jurisdiction under any other statute, the court is not likely to find it persuasive. The leading case is City of Highland Park v. Train, 519 F.2d 681 (7th Cir. 1975), cert. denied, 421 U.S. 927 (1976). In Highland Park, the plaintiffs filed suit to have the EPA promulgate indirect source and significant deterioration regulations under the Clean Air Act in an attempt to prevent construction of a shopping mall and attendant road expansion. The plaintiffs based jurisdiction on sections 304 and 1331(a). The court held that because the plaintiffs had provided no notice what-soever, it could not exercise jurisdiction under either section 304 or section 1331(a). The court reasoned that "the savings provision, expressing the general intention of Congress not to disturb existing rights to seek relief, does not have the affirmative effect of removing conditions which existing law imposes upon the exercise of those rights." Id. at 693. The court further reasoned that since section 304 was an adequate jurisdictional basis for the plaintiffs' claim, they were required to use that and nothing else. Id.

This reasoning is not without force, but the Highland Park court failed to read section 304(e) for its plain meaning. The court's analysis imposes a sixty-day notice requirement on section 1331(a) in Clean Air Act cases, even though section 304(e) expressly preserves "any right" that a person may have under "any statute." The right to bring suit under section 1331(a) as it is written must be considered as a right preserved by section 304(e). In addition, there does not appear to be a valid basis for making section 304 the exclusive jurisdictional basis for Clean Air Act suits when its own terms provide to the contrary. The court in Westbrook's case, therefore, will probably reject the Highland Park reasoning and exercise jurisdiction over the plaintiff's Clean Air Act claim under section 1331(a).

CONCLUSION

The court probably does not have citizen suit jurisdiction, but it probably does have federal question jurisdiction. The Clean Air Act requires that a plaintiff in a citizen enforcement suit must provide the defendant with sixty days' notice before filing suit. The plaintiff in the present case failed to meet the sixty-day requirement because it provided only thirty-seven days' notice. The substantial compliance exception to this requirement, which applies when a defendant responds to the notice by stating that it will take no further action prior to the end of the notice period, is inapplicable here. The defendant responded to the notice by stating it was taking corrective action and

would continue to do so before the end of the period.
A second exception, constructive compliance, will most
likely be rejected by the court. This little-used theory
permitting notice after suit is filed is of questionable
legal validity because it effectively renders the notice
period meaningless in most cases.

The court, however, probably has federal question
jurisdiction over the plaintiff's suit. The plaintiff
has met the statutory requirements for federal question
jurisdiction because the amount in controversy exceeds
$10,000 and the claim arises under federal law. In addi-
tion, such jurisdiction is a permissible alternative to
citizen suit jurisdiction. The better reasoned cases
have concluded that the citizen suit provision was
intended to expand rather than restrict the existing
bases of federal jurisdiction over suits to enforce the
Act. This interpretation is confirmed by the savings
clause in the Act, which preserves any right a person may
have under any other statute. The plaintiff's failure to
provide the requisite sixty-day notice is thus irrelevant
to federal question jurisdiction.

14

UNITED STATES COURT OF APPEALS
FOR THE THIRTEENTH CIRCUIT

No. 80-152

WESTBROOK NEIGHBORHOOD ASSOCIATION,
Appellant,

vs.

ELLISON RECYCLING, INC.,
Appellee.

ON APPEAL FROM THE
UNITED STATES DISTRICT COURT
FOR THE DISTRICT OF SUPERIOR

BRIEF FOR APPELLANT

Truman LaFoote
1602 Cass Avenue
Suite 411
Detroit, Michigan 48202

INDEX

i

340

AUTHORITIES CITED

OPINIONS BELOW

The opinion of the United States District Court for the District of Superior is unreported, and contained in the Transcript of Record. (R. at 22-25.)

JURISDICTION

The judgment of the United States District Court for the District of Superior was entered on August 8, 1980. The appeal was filed on August 20, 1980, and was granted on December 1, 1980. The jurisdiction of this Court is invoked under 28 U.S.C. § 1291 (1976).

STATUTES INVOLVED

The texts of the following statutes relevant to the determination of the present case are set forth in the Appendix: Clean Air Act, §§ 304(a), 304(a)(1), 304(b)(1), 304(e), 42 U.S.C. §§ 7604(a), 7604(a)(1), 7604(b)(1), 7604(e) (Supp. III 1979); 28 U.S.C. § 1331(a) (1976).

STANDARD OF REVIEW

This is an appeal from a decision to grant the defendant's motion to dismiss for lack of subject matter jurisdiction under Fed. R. Civ. P. 12(b)(1). The district court's decision is subject to de novo review. See Massachusetts v. United States Veterans Admin., 541 F.2d 119 (1st Cir. 1976) (applying de novo review).

QUESTIONS PRESENTED

I. Whether the district court erred in refusing to exercise citizen suit jurisdiction under the Clean Air Act when the plaintiff substantially complied with the Act's sixty-day notice provision by giving notice and bringing suit only when the defendant's response indicated that waiting further would be futile.

1

II. Whether the district court erred in refusing to exercise citizen suit jurisdiction under the Clean Air Act when the plaintiff constructively complied with the Act's sixty-day notice provision because more than sixty days elapsed between the notice and the district court's first hearing on the case.

III. Whether the district court erred in declining to exercise federal question jurisdiction over a citizen enforcement action under the Clean Air Act, when the plaintiff has met the requirements for federal question jurisdiction and the Act expressly states that it does not restrict any right a person may have under any statute or common law.

STATEMENT OF FACTS

The Appellant, Westbrook Neighborhood Association (Westbrook), is an organization of approximately 250 members, most of whom are residents and landowners in and around the town of Westbrook, Superior. The Appellee, Ellison Recycling, Inc. (Ellison), is a corporation that has its sole plant located on the outskirts of Westbrook. (R. at 1-2.)

On April 15, 1980, one day after the plant commenced operation, local residents, many of them members of Westbrook, began complaining of intermittent, noxious odors from plant emissions. These emissions in all likelihood contained several substances with carcinogenic, mutagenic, and toxic properties. On the same day, Westbrook wrote the company and the Superior Air Resources Board, asking them to take measures to correct the problem. Neither the company nor the Board responded. (R. at 2, 22-23.)

The odors continued. On May 20, 1980, Westbrook again wrote the company and requested that it take some action to reduce the pollution. Westbrook informed the company that unless action was taken within sixty days a

suit would be filed against it for violation of section
33.1301 of the Superior Administrative Code. (R. at
10-12.)   That section prohibits any person from dis-
charging into the atmosphere visible contaminants with
a density of more than 20% opacity for more than three
minutes in any twenty-four hour period.   Opacity measures
darkness of the smoke or emissions from a polluting
source. (R. at 8-9.)   Westbrook sent copies of that
letter to the Board and to the United States Environmental Protection Agency (EPA). (R. at 10.)

The excess emissions were not abated, and Ellison's
response did not come until more than one month later.
On June 22, 1980, the company informed Westbrook that it
had recently hired a consultant to make a survey of
pollution control technology and that it "hoped" to
install control equipment that would reduce emissions to
comply with the regulation.   The consultant, however,
was not scheduled to report back to the company until
July 15, 1980, three months after the plant had begun
polluting the air and only five days before the end of
the notice period.   Although the number of violations
diminished somewhat after April because of "minor
adjustments ... in the shakedown process," the company
violated the regulation fifty-seven separate times
between April 15 and June 25.   There were twenty-eight
violations in April, seventeen in May, and twelve in the
first twenty-five days of June.   The pollution was
causing extensive corrosion to buildings and automobiles
in the neighborhood. (R. at 3.)   Neither the Board nor
the EPA responded to the notice. (R. at 10.)

Finally, on June 26, 1980, Westbrook filed suit for
declaratory and injunctive relief in federal district
court, alleging violations of the opacity regulation.
The complaint also stated that neither the Board nor the
EPA was prosecuting Ellison for these violations.   Westbrook predicated jurisdiction on the citizen suit provi-

sion of the federal Clean Air Act, 42 U.S.C. § 7604, and
on federal question jurisdiction, 28 U.S.C. § 1331(a).
(R. at 1-4.)   Several members of Westbrook were by that
time damaged in excess of $10,000 each by emissions from
Ellison's plant. (R. at 3.)

The court heard argument on Westbrook's motion for
a preliminary injunction and Ellison's motion to dismiss
on July 28, 1980.   The court did not hear any testimony
or receive any affidavits or other evidence, however,
including evidence on the continuing nature of the violations.   On August 8, 1980, the court granted Ellison's
motion to dismiss. (R. at 22-25.)

SUMMARY OF ARGUMENT

The district court erred in dismissing this case for
want of jurisdiction.   The court had jurisdiction under
section 304 of the federal Clean Air Act, which provides
jurisdiction for citizen enforcement actions against
violators of the Act when the plaintiff has given sixty
days' advance notice of the suit.   Westbrook substantially
complied with the sixty-day notice provision by giving
notice and bringing suit only after Ellison implied that
waiting longer would be futile.   Ellison's response
stated that a consultant would not report until several
days before the end of the notice period, indicating that
no action would occur before the end of the period, if at
all.   The purpose of the notice period, promoting out-of-
court settlements when possible, was served, since waiting
the entire period would have been pointless and counterproductive.

Westbrook also constructively complied with the
sixty-day notice provision because more than sixty days
elapsed between the formal notice and the date of the
court's first hearing in the case.   In fact, Westbrook's
prior complaints and requests for action, coupled with
the period after formal notice, provided Ellison with

more than 100 days of notice to correct its air pollution
problem.

Finally, even if Westbrook failed to comply with the
sixty-day notice provision, the district court erred
because Westbrook met the requirements of federal
question jurisdiction as an independent basis for the
lawsuit. Several members of Westbrook were damaged in
excess of $10,000 each by Ellison's emissions, and
Westbrook brought this suit under federal law. Section
304 expands the opportunities of citizens to bring
actions to enforce the Act because it is expressly
available to plaintiffs regardless of the amount in
controversy. At the same time, section 304 expressly
preserves "any right" that any person may have to proceed
under "any statute," thus permitting the assertion of
independent jurisdictional bases. Because Westbrook met
the requirements for federal question jurisdiction, the
district court should have permitted Westbrook to seek
relief on the merits.

ARGUMENT

I.   THE DISTRICT COURT ERRED IN REFUSING TO EXERCISE
     CITIZEN SUIT JURISDICTION UNDER SECTION 304 OF THE
     CLEAN AIR ACT.

The nation's serious efforts to prevent and control
air pollution and its adverse effects on human health
and the environment began with the passage of the 1970
Clean Air Act Amendments, 42 U.S.C. §§ 7401-7626 (Supp.
III 1979). The basic purpose of the Amendments, Congress
stated, is "to protect and enhance the quality of the
Nation's air resources so as to promote the public
health and welfare and the productive capacity of its
population." 42 U.S.C. § 7401(b)(1) (Supp. III 1979).
Congressional concern about controlling air pollution
was so great that Congress took the unprecedented step
of permitting citizens to aid in the enforcement
process. This step was necessary, observed the late

5

Senator Philip A. Hart, because "the Government simply is not equipped to take court action against the numerous violations of legislation of this type which are likely to occur." 116 Cong. Rec. 33,104 (1970).

Section 304(a) of the Act, 42 U.S.C. § 7604(a), permits "any person" to bring a civil action against any other person alleged to be in violation of "an emission standard or limitation under this act." Although section 304(b) of the Act, 42 U.S.C. § 7604(b), provides for sixty days' advance notice to the potential defendant, section 304 was intended to widen citizen participation in the enforcement of the Act by removing technical hindrances to jurisdiction. Natural Resources Defense Council v. Train, 510 F.2d 692 (D.C. Cir. 1975). The district court's elevation of form over substance is thus wholly at odds with both the intent and language of the Act.

A.   The plaintiff substantially complied with the sixty-day notice provision by bringing suit only after the defendant's response indicated that corrective action was highly unlikely before the period expired.

Congress intended the sixty-day notice provision to give industrial polluters and governmental agencies an opportunity to administratively resolve problems and avoid lawsuits. S. Rep. No. 1196, 91st Cong., 2d Sess. 37 (1970). When the potential defendant indicates prior to the expiration of the notice period that it will take no action on the matter before the end of that period, the purpose of the sixty-day notice provision has been served and the plaintiff may immediately bring suit. Massachusetts v. United States Veterans Admin., 541 F.2d 119 (1st Cir. 1976); Natural Resources Defense Council v. Callaway, 524 F.2d 79 (2d Cir. 1975).

In Callaway, the plaintiffs brought suit under the Federal Water Pollution Control Act (FWPCA), 33 U.S.C.

§§ 1251-1376 (1976 & Supp. III 1979), and the Marine
Research, Protection, and Sanctuaries Act, 33 U.S.C.
§§ 1401-1444 (1976), seeking to enjoin the use of an
ocean disposal site for dredge materials. Both statutes
have a citizen suit provision identical to section 304
in all material respects. The district court dismissed
the action because the plaintiffs filed suit only forty-
eight days after giving notice. The court of appeals
reversed, holding that the plaintiffs had substantially
complied with the notice provision. 524 F.2d at 83.
The court reasoned that the purpose of the notice provision had been served because the EPA and other agencies
were given notice of the alleged violations, and that
the defendants indicated no action would be taken before
the suit was commenced. 524 F.2d at 84 n.4.

Similarly, in Conservation Society v. Secretary of
Transportation, 508 F.2d 927 (2d Cir. 1974), vacated on
other grounds, 423 U.S. 809 (1975), the court of appeals
held that Congress did not intend the sixty-day notice
provision to erect an absolute barrier to earlier suits
by private citizens. The court described the district
court's dismissal of a citizen suit claim for failure to
comply with the notice provision as a "crabbed
construction" of the provision. Id. at 938 n.62.

Westbrook, like the plaintiffs in Callaway, substantially complied with the sixty-day notice provision
by not bringing suit until Ellison stated, in effect,
that waiting longer would be futile. Ellison responded
to Westbrook's May 20, 1980, notice by stating that it
had hired a consultant to study technological options
and that the consultant's report was due July 15.
Ellison said only that it "would know better what to do"
after it saw the report, indicating that Ellison would
not begin to formulate options until immediately before
the sixty-day period expired. Although Ellison said it
"hoped" to install better controls, it did not make a

7

firm commitment to resolve its severe air pollution problems, nor did Ellison commit itself to a timetable for resolving them.

During this period, moreover, the number of opacity violations stabilized. Ellison made some progress in controlling its emissions after it violated the opacity regulation twenty-eight times in the last half of April, but there were seventeen violations in May and twelve in the first twenty-five days of June. Ellison's inability to further improve air quality after April 30 indicated that "minor adjustments ... in the shakedown process" were insufficient to meet the opacity limitation. Westbrook had every reason to believe that the controls described in the consultant's report would be necessary. During this entire period, in addition, emissions from Ellison's plant were causing economic and potentially severe health injury to the members of Westbrook; several members alleged damage of more than $10,000 each. These emissions in all likelihood contained many toxic, muta-genic, and carcinogenic substances. Westbrook was amply justified in bringing suit before the sixty-day period formally expired.

This case is thus different from Massachusetts v. United States Veterans Administration, 541 F.2d at 119, which involved a citizen suit for civil penalties to correct a past failure rather than injunctive relief to correct a continuing one. In Massachusetts, the plaintiff brought suit after only forty days' notice, claiming that a veterans hospital had violated a permit requirement under the FWPCA. The court affirmed the dismissal of the plaintiff's claim because the plaintiff had not shown that waiting the full period would be futile. Increased administrative action, the court reasoned, might resolve the problem just as quickly. Id. at 121-22. In the present case, however, an injunction against the operation of Ellison's plant or even a court order expediting compliance would have resolved this problem far more

quickly than administrative action. In light of
Ellison's unwillingness to take significant corrective
action during the notice period, Westbrook had ample
evidence of futility.

Cases requiring strict compliance with the sixty-day
notice provision are distinguishable because they usually
involve either plaintiffs who make no attempt whatsoever
to give notice before filing suit or special considerations applicable only to governmental defendants. In
City of Highland Park v. Train, 519 F.2d 681 (7th Cir.
1975), cert. denied, 424 U.S. 927 (1976), the court of
appeals affirmed the dismissal of a section 304 claim
because the plaintiffs gave no notice at all to the
defendants. Courts have repeatedly dismissed citizen
suit claims by plaintiffs who provided no notice whatsoever. E.g., City of Evansville v. Kentucky Liquid
Recycling, Inc., 406 F.2d 1008 (7th Cir. 1979), cert.
denied, 444 U.S. 1025 (1980); Pinkney v. Ohio Envtl.
Protection Agency, 375 F. Supp. 305 (N.D. Ohio 1974).
These courts did not require strict (as opposed to
substantial) compliance; they merely rejected claims by
plaintiffs who made no effort to obey the law. Because
Westbrook made an effort to comply with the law, these
decisions are inapplicable.

The concerns in these cases are also inapplicable to
private defendants. The court in West Penn Power Co. v.
Train, 378 F. Supp. 941 (W.D. Penn. 1974), dismissed a
citizen suit claim by plaintiffs who failed to give any
notice, relying on the sovereign immunity principle that
the terms of congressional consent to sue the government
must be strictly construed. See also Smoke Rise, Inc.
v. Washington Suburban Sanitary Comm'n, 400 F. Supp.
1364 (D. Md. 1974) (strict compliance required by sovereign immunity). Similarly, the court in Highland Park
reasoned that the notice requirement was designed to
give the EPA time to respond to complex lawsuits and
minimize the interruption of the ongoing regulatory

9

process caused by lawsuits. 519 F.2d at 690. Both of
these concerns are inapplicable to the present case.

The few remaining cases requiring strict compliance,
e.g., Loveladies Property Owners Ass'n v. Raab, 430 F.
Supp. 276 (D.N.J. 1975), aff'd, 547 F.2d 1162 (3d Cir.
1976), are wrongly decided because they place technical
considerations before substance in interpreting a
statutory provision designed to involve citizens in the
enforcement process. The danger of elevating form over
substance in statutory interpretation was recognized at
an early date by the Supreme Court when it stated, "A
thing may be within the letter of the statute and yet not
... within the intention of its makers." Church of the
Holy Trinity v. United States, 143 U.S. 457, 459 (1892),
cited in United Housing Found., Inc. v. Forman, 421 U.S.
847, 849 (1975).

Air pollution control is more important than procedural nicety. The undeniable effect of the district
court decision is to force members of Westbrook to
breathe and live with obnoxious and health-damaging
emissions from Ellison's plant for a longer period than
they would have to otherwise. Westbrook could file
another notice, wait sixty days, and bring suit again,
but its members would continue to suffer through an
additional two months of pollution, a penalty manifestly
inconsistent with the spirit of the Clean Air Act.
Westbrook substantially complied with the sixty-day
notice requirement, and the district court should thus
have heard its claim.

B.   The plaintiff constructively complied with the
     sixty-day notice requirement of section 304
     because sixty days elapsed between the notice
     and the district court's first hearing on the
     case.

Even if section 304(b) rigidly requires sixty days'
notice, Westbrook complied with that requirement because

sixty days elapsed between the notice and the court's
first hearing. In City of Riverside v. Ruckleshaus,
4 Env't Rep. Cas. (BNA) 1728 (C.D. Cal. 1972), the
plaintiffs sued the Administrator of the EPA for his
failure to publish an air quality implementation plan.
The court held it had jurisdiction because sixty days
passed between the filing of the complaint and the date
that the hearing on the plaintiffs' request for a preliminary injunction was complete. The court reasoned
that the EPA had the beneficial effect of the sixty-day
notice provision during this time. 4 Env't Rep. Cas. at
1731. In National Sea Clammers Ass'n v. City of New York,
616 F.2d 1222, 1226 (3d Cir. 1980), the court noted that
it would be permissible to "adopt the pragmatic approach,"
requiring merely that sixty days elapse prior to district
court action on the complaint.

The underlying reasons for this "pragmatic approach"
are sound. First, impermissible pollution occurs
throughout the inherent delay between the time when the
complaint is filed and the time when the district court
takes action on it. Second, potential defendants often
receive notice of the violation long before formal notice
is sent and thus have an early opportunity to correct the
problem. Save Our Sound Fisheries Ass'n v. Callaway,
429 F. Supp. 1136, 1143-44 n.11 (D.R.I. 1977). Third,
negotiation or resolution of a violation can occur as
easily after suit is filed as before.

This "pragmatic approach" should be applied here.
Ellison knew on April 15 that its emissions were causing
problems and learned a short time later that it was
violating the state's opacity limitation. The district
court held its hearing on Westbrook's motion for a preliminary injunction and Ellison's motion to dismiss on
July 28, 1980, sixty-nine days after Westbrook gave
notice on May 20 and about 104 days after it first
learned of the violations. Ellison thus had far more

11

than the sixty days provided by section 304(b) to correct
its violations. To require even more time would prolong
a serious problem, discourage settlement of litigation,
and encourage industrial dischargers to ignore citizen
complaints until receiving formal notices under section
304(a). Congress intended the contrary in creating
section 304.

II. THE DISTRICT COURT ERRED IN REFUSING TO EXERCISE
    FEDERAL QUESTION JURISDICTION.

    A. The amount in controversy exceeds $10,000 and
        the case arises under the Federal Clean Air Act.

Section 1331(a) of the Judicial Code, 28 U.S.C.
§ 1331(a) (1976), provides that the federal district
courts shall have jurisdiction in civil suits against
private parties when the amount in controversy exceeds
$10,000 and the case arises under federal law. The
district court erred in denying jurisdiction under
section 1331(a) because Westbrook unmistakably met its
requirements. First, Westbrook alleged that each of
several members were damaged in excess of $10,000 by
unlawful emissions from Ellison's plant. Second, the
matter arises under federal law because the Clean Air
Act requires State Implementation Plans to be federally
approved and federally enforceable. Citizens Ass'n v.
Washington, 383 F. Supp. 136 (D.D.C. 1974). The opacity
limitation is part of the Superior State Implementation
Plan under the Clean Air Act.

    B. The language and purpose of section 304 permit
        independent assertion of federal question juris-
        diction for citizen enforcement suits under the
        Clean Air Act.

Regardless of whether Westbrook complied with the
sixty-day notice provision of Section 304(b), the
district court should have heard its claim under section
1331(a). Section 304(e) of the Clean Air Act expressly

12

preserves such independent jurisdictional bases for
citizen enforcement lawsuits:

> Nothing in this section shall restrict <u>any right</u>
> which any person (or class of persons) may have
> under <u>any statute</u> or common law to seek enforcement
> of any emission standard or limitation or to seek
> any other relief (including relief against the
> Administrator or a State agency).

42 U.S.C § 7604(e) (Supp. III 1979) (emphasis added).
Congressional intent to preserve existing bases of jurisdiction while providing another basis of jurisdiction is
central to the meaning of section 304.

Section 304(a), which expressly provides for jurisdiction without regard to the amount in controversy, was
particularly intended for those persons who could not
meet the $10,000 requirement of section 1331(a), but who
nonetheless had a legitimate need to bring an enforcement
action. <u>National Sea Clammers</u>, 616 F.2d at 1222. In
<u>National Sea Clammers</u>, the plaintiffs brought suit under
the FWPCA, claiming that the defendants had adversely
affected shellfish populations by improperly permitting
sewage to be dumped into the Atlantic Ocean. In rejecting
the defendant's claim that the citizen suit provision of
the FWPCA precludes the assertion of section 1331(a) jurisdiction, the court observed that the "more persuasively
reasoned cases" recognize that the citizen suit provision
gives the district court jurisdiction over a new class
of plaintiffs and "preserves jurisdiction over the pre-
existing right of injured parties to sue to enforce the
Act."   616 F.2d at 1228.

Similarly, the Court of Appeals for the District of
Columbia Circuit in <u>Natural Resources Defense Council v.
Train</u>, 510 F.2d 692 (D.C. Cir. 1975), held that the
plaintiff could bring an action under section 1331(a),
notwithstanding its failure to give sixty days' notice.
The legislative history, the court said, reflected a
deliberate choice by Congress to widen citizen access to

the courts as a supplemental and effective assurance that
the Act would be implemented and enforced. Id. at 700.
The court further reasoned that the provisions of section
304(b) were not intended to restrict or to curtail
federal court jurisdiction over suits that would have
been maintainable even in the absence of section 304.
Id. at 701.

Section 304(a), therefore, expands the opportunities
citizens have to participate in the enforcement of the
federal Clean Air Act. When there are existing jurisdictional bases such as section 1331(a), plaintiffs have
the option of proceeding under either section 1331(a) or
section 304(a). Because Westbrook met the jurisdictional
requirements of section 1331(a), the district court
should have allowed the suit to proceed.

Cases to the contrary ignore this option and render
section 304(e) meaningless. These cases are premised
largely on a view that congressional delineation of a
judicial review scheme within a statute means the scheme
should be exclusive. E.g., Loveladies Property Owners
Ass'n v. Raab, 430 F. Supp. 276, 281 (D.N.J. 1975),
aff'd, 547 F.2d 1162 (3d Cir. 1976) (citing Weinberger v.
Salfi, 422 U.S. 749 (1975)). In Weinberger, the Court's
decision that section 1331(a) could not be asserted as a
jurisdictional base for benefit claims arising under the
Social Security Act was based on language in that Act
expressly prohibiting the use of section 1331(a) for that
purpose. There is no indication, however, that Congress
intended section 304 to be the exclusive grant of jurisdiction for claims under the Clean Air Act. Indeed,
section 304(e) says the opposite.

There is also no merit to the reasoning in City of
Highland Park for the exclusiveness of section 304. The
court there held, in effect, that the Clean Air Act imposes
the sixty-day notice provision of section 304(b) on section
1331(a). The court stated, "The saving provision, expressing the general intention of Congress not to disturb exist-

14

ing rights to seek relief, does not have the affirmative
effect of removing conditions which existing law imposes
upon the exercise of these rights." 519 F.2d at 693.
The court's description of section 304 as "existing law"
fails to recognize that section 1331(a) existed long before
the Clean Air Act and converts the savings clause into a
powerful weapon to preclude other rights of relief--an
interpretation that is totally at odds with congressional
intent.   It is not necessary to remove any additional
conditions from section 1331(a) because section 304(e)
prevents their imposition in the first place.

　　　Section 304(e) expands rather than narrows the range
of jurisdictional options available to citizen plaintiffs.
Because Westbrook met the requirements of section 1331(a),
the district court should have exercised jurisdiction
over its claim.

CONCLUSION

　　　For all of the foregoing reasons, the judgment of
the United States District Court for the District of
Superior should be reversed and remanded for proceedings
on the merits.

　　　　　　　　　　　　Respectfully submitted,

　　　　　　　　　　　　Truman La Foote
　　　　　　　　　　　　‾‾‾‾‾‾‾‾‾‾‾‾‾‾‾‾‾‾‾‾‾‾‾‾
　　　　　　　　　　　　TRUMAN LAFOOTE
　　　　　　　　　　　　Attorney for Appellant

　　　　　　　　　　　　1602 Cass Avenue
　　　　　　　　　　　　Suite 411
　　　　　　　　　　　　Detroit, Michigan 48202
　　　　　　　　　　　　(313) 577-5646

November 3, 1980

APPENDIX

Clean Air Act

Section 304(a), 42 U.S.C. § 7604(a):

> The district courts shall have jurisdiction, without
> regard to the amount in controversy or the citizen-
> ship of the parties, to enforce such an emission
> standard or limitation, or such an order, or to
> order the Administrator to perform such act or duty,
> as the case may be.

Section 304(a)(1), 42 U.S.C. § 7604(a)(1):

> Except as provided in subsection (b) of this section,
> any person may commence a civil action on his own
> behalf--

> (1) against any person (including (i) the United
>   States, and (ii) any other governmental instru-
>   mentality or agency to the extent permitted by
>   the Eleventh Amendment to the Constitution) who
>   is alleged to be in violation of (A) an emission
>   standard or limitation under this chapter or
>   (B) an order issued by the Administrator or a
>   State with respect to such a standard or limita-
>   tion ....

Section 304(b)(1), 42 U.S.C. § 7604(b)(1):

> No action may be commenced--

> (1) under subsection (a)(1) of this section--

> > (A) prior to 60 days after the plaintiff has
> >   given notice of the violation (i) to the
> >   Administrator, (ii) to the State in which
> >   the violation occurs, and (iii) to any
> >   alleged violator of the standard, limita-
> >   tion, or order, or

> > (B) if the Administrator or State has commenced
> >   and is diligently prosecuting a civil action
> >   in a court of the United States or a State
> >   to require compliance with the standard,
> >   limitation, or order ....

Section 304(e), 42 U.S.C. § 7604(e):

> Nothing in this section shall restrict any right
> which any person (or class of persons) may have
> under any statute or common law to seek enforcement
> of any emission standard or limitation or to seek
> any other relief (including relief against the
> Administrator or a State agency).

Judicial Code

28 U.S.C. § 1331(a):

> The district courts shall have original jurisdiction
> of all civil actions wherein the matter in contro-
> versy exceeds the sum or value of $10,000, exclusive
> of interest and costs, and arises under the Consti-
> tution, laws, or treaties of the United States,
> except that no such sum or value shall be required
> in any such action brought against the United States,
> any agency thereof, or any officer or employee there-
> of in his official capacity.

UNITED STATES COURT OF APPEALS
FOR THE THIRTEENTH CIRCUIT

No. 80-152

WESTBROOK NEIGHBORHOOD ASSOCIATION,
Appellant,

vs.

ELLISON RECYCLING, INC.,
Appellee.

ON APPEAL FROM THE
UNITED STATES DISTRICT COURT
FOR THE DISTRICT OF SUPERIOR

BRIEF FOR APPELLEE

Amy Scroggins
880 Woodward Avenue
Detroit, Michigan 48202

INDEX

AUTHORITIES CITED

OPINIONS BELOW

The opinion of the United States District Court for the District of Superior is unreported, and contained in the Transcript of Record. (R. at 22-25.)

JURISDICTION

The judgment of the United States District Court for the District of Superior was entered on August 8, 1980. The appeal was filed on August 20, 1980, and was granted on December 1, 1980. The jurisdiction of this Court is invoked under 28 U.S.C. § 1291 (1976).

STATUTES INVOLVED

The texts of the following statutes relevant to the determination of the present case are set forth in the Appendix: Clean Air Act, §§ 304(a), 304(a)(1), 304(b)(1)(A), 304(e), 42 U.S.C. §§ 7604(a), 7604(a)(1), 7604(b)(1)(A), 7604(e) (Supp. III 1979); 28 U.S.C. § 1331(a) (1976).

STANDARD OF REVIEW

This is an appeal from a decision to grant the defendant's motion to dismiss for lack of subject matter jurisdiction under Fed. R. Civ. P. 12(b)(1). When subject matter jurisdiction is challenged, the plaintiff has the burden of showing that jurisdiction exists. Mortensen v. First Fed. Sav. & Loan Ass'n, 549 F.2d 884, 891 (3d Cir. 1977). The district court's decision that the plaintiff did not meet this burden is subject to de novo review. See Massachusetts v. United States Veterans Admin., 541 F.2d 119 (1st Cir. 1976) (applying de novo review).

QUESTIONS PRESENTED

I. Whether the district court properly declined citizen suit jurisdiction because a provision of the Clean Air Act expressly conditions jurisdiction on sixty days' advance notice by the plaintiff, and the plaintiff provided only thirty-seven days' notice.

II. Whether the district court properly declined citizen suit jurisdiction because the plaintiff failed to substantially comply with the sixty-day notice requirement by bringing suit prior to the expiration of the notice period when the defendant was taking corrective measures and had so informed the plaintiff.

III. Whether the district court properly declined federal question jurisdiction in a suit brought under the Clean Air Act because the citizen suit provision of that Act, which provides an adequate procedure for judicial review, is the exclusive basis of jurisdiction for such suits.

STATEMENT OF FACTS

Ellison Recycling, Inc. (Ellison) is a small company engaged in the business of recycling oil. The firm converts waste oil from steel treatment plants, car repair facilities, and small shops into usable oil by removing the contaminants. The company operates its only plant on the outskirts of Westbrook. (R. at 2, 18-19.)

Ellison began operation on April 14, 1980. On April 15, 1980, Ellison received complaints from Appellant Westbrook Neighborhood Association (Westbrook), a citizens' organization, and the Superior Air Resources Board about intermittent odors from the plant. The Board informed Westbrook that the plant's emissions were not regulated by its State Implementation Plan under the federal Clean Air Act except for the opacity requirement of section 33.1301 of the State Administrative Code. (R. at 2.) That section prohibits any person from dis-

charging into the atmosphere a visible air contaminant
with a density of more than 20% opacity for more than
three minutes in any twenty-four hour period. (R. at
8-9.)   Opacity is a measure of the darkness of the
emissions. Ellison made many changes in its plant
during the first few weeks of operation to reduce such
emissions.   Although there were twenty-eight violations
of the opacity requirement in April, Westbrook alleged
only seventeen in May. (R. at 2.)

   Notwithstanding this improvement, Westbrook sent
Ellison a letter on May 20, 1980, stating its intent to
file suit against Ellison unless Ellison complied with
the opacity requirements within sixty days. (R. at 10-12.)
Westbrook sent copies of the letter to the Board and to
the United States Environmental Protection Agency (EPA).
In response to this letter, Ellison wrote Westbrook on
June 22, 1980, stating that it had hired a consultant
to conduct a national search of air pollution control
technologies available to oil recycling plants.   Ellison
stated that it hoped to install equipment that would
reduce emissions far more than the opacity regulation
required, and that it would know better what to do after
the consultant reported back on July 15, 1980.   Ellison
stated that it had already made progress in reducing
emissions and that it had been meeting with the Board's
staff. (R. at 15-16.)

   On June 26, 1980, only four days after Ellison's
response, and only thirty-seven days after Ellison
received notice, Westbrook filed suit in federal district
court seeking declaratory and injunctive relief against
Ellison for violations of the opacity requirement.
(R. at 1-4.)   Westbrook charged only twelve violations
of the requirement to that date. (R. at 3.)   In response,
Ellison filed a motion to dismiss under Fed. R. Civ. P.
12(b)(1) for lack of subject matter jurisdiction.

On July 28, 1980, the court heard argument on
Westbrook's motion for a preliminary injunction and
Ellison's motion to dismiss. The court received no
evidence. On August 8, 1980, the court dismissed the
case. The court concluded that jurisdiction under the
citizen suit provision of the Clean Air Act was improper
because Westbrook had filed suit before expiration of the
requisite sixty-day waiting period required by the Act.
The court also refused to exercise federal question
jurisdiction. The court reasoned that Congress intended
the citizen suit provision of the Clean Air Act to be the
exclusive basis of jurisdiction for citizen enforcement
suits under that Act. (R. at 22-25.)

SUMMARY OF ARGUMENT

The district court properly dismissed this case for
want of jurisdiction because Westbrook ignored the
thoughtful and orderly procedure Congress established for
citizen enforcement claims under the Clean Air Act.
Although the Clean Air Act provides for citizen suits
against alleged violators of the Act, it conditions that
jurisdictional grant on strict compliance with a sixty-
day advance notice requirement. Westbrook failed to comply
with that requirement because it gave only thirty-seven
days' advance notice. Congress intended the provision to
avoid unnecessary litigation and minimize interference
with the enforcement process. That intent would have
been frustrated by a premature lawsuit.

Even if it were possible to abrogate the language
and intent of Congress by permitting jurisdiction when a
plaintiff substantially complied with the sixty-day
notice requirement, jurisdiction would still have been
improper. Substantial compliance can occur only when
the potential defendant responds to the notice prior to
the end of the sixty-day period that it plans to take no
action on the notice. In this case, however, Ellison

4

made significant progress in reducing emissions simply
by making changes in its operation.   In addition,
Ellison hired a consultant to investigate control
technologies and hoped to reduce its emissions beyond
the requirements of state law.   Since Ellison's response
to Westbrook's notice states these facts, Westbrook
cannot reasonably claim that waiting until the end of
the notice period would have been futile.

Westbrook's failure to meet the sixty-day notice
requirement closed the only jurisdictional door open to
it because the citizen suit provision of the Clean Air
Act is the exclusive jurisdictional basis for such
lawsuits.   Any other conclusion would permit the notice
requirement to be easily eluded and frustrate congressional
intent to avoid premature lawsuits.   When Congress has
prescribed adequate procedures for judicial review under
a statutory scheme, these procedures are exclusive.

ARGUMENT

I.   THE DISTRICT COURT PROPERLY DECLINED JURISDICTION
     UNDER THE CITIZEN SUIT PROVISION OF THE CLEAN AIR
     ACT.

The most fundamental attribute of the federal courts
is their limited jurisdiction.   They are empowered to
hear only those cases that are within constitutional
limits of the judicial power of the United States and
that have been entrusted to them by a jurisdictional
grant of Congress.   Charles Alan Wright, The Federal
Courts § 7 (3d ed. 1976).   When Congress provides a
statutory method for obtaining review of administrative
decisions, that method must be strictly adhered to.
Loveladies Property Owners Ass'n v. Raab, 430 F. Supp.
276 (D.N.J. 1975), aff'd, 547 F.2d 1162 (3d Cir. 1976).
Because Westbrook failed to follow the statutory scheme
in this case, the district court properly declined to
exercise jurisdiction over the claim.

A. <u>The plaintiff violated the sixty-day notice
   requirement for citizen suits by providing the
   defendant only thirty-seven days' notice before
   filing suit.</u>

Section 304(a)(1) of the Clean Air Act, 42 U.S.C.
§ 7604(a)(1) (Supp. III 1979), provides a jurisdictional
basis for citizens to bring actions against persons
alleged to be violating emissions standards or limitations
under the Act. Jurisdiction is proper "without regard
to the amount in controversy or the citizenship of the
parties." 42 U.S.C. § 7604(a). Section 304(b)(1)(A),
however, provides that

> no action may be commenced prior to 60 days after
> the plaintiff has given notice of the violation
> (i) to the Administrator, (ii) to the State in which
> the violation occurs, and (iii) to any alleged
> violator of the standard, limitation, or order.

42 U.S.C. § 7604(b)(1)(A) (Supp. III 1979).

In the present case, the district court correctly
refrained from exercising jurisdiction under section 304.
Westbrook filed suit on June 26, 1980, after giving
notice on May 20. Westbrook failed to comply with the
statutory requirement because only thirty-seven of the
required sixty days had elapsed.

The legislative history of section 304 shows that
Congress intended the sixty-day notice period to be
scrupulously observed. The Conference Committee for the
Act doubled the thirty-day notice period contained in the
Senate bill to sixty days. H.R. Rep. No. 1783, 91st
Cong., 2d Sess. at 55-56 (1970). The Conference Report
stated, "Prior to commencing any action in the district
courts, the plaintiff <u>must</u> have provided the violator,
the Administrator, and the State with sixty days' notice."
<u>Id.</u> at 56 (emphasis supplied).

The great majority of courts have recognized the
importance of strictly complying with the sixty-day
notice requirement. In <u>City of Highland Park v. Train</u>,

6

519 F.2d 681 (7th Cir. 1975), <u>cert. denied</u>, 424 U.S.
927 (1976), the court affirmed the dismissal of a
section 304 claim because of the plaintiff's failure to
comply with the sixty-day notice requirement, observing
that Congress's intention would be frustrated if the
statutory mandate of section 304(b)(1)(A) were ignored.
519 F.2d at 691. Courts have applied this rule in
citizen suits against industrial sources, <u>City of
Evansville v. Kentucky Liquid Recycling, Inc.</u>, 604 F.2d
1008 (7th Cir. 1979), <u>cert. denied</u>, 444 U.S. 1025
(1980). They have also applied this rule when the
plaintiffs gave fewer than sixty days' notice, <u>Smoke
Rise, Inc. v. Washington Suburban Sanity Commission</u>,
400 F. Supp. 1369 (D. Md. 1974); when the plaintiffs gave
the EPA Regional Administrator sixty days' notice before
filing their amended complaint, <u>Raab</u>, 430 F. Supp. at
276; and when the plaintiff gave no notice at all,
<u>Pinkney v. Ohio Environmental Protection Agency</u>, 375 F.
Supp. 305 (N.D. Ohio 1974). In each case, failure to
strictly comply with the sixty-day notice requirement
was fatal to citizen suit jurisdiction.

Congress had good reason for requiring strict
compliance with this notice requirement. First, the
full notice period provides an opportunity for the
parties to settle the problem, making it less likely
that unnecessary lawsuits will add to the burden of the
courts. S. Rep. No. 1196, 91st Cong., 2d Sess. 37
(1970). Second, the notice period provides an opportunity for government lawyers to more smoothly integrate
the interruption caused by a citizen suit into their
overall enforcement concerns. <u>City of Highland Park</u>,
519 F.2d at 690. The government is necessarily involved
in any citizen enforcement action, whether it is a formal
party or not, because a suit affects its enforcement
efforts. Third, a precise sixty-day period decreases
the judicial time required to process a citizen suit;

plaintiffs either give proper notice or they do not. For a similar reason, Congress set forth an "objective evidentiary standard" in section 304, requiring plaintiffs to allege specific violations under the Act rather than generalized claims of pollution. S. Rep. No. 1196, 91st Cong., 2d Sess. at 36 (1970).

Finally, strict compliance is fundamentally equitable because of the substantial power granted to citizen suit plaintiffs against persons alleged to be violating the statute. In Tennessee Valley Authority v. Hill, 437 U.S. 153 (1978), the plaintiffs brought suit under a provision of the Endangered Species Act modeled after section 304 to prevent completion of the Tellico Dam and the consequent destruction of the snail darter, a fish species protected by that Act. The Court affirmed an order permanently enjoining completion of the dam because the statutory language permitted no exceptions, and in so doing brushed aside arguments that the result would cost millions of dollars and preserve a species of minimal value. Congress, the Court said, "has spoken in the plainest of words." 437 U.S. at 195. When plaintiffs seek compliance with the letter of the law through such drastic means as prohibiting completion of a nearly finished dam or enjoining the operation of an oil recycling plant, they must comply with the jurisdictional language conditioning their right to do so.

Cases sustaining citizen suit jurisdiction on "substantial" or "constructive" compliance ignore the language and purposes of section 304. The Second Circuit has permitted jurisdiction when there was "substantial compliance" with the sixty-day notice requirement, but only when that issue was peripheral, if relevant at all, to the decision. The substantial compliance theory, which permits jurisdiction after fewer than sixty days' notice when the purpose of the notice period had been served, originated in dicta in Conservation Society v.

<u>Secretary of Transportation</u>, 508 F.2d 927 (2d Cir. 1974),
<u>vacated on other grounds</u>, 423 U.S. 809 (1975). Although
the court stated that the sixty-day notice provision was
not intended to be an "absolute barrier" to an earlier
suit, that statement was premised largely on the court's
view that other jurisdictional bases were available. In
addition, the court never held that the district court
wrongly denied jurisdiction for failure to strictly
comply with the sixty-day requirement; it only assumed
there was jurisdiction under some statutory provision to
reach a substantive question. The same court of appeals,
in <u>Natural Resources Defense Council v. Callaway</u>, 524
F.2d 79 (2d Cir. 1975), was similarly influenced by its
erroneous assumption that there were jurisdictional bases
other than the citizen suit provision, an assumption
discussed in Argument II of this brief.

Substantial compliance also makes poor policy. The
<u>Callaway</u> court's footnote that the purposes of the sixty-
day notice requirement are served when the potential
defendant says "no action will be taken," 524 F.2d at 84
n.4, permits a plaintiff to seize on the slightest
negative response, or even an ambiguous response, as
an excuse for a premature lawsuit. In this case, for
example, Westbrook claims futility notwithstanding
Ellison's continuing and fruitful effort to reduce
violations. The "substantial compliance" principle also
hinders pre-lawsuit communications between the parties,
makes it difficult for potential defendants to communicate anything short of total agreement with those giving
notice, and raises difficult and unnecessary questions
about how much notice is enough.

The slipperiness of this concept is illustrated by a
closely related theory extending jurisdiction if the
plaintiff gave notice sixty days before the court's first
hearing in the citizen suit, rather than sixty days
before filing suit. This "constructive compliance"

theory was applied in City of Riverside v. Ruckelshaus, 4 Env't Rep. Cas. (BNA) 1728 (C.D. Cal. 1972), and has not been applied since. Dicta in National Sea Clammers Ass'n v. City of New York, 616 F.2d 1222 (3d Cir. 1980), states that such an interpretation would be "entirely permissible," but the court in that case added that it "need not pass upon this proposition" because it found independent jurisdiction under another statute. 616 F.2d at 1226.

The decision in the Riverside case was wrong because it abrogates the language of section 304(a) requiring sixty days' notice before any action "may be commenced." It would permit a plaintiff to ignore the sixty-day notice period before filing suit, since sixty days almost certainly would pass by the time the court began to hear the case. As the court in City of Highland Park observed, Rule 12(b) of the Federal Rules of Civil Procedure provides sixty days for the federal government to respond to complaints in lawsuits where it is a defendant. 519 F.2d at 690. Although the same rule provides only twenty days for other parties to respond, Congress intended the notice provision to supplement, rather than replace, these and other response periods in the litigation process. Section 304(b)(1)(A) provides a workable and efficient notice procedure, and the district court properly dismissed Westbrook's complaint for failure to comply with it.

B. The plaintiff failed to substantially comply with the sixty-day notice requirement by bringing suit prior to the end of that period when the defendant was taking corrective action and so informed the plaintiff.

Even if it were proper to abrogate the statutory language by permitting jurisdiction under section 304(a)(1) when a plaintiff provides fewer than sixty

days' notice, Westbrook did not "substantially comply"
with the sixty-day requirement here. This case is
analogous to the situation in <u>Massachusetts v. United
States Veterans Administration</u>, 541 F.2d 119 (1st Cir.
1976), which involved a citizen suit under the Federal
Water Pollution Control Act (FWPCA), 33 U.S.C. §§ 1251-
1376 (1976 & Supp. III 1979), because of the alleged
failure of a veterans hospital to comply with the timetable in a permit for connecting to a municipal sewage
system.   (The FWPCA contains a citizen suit provision
that is similar to the one in the Clean Air Act.) The
state brought a citizen suit after giving only forty
days' notice, claiming that notice would not cure past
violations of the permit condition. The court of appeals
affirmed the dismissal of the citizen suit claim, holding
that there was no claim of futility sufficient to raise
the issue of constructive compliance. 541 F.2d at 121-22.
The court reasoned, "[E]ven conceding that no administrative action could cure the failure of the VA to meet past
deadlines for planning and construction of the sewer
tie-in, increased administrative attention could still
expedite the completion of the project." <u>Id.</u> at 121.

Westbrook did not substantially comply with the
sixty-day notice requirement because Ellison was and is
taking corrective actions, and so informed Westbrook
prior to the end of the notice period. Westbrook's
complaint alleged twenty-eight violations of the opacity
limitation in the Superior regulations in the last half
of April, seventeen in May, and only twelve in the first
twenty-five days of June. Ellison was thus making significant progress in meeting the opacity regulation, the
only regulation addressed in the complaint. In addition,
Ellison responded to the notice on June 22 by stating
that it had hired a consultant to examine different
control technologies and that it hoped to install equipment that would reduce emissions even below levels

11

required by the opacity regulation. Ellison wrote that it would know better what to do after receiving the consultant's report on July 15, five days before the end of the notice period. Westbrook brought suit four days later, without waiting for the consultant's report and without asking for any clarifications, even though Ellison was resolving a difficult technical problem.

Even if Ellison's response can be considered ambiguous, Westbrook cannot claim frustration. In Veterans Administration, the court suggested that there can be no substantial compliance if it is possible that some administrative action "could" correct the problem. 541 F.2d at 121. Because in Ellison's case there was a possibility--and a strong one--of further corrective measures being taken, the substantial compliance theory is inapplicable.

This situation thus is far different from that in Callaway, because Ellison did not say that "no action" would be taken. The plaintiffs in Callaway brought a citizen suit under FWPCA and the Marine Research, Protection, and Sanctuaries Act, 33 U.S.C. §§ 1401-1444 (1976), to enjoin the use of an ocean disposal site for dredge materials. The court of appeals reversed the district court's dismissal of the case because of the plaintiffs' failure to provide more than forty-eight days' notice, reasoning that the refusal of the defendants to take any action meant that waiting any longer would be futile. 524 F.2d at 79. When a potential defendant responds positively, or at worst ambiguously, to formal notice, there can be no reasonable claim of frustration. In the present case, Ellison had not stated that "no action" would be taken. To the contrary, Ellison responded that it was studying what steps it could take to remedy the problem. Westbrook, therefore, had no basis for a premature lawsuit.

12

II. THE DISTRICT COURT PROPERLY DECLINED FEDERAL QUESTION
    JURISDICTION BECAUSE THE CITIZEN SUIT PROVISION OF
    THE CLEAN AIR ACT IS THE EXCLUSIVE JURISDICTIONAL
    BASIS FOR CITIZEN ENFORCEMENT ACTIONS UNDER THAT ACT.

Plaintiffs in a citizen suit cannot claim alternative
jurisdictional bases to avoid the sixty-day notice requirement. "If Congress has provided adequate procedures for
judicial review within a given statutory scheme, the
prescribed procedures are exclusive." Pinkney v. Ohio
Envtl. Protection Agency, 375 F. Supp. 305, 309 (N.D. Ohio
1974).

When a statute provides a specific procedure for
obtaining judicial review of claims under the statute, a
plaintiff may not raise those claims under other jurisdictional statutes. In Weinberger v. Salfi, 422 U.S.
749 (1975), the Court held that section 405(g) of the
Social Security Act, 42 U.S.C. § 405(g) (1976), provided
the sole jurisdictional basis for benefit claims under
that Act. Because the Social Security Act contains a
series of procedural steps that an aggrieved claimant
must follow before bringing action in federal district
court, the Court concluded that the plaintiffs were
barred from bringing those same claims under general
federal question jurisdiction. The Court reasoned that
when there is an orderly administrative mechanism, it is
counterproductive to permit plaintiffs to circumvent its
requirements by relying on other jurisdictional statutes.
Id. at 757-59. Similarly, the claimant in Califano v.
Sanders, 430 U.S. 99 (1977), a case that also dealt with
section 405(g), was barred by procedural irregularities
from seeking judicial review under that Act. The Court
held that he could not rely on the Administrative Procedure Act, 5 U.S.C. §§ 701-06 (1976), as an alternative
jurisdictional basis. Id. at 985.

In the present case, the Clean Air Act provides an
adequate procedure for judicial review. The Act expressly

allows citizens to sue to enforce the provisions of the
Act, but it conditions this right on waiting sixty days
before bringing suit. As in Califano and Weinberger,
plaintiffs seeking relief under the Clean Air Act must
adhere to the prescribed procedural steps. The district
court properly refused to permit Westbrook to circumvent
the notice requirement by simultaneously claiming federal
question jurisdiction under 28 U.S.C. § 1331(a) (1976).

Section 304(e) of the Clean Air Act, 42 U.S.C.
§ 7604(e) (Supp. III 1979), which provides that "[n]othing
in this section shall restrict any right which any person
(or class of persons) may have under any statute or
common law," does not preserve additional jurisdictional
bases for declaratory and injunctive relief. Rather, the
legislative history of section 304(e) shows that Congress
intended it primarily to preserve common law actions for
damages. The Senate Committee emphasized that section
304 contains no provision "for the recovery of property
or personal damages. It should be noted, however, that
the section would specifically preserve any rights or
remedies under any other law. Thus, if damages could be
shown, other remedies would remain available." S. Rep.
No. 1196, 91st Cong., 2d Sess. 38 (1970). Congress thus
required sixty days' advance notice for enforcement
actions brought under the Clean Air Act pursuant to
section 304(b)(1)(A), while preserving common law actions
for damages caused by air pollution through section 304(e).

Even if section 304(e) preserves other jurisdictional
statutes for citizen enforcement claims, it conditions
their use on compliance with section 304(b). In City of
Highland Park, the court specifically concluded that
section 304(e) does not permit citizen suit plaintiffs to
seek jurisdictional refuge in section 1331(a). The court
reasoned that, although the savings provision expressed
the general intention of Congress not to disturb existing

14

rights to seek relief, it did not remove conditions that
existing law imposes on the exercise of those rights.
519 F.2d at 693. The court then held that section 304(b)
was "existing law," which imposed its jurisdictional
prerequisites--including proper notice--on section
1331(a). Accord Pinkney, 375 F. Supp. at 305.

There is thus no merit to the distinction in
National Sea Clammers Ass'n v. City of New York, 616
F.2d 1222 (3d Cir. 1980), between "injured" parties, who
can bring actions under both the citizen suit provision
and section 1331(a), and "non-injured" parties, who are
limited to citizen suit jurisdiction. The legislative
history contains no indication that Congress intended
two classes of plaintiffs to be involved in citizen
enforcement action. The policy considerations behind the
sixty-day notice requirement--administrative resolution
of issues, minimal disruption of the administrative
process, and minimal court clogging--are applicable
to all plaintiffs regardless of the degree of their
"injury." This artificial distinction may well encourage
potential plaintiffs to ignore section 304 altogether
and proceed under section 1331(a)--a result manifestly
at odds with congressional intent.

When Congress provides a means of judicial review,
the means specified are exclusive and must be followed.
Congress permitted Westbrook to sue under section 304
and only under section 304. Westbrook's failure to provide the required sixty days' notice before filing suit
precluded the district court from exercising jurisdiction
under the citizen suit provision of the Clean Air Act.
This Court should therefore find that the district court
correctly refused to exercise federal question jurisdiction over the claim.

CONCLUSION

For all the foregoing reasons, the judgment of the United States District Court for the District of Superior should be affirmed.

Respectfully submitted,

Amy Scroggins

AMY SCROGGINS
Attorney for Appellee

880 Woodward Avenue
Detroit, Michigan 48202
(313) 577-7424

November 3, 1980

APPENDIX

Clean Air Act

Section 304(a), 42 U.S.C. § 7604(a):

> The district courts shall have jurisdiction, without
> regard to the amount in controversy or the citizen-
> ship of the parties, to enforce such an emission
> standard or limitation, or such an order, or to
> order the Administrator to perform such act or duty,
> as the case may be.

Section 304(a)(1), 42 U.S.C. § 7604(a)(1):

> Except as provided in subsection (b) of this section,
> any person may commence a civil action on his own
> behalf--

> (1) against any person (including (i) the United
>   States, and (ii) any other governmental
>   instrumentality or agency to the extent
>   permitted by the Eleventh Amendment to the
>   Constitution) who is alleged to be in violation
>   of (A) an emission standard or limitation under
>   this chapter or (B) an order issued by the
>   Administrator or a State with respect to such
>   a standard or limitation ....

Section 304(b)(1), 42 U.S.C. § 7604(b) (1):

> No action may be commenced--

> (1) under subsection (a)(1) of this section--

>   (A) prior to 60 days after the plaintiff has
>   given notice of the violation (i) to the
>   Administrator, (ii) to the State in which
>   the violation occurs, and (iii) to any
>   alleged violator of the standard, limitation,
>   or order, or

>   (B) if the Administrator or State has commenced
>   and is diligently prosecuting a civil action
>   in a court of the United States or a State
>   to require compliance with the standard,
>   limitation, or order ....

Section 304(e), 42 U.S.C. § 7604(e):

Nothing in this section shall restrict any right
which any person (or class of persons) may have
under any statute or common law to seek enforcement
of any emission standard or limitation or to seek
any other relief (including relief against the
Administrator or a State agency).

Judicial Code

28 U.S.C. § 1331(a):

The district courts shall have original jurisdiction of all civil actions wherein the matter
in controversy exceeds the sum or value of $10,000,
exclusive of interest and costs, and arises under
the Constitution, laws, or treaties of the United
States, except that no such sum or value shall be
required in any such action brought against the
United States, any agency thereof, or any officer
or employee thereof in his official capacity.

Appendix G

SELECTED BOOKS ON STYLE AND GRAMMAR

Stephen V. Armstrong & Timothy P. Terrell, *Thinking Like a Writer: A Lawyer's Guide to Effective Writing and Editing* (Clark Boardman Callaghan 1992).

Gertrude Block, *Effective Legal Writing* (4th ed., Foundation Press 1992).

Alan L. Dworsky, *The Little Book on Legal Writing* (2d ed., Fred B. Rothman & Co. 1992).

H. Ramsey Fowler & Jane E. Aaron, *The Little, Brown Handbook* (5th ed., Harper Collins 1992).

H. W. Fowler, *A Dictionary of Modern English Usage* (Sir Ernest Gower rev., Oxford University Press 1965).

Tom Goldstein & Jethro K. Lieberman, *The Lawyer's Guide to Writing Well* (McGraw-Hill 1989).

C. Edward Good, *Mightier Than the Sword: Powerful Writing in the Legal Profession* (Blue Jeans Press 1989).

Diana Hacker, *A Writer's Reference* (2d ed., St. Martin's Press 1992).

Hollis T. Hurd, *Writing for Lawyers* (Journal Broadcasting & Communications 1982).

Edward D. Johnson, *The Handbook of Good English* (rev. ed., Washington Square Press 1991).

Glenn Leggett et al., *Prentice Hall Handbook for Writers* (11th ed., Prentice Hall 1991).

David Mellinkoff, *Legal Writing: Sense and Nonsense* (West 1982).

Mary Bernard Ray & Jill J. Ramsfield, *Legal Writing: Getting It Right and Getting It Written* (2d ed., West 1993).

William Strunk, Jr. & E. B. White, *Elements of Style* (3d ed., Macmillan 1979).

Texas Law Review, *Manual on Style* (7th ed., Texas Law Review Association 1992).

Joseph M. Williams, *Style: Ten Lessons in Clarity and Grace* (3d ed., Scott Foresman 1989).

Richard C. Wydick, *Plain English for Lawyers* (3d ed., Carolina Academic Press 1994).

Bibliography

SOURCES OF LAW

THE CASES AND STATUTES in this book are used only to illustrate specific principles of legal writing and legal method. Although they are not intended to teach substantive rules of law, they are based on or inspired by real cases and statutes which are too lengthy to be reproduced in full. This section is provided to show where the ideas for the illustrations and exercises were derived. When an exercise or example is based on an earlier one, no additional authority is provided.

Chapter 1

The text and Exercise 1-A require no comment. Exercise 1-B is inspired by *People v. Utica Daw's Drug Store Co.*, 225 N.Y.S.2d 128 (App. Div. 1962), and *People v. Walker*, 200 N.E.2d 779 (N.Y. 1964).

Chapter 2

The evidentiary rule in Exercise 2-A is based on Model Rule of Evidence 404. Case examples are based on *Lovely v. United States*, 169 F.2d 386 (4th Cir. 1948); *Velez v. State*, 762 P.2d 1297 (Alaska Ct. App. 1988); and *State v. Cox*, 787 P.2d 4 (Utah Ct. App. 1990). A representative law review article is Dana Berliner, *Rethinking the Reasonable Belief Defense to Rape*, 100 Yale L.J. 2687 (1991).

The case examples in Exercise 2-B are drawn from *Northern Insurance Co. v. Aardvark Associates*, 942 F.2d 189 (3d Cir. 1991); *United States Fidelity & Guaranty Co. v. T. K. Stanley, Inc.*, 764 F. Supp. 81 (S.D. Miss. 1991); *Claussen v. Aetna Casualty & Surety Co.*, 380 S.E.2d 686 (Ga. 1989); and *Just v. Land Reclamation, Ltd.*, 456 N.W.2d 570 (Wis. 1990). The references to secondary authority are drawn from various sources, including Sharon M. Murphy, *The "Sudden and Accidental" Exception to the Pollution Exclusion Clause in Comprehensive General Liability Insurance Policies: The Gordian Knot of Environmental Liability*, 45 Vand. L. Rev. 161 (1991), and authorities cited therein.

Chapter 3

The first case in the text, *State v. Jones*, is based on *United States v. Castillo*, 524 F.2d 286 (10th Cir. 1975), and *State v. Baxter*, 208 S.E.2d 696 (N.C. 1974).

The burglary case under Part 2 is based on *State v. Crawford*, 80 N.W. 193 (N.D. 1899).

The case under Part 3 is based on *Jackson v. Brown*, 164 N.W.2d 824 (Iowa 1969).

The wills case under Part 4 is drawn from *Brown v. Union Trust Co.*, 98 N.E.2d 901 (Ind. 1951).

The corporation case under Part 4 is based on the reasoning in *Decker v. Juzwik*, 121 N.W.2d 652 (Iowa 1963), although the court in that case concluded the promoters were not liable because there was a novation of the contract by the corporation.

The case under Part 5 is drawn from *Stratton v. Mt. Hermon Boys' School*, 103 N.E. 87 (Mass. 1913).

The case and sample case brief after Part 8 are based on *Jones v. City of Atlanta*, 363 S.E.2d 254 (Ga. 1988).

Exercise 3-A is derived from the principles stated in *Missouri Federation of the Blind v. National Federation of the Blind*, 505 S.W.2d 1 (Mo. Ct. App. 1973), and *Powell v. Zuckert*, 366 F.2d 634 (D.C. Cir. 1966).

Exercise 3-B is drawn from W. Page Keeton et al., *Prosser and Keeton on the Law of Torts* § 70 (5th ed. 1984).

Exercise 3-C was inspired by *State v. Glover*, 50 S.W.2d 1049 (Mo. 1932), and *Commonwealth v. Redline*, 137 A.2d 472 (Pa. 1958). *But see Commonwealth v. Lang*, 426 A.2d 691 (Pa. Super. Ct. 1981).

Chapter 4

The cases in the text are based on *Johnston v. Harris*, 198 N.W.2d 409 (Mich. 1972), and *Samson v. Saginaw Professional Building*, 224 N.W.2d 843 (Mich. 1975).

Exercise 4-A is based on a line of cases typified by *Wyman v. Newhouse*, 93 F.2d 313 (2d Cir. 1937). *See generally* Annotation, *Attack on Personal Service as Having Been Obtained by Fraud or Trickery*, 98 A.L.R.2d 551 (1964).

Exercise 4-B is modeled on a trilogy of Rhode Island decisions: *State v. Welford*, 72 A. 396 (R.I. 1909); *State v. Scofield*, 138 A.2d 415 (R.I. 1958); and *State v. Lunt*, 260 A.2d 149 (R.I. 1969).

Exercise 4-C is drawn from *Ellis v. Butterfield*, 570 P.2d 1334 (Idaho 1977), and *Skendzel v. Marshall*, 339 N.E.2d 57 (Ind. 1975).

Exercise 4-D was inspired primarily by *Williams v. Walker-Thomas Furniture Co.*, 350 F.2d 445 (D.C. Cir. 1965).

Chapter 5

The statutes in the text are 28 U.S.C. §§ 1332(a) and 1333 (1988).

The cases in the text were inspired by *Sisson v. Ruby*, 497 U.S. 358 (1990) (admiralty jurisdiction); *Executive Jet Aviation, Inc. v. City of Cleveland*, 409 U.S. 249 (1972) (admiralty jurisdiction); *Taylor v. Vallelunga*, 339 P.2d 910 (Cal. Ct. App. 1959) (emotional distress); *Whitley v. Andersen*, 551 P.2d 1083 (Colo. Ct. App. 1976) (battery); and *Restatement (Second) of Torts § 13* (1965).

The authority in Exercise 5-A is based on *Soldano v. O'Daniels*, 190 Cal. Rptr. 310 (Ct. App. 1983); *Timmons v. Bostwick*, 82 S.E. 29 (Ga. 1914); *Olson v. Rasmussen*, 8 N.W.2d 668 (Mich. 1943); and *Lucy v. Zehmer*, 84 S.E.2d 516 (Va. 1954). The principles find some support in John Calamari & Joseph Perillo, *The Law of Contracts* §§ 2-3, 2-20(e), 4-4 (3d ed. 1987).

Exercise 5-B is derived from Mich. Comp. Laws. Ann. §§ 15.231–.246 (West 1981); Tex. Gov't Code Ann. §§ 552.021, .108 (West Supp. 1994); *Ayers v. Lee Enterprises, Inc.*, 561 P.2d 998 (Or. 1977); and *Houston Chronicle Publishing Co. v. City of Houston*, 531 S.W.2d 177 (Tex. Civ. App. 1975).

Chapter 6

The cases in the text are based on *Ball v. White*, 143 N.W.2d 188 (Mich. 1966); *Barnes v. Clayton House Motel*, 435 S.W.2d 616 (Tex. Civ. App. 1968); *Anderson v. Cramlet*, 789 F.2d 840 (10th Cir. 1986); and Bruce W. Sanford, *Libel and Privacy* §§ 6.2 -.3 (2d ed. 1993).

Exercise 6-B is drawn from *Cooper v. Sisters of Charity*, Inc., 272 N.E.2d 97 (Ohio 1971); *Hicks v. United States*, 368 F.2d 626 (4th Cir. 1966); and *Walden v. Jones*, 439 S.W.2d 571 (Ky. 1968).

The cases in Exercise 6-C are based on *Miles v. A. Arena & Co.*, 73 P.2d 1260 (Cal. Ct. App. 1937); *Fontainebleau Hotel Corp. v. Forty-Five Twenty-Five,Inc.*, 114 So. 2d 357 (Fla. Dist. Ct. App. 1959); *Moellering v. Evans*, 22 N.E. 981 (Ind. 1889); and *Sherk v. Indiana Waste Systems, Inc.*, 495 N.E.2d 815 (Ind. Ct. App. 1986).

Chapter 7

The open meetings example in the text is drawn from Mich. Comp. Laws Ann. §§ 15.262(a)–(b), 15.263(1) (West 1981 & Supp. 1993), and *News-Journal Co. v. McLaughlin*, 377 A.2d 358 (Del. Ch. 1977). The example illustrating *ejusdem generis* is taken from *Martin v. Holiday Inns, Inc.*, 245 Cal. Rptr. 717 (Ct. App. 1988).

Exercise 7-C was suggested by *Peralta Community College District v. Fair Employment & Housing Commission*, 801 P.2d 357 (Cal. 1990).

Exercise 7-D is based on Mich. Ct. R. 2.209 and *D'Agostini v. City of Roseville*, 240 N.W.2d 252 (Mich. 1976).

Exercise 7-E was inspired by Mich. Comp. Laws Ann. §§ 169.252, .269 (West 1989); N.J. Stat. Ann. §§ 19:44A-29(b) (West Supp. 1981); *Buckley v. Valeo*, 424 U.S. 1 (1976); and *Common Cause v. New Jersey Election Law Enforcement Commission*, 377 A.2d 643 (N.J. 1977).

Chapter 8

The cases in the text came from *Payne v. Palm Beach County*, 395 So. 2d 1267 (Fla. Dist. Ct. App. 1981), and *Town of Belleair v. Taylor*, 425 So. 2d 669 (Fla. Dist. Ct. App. 1983).

Chapter 9

The cases in the text under Part 1 are based on Wayne R. LaFave & Austin W. Scott, *Criminal Law* §§ 7.16, 8.11(d) (2d ed. 1986).

The cases in the text under Part 2 are drawn from *Bartram v. Zoning Commission*, 68 A.2d 308 (Conn. 1949); *Rodgers v. Village of Tarrytown*, 96 N.E.2d 731 (N.Y. 1951); *Thomas v. Town of Bedford*, 214 N.Y.S.2d 145 (Sup. Ct. 1961); and *D'Angelo v. Knights of Columbus Building Association*, 151 A.2d 495 (R.I. 1959).

The case under Part 3 is drawn from *Thompson v. Enz*, 154 N.W.2d 473 (Mich. 1967), and *In re County Ditch No. 34*, 170 N.W. 883 (Minn. 1919).

The problem used under Part 4 is based on section 102(2)(C) of the National Environmental Policy Act of 1969, 42 U.S.C. § 4332(2)(C) (1988).

Exercise 9-A was inspired by *In re Estate of Kamesar*, 259 N.W.2d 733 (Wis. 1977), and *In re Estate of Malnar*, 243 N.W.2d 435 (Wis. 1976).

Exercise 9-B was inspired by sections 109 and 304 of the Clean Air Act, 42 U.S.C. §§ 7409, 7604 (1988 and Supp. III 1991); Mich. Admin. Code r. 336.1401(1) (1980); *Jost v. Dairyland Power Co-op*, 172 N.W.2d 647 (Wis. 1969); *Amphitheaters, Inc. v. Portland Meadows*, 198 P.2d 847 (Or. 1948); and W. Page Keeton et al., *Prosser and Keeton on the Law of Torts* § 88-89 (5th ed. 1984).

Chapter 10

The common law illustration under Part 1 was inspired by the principles in *Henderson v. Fisher*, 46 Cal. Rptr. 173 (Ct. App. 1965). The statutory illustration is based on Federal Water Pollution Control Act § 505, 33 U.S.C. § 1365 (1988).

The illustration under Part 2 is drawn from section 107 of the Comprehensive Environmental Response, Compensation, and Liability Act of 1980, 42 U.S.C.A. § 9607(a) (West Supp. 1993), and section 701(a) of the Hazardous Sites Cleanup Act, 35 Pa. Cons. Stat. Ann. § 6020.701(a) (1993).

The illustration under Part 3 is based on 28 U.S.C. § 1332(a) (1988) and *Zahn v. International Paper Co.*, 414 U.S. 291 (1973). Although the amount in controversy has been changed by statute since *Zahn*, the basic premise remains the same. *See Bassett v. Toyota Motor Credit Corp.*, 818 F. Supp. 1462 (S.D. Ala. 1993);

Kennedy v. Commercial Carriers, Inc., 739 F. Supp. 406 (N.D. Ill. 1990); *Coleman v. Southern Norfolk*, 734 F. Supp. 719 (E.D. La. 1990).

The cases cited under Part 4 are based on *Chandler v. Hospital Authority*, 500 So. 2d 1012 (Ala. 1986); *Birmingham Baptist Hospital v. Crews*, 157 So. 224 (Ala. 1934); *Wilmington General Hospital v. Manlove*, 174 A.2d 135 (Del. Super. Ct. 1961); *O'Neill v. Montefiore Hospital*, 202 N.Y.S.2d 436 (App. Div. 1960); and *Valdez v. Lyman-Roberts Hospital*, 638 S.W.2d 111 (Tex. Ct. App. 1982).

The illustration under Part 5 is drawn from *Wilhite v. Mays*, 235 S.E.2d 532 (Ga. 1977), and *Stambovski v. Ackley*, 572 N.Y.S.2d 672 (App. Div. 1991).

Chapter 11

The illustration under Part 1 is based on Federal Water Pollution Control Act § 505, 33 U.S.C. § 1365 (1988).

The illustration under Part 2 is drawn from *Walters v. Department of Transportation*, 474 A.2d 66 (Pa. Commw. Ct. 1984). *But see Capuzzi v. Heller*, 558 A.2d 596 (Pa. Commw. Ct. 1989), which required that a government employee actually be driving in order for the vehicle exception doctrine of governmental immunity to apply.

The illustration under Part 3 was inspired by *Rose v. Chaikin*, 453 A.2d 1378 (N.J. Super. Ct. Ch. Div. 1982).

The illustration under Part 4 is drawn from *Meadows v. F.W. Woolworth Co.*, 254 F. Supp. 907 (N.D. Fla. 1966), and *Coblyn v. Kennedy's, Inc.*, 268 N.E.2d 860 (Mass. 1971).

Chapter 12

The illustration under Part 1 is loosely based on *Machinery Hauling, Inc. v. Steel of West Virginia*, 384 S.E.2d 139 (W. Va. 1989).

The illustration under Part 2 is based on *Ingram v. Peachtree South, Ltd.*, 355 S.E.2d 717 (Ga. Ct. App. 1987), and *Rosa v. Dunkin' Donuts*, 583 A.2d 1129 (N.J. 1991).

The illustration under Part 3 is based on *Frampton v. Central Indiana Gas Co.*, 297 N.E.2d 425 (Ind. 1973), and *Petermann v. International Brotherhood of Teamsters, Local 396*, 344 P.2d 25 (Cal. Ct. App. 1959).

The first illustration under Part 4 was suggested by a line of cases including *Dolcy v. Rhode Island Joint Reinsurance Association*, 589 A.2d 313 (R.I. 1991); *Morgan v. Cincinnati Insurance Co.*, 307 N.W.2d 53 (Mich. 1981); and *Cooperative Fire Insurance Association v. Domina*, 399 A.2d 502 (Vt. 1979).

The second illustration under Part 4 is based on Fed. R. Civ. P. 24 and *McElrea v. Volt Information Sciences, Inc.*, 119 F.R.D. 630 (E.D. Pa. 1987).

Exercise 12-A is based on *Meminger v. State*, 287 S.E.2d 296 (Ga. Ct. App. 1981), *rev'd on other grounds*, 292 S.E.2d 681 (Ga. 1982); *Choate v. State*, 279 S.E.2d 459 (Ga. Ct. App. 1981); and *Fann v. State*, 266 S.E.2d 307 (Ga. Ct. App. 1980). *Choate* and *Fann* were superseded by a statutory amendment that is now codified at Ga. Code Ann. § 16-8-41 (1992).

Exercise 12-B is based on *ANR Production Co. v. Westburne Drilling, Inc.*, 581 F. Supp. 542 (D. Colo. 1984); *Cain v. Cleveland Parachute Training Center*, 457 N.E.2d 1185 (Ohio Ct. App. 1983); *Phibbs v. Ray's Chevrolet Corp.*, 357 N.Y.S.2d 211 (App. Div. 1974); and *Schutkowski v. Carey*, 725 P.2d 1057 (Wyo. 1986).

Chapter 13

Exercise 13-A is based on *Tyus v. Booth*, 235 N.W.2d 69 (Mich. Ct. App. 1975), and *Hersh v. Kentfield Builders, Inc.*, 172 N.W.2d 56 (Mich. Ct. App. 1969), *rev'd on other grounds*, 189 N.W.2d 286 (Mich. 1971).

Chapter 14

The illustration under Part 1 is based on *Branch v. Western Petroleum, Inc.*, 657 P.2d 267 (Utah 1982).

Exercise 14-A(1) is based on *Blumenfeld v. Borenstein*, 276 S.E.2d 607 (Ga. 1987).

Exercise 14-A(2) is based on *Roe v. Catholic Charities*, 588 N.E.2d 354 (Ill. Ct. App. 1992), and *Burr v. Board of County Commissioners*, 491 N.E.2d 1101 (Ohio 1986).

Chapter 15

The injunction rule alluded to several times in the chapter is drawn from cases such as *People v. Black's Food Store*, 105 P.2d 361 (Cal. 1940).

Chapter 16

The illustration under Part 1 is based on *Komatsy Ltd. v. Staton Steamship Co.*, 674 F.2d 806 (9th Cir. 1992).

The illustration under Parts 2 and 3 was inspired by the Municipal Waste Planning Recycling and Management Act § 902, 43 Pa. Cons. Stat. Ann. § 4000.902 (Supp. 1993).

Chapter 17

The illustration in the text is derived from the principles stated in *Canell v. Arcola Housing Corp.*, 65 So. 2d 849 (Fla. 1953) (express easement), and *Romanchuk v. Plotkin*, 9 N.W.2d 421 (Minn. 1943) (implied easement by necessity).

Exercise 17-A is similar to *Kline v. Burns*, 276 A.2d 248 (N.H. 1971).

Chapter 18

The illustration in the text is based on W. Page Keeton et al., *Prosser and Keeton on the Law of Torts* § 11 (5th ed. 1984).

Exercise 18-A is based on the English Statute of Frauds entitled "An Act for the Prevention of Frauds and Perjuries," 29 Charles II, c.3 (1677). The sale of land case is based on the principles contained in John Calamari & Joseph Perillo, *The Law of Contracts §§ 19-26, 19-35* (3d ed. 1987). The dance case is inspired by *Vokes v. Arthur Murray, Inc.*, 212 So. 2d 906 (Fla. Dist. Ct. App. 1968).

Chapter 19

The quotation under Part 4 is adapted from the "opinions below" section in the petitioner's brief in *MCI Telecommunications Corp. v. American Telephone & Telegraph Co.*, No. 93-356 (U.S. filed Sept. 2, 1993).

The first quotation under Part 5 is adapted from the "jurisdiction" section in the petitioner's brief in *Griffin v. United States*, 112 S. Ct. 466 (1991) (No. 90-6352).

Chapter 20

The statute described under Parts 1 and 2 is drawn from Mich. Comp. Laws Ann. §§ 168.951, .952, .955 (West 1989). *See also Woods v. Clerk of Saginaw County*, 264 N.W.2d (Mich. Ct. App. 1978). The cases under Part 3 are based on the discussion in *People v. Kelly*, 549 P.2d 1240 (Cal. 1976).

The illustration under Part 4(a) is based on 28 U.S.C. § 1337 (1988) and the Federal Noise Control Act, 42 U.S.C.A. §§ 4901–4918 (West 1983).

The cases cited under Part 4(b) are *Kopischke v. First Continental Corp.*, 610 P.2d 668 (Mont. 1980), and *Bentzler v. Braun*, 149 N.W.2d 626 (Wis. 1967).

The illustration under Part 4(c) is inspired by *State Bar v. Geralds*, 263 N.W.2d 241 (Mich. 1978), and *State Bar v. Williams*, 228 N.W.2d 222 (Mich. 1975), *modified*, 240 N.W.2d 246 (Mich. 1976).

The illustration under Part 5(a) is inspired by *People v. Valentine*, 169 P.2d 1 (Cal. 1946).

The example under Part 5(b) is based on section 8 of the Michigan Township Rural Zoning Act, Mich. Comp. Laws Ann. § 125.282 (West 1986), and *Stadle v. Township of Battle Creek*, 77 N.W.2d 329 (Mich. 1956).

Exercises 20-A and 20-B were inspired by 75 Pa. Cons. Stat. Ann. § 3301(a) (1977); *Hamilton v. Glemming*, 46 S.E.2d 438 (Va. 1948); *Stoll v. Curry*, 175 A. 724 (Pa. Super. Ct. 1934).

Exercise 20-C is based on *Gibson v. Gibson*, 479 P.2d 648 (Cal. 1971); *Pedigo v. Rowley*, 610 P.2d 560 (Idaho 1980); and *Cole v. Sears Roebuck & Co.*, 177 N.W.2d 866 (Wis. 1970).

Chapter 21

The Williams Act cited under Part 1 is located at 15 U.S.C. §§ 78m(d),(e), 78n(d)–(f) (1988). The cases are *Kewanee Oil Co. v. Bicron Corp.*, 416 U.S. 470 (1974); *Perez v. Campbell*, 402 U.S. 637 (1971); and *Hines v. Davidowitz*, 312 U.S. 52 (1941).

The illustration under Part 2 is based on Mich. Comp. Laws Ann. §§ 691.1201–1207 (West 1987 & Supp. 1993), and *West Michigan Environment Action Council, Inc. v. Natural Resources Commission*, 275 N.W.2d 538 (Mich. 1979).

The illustration under Part 3 was inspired by Mich. Comp. Laws Ann. §§ 333.13501–.13536 (West 1992). It is based on *Tennessee Valley Authority v. Hill*, 437 U.S. 153, 193–95 (1978), and *Hecht Co. v. Bowles*, 321 U.S. 321 (1944).

Exercise 21-A is based on *Prows v. Industrial Commission*, 610 P.2d 1362 (Utah 1980).

Chapter 22

The statute in the text is the Equal Employment Opportunity Act of 1972, 42 U.S.C.A. §§ 2000e to 2000e-17 (West 1981 & Supp 1993).

The case in the text was inspired by and is a combination of *Berg v. Richmond Unified School District*, 528 F.2d 1208 (9th Cir. 1975), *vacated*, 434 U.S. 158 (1977), and *Drew v. Liberty Mutual Insurance Co.*, 480 F.2d 69 (5th Cir. 1973), *cert. denied*, 417 U.S. 935 (1974).

Exercise 22-A is based on *Bernstein v. Kapneck*, 417 A.2d 456 (Md. Ct. Spec. App. 1980); *Thomas v. Erie Insurance Exchange*, 182 A.2d 823 (Md. 1962); *Hall v. Strom Construction Co.*, 118 N.W.2d 281 (Mich. 1962); and *Le Francois v. Hobart College*, 31 N.Y.S.2d 200 (N.Y. Sup. Ct. 1941), *aff'd*, 39 N.E.2d 271 (N.Y. 1941).

Chapters 23 and 24

The Miller/Chisholm/Aaron problem in the text was inspired by the following cases: *Cook v. Stansell*, 411 S.E.2d 844 (W. Va. 1991); *Reager v. Anderson*, 371 S.E.2d 619 (W. Va. 1988); *Board of Education v. Zando, Martin & Milstead, Inc.*, 390 S.E.2d 796 (W. Va. 1990); *Cline v. White*, 393 S.E.2d 923 (W. Va. 1990); *Missouri Pacific Railroad Co. v. Whitehead & Kales Co.*, 566 S.W.2d 466 (Mo. 1978); *Iowa v. Norfolk & Western Railway Co.*, 753 S.W.2d 891 (Mo. 1988); and *Greenstreet v. Rupert*, 795 S.W.2d 539 (Mo. Ct. App. 1990).

Index

395